THE HANDBOOK OF ETHNIC MEDIA IN CANADA

The Handbook of Ethnic Media in Canada

Edited by

Daniel Ahadi, Sherry S. Yu,

and Ahmed Al-Rawi

McGill-Queen's University Press

Montreal & Kingston • London • Chicago

© McGill-Queen's University Press 2023

ISBN 978-0-2280-1926-8 (cloth)
ISBN 978-0-2280-1927-5 (paper)
ISBN 978-0-2280-1936-7 (ePDF)
ISBN 978-0-2280-1937-4 (ePUB)

Legal deposit fourth quarter 2023
Bibliothèque nationale du Québec

Printed in Canada on acid-free paper that is 100% ancient forest free (100% post-consumer recycled), processed chlorine free

This book has been published with the help of a grant from the Canadian Federation for the Humanities and Social Sciences, through the Awards to Scholarly Publications Program, using funds provided by the Social Sciences and Humanities Research Council of Canada. Funding was also received from the University Publications Fund, Office of the Vice-President, Research, Simon Fraser University.

Funded by the Government of Canada | Financé par le gouvernement du Canada | Canada

We acknowledge the support of the Canada Council for the Arts.
Nous remercions le Conseil des arts du Canada de son soutien.

McGill-Queen's University Press in Montreal is on land which long served as a site of meeting and exchange amongst Indigenous Peoples, including the Haudenosaunee and Anishinabeg nations. In Kingston it is situated on the territory of the Haudenosaunee and Anishinaabek. We acknowledge and thank the diverse Indigenous Peoples whose footsteps have marked these territories on which peoples of the world now gather.

Library and Archives Canada Cataloguing in Publication

Title: The handbook of ethnic media in Canada / edited by Daniel Ahadi, Sherry S. Yu, and Ahmed Al-Rawi.
Other titles: Ethnic media in Canada
Names: Ahadi, Daniel, editor. | Yu, Sherry S., editor. | Al-Rawi, Ahmed K., editor.
Description: Includes bibliographical references and index.
Identifiers: Canadiana (print) 20230473601 | Canadiana (ebook) 2023047361X | ISBN 9780228019268 (cloth) | ISBN 9780228019275 (paper) | ISBN 9780228019367 (ePDF) | ISBN 9780228019374 (ePUB)
Subjects: LCSH: Ethnic mass media—Canada.
Classification: LCC P94.5.M552 C22 2023 | DDC 302.23089/00971—dc23

This book was typeset in 10.5/13 Sabon Pro.

Contents

Tables and Figures

TABLES

FIGURES

THE HANDBOOK OF ETHNIC MEDIA IN CANADA

INTRODUCTION

Ethnic Media in Canada: Governance, Practice, and Integration

Daniel Ahadi, Sherry S. Yu, and Ahmed Al-Rawi

Ethnic media research has been active in Canada over the past few decades (see, e.g., Ahmed and Veronis 2017; Black and Leithner 1988; Hirji 2010; Karim 2003; Murray, Yu, and Ahadi 2007; Yu 2018). With the emergence of new technologies, including social media, and the increasing rates of immigration to Canada, ethnic media outlets further flourished in diverse languages. Studies have found that ethnic media play various functions, including preserving the culture of their respective ethnic communities, uniting and strengthening the sense of community, providing an alternative to mainstream media, and offering basic information that is vital to settlement and civic engagement of ethnoracial communities.

Building on this body of literature, a more in-depth investigation is timely, considering not only the increasingly complicated layers of identity and belonging – along lines of ethnicity, race, gender, religion, language, nationality, and citizenship, among other traits – but also the subsequent challenges of the reciprocal or two-way integration of majority and minority populations in Canada. This volume emerges in the critical time that requires (1) a timely intervention of ethnic media in increasingly complicated race relations in Canada and elsewhere, and (2) a timely reflection of ethnic media research in Canada in the changing mediascape from analogue to digital media and the subsequent need for the reconceptualization of ethnic media and new methodological approaches to ethnic media research. The following two sections will provide more details about these developments.

SITUATING ETHNIC MEDIA IN A BROADER SOCIO-POLITICAL CONTEXT

This handbook is compiled amidst ongoing majority–minority conflicts in Canada as well as elsewhere, and within the context of the unprecedented global pandemic and the subsequent increasing racism, especially against Asians and Muslims. To begin with, the majority–minority conflict is a long-standing issue. The public debates on rising xenophobia in Canada (Khan, Zainuddin, and Mahi 2021) have added intensity to the ongoing debate on the continued exclusion of racialized individuals and their stories in mainstream media. The COVID-19 pandemic has further exacerbated racism against Asian and Muslim communities. According to numerous reports, from both news media and academic research, there has been a sharp rise in anti-Asian racism in Canada (Guo and Guo 2021). In online forums, news websites, and social media sites, these xenophobic sentiments have been remarkably visible, especially under the auspices of anonymity. Certainly, these sentiments are not limited to the online environment alone. In Vancouver, for example, there has been a 700 per cent increase in hate crimes against Asians (Baylon and Leyland 2021). The same offline violence applies to other groups like Muslims who have also been targeted for many years in real life and on social media. On 6 June 2021, for example, a Muslim family was brutally attacked in London, Ontario, and four family members were killed (Jackson 2021). Four years earlier, in 2017, a gunman opened fire in a Quebec City mosque during prayer and killed six worshipers (Mahrouse 2018).

Public debates on the country's reckoning with cultural genocide against its Indigenous population (Austen 2021) have added further momentum to the ongoing debate on racialization and exclusion. In 2021, Canada also came face-to-face with its awful legacy of cultural genocide and ethnic cleansing of its Indigenous populations when mass graves of children were discovered at the site of several former Indian Residential Schools in British Columbia, Saskatchewan, and Manitoba. It is likely that further discoveries will be made at the over 130 residential school sites in Canada (BBC 2021). Despite the damning report from the Truth and Reconciliation Commission (TRC) issued six years earlier in 2015, and the much-publicized survivor testimonies as well as federal and provincial governments' commitments to implement the recommendations of the TRC report, the revelations of mass graves of children came as a rude awakening for non-Indigenous Canadians, especially to the realities of the genocidal state policies of Canada. Even to this day, such policies continue in various forms, depriving many Indigenous communities of basic life necessities such as access to clean water, healthcare, education, and land sovereignty, and incarcerating them at an alarmingly disproportionate rate (Jacobs, Gallagher, and Heydt 2018).

Lastly, this handbook arises when ethnic media as an exercise of self-representation has historically emerged not only as a means to assist with integration but also as a response to exclusion from the mainstream media. While the representation of racialized and minoritized groups is on the rise in the 2020s, there is still a gross under- or misrepresentation of non-white groups in mainstream media. One of the alarming areas of decline is in coverage of local and international news in Canadian media. Lindgren (2020) reports that hundreds of local news outlets have either shut down or been consolidated in takeovers by large media companies, adding to the already existing deficit in quality journalism at the local level. Similarly, for international news, there is a lack of coverage of news "from home" – a sentiment commonly reflected in studies on ethnic media in Canada (Ahadi and Murray 2009). Certainly, the need for news from home is satisfied increasingly by homeland media rather than local ethnic media in the digital age, setting aside the discussion on digital divides within ethnic groups. However, the lack of international news in mainstream media conversely means an information gap within the majority population about news concerning regions where minorities come from and the subsequent lack of cultural knowledge about people with whom they coexist.

SITUATING THIS VOLUME IN THE CONTEXT OF ETHNIC MEDIA RESEARCH

This volume responds to the lack of comprehensive collections of ethnic media research on this scale with a specific focus on Canada. Special attention is given to theories, methodologies, policies, and case studies concerning ethnic media to offer insights on the nature and implications of policy making, production, and consumption related to ethnic media in Canada. Specifically, the focus is on how policy makers, journalists, media practitioners, industry stakeholders, and audiences in Canada engage with ethnic media, and what this media sector means for socio-cultural, economic, and political integration, or lack thereof.

We use the term "ethnic media" to refer to communication initiated mainly by and/or for ethnoracial minorities. While we acknowledge various terms used by scholars in media and communication research to refer to media practices by this population, it is our deliberate decision to use the term ethnic media for a few reasons. Broadly speaking, minority media, as defined by Dayan (1998), function as a means of preserving the community's cultural specificity. Browne's (1996) description of ethnic media, on the other hand, points out that there are certain functions common to ethnic media despite variations in multicultural politics and policies across nations: ethnic media are found to (1) rescue the language; (2) increase self-esteem; (3) combat negative images and stereotypes; (4) work for greater social cohesiveness, and through this for political influence; (5) provide a visible and audible symbol for the ethnic society; (6) provide an outlet for creative production; and finally, (7) provide a source of employment for the immigrant population.

The wide use of the term ethnic media also may have to do with the experience of mobility which changes the meaning of home, belonging, and nation. Members of an exilic community living with the trauma of displacement from home become more consciously ethnic than they were when they lived at home (hooks 2009). Nancy Fraser (1992) and Iris Marion Young (2000) attribute this phenomenon partially to the continued racialization and exclusion of newcomers and minoritized groups in Western immigrant-receiving societies like Canada. For bell hooks (2009), although not an immigrant, it was her accent and "strange" customs and habits as a Black Kentuckian Southerner that made her stand out among White Californians at Stanford University during her university years.

This emphasis on ethnic identity is also mirrored in diasporic communities across the globe. To remedy the sense of exclusion, newcomers have historically created a small version of their original homelands by occupying sections of mainly urban areas to set up shops, restaurants, and services to serve the needs of their own ethnic community. The experience of having strong attachments to one's own ethnic origin in diaspora has also been attributed to language barriers, especially in early years of settlement (Min and Kim 2000; Sanders 2002). For practical reasons, members from diasporic communities retain their cultural heritage and language and acquire day-to-day information about their community and their homeland through ethnic networks. James Clifford's influential essay "Diasporas" (1994) further argued that members of diasporic communities retain their cultural heritage by maintaining ties with the homeland and the local diasporic community in new societies. The experience of loss of homeland, culture, and ethnic heritage, according to Clifford, is compensated for by staying together with people who share the experience of displacement. The fantasy of an eventual return to the homeland also strengthens one's desire to retain parts of the ethnic culture.

Whatever the cause may be for this turn to the ethnic, ethnic "communication infrastructures" (Marques and Santos 2004, 3; Matei, Ball-Rokeach, Wilson, Gibbs, and Hoyt 2001) in the country of settlement play an important role. Generally, the debates surrounding ethnic media fall within two broader streams. The integrative stream acknowledges ethnic media's role in helping the integration of minority groups into the mainstream culture and fostering ethnic cohesion and cultural maintenance through their symbolic function as mediators of identities and their connective function as mediators of information (Deuze 2006). These media also enhance the public sphere in their role of encouraging debate on different issues that are relevant to ethnic groups. On the other hand, the non-integrative stream expresses concerns ethnic media's divisive role, as it may further alienate minority groups from mainstream culture, ultimately hindering their integration (Deuze 2006).

Increasingly, there is recognition of ethnic media's complementary role to mainstream media, reflecting the convergence culture in what Annabelle Sreberny (2005, 443) calls "not only, but also." In other words, ethnic media provide an alternative perspective to what is already covered in mainstream media. In this regard, ethnic journalism is seen to be capable of altering the hierarchy of access to news by focusing on ethnic groups rather than those who have historically been in a position of privilege and power. This is achieved in the way that the different media platforms provide an outlet for self-representation and a space to voice concerns and highlight the important issues relevant to specific minority groups.

These streams of thought, however, confirm the conventional notion of ethnic media as media *by* and *for* ethnoracial minorities. In this volume, we strive to challenge the conceptual boundaries of ethnic media by inviting scholars to revisit ethnic media from critical perspectives. For example, is the term "ethnic media" still theoretically relevant? What are the methodological challenges and innovative approaches that need to be considered when studying ethnic media, especially in the digital age, with the increasing involvement of second-generation migrants (and beyond) who are part of this turn to the ethnic?

This volume also acknowledges the need for more research on the historical account of ethnic media and the role of policies, regulations, and industry codes in ethnic media operation and journalism. The work of ethnic media in Canadian politics dates back to the late 1800s in Canada (Burnet and Palmer 1988); however, their significance in Canadian journalism is often underestimated. The historical account also refers to examining the development of ethnic media in a chronological sense, specifically the transition from analogue to digital in the changing mediascape. Similarly, the Ethnic Broadcasting Policy (CRTC 1999) stipulates what ethnic broadcasting should provide; however, does this media policy or do any others properly address the actual needs of ethnic media production and consumption on the ground?

Further, this volume acknowledges the need for more research on the role of ethnic media in intercultural communication. Ethnic media tend to be studied in isolation as media for ethnic communities with less attention paid to their integrative role. Related to this area of research are the growing digital spaces created by younger generations whose in-betweenness or hyphenated identities not only allow them to find ways to establish communicative spaces for those of similar backgrounds, but also enable them to reach out to a broader audience.

Such acknowledgment and intention to fill these gaps in ethnic media literature that originated in Canada enable this volume to address the conceptual, methodological, historical, policy-related, and intercultural concerns of ethnic media research. Before delving into the details of the volume's structure in the following section, we would like to highlight two points: that is, new concepts and emerging types of ethnic media this volume introduces. First, for the new concepts, Fleras's discussion of "postmulticultural" and "postethnic" (chapter 1) provides a new theoretical framework to situate current scholarship which is largely limited to ethnic, rather than post-ethnic, orientation. Yu and Ahadi's work (chapter 2) also offers new conceptual and methodological interpretations on ethnic media research. The chapter reminds us of ethnic media's unique nature as being both local and transnational, ethnic versus diasporic, and immigrant versus ethnic minority, and the subsequent multiple perceptions of belonging and hybridity of populations, and that such nature requires a more nuanced approach to ethnic media as a site and subject of research. Hayward's work (chapter 4) also offers new conceptual and methodological interpretations through the application of "cultural brokerage" from anthropology. Such an interdisciplinary approach to ethnic media research is much needed in order to understand the multifaceted nature of ethnic media and the various socio-cultural and regulatory environments within which they operate and evolve, particularly within the Canadian context.

Second, this volume also introduces emerging types of ethnic media. We call these media "emerging," not because they have not existed before but because they have come to recent research attention. One of such types is "religious ethnic media" through the analysis of media texts produced by religious organizations within ethnic communities (see further details in the next section for Karim's work in chapter 10 and Datta and Chakraborty's work in chapter 14). Ethnic media content analyzed thus far has focused largely on news and entertainment media. The focus on media content by religious organizations is new within the Canadian context and invites more research in this area. Another new concept is "second-generation media" that suggests the intercultural potential of ethnic media (see further details in the next section for Jiwani and Bernard-Brind'Amour's work in chapter 11 and Bains's work in chapter 12). Situated between traditional ethnic media by and mainly for first-generation immigrants, on the one hand, and mainstream media on the other, these media create a space of interruption and advocacy for hyphenated Canadians, which neither traditional ethnic media nor mainstream media enable them to do. The emphasis on the intersectionality of gender, ethnicity, and generation – from the perspectives of second-generation children of immigrants – responds to varying experiences of members of ethnic communities and expands the boundary of ethnic media as a field and subject of research.

Certainly, there are areas that this volume has not been able to adequately offer. Despite the breadth of ethnic communities covered in the volume, research on Black media is lacking with only one chapter featuring Black media in a comparative study with South Asian media (see Douai and Perry's work in chapter 13). The failure to achieve a fair balance of representation across ethnic communities is mainly due to the lack of responses from the research community despite the editors' repeated attempts to include Black media research. We hope that future volumes on ethnic media will fill this gap.

STRUCTURE OF THE VOLUME

This volume brings together research from senior and junior scholars in the field of communication studies in Canada, including graduate students. Based on the chapters contributed, we have devised the following three sections. The first section of the volume discusses ethnic media and governance. In general, ethnic media are often conditioned by a myriad of forces, including waves of migration, the demographic profiles of ethnic groups, and immigration, multiculturalism, and media policies. This section considers the policies that inform ethnic media practices in Canada. Prior to the introduction of case study chapters, the two opening chapters discuss some of the overarching epistemological and methodological issues that researchers in the field of ethnic media studies face. Fleras in chapter 1 opens a discussion on ethnic media with a multicultural framework, specifically on the role that the official Canadian multiculturalism policy plays in safeguarding and nourishing the ethnic media sector in Canada, by framing the two as mutually complementary in continuing to shape and define Canadian national identity as a multi-ethnic country. Fleras's suggestion of a "postmulticultural" and "postethnic" framework for ethnic media research in the digital age is both supported and challenged by the case studies examined in this volume. Yu and Ahadi in chapter 2 provide a critical intervention in the study of ethnic media by considering how the definition of ethnic media requires re-conceptualization in the digital age, and what new methodological inquiries have emerged in ethnic media research as a result of this shift. In chapter 3, Ng explores the role of Canadian broadcasting and multiculturalism policies in ethnic media practices in fostering transnational connections and identity-making in the Chinese community through in-depth interviews with Chinese-language media workers. In chapter 4, Hayward uses the notion of "cultural brokerage" and explores how the process of translation and the operation of regulations across different jurisdictions work, how cultural products embody such practices, and finally, what that means for ethnic media in Canada.

The second section of the volume deals with ethnic media practices. By the late 1800s, there were dozens of newspapers serving the Caribbean, Chinese, Icelandic, Italian, and Japanese communities in Canada, to name a few, and some of these media established alliances with political parties (Burnet and Palmer 1988; Yarhi and Walkom 2017). This section focuses on various practices of ethnic media in Canada and their roles in ethnoracial communities. Some chapters offer a historical account of ethnic media of respective communities. Bukhari in chapter 5 provides an overview of various types and usages of South Asian ethnic media in Canada including radio, television, and print media, with a focus on their linkages with audiences, through interviews with media producers and focus group discussions with audiences. Al-Rawi in chapter 6 explores the history of Arab-language publications by identifying the first Arab Canadian newspaper, *The Canadian Office*, and then focusing on the case study of *Hona London* (This is London) through a digital textual analysis, aiming at understanding the importance and functions of the identified topics. In chapter 7, Zylinski traces the history and function of media for the Polish community, as well as their move from analogue to digital platforms. Sanzone and Principe's study of Italian media in chapter 8 also traces the history and investigates the past and the present form and function of Italian media in Canada. This is achieved by comparing the media's role as a connector to the political sphere in Italy in the early days of settlement from the early 1900s to the 1970s when they shifted focus to cover more domestic politics, linking the community to the political landscape here in Canada, and more recently, when new digital initiatives emerged. In chapter 9, Moore and Whitehead take us through a historical journey in the practice and the role of film advertising in diasporic cinemas in urban Canada and reveal the evidence of an intercultural mediascape years before and after the official promotion of pluralistic Canadian citizenship. In chapter 10, Karim explores the official and non-official Ismaili online media, specifically their mandates, content, interaction with each other and with audiences and the degree to which these media challenge the authority and leadership of the Ismaili Imam and the institutional system.

Finally, the third section of the volume deals with ethnic media and the issue of integration and the intercultural potential of ethnic media. The focus is on ethnic media practices broadly in the context of what has been referred to in the literature as the "connective" and "symbolic" functions of ethnic media, that is, media's ability to inform members of communities about day-to-day news and community activities, as well as to foster a sense of belonging to the broader society respectively (Matsaganis and Ahadi 2018). As mediators of identity, ethnic media can play a significant role in the ability to maintain a cultural identity while integrating into multicultural societies such as Canada. Contributors in this section provide several case studies of how ethnic media can play this integrative role in the communities which they serve. In chapter 11, Jiwani and Bernard-Brind'Amour trace the inception and development of *Rungh* from the *South Asian Quarterly of Culture, Comment and Criticism* in Vancouver into a multifaceted pan-ethnoracial online medium of the Rungh Cultural Society. In chapter 12, Bains explores the role of the online South Asian collective Didihood: The Sisterhood of South Asian Creatives in Canada as a site of resistance, community building, and knowledge exchange within the South Asian community. In chapter 13, Douai and Perry explore the role of ethnic media in crime coverage through a qualitative analysis of Black and South Asian newspapers in the Greater Toronto Area. In chapter 14, Datta and Chakraborty explore the meaning of "being and living as a Hindu" in Canada and the relationship with Canadian identity through an analysis of festival literature in the form of magazines, souvenirs, leaflets, and pamphlets as ethnic media. The authors investigate the degree to which the Hindutva identity or political Hinduism shapes or is shaped by these mediated forms of expression in the faith-based community. In the final chapter of this volume, chapter 15, Miftari offers the perspective of an ethnic media practitioner (unlike the scholarly observations shared in the previous chapters) by exploring new initiatives developing alongside traditional ethnic media. The analysis of services targeting a broader audience or specialized clients suggests new consumers of ethnic news for varying purposes, including civic engagement and political/corporate interests.

The chapters collected for this volume are intended to critically reflect on ethnic media on various levels, from theoretical inquiries and methodological approaches to policy interventions, journalistic practices, and everyday consumption, and identify areas for further research. The findings from the chapters are also meant to suggest areas for further conversation, not only in the research community but also policy, industry, and journalistic communities, as we move forward with ongoing majority–minority issues and seek ways to proactively and productively discuss them. We hope that this latest collection on ethnic media research in Canada will serve as useful groundwork for the systematic research of this media sector for interested scholars.

REFERENCES

Ahadi, Daniel, and Catherine A. Murray. 2019. "Urban Mediascapes and Multicultural Flows: Assessing Vancouver's Communication Infrastructure." *Canadian Journal of Communication* 34 (4): 587–612.

Ahmed, Rukhsana, and Luisa Veronis. 2017. "Multicultural Media Use and Immigrant Settlement: A Comparative Study of Four Communities in Ottawa, Canada." *Journal of International Migration and Integration* 18 (2): 587–612.

Austen, Ian. 2021. "With Discovery of Unmarked Graves, Canada's Indigenous Seek Reckoning." *New York Times*, 26 June 2021. https://www.nytimes.com/2021/06/26/world/canada/indigenous-residential-schools-grave.html.

Baylon, John, and Leyland Cecco. 2021. "Attacks Make Vancouver 'Anti-Asian Hate Crime Capital of North America." *Guardian*, 23 May 2021. https://www.theguardian.com/world/2021/may/23/vancoucer-anti-asian-hate-crimes-increase.

BBC. 2021. "Canada: 751 Unmarked Graves Found at Residential School." BBC News Online, 24 June 2021. https://www.bbc.com/news/world-us-canada-57592243.

Black, Jerome H., and Christian Leithner. 1988. "Immigrants and Political Involvement in Canada: The Role of the Ethnic Media." *Canadian Ethnic Studies/Études éthniques au Canada* 20 (1): 1–20.

Browne, Donald R. 1996. *Electronic Media and Indigenous Peoples: A Voice of Our Own?* Iowa: Iowa State University Press.

Burnet, Jean R., and Howard Palmer. 1988. *Coming Canadians: An Introduction to a History of Canada's Peoples*. Toronto: McClelland and Stewart.

Clifford, James. 1994. "Diasporas." *Cultural Anthropology* 9 (3): 302–38.

CRTC (Canadian Radio-television and Telecommunications Commission). 1999. "Ethnic Broadcasting Policy." Public Notice CRTC 1999-117. Ottawa, ON: CRTC. http://www.crtc.gc.ca/eng/archive/1999/PB99-117.HTM.

Dayan, Daniel. 2002. "Particularistic Media and Diasporic Communications." In *Media, Ritual and Identity*, edited by James Curran and Tamar Liebes, 113–23. London: Routledge.

Deuze, Mark. 2006. "Ethnic Media, Community Media and Participatory Culture." *Journalism* 7 (3): 262–80.

Fraser, Nancy. 1992. "Rethinking the Public Sphere: A Contribution to the Critique of Actually Existing Democracy." In *Habermas and the Public Sphere*, edited by Craig Calhoun, 109–42. Cambridge, MA: MIT Press.

Guo, Shibao, and Yan Guo. 2021. "Combating Anti-Asian Racism and Xenophobia in Canada: Toward Pandemic Anti-Racism Education in Post-COVID-19." *Beijing International Review of Education* 3 (2): 187–211.

Hirji, Faiza. 2010. *Dreaming in Canadian: South Asian Youth, Bollywood, and Belonging*. Vancouver: UBC Press.

hooks, bell. 2009. *Belonging: A Culture of Place*. London: Routledge.

Jackson, Hannah. 2021. "'Brutal and Horrific': Condolences Pour in for Muslim Family Killed in London, Ont. Attack." Global News, 7 June 2021. https://globalnews.ca/news/7928449/london-vehicle-attack-reaction/.

Jacobs, Bette, Meghan Gallagher, and Nicole Heydt. 2018. "At the Intersection of Health and Justice: How the Health of American Indians and Alaska Natives Is Disproportionately Affected by Disparities in the Criminal Justice System." *Belmont Law Review* 6:41–77.

Karim, Karim H., ed. 2003. "Mapping Diasporic Mediascapes." In *The Media of Diaspora: Mapping the Globe*, 16–32. New York: Routledge.

Khan, Shamim Ahmed, Mohammad Zainuddin, and Masnun Mahi. 2021. "Rising Xenophobia and Anti-Asian Racism amid COVID-19: A Theoretical Lens." *ICS Analysis* 133: 1–12.

Lindgren, April. 2020. "Local News Is Being Decimated during One of Its Most Important Moments." *Policy Options*, 27 May 2020. https://policyoptions.irpp.org/magazines/may-2020/local-news-is-being-decimated-during-one-of-its-most-important-moments/.

Mahrouse, Gada. 2018. "Minimizing and Denying Racial Violence: Insights from the Québec Mosque Shooting." *Canadian Journal of Women and the Law* 30 (3): 471–93.

Marques, M. Margarida, and Rui Santos. 2004. "Top-Down and Bottom-Up Reconsidered: The Dynamics of Immigrant Participation in Local Civil Society." In *Citizenship in European Cities: Immigrants, Local Politics and Integration Policies: Diversity and Convergence in European Cities*, edited by Karen Kraal, Steven Vertovec, and Rinus Penninx, 107–26. London: Routledge.

Matei, Sorin, Sandra J. Ball-Rokeach, Mary Wilson, Jennifer Gibbs, and Elizabeth Gutierrez Hoyt. 2001. "Metamorphosis: A Field Research Methodology for Studying Communication Technology and Community." *Electronic Journal of Communication* 11 (2): 1–35.

Matsaganis, Matthew D., and Daniel Ahadi. 2017. "Ethnic Media and Acculturation." In *The International Encyclopedia of Intercultural Communication*, edited by Young Yun Kim, 1–10. New York: Wiley-Blackwell.

Min, Pyong Gap, and Rose Kim. 2000. "Formation of Ethnic and Racial Identities: Narratives by Young Asian-American Professionals." *Ethnic and Racial Studies* 23 (4): 735–60.

Murray, Catherine, Sherry S. Yu, and Daniel Ahadi. 2007. "Cultural Diversity and Ethnic Media in BC. A Report to the Canadian Heritage Western Regional Office." Centre for Policy Studies on Culture and Communities. Vancouver, BC: Simon Fraser University.

Sanders, Jimy M. 2002. "Ethnic Boundaries and Identity in Plural Societies." *Annual Review of Sociology* 28: 327–57.

Sreberny, Annabelle. 2005. "'Not Only, but Also': Mixedness and Media." *Journal of Ethnic and Migration Studies* 31 (3): 443–59.

Yarhi, Eli, and Thomas Walkom. 2017. "Newspapers in Canada: 1800s–1900s." *The Canadian Encyclopedia*, 24 October 2017. https://www.thecanadianencyclopedia.ca/en/article/newspapers-in-canada-1800s1900s.

Young, Iris Marion. 2000. *Inclusion and Democracy*. Oxford: Oxford University Press.

Yu, Sherry S. 2018. *Diasporic Media beyond the Diaspora: Korean Media in Vancouver and Los Angeles*. Vancouver and Toronto: UBC Press.

PART ONE

Ethnic Media and Policies: Governance of Media Practices

CHAPTER ONE

Ethnic Media and Canadian Multiculturalism: An Inclusive Canada-Building Tandem ... For Now

Augie Fleras

INTRODUCTION: FRAMING THE MULTICULTURALISM/ETHNIC MEDIA NEXUS

The relationship between an official multiculturalism and Canada's ethnic media[1] has rarely attracted the kind of academic attention it so richly deserves (see Hayward 2019; Yu and Murray 2007). Yet there is no mistaking parallels in the animating logic – and the public reaction – that underscores both domains. For some, an official multiculturalism policy framework and Canada's ethnic media are inherently regressive in delaying the integration of immigrants and the accommodation of minorities (see Yu 2018a for discussion). Both are accused of intensifying social divisions in Canada through the creation of segregated communities or the retention of illiberal values (Budarick 2019). For others, the interplay of multiculturalism with a robust ethnic media sphere forges a commitment to a more inclusive Canada (see Karim 2002 for discussion). Consider how applying a social capital lens yields insight into the genesis and development of multiculturalism as a governance model for bonding (inward-looking) and bridging (outward-oriented) – an agenda that persists into the present, albeit more often framed in the normative language of integration and inclusion. Similarly, vast differences in their style, focus, content, and audience base (see Ahmed and Veronis 2017; Griffith 2019; Matsaganis, Ball-Rokeach, and Katz 2010) have not dissuaded ethnic media from embodying the social capital logic of bridging and bonding (Bucholtz 2019). Not only do ethnic media create a bond by binding ethnic, immigrant, and racialized minorities into a lived community, but the approximately 800 ethnic media outlets in Canada (Todd 2019) also serve as a springboard in bridging a pathway to society at large. Still, while ethnic media are thought to complement the inclusive logic of Canada's integrative multiculturalism, the jury is out on whether or not this mutually reciprocating relationship is sustainable in a vastly more complex and contested world.

The interplay of an ethnicity-themed multiculturalism with the multicultural logic of ethnic media may be framed as a partnership in Canada-building. Ethnic media that bond and bridge are shown to be reflective of and consistent with an official multiculturalism in advancing an inclusive Canada through immigrant integration and minority accommodation (Fleras 2021). Moreover, while an ethnic component no longer consciously informs it, Canada's multicultural logic remains tethered to the ethnicity principle. That is, those confident in their ethnocultural heritage – achieved in part through involvement with ethnic media – will be better and more accommodative Canadians by virtue of identifying with Canada through their ethnicity (Berry, Kalin, and Taylor 1977).[2] Nevertheless, despite their roles as partners in Canada-building, both an official multiculturalism and ethnic media confront a looming crisis of legitimacy – namely, an identity crisis ("who are we?") and a crisis of confidence ("what should we be doing?"). Just as multiculturalism as a political project is no longer conceptually attuned to the puzzles of a postmulticultural world, so too are ethnic media in danger of losing relevance because of changes to how people see, think, and do ethnicity. Effectively, this places pressure on applying a postethnic mindset to reset ethnic media. In short, just as an official multiculturalism will struggle to gain traction in coping with the complexities of a postmulticultural world, so too must an ethnic media scramble to reclaim credibility among those who resent being entombed in ethnic silos that gloss over their connections, commitments, and crossings which traverse a local/national/global nexus (Li 2019; Fleras 2019a, b).

In acknowledging the reality of an unruly world that disrupts a business-as-usual model, this chapter explores the complementary yet increasingly unsettled relationship between Canadian multiculturalism and Canada's ethnic media. The chapter begins by discussing how the mosaic logic of an official multiculturalism is being de-legitimized by the shifting realities and complex demands of a postmulticultural world. It then demonstrates how the multicultural logic of Canada's ethnic media is under pressure because of changes to how we approach ethnicity as a discourse and lived reality. Applying a postethnicity lens to ethnic media is shown to render the domain more receptive to the postmulticultural dynamics of complex diversities, fluid and multiple identities, transmigrant mobilities, and transnational webs of connection. The chapter concludes accordingly: ethnic media may need to reinvent themselves by building on their positives (i.e., they are well-positioned as niche markets beyond the homogenizing logic of a mainstream media) while moving positively forward along a postethnic ethic – if only to stay relevant by reconnecting with new audiences while relying on their traditional base. It remains to be seen if the tandem of ethnic media and an official multiculturalism as discursive partners in Canada-building can be repurposed for making the transition to a world infinitely more complex than before.

OFFICIAL MULTICULTURALISM: BRIDGING AND BONDING AS INCLUSIVE CANADA-BUILDING

Canada's official multiculturalism was launched in 1971 when the Liberal prime minister, Pierre Elliott Trudeau, announced a policy of multiculturalism within a bilingual framework. Trudeau envisaged a Canada in which members of different ethnic communities coexisted as components of a national mosaic, without reneging on their commitment to Canada or discarding their cultural heritage or ethnic attachments. Four major principles underscored this political project in realigning Canada around a multicultural axis:

- *Equality of status*: Canada does not have an official culture; all cultures are equal.
- *Canadian identity*: Diversity lies at the heart of Canadian identity.
- *Personal choice*: Individuals have the right to identify with the cultural tradition of their choice.
- *Protection of individual rights*: Individuals have the right to be free from discrimination.

To put these principles into practice, the government proposed a package of initiatives to (1) assist those cultural groups that demonstrated a commitment to *share and contribute* to Canada; (2) assist the members of all cultural groups to overcome cultural barriers to *full participation and equal involvement* in Canadian society; (3) promote *creative encounters and exchanges* among all Canadian cultural groups; and (4) assist immigrants to acquire at least one of Canada's official languages, English or French, to ensure full and equal participation. Even a cursory reading of these objectives – namely, the tropes of "share and contribute," "full participation and equal involvement," and "creative encounters and exchanges" – should make it abundantly clear that an official multiculturalism originated and evolved in defence of a participatory ethnicity as a pathway for belonging and identity in an inclusive Canada (Fleras 2021). Rather than use this as an excuse to hunker down and self-isolate under multiculturalism, ethnic groups were expected to interact and share their cultural heritage (i.e., visual and performing arts) in an effort to make Canada strong.

The logic of an official multiculturalism pivoted on the principle of inclusiveness. It aimed at legitimizing the bonding of ethnic Canadians to their ethnicity while promoting this bond as a bridge to other ethnic groups and, more importantly, to Canadian society. The bonding and bridging dimensions of an ethnicity-forward multiculturalism pursued two goals. First, it sought to eliminate those historical exclusions anchored in ethnocultural prejudices, not by promoting ethnicity per se, but by securing peoples' involvement and contribution to Canada through their ethnicity (Fleras 2016). To express this differently, anybody could belong to, participate in, contribute to, and identify with Canada without forsaking their ethnicity or incurring an ethnic penalty. Not only did an official multiculturalism promote ethnicity as a medium for engaging other Canadians, it also sought to make immigrant ethnicity irrelevant as a predictor of success or a mark of failure (Kymlicka 2012). Second, an official multiculturalism promoted a new symbolic order of governance that respected immigrants' ethnicity differences in facilitating the pace of their integration into Canada. This commitment was predicated on the goal of respecting ethnic heritages while, at the same time, depoliticizing ethnicity to make it safe for Canada, yet safe from Canada. The ethnicity principle also assumed that migrants and minorities were more likely to emotionally embrace Canada if they took pride in their cultural traditions as grounds for regulating the pace of adjustment and integration (Adams 2007; Berry, Kalin, and Taylor 1977).

Canada continues to support a multicultural agenda that recognizes ethnocultural differences ("bonding") while fostering intercultural relations ("bridging") in advancing an inclusive society ("binding") (Berry 2013). The *Annual Report on the Operation of the Canadian Multiculturalism Act, 2016–2017* (Canadian Heritage 2018, 4) reinforced this commitment to inclusiveness through an ethnic coexistence when it claimed: "the Government of Canada recognizes the diversity of Canadians ... as a fundamental characteristic of Canadian society and is committed to a policy of multiculturalism designed to improve and enhance the multicultural heritage of Canadians while working to achieve the equality of all Canadians." The 2018–19 annual report also drew attention to the centrality of intercultural/interfaith understanding, including the importance of cross-cultural interaction as the cornerstone of its multiculturalism grants and contributions program. Additionally, consider how the 2016–17 funding guidelines for the Multiculturalism Directorate's Inter-Action component confirmed support of "projects that encourage positive interaction between cultural, religious, and ethnic communities in Canada and projects that promote the expression of Canada's multiple identities. This interaction, through the inclusion and the welcoming of diverse Canadians is intended to increase participants' sense of belonging and attachments to Canada" (Canadian Heritage 2018). It is against this backdrop of an inclusive multicultural logic for Canada-building that provides a context for Canada's ethnic media.

MULTICULTURALISM UNDER SIEGE: A LOOMING LEGITIMACY CRISIS

Canada may well exemplify the world's quintessential multicultural regime in advancing the principle of a tolerant coexistence (Marche 2016, 2018; Biscahie 2019; Fleras 2021). Yet Canadian multiculturalism is also situated within the broader context of a global dynamic that may unsettle the legitimacy of a multicultural governance model. The reality is that we no longer live in a multicultural mosaic of fixed and bounded ethnicities within a closed national frame (if we ever did); ours is now a postmulticultural world of accelerated changes, complex diversities, and networked mobilities (Fleras 2019a). A national multiculturalism that endorsed a mosaic model of ethnicity no longer carries as much authority or conviction.

Nor is there as much respect for a state-driven multiculturalism that embraced a one-way path to migrant integration, the inevitability of permanent settlement, the citizenization of newcomers, and a standardized diversity governance (Triandafyllidou 2017). That it is neither conceptually affixed to the demands of the "small picture" (the local) nor thematically aligned with the realities of the "big picture" (the global) points to a governance paradox. English Canada's multiculturalism model must contend with a more cosmopolitan mindset that emphasizes a universalistic ethic for all of humanity over the specificities of the national (Bradley 2013). Yet, this domain is being eroded by a locally driven and community-led governance model that commits to the convivial practices of interculturalism at lived levels, including a connectedness to others through a two-way process of constructive engagement (Zapata-Barrero 2017; Mansouri, Elias, and Sweid 2017; Fleras 2019a). A bounded multiculturalism finds itself drifting into a kind of governance "limbo," both incapable of addressing the lived complexities of everyday urban life, yet poorly positioned to engage the broader dynamics and demands of a local/national/global nexus.

The conclusion seems inescapable. Canada's multicultural regime is increasingly undone by diametrically opposed tensions. A commitment to a more diverse and increasingly inclusive governance agenda is offset by a multicultural logic that is conceptually flawed in responding to the disruptive realities and unprecedented demands of an emergent postmulticultural world. Such an apparent contradiction ups the ante to rethink and reset multiculturalism by reassessing the concept of diversity governance in a world that is disappearing. The mosaic metaphor that underlined the homogenizing logic of an official multiculturalism exposes the shortcomings of a one-size-fits-all approach to governance (Biscahie 2019). Concepts and assumptions that once informed multiculturalism – from ethnicity to integration to citizenship – are now dismissed as simplistic and naïve. Worse still, they are perceived as contrary to the norms of good governance in a profoundly more complex and chaotic environment (Kymlicka 2015; also, Triandafyllidou 2017).

Certainly, the worth of Canada's official multiculturalism as a preferred governance model should not be discounted. Much of value can be pitched in defence of its role in the remaking of Canada's national imaginary along more inclusive lines (Ruble 2018). From an openly Eurocentric society embedded in a settler colonial regime,

Canada now commits to the multicultural principles of diversity, inclusion, and equality, regardless of, or perhaps precisely because of, peoples' race, ethnicity, or nationality. Nevertheless, there is a danger of multiculturalism becoming irrelevant in aspiring to the postmulticultural ideal of living together with/in/through a complexity of differences. What is proposed instead is a governance model that folds the positives of an official multiculturalism into a framework more aligned with a postmulticultural commitment to (a) a multiversal world of diversities-within-diversities, (b) an intercultural-based inter-existence rather than a passive coexistence, (c) a local/national/global nexus as a respatialized governance framework, and (d) the more fluid and contested demands of the new ethnicity ("postethnicity"). This intriguing mix of hope and despair makes it more important than ever to rethink and theorize the relational status of ethnic media in transitioning from a multicultural milieu to a postmulticultural matrix.

ETHNIC MEDIA: BINDS THAT BOND, BONDS THAT BRIDGE

Ethnic media – defined as print, broadcast, or digital media produced by, for, and about ethnic, racialized, diasporic, and immigrant minorities (Yu and Matsaganis 2019; Papoutsaki and Kolesova 2017) – are a formidable feature of Canada's mediascape (Kim 2020). And like Canada's official multiculturalism, whose principles they embody and embed, ethnic media are also predicated on the multicultural logic of bonding ("look in") and bridging ("act out") (Fleras 2009, 2015). The bonding logic of ethnic media as social capital for ethnocultural communities embraces two dimensions: reactive and proactive; the bridging logic is two-dimensional as well: outward and inward. Bonding as reactive reflects minority resentment of and reaction to their exclusion as subjects in the mainstream news media (Ferrer and Retis 2019; Husband 2005). As a counter-narrative that challenges conventional representation (Douai and Perry 2018), ethnic media provide a much-needed corrective to mainstream media coverage, which is inclined to frame minority stories around the themes of hyper-visibility (minorities as "problem people" or "othered") or hyper-*in*visibility (minorities as "irrelevant" or "non-existent") (Clark 2014; Fleras and Kunz 2001; Mahtani 2002; Perrigoe and Eid 2014).

Conversely, ethnic media proactively strive to celebrate minority accomplishments and success stories (Luo 2016). They not only secure a buffer from the stereotyping and distortions which plague mainstream diversity content, but also offer hope through positive narratives which unify an imagined community around a sense of pride and belonging. No less critical is the role of ethnic media in supplying a "news-minorities-can-use" content that speaks to minority anxieties and aspirations in a relatable language (Gerson and Rodriguez 2018). In communities desperate for information about policies and programs that impact their lives, ethnic media are better positioned to convey more nuanced communication than, for example, a tone-deaf and top-down government communiqué (Budarick 2019; Jeyasundarum 2020; Li 2019). They offer ethnically diverse communities trusted and in-language insights about community health, perhaps no more so than through culturally inflected and language-specific updates regarding the dangers of the COVID-19 pandemic (Brar 2021; Kim 2020). Lastly, in debunking their so-called isolationist logic, including allegations that they intensify social divides by fostering parallel communities or delaying integration, ethnic media may enrich citizenship education by enhancing civic engagement (Yu and Ahadi 2010; Griffith 2019).

Ethnic media as bridging capital also play an outward- and inward-looking role. Outwardly, they provide an information roadmap for facilitating a connection between what is happening "in here" with what is happening "over there." They further cater to a niche audience who want to know what is happening in their homeland or within their ethnic enclaves, how to negotiate a fitting into Canada for those unfamiliar with the normative lay of the land, when and where to rebuild social networks, and how to locate and access available local resources (Abraham 2017; Luo 2016; Walane 2017). Of particular importance are information tip sheets for coping with a strange new world without becoming entangled in a byzantine maze of government red tape or balky service agencies (Gerson and Rodriguez 2018). Ethnic media also provide communities with an outlet and a voice to articulate their needs and concerns to the general public, provide a much-needed alternative perspective to the public domain, and a secure space for those who desire to participate and contribute as societal stakeholders (Yu and Matsaganis 2019; Griffith 2019). In turn, mainstream media may look to ethnic media for access to high impact stories within ethnic communities of relevance to Canada and Canadians (Todd 2019). By offering different perspectives, opinions, and narratives, ethnic media provide coverage that transcends the usual storylines, therefore procuring a fuller understanding of controversial issues, such as the "truckers' blockade" in Ottawa in 2022 (NCM News Desk 2022).

Inwardly, ethnic media offer a platform for mobilizing a community into action for bridging the gap. They embody a marker of identity through coverage that connects community members around a cultural idiom they can understand and in a language (or tone) to which they can relate.[3] Pitching an issue in a readily recognizable format not only strengthens identities and commitments, particularly since mainstream media tend to dispel minority issues or negatively frame them, ethnic media also eases the adjustment process by cushioning the blows in settling down, fitting in, and moving up. News from their homeland taps into peoples' longing for content while softening the blows of transitioning from there to here, especially for those who remain emotionally invested in their country of origin (Douai and Perry 2018). In re-rooting their floating lives along cultural borderlines, ethnic media forge an in-between space, a kind of interstitial zone, which interweaves dislocation with relocation, division with connection, integration with hybridity, the local with the global (Luo 2016), and assimilation with resistance (Ferrer and Retis 2019). Bridging the transition of minority members from the margins to the centre demonstrates how ethnic media draw attention to issues of social injustice and institutional exclusion. This activist ethic reinforces their inward–outward role as a catalyst which galvanizes the community into action over local concerns. It also serves as a reminder that ethnic media do more than simply report the facts. They provide a public service by conveying information in ways that strike a chord for new and established migrants, while assuming a responsibility for defending or advancing minority rights (Gerson and Rodriguez 2018).

In sum, ethnic media play a critical role in Canada-building (bridging) through community empowerment (bonding). As many have noted, including the tireless defender of ethnic media, Madeline Ziniak (NCM News Desk 2020), members of Canada's 250 or so ethnic communities rely on ethnic media to keep them informed of developments in their homeland and their country of settlement. This dual focus demonstrates how newcomers to Canada occupy two states of being and belonging. On one side is their achieved status as new Canadians, which is full of challenges, anxieties, and aspirations; on the other side is their ascribed status as members of a homeland which pulsates with the richness of history, relationships, familiarity, and memories (Matta 2019). Certainly, the use and popularity of ethnic media both within and across ethnocultural groups is highly varied and contextual, depending on numerous factors including length of residence in Canada (Ahmed and Veronis 2017; Matsaganis, Ball-Rokeach, and Katz 2010). Economies of scale may also prove a problem. As one survey respondent explained, in predicting a looming crisis because of a shrinking ethnic market, ethnic media are likely to decline with the passing of the current generation and the emergence of a new generation more inclined toward the Canadian economy (Lindgren, 2011). Despite this doomsday scenario, the contribution of ethnic media to Canadian multiculturalism should not be discounted. This is due, in part, to the anticipated admission of nearly 1.5 million newcomers to Canada between 2023 and 2025 who will continue to rely on trusted sources of information. In rising to the challenge of meeting newcomers' needs, ethnic media constitute a Canada-building strength that complements the integrative logic of an official multiculturalism in the service of an inclusive Canada.

The relationship between multiculturalism and ethnic media should be framed as mutually complementary and reciprocally reinforcing. However, this relationship may be on the verge of unravelling for reasons that are partly beyond control of both. Ethnic media and an official multiculturalism are rooted in a perception of ethnicity as a mosaic of fixed, uniform, and discreet cultural tiles. Previously, minorities were slotted into precast ethnicity boxes in which identities were deemed to be stuck, static, and singular (Matejskova and Antonsich 2015). Multicultural discourses assumed an almost essentialized understanding of immigrant ethnicity as primordial and immutable, with members locked into hermetically sealed silos of separation. Ethnic media content was also predicated on the essentialist assumptions of an identifiable ethnocultural community that could be catered to and counted on as long as the news narrative emphasized the ethnic component. But what happens when the "ethnic" in ethnic media no longer means what it once did because of shifts in how people perceive, conceptualize, or experience ethnicity? How will ethnic media target ethnic communities who may exhibit more internal variation and less consensus than the differences and disagreements between ethnic groups? What will become of ethnic media now that the ethnic media/multiculturalism nexus is less sustainable in a reconfigured world?

FROM A MULTICULTURAL WORLD TO A POSTMULTICULTURAL WORLD

All the polite fiction aside, references to the fiftieth anniversary of Canada's official multiculturalism cannot conceal an inconvenient fact (Fleras 2021). Canadians no longer occupy a multicultural world that upholds a simplistic view of ethnicity and ethnic diversity. They no longer define immigration as a one-way linear process that severs links with the past in adjusting to the present, embrace the goal of a singular identity and national belonging around a uniform citizenship, or envision society as a mosaic of thick ethnic communities that are bounded, homogeneous, and perpetually fixed (Hollinger 2006; Latham 2008). Nor do Canadians live in a multicultural world that espouses an ordered social reality as linear, logical, and unproblematic ("inward-looking"), yet one increasingly at odds with the realities of a changing and hyperdiverse world, while more conceptually consistent with a network of flows rather than a space of places. More accurately, Canadians now exist in a world that is postmulticultural in logic, process, and outcomes, whose distinctive way of conceptualizing and responding to complex ethnodiversities exerts pressure on reassessing multiculturalism as a governance model (Fleras 2019a).

At the forefront of any reassessment are changes in global mobilities. The spread, speed, and scale of migrant movements, the volume and scope of new mobility patterns, the changing dynamic of global migration, and the pluralization of ethnic diversities, have combined to transform the governance of complex diversities into a daunting challenge (Spoonley and Tolley 2012). The seemingly ceaseless movement of people has amplified global anxieties over a "coming anarchy" in redefining the conventional markers of identity and belonging, and of unity and security (Haas, Castles, and Miller 2020). Consider immigrants and immigration as a case in point. Not only do newcomers increasingly identify with multiple identities across national borders as they settle into their new homeland, they remain in the vanguard of constructing diasporic linkages that offer solidarity, support, information, and identity across multiple domains without necessarily abandoning an attachment to their homeland or commitment to the host country in which they settle (Pieterse 2006). Not only do the dynamics of transmigration and transnationalism unhinge conventional notions of diversity governance, but the crossing and connections of diasporic and transmigrant mobilities are known to be disruptive because they: (a) blur a defence of territorial boundaries, (b) accelerate cross-border movements of migrants in search of safety or success, (c) transform public space into a contested site of clashing viewpoints, (d) transfer identities and belongings away from an exclusive national focus into more nebulous forms, and (e) complicate the search for accommodation models that combine the values of diversity and inclusion with that of societal unity and national identity (Ang 2011, 2014).

Even the concept of ethnic integration acquires a different tactic in a postmulticultural world (Fleras 2019b). Integration was traditionally defined as a one-way process of migrant admission into, their adjustment to, and an acceptance by a host society. However, the onset of a postmulticultural world unspools a European (or national) model of migration and integration as well as the related concepts of citizenship, inclusion, and integration (Cherti and McNeil 2012; Grzymala-Kazlowska and Phillimore 2018). Whereas reference to integration once employed a binary language of us/them to describe the linear progress of merging into a single majority culture, a new integration narrative differs in exposing the process of adjustment as more enigmatic and elusive (Fleras 2016). A new analytic framework is proposed that reflects the complexities of a "reimagined integration" involving a contested interplay of homeland identity and ethnic roots within a negotiated national identity against the backdrop of a local/national/global frame of reference (Hiebert 2015). A postintegration discourse also draws attention to how the idea of integration involves those in the mainstream who, too, must adopt a new integrative mindset by adjusting to the riddles and realities of a postmulticultural world (Foroutan 2015). As well, a postintegration mindset attends to migrant experiences beyond that of settlement and adaptation, in effect shifting the focus of integration from a fixed destination to a fluid process along a lengthy and often difficult journey. Such a shift opens the way for a discursive reframing of integration from that of a noun to a verb – namely, integration not as a destination of immutable beliefs (a thing), but a dynamic of mutable practices whose very nature is to change and be changed (a process) (Appiah 2018). Finally, reference to postintegration reinforces the value of an intersectionality lens with which to describe the interplay of ethnicity with other markers of identity such as gender and class as they intersect to amplify often negative outcomes (Grzymala-Kazlowska and Phillimore 2017).

The fact that we no longer live in a multicultural world is arguably true (Fleras 2019a). Ours is increasingly becoming a postmulticultural world whose mutating realities and messy demands are eroding the legitimacy of a mosaic multiculturalism as a diversity governance (Gozdecka, Ercan, and Kmak 2014; Biscahie 2019). The impact of a postmulticultural world in reshaping identity, belonging, and governance is no less significant than changes in reframing the idea of ethnodiversity as a lived experience (Biscahie 2019). However, a postmulticultural world of multiple identities, complex diversities, global mobilities, and despatialized domains is proving difficult to theorize when coaxing insights from explanatory frameworks designed for another era (Zapata-Barrero 2017). For example, a globalized world where over a quarter of a billion people reside outside their homeland, while digital technology transforms borders into wafer-thin membranes, raises questions about the viability of a bounded multiculturalism in a freewheeling era of transbounded ties, transmigratory movements, transnational webs of connections, and translocal identities. Not surprisingly, the ethnicity-forward logic of a mosaic multicultural model no longer resonates with authority among those who bristle at the prospect of being locked into its myopic gaze. Doug Saunders (2013) writes of second-generation young Canadians who dismiss an official multiculturalism as a demeaning and obsolete straitjacket when endorsing an ethnicity that is thought to define destiny: "This is the post-immigrant shift: For the first generation, multiculturalism was a way to feel part of the national whole; for the second, it often feels like a barrier to such inclusion. For this new comfortably inclusive Canada, we need a new vocabulary: More 'multi,' less 'culturalism.'"

Having exhausted some of its social capital and public legitimacy, what are the options for an official multiculturalism as a political project? Furthermore, what is to become of ethnicity – and by extension, ethnic media – as a business practice and an ideological tool in an evolving world of complex yet fluid ethnic diversities? No more so, it might be argued, than one in which migrant notions of identity and belonging are increasingly decoupled from conventional anchors, when a one-size-fits-all accommodation no longer make sense in a multiversal world of varied diversities, and where a diminishing national commitment to the mosaic of living together with differences (a tolerant coexistence) exerts pressure on crafting a new lived reality (a cooperative inter-existence) for living together with/in/through complex differences. Similarly, just as an official multiculturalism will struggle to gain traction in dealing with the turmoil of a postmulticultural world, so too must an ethnic media scramble to recapture their credibility among those who resent confinement to silos which exclude their complex identities and convoluted belongings, yet look to ethnicity to ground their rootless realities (Li 2019; Fleras 2019a).

FROM ETHNICITY TO POSTETHNICITY

Of those discursive shifts associated with a postmulticultural world, few can match the enormity of changes to how we see, think, and talk about ethnicity. An emergent postmulticultural world poses a challenge for both an official multiculturalism and ethnic media whose governance logic reflects conventional ethnicity tropes. The mosaic metaphor of bounded ethnic entities is giving way to a kaleidoscopic narrative of identity and belonging around a postethnic lens. Reference to a postethnicity as the new ethnicity confirms the possibility of a third space, born out of the lived realities of those diasporic members who must navigate a shifting world of neither here (receiving society) nor there (host country), but somewhere in between (Karim and Al-Rawi 2018). Unlike a corporate ("groupist") ethnicity model that shackles people around their ethnicity and ancestry (Brubaker 2004), a postethnic mindset commits to ethnicity as but one of many strands of a multi-plaited identity (Ang 2011; Hollinger 2006). Belongings and attachments in a postethnic world are layered, contextual, and relational since membership in one group does not preclude involvement in multiple forms of identification and affiliation (Ang 2014). Members of ethnic minority groups are no longer assumed to be locked into similar outlooks or shared experiences that obscure in-group differences (James and Turner 2017). To the contrary, members who claim an ethnic heritage may reflect as much intra-group variation and internal conflicts as that which exists between ethnic groups. Nor can political responses to the hopes and anxieties of ethnic minorities be slotted into conventional governances and generic (one-size-fits-all) policies that standardize as they homogenize (Malik 2012). Instead, postethnic identities are reconfigured as fluid and flexible rather than reified, open-ended rather than deterministic, complex rather than reductionist, contextual rather than categorical, and experiential rather than essentialistic. These identities also tend to be voluntaristic rather than ascribed, inasmuch as individuals decide on their degree of ethnic involvement instead of having it imposed from above or enforced from within (Tasan-Kok, Van Kempen, Raco, and Bolt 2013; Hollinger 2006).

A postethnicity turn raises the question of whether the cookie-cutter logic of a mosaic multiculturalism as governance is sustainable in a postmulticultural world. Reference to a mosaic metaphor envisaged ethnicity and ethnic communities as fixed and final while downplaying the mainstream "grouting" that kept every tile in its place. The principle of a tolerant coexistence under a mosaic metaphor tended to reify and essentialize ethnocultures as rigid, homogeneous, and unchanging wholes with fixed boundaries when, in reality, they are fluid, creative and changing, internally contested, accommodative of multiple and intersecting identities, and selectively permeable (Werbner 2012). Under the banner of a mosaic multiculturalism, central authorities managed the dynamics of ethnodiversity by slotting individuals into ethnic, racial, or cultural boxes, defined ethnic needs and interests around placement in these cultural tiles, and sanctioned these compartments as if they were a monolithic community with a single voice and uncontested viewpoints. These ethnic straitjackets were then deployed to formulate public policy and institutional programs, and in the process, reinforced those very divisions multiculturalism sought to manage (Malik 2015; Werbner 2012).

A legitimacy crisis is looming for those multicultural governance agendas that commit to a conventional ethnicity (Ang 2011, 2014). Their worth as rigid categories or reified groups as explanatory frameworks are unlikely to tap into networks, idioms, and routines that are relational, processual, hybridic, and fragmented (Brubaker 2004). Young people and second-generation migrants may no longer identify solely in terms of their ethnicity preferring, instead, to define themselves along lifestyle choices related to brands, friendship, travels, and social media (Cantle 2016; Khan 2017). Identities, loyalties, and belongings traverse and transcend national borders as intergenerational Canadians settle into new spaces which span a local/national/global domain; construct social networks that offer solidarity, support, information, and community, and participate across multiple universes-within-universes (multiverses) without necessarily discarding an attachment to the normative expectations of the host country (Pieterse 2006). A sense of nuance is critical in articulating a new identity when discursively framed as a hyphen which links a homeland with a "hostland" (Luo 2016). Ethnicity for young Canadians may partly inform their complex and dynamic identity across multiple cultural spaces. Yet for those whose ethnicity is not all-consuming as a dominant category of identity, it should neither define who they are nor lock them into strict ethnic scripts, in effect expressing a core postethnic principle: *don't judge me because of my ethnicity, but never forget where I came from* (Malik 2012; Ang, Brand, Noble, and Sternberg 2006).

Reference to postethnicity as an interpretive lens does not imply a rejection of ethnicity per se. Ethnicity remains important as a marker and container of personal or group identity, informal networks, social status, cultural meanings, and political mobilization in times of duress. Nor does postethnicity as an explanatory frame discredit the existence of ethnic communities or downplay the centrality of ethnic group identities. What the idea of postethnicity rejects is an uncritical reliance on the primacy of ethnicity as the exclusive unit of analysis, its centrality as the core component in the representation of diversity, or its status as the primary determinant of peoples' lives and life chances. Simplistic narratives of ethnicity are spurned because they rarely capture the complex lived realities of those whose lives and life chances flourish amidst a context of fusions, fissures, and flows. Ethnic narratives that draw on narrow and elitist versions no longer hold sway, especially when they superimpose static and dated representations of ethnicity at odds with the shifting realities of those whose connectedness to the homeland or traditional ethnicity is varied and conditional. A postethnic discursive shift eclipses these concepts. A reframing of ethnicity as an unstable social construct rather than fixed and foundational incorporates peoples' diverse differences across a dynamic constellation of flexible arrangements and fluid relationships (Hollinger 2006; Brubaker 2004; Cherti and McNeil 2012). Yet, the combination of these dynamics and demands poses a challenge for conventional ethnic media who must find a third space that addresses the concerns of those for whom immigrant ethnicity matters alongside the reality of those for whom homeland ethnicity is largely a default option.

TOWARD A POSTETHNIC ETHNIC MEDIA

Canada is routinely cast as a principled multicultural society with a lively ethnic media sector that complements a difficult political project (Murray 2008; Fleras 2015). It is increasingly unsettled by the realities and demands of a world both postmulticultural and postnational[4] that exposes flaws in an official multiculturalism while realigning how we see, think, and talk about ethnicity (Latham 2008; Fleras 2019b).[5] Such a perceptual/conceptual shift raises the spectre of whether the tandem of ethnic media and a mosaic multiculturalism are up to the challenges of a postmulticultural Canada. Attention is also drawn to whether an ethnic media in a postmulticultural world can defuse a growing crisis over their status (an identity crisis over what they are) and their role (a crisis of confidence over what they should be doing). That is, an ethnic media may have taken root in Canada because it complied with the integrative logic of an inclusive multiculturalism. The question now is whether ethnic media as a marker of communication, identity, and integration will remain relevant in a Canada that increasingly resembles a postmulticultural world yet remains tethered to an official multiculturalism as an ethnodiversity governance?

The emergence of a postmulticultural Canada offers the possibility of a postethnic ethnic media that moves beyond earlier conventions of bridging and bonding. An evolving context that is no longer multicultural but increasingly postmulticultural as reality and discourse – that is, it embraces the priority of the transnational, cosmopolitan, pluralized, and lived – exposes gaps in ethnic media when disconnected from those who resist being pigeon-holed into a standardized ethnic box. Ethnic media also fail to capitalize on the growing tendency for second-generation Canadians to construct new identities at the confluence of traditional ethnicity, their lived experiences as racialized Canadians, and their membership in far-flung diasporic communities (Li 2019). By contrast, the politics of postethnicity speaks to this reality of engaging a complexity of ethno-differences across a virtual domain that spurns convention yet spans the nexus of a local/national/global dynamic. A postethnic turn also disturbs the niche-based logic of ethnic media, the majority of which dwell on a single ethnic group by catering to their respective interests in isolation from others (Karim 2002). But despite mounting concerns over marketability in a postmulticultural world, there will always be a market for an ethnic media that never forgets its ethnic roots (Abraham 2017). A Canada that projects an unprecedented number of new admissions (i.e., permanent residents) in the foreseeable future will generate a constant supply of audiences eager to identify with traditional ethnicity as a basis to bond within and bridge beyond. Moreover, while the internet continues to challenge and change ethnic media in terms of content production and distribution, relationship to audiences, and the viability of established revenue streams, digital ethnic media will remain central as a bonding and bridging platform that moves with the times (Erdem 2018; Ali 2022).

The idea of a postethnic ethnic media confronts new challenges that, in some ways, are not wholly different from that of mainstream media. The COVID-19 pandemic has exposed and exacerbated the difficulties of conducting media business and remaining viable in a digital age, especially as notions of public trust and traditional authority begin to unravel. Both are coping with the drift of advertising dollars to other platforms, the monetization of digital content, the emergence of new business models, and proliferation of new communication technologies that disrupt the production, distribution, and consumption of information (Yu and Matsaganis 2019). However, adjustments in how ethnic media connect to audiences in the digital age do not address a core paradox. Traditional ethnic media may be too broad-brushed to capture the micro-realities of a multiversal world of in-group diversities. Conversely, they may be too narrowly regimented as an inward-looking enterprise for dealing with the macro-realities of a networked and mobile world of coming and going. A context of complex and shifting ethnicities puts pressure on customizing content by recalibrating it around people's real-life experiences while simultaneously expanding a localized ethnicity gaze to embrace a global outreach and cosmopolitan mindsets. At minimum, a postethnic ethnic media must (a) resist tendencies to over-ethnicize peoples' social identities; (b) soften groupist conceptions of ethnocultural membership; (c) recognize ethnocultural communities as socially constructed and internally contested; (d) acknowledge the intersectionality of ethnicity with other devalued identity markers such as gender, race, and class; (e) commit to a world that is simultaneously more ethnically hyperdiverse yet less ethnically localized as patterns of identity and belonging traverse new spatialized domains; and (f) approach ethnicity, discursively speaking, as a process ("a verb") rather than a thing ("a noun") (Fleras 2018). At best, the possibility of a postethnic ethnic media must reach out to an evolving audience base that de-essentializes ethnicity by focusing on inter-group dynamics and problem-solving cooperation as grounds for living together – not only with differences (a tolerant coexistence) but also in and through a complexity of lived differences as part of a cooperative inter-existence (Fleras 2019a).

How, then, should postethnic ethnic media reinvent themselves to take advantage of changing technology and a shifting audience base that defines itself as Canadian yet globally cosmopolitan without losing its ethic of ethnicity (Yu and Matsaganis 2019)? At the outset, no one is suggesting that the ethnic media "baby" be expelled from the postethnic bathwater. Reference to a postethnic media as a major reset is not a repudiation of ethnic media as much as a commitment to re-energize by capitalizing on their strengths in moving positively forward. Nor does this new ethnic media as an explanatory framework neglect the viability of ethnic communities or dare to downplay the salience of ethnic identities. Ethnicity still matters, albeit in ways that tap into the messy demands and unruly realities of a postmulticultural world. A postethnic ethnic media will continue to embrace the inclusive (reactive/proactive, inward/outward) logic of an ethnic media in terms of "constructing buffers," "creating bonds," "removing barriers," and "building bridges" (Fleras 2009). But they must also reboot to become more responsive to the imperatives of a postmulticultural world which is no longer conceptually attuned to the ethnicity logic of an official multiculturalism or the multicultural logic of ethnic media. Anita Li (2019) – a self-identified second-generation Canadian-born Chinese – pursues a similar line of reasoning to ethnic media. According to Li, ethnic media may have worked for her immigrant parents' generation, but it does not apply to a cohort who grew up in an era of multiplicity, hybridity, and mobility. She writes: "To me, ethnic media is for my immigrant parents' generation, not my friends and peers who grew up here. Unfortunately, these two audiences have been traditionally conflated, so there's a gaping hole where news coverage should be for young, diverse Canadians."

Finally, initiatives under a postethnic ethnic media must be aimed at constructing inter-ethnic linkages that foster intercultural dialogue in advancing a lived inter-existence beyond a specific ethnic locale. They must focus on forging intra-ethnic connections that diverge from yet draw on parental ethnicity to negotiate identities around people's lived spaces. Of particular note is the necessity to engage the community through an interactive and hyperlocal journalism that encourages a reshaping of the narrative for affecting change over issues which matter most (Ali 2022). A postethnic media must also consider the need to assume and align with a trans-ethnic perspective to take advantage of a transnational demographic that readily negotiates borders by transcending them. The use of digital technologies such as mobile news apps will also empower a new ethnic media to capitalize on community links as a stepping stone to a broader public sphere, in effect prompting the younger generation to connect, share, and mobilize in a diversifying complex world of "here," "there," and "everywhere" (Deuze 2006; Al-Rawi 2019; Yu and Matsaganis 2019).

CONTINUITY-IN-CHANGE: "PLUS ÇA CHANGE, C'EST LA MÊME CHOSE"

This chapter contends that we no longer live in a multicultural world but in the grip of a postmulticultural world. The logic and rationale behind a bounded and managed multiculturalism are now perceived as thematically inconsistent with the discordancy that drives this new governance agenda (Fleras 2021). Moves to defuse a looming governance crisis must build on the positives of a Canadian multiculturalism while moving positively forward along a postmulticultural pathway. A similar line of argument applies to the concept of ethnic media. In that we no longer commit to an ethnic world in terms of how people perceive and receive ethnicity and its governance, the multicultural logic of Canada's ethnic media is disconnected from the imperatives of a postmulticultural world, in effect putting pressure on applying a postethnicity lens to clarify what is occurring, and how and why. Just as ethnic media reflected, reinforced, and advanced the inclusionary logic of Canada's official multiculturalism, so too must a postethnic ethnic media adapt to a Canada less multicultural but more postmulticultural in framing the new ethnicity. Of course, reference to a postethnic ethnic media is not about abandoning ethnic media. Rather, it is a recognition that the concept of a multiculturally normed ethnic media may have reached its limit as a tool of integration, identity, and communication in a world of "posts," "trans," and "isms."

The theme of continuity-in-change strikes as appropriate. A postethnic ethnic media must capitalize on the logic and strength of ethnic media as a platform for moving forward. They will need to reinvent themselves by becoming more inward-looking while bonding around a complexity of diverse differences. Content must be customized and circulated in ways that interact with the lived realities of migrants and minorities who thrive, identify, and engage a networked and digitalized reality beyond the boundedness of conceptual categories and conventional borders. A postethnic ethnic media must also be poised toward a more outward orientation by bridging the local with the transnational and the cosmopolitan by way of the national. A readjustment in the multicultural logic of ethnic media is critical in moving from ethnicity to postethnicity, from silos to connections, from niches to networks, from diversity to hyperdiversity, and from coexistence to inter-existence. The implications of such a discursive shift are promising. Thinking outside the ethnicity/multicultural box may empower ethnic media to leverage the postethnic idea in a postmulticultural Canada into a winning combination.

NOTES

1 The term *ethnic media* represents a catch-all phrase encompassing a range of references that also include: multicultural, multilingual, alternative and community, third language, immigrant, transcultural, and diasporic (Papoutsaki and Kolesova 2017). Of the approximately 800 ethnic media outlets in Canada, 60 per cent are based in Ontario, about one-third operate in a South or East Asian language while another third use a European language, and they provide coverage of major national issues including election issues and trends (Griffith 2019). I have argued elsewhere (Fleras 2014), based on Riggins's (1992) prescient notion, that mainstream media may be framed as ethnic media – albeit not consciously so – insofar as content is organized around the realities and interests of a white ethnicity. That, in turn, suggests the possibility of defining ethnic media as media that have been "ethnicized" rather than a naturally occurring phenomenon "out there."

2 One is reminded of a comment by Canada's governor-general Lord Tweedsmuir when, in 1936, he proclaimed to an audience, "You will all be better Canadians for being also good Ukrainians." The gist of this statement, which suggests you will become better Canadians by

capitalizing on your ethnicity (Wolters-Fredland 2005), informs the logic of Canada's multicultural governance model.

3 Based on 2016 Statistics Canada data, the Peel Region outside Toronto possesses the lowest percentage of the population who speak English at home (61 per cent); 4 per cent of Peel's population had no working knowledge of either English or French.

4 Prime Minister Justin Trudeau's reference to Canada as the world's first postnational state ("no core identity, no mainstream") in a 2015 *New York Times* interview would appear to align with reference to Canada's postmulticulturality (see Biscahie 2019 for a critique of Trudeau's claim).

5 I have suggested elsewhere (Fleras 2021) that there is nothing inherently wrong with the idea of multiculturalism in Canada. Rather, an official multiculturalism as a modernist idea and twentieth century ideal is losing credibility because the world has changed in ways that render a state-sanctioned multicultural governance increasingly outside the realities and demands of a postmulticultural world.

REFERENCES

Abraham, George. 2017. "A Cultural Policy that Overlooks Multiculturalism." *Policy Options*, 19 October 2017. https://policyoptions.irpp.org/magazines/october-2017/a-cultural-policy-that-overlooks-multiculturalism/.

Adams, Michael. 2007. *Unlikely Utopia*. Toronto: Penguin Press.

Ahmed, Rukhsana, and Luisa Veronis. 2017. "Multicultural Media Use and Immigrant Settlement: A Comparative Study of Four Communities in Ottawa, Canada." *Journal of International Migration and Integration* 18 (2): 587–612.

Ali, Adena. 2022. "New Ventures Helping to Fill the Gaps in Canadian Media." *Toronto Star*, 15 March 2022. https://www.thestar.com/business/2022/03/14/new-media-ventures-continue-to-pop-up-in-canada-and-theyre-helping-fill-gaps.html.

Al-Rawi, Ahmed. 2019. "Mobile News Apps as Sites of Transatlantic Ethnic Mediascapes." *The Journal of International Communication* 26 (1): 73–91.

Ang, Ien. 2011. "Ethnicities and Our Precarious Future." *Ethnicities* 11 (1): 27–31.

– 2014. "Beyond Chinese Groupism: Chinese Australians between Assimilation, Multiculturalism, and Diaspora." *Ethnic and Racial Studies* 37 (7): 1184–96.

Ang, Ien, Jeff Brand, Greg Noble, and Jason Sternberg. 2006. *Connecting Diversity: The Paradoxes of Australian Multiculturalism*. NSW, Australia: Special Broadcasting Services Corporation. http://media.sbs.com.au/sbscorporate/documents/Connecting_Diversity.pdf.

Appiah, Kwame Anthony. 2018. *The Lies That Bind: Rethinking Identity*. New York: W.W. Norton.

Berry, John. 2013. "Research on Multiculturalism in Canada." *International Journal of Intercultural Relations* 37 (6): 663–75.

Berry, John, Rudolf Kalin, and Donald Taylor. 1977. *Multiculturalism and Ethnic Attitudes in Canada*. Ottawa, ON: Minister of Supply and Services.

Biscahie, Thibault. 2019. "Beyond the Mosaic: Justin Trudeau and the Postnational Chimera." *London Journal of Canadian Studies* 34 (3): 22–42.

Bradley, William. 2013. "Is There a Post-Multiculturalism?" *Studies on Multicultural Societies* 19. Afrasian Research Centre, Ryukoku University.

Brar, Arnanpeet. 2021. "I Went on Punjabi Radio to Share COVID Information with My Community. I Learned That Multicultural Media Has Been Kept in the Dark." *Toronto Star*, 6 January 2021. https://www.thestar.com/opinion/contributors/2021/01/06/i-went-on-punjabi-radio-to-share-covid-information-with-my-community-i-learned-that-multicultural-media-has-been-kept-in-the-dark.html.

Brubaker, Rogers. 2004. "Ethnicity without Groups." In *Ethnicity, Nationalism, and Minority Rights*, edited by Stephen May, Tariq Modood, and J. Squires, 50–77. Cambridge: Cambridge University Press.

Bucholtz, Ianis. 2019. "Bridging Bonds: Latvian Migrants' Interpersonal Ties on Social Networking Sites." *Media, Culture & Society* 41 (1): 104–19.

Budarick, John. 2019. "Ethnic Media Are Essential for New Migrants and Should Be Better Funded." *The Conversation*, 23 April 2019. https://theconversation.com/ethnic-media-are-essential-for-new-migrants-and-should-be-better-funded-115233.

Canadian Heritage. 2018. *Multiculturalism from Now and Into the Future. Annual Report on the Operation of the Canadian Multiculturalism Act 2016–2017*. Ottawa, ON: Canadian Heritage. https://www.canada.ca/en/canadian-heritage/corporate/publications/plans-reports/annual-report-canadian-multiculturalism-act-2016-2017.html.

Cantle, Ted. 2016. "Interculturalism: Learning to Live in Diversity." *Ethnicities* 16 (3): 471–79.

Cherti, M., and C. McNeil. 2012. *Rethinking Integration. Briefing.* London: Institute for Public Policy Research. https://www.ippr.org/files/images/media/files/publication/2012/10/rethinking-integration_Oct2012_9761.pdf.

Clark, Brad. 2014. "'Walking Up a Down-Escalator': The Interplay between Newsroom Norms and Media Coverage of Minority Groups." *InMedia*, 17 September 2014. http://inmedia.revues.org/749.

Deuze, Mark. 2006. "Ethnic Media, Community Media, and Participatory Culture." *Journalism* 7 (3): 262–80.

Douai, Aziz, and Barbara Perry. 2018. "A Different Lens? How Ethnic Minority Media Cover Crime." *Canadian Journal of Criminology and Criminal Justice* 60 (1): 96–121.

Erdem, Bora. 2018. "How Can Social Media Be Helpful for Immigrants to Integrate into Society in the US." *European Journal of Multidisciplinary Studies* 3 (3): 74–82.

Ferrer, Alicia Ferrández, and Jessica Retis. 2019. "Ethnic Minority Media: Between Hegemony and Resistance." *Journal of Alternative and Community Media* 4 (3): 1–11.

Fleras, Augie. 2009. "Theorizing Multicultural Media as Social Capital: Crossing Borders, Constructing Buffers, Creating Bonds, Building Bridges." *Canadian Journal of Communication* 34 (4): 725–29.

– 2014. "Theorizing Minority Misrepresentation: Framing Mainstream Media as White Ethnic Media." Presentation at the Media and Integration Conference, sponsored by the Jewish Museum and Council of Migration, Berlin, Germany, 27 November 2014. Also presented at the European Centre for Minority Issues, Flensburg, Germany, 2 December 2014.

– 2015. "Multicultural Media in a Post-Multicultural Canada? Rethinking Integration." *Global Media Journal, Canadian Edition* 8 (2): 25–47.

– 2016. *Unequal Relations: A Critical Introduction to Race, Ethnic, and Aboriginal Dynamics in Canada.* 8th ed. Toronto: Pearson.

– 2018. *Citizenship in a Translational Canada.* New York: Peter Lang.

– 2019a. *Postmulticulturalism: Realities, Discourses, Practices.* New York: Peter Lang.

– 2019b. "Fifty Years of Canadian Multiculturalism: Accounting for Its Durability, Theorizing the Crisis, Preparing for the Future." *Canadian Ethnic Studies* 48 (3): 1–23.

– 2021. *Multiculturalism @50: Retrospect, Perspectives, Prospects.* Leiden: Brill.

Fleras, Augie, and Jean Lock Kunz. 2001. *Media and Minorities in Canada.* Toronto: Thompson Publishing.

Foroutan, Naika. 2015. "Paradigm Shift." BPD. https://www.bpb.de/themen/migration-integration/kurzdossiers/205297/paradigm-shift/.

Gerson, Daniela, and Carlos Rodriguez. 2018. "Going Forward: How Ethnic and Mainstream Media Can Collaborate in Changing Communities." *American Press Institute*, 19 July 2018. https://www.americanpressinstitute.org/publications/reports/strategy-studies/ethnic-and-mainstream-media-collaborations-in-changing-communities/.

Gozdecka, Dorota A., Selen A. Ercan, and Magdalena Kmak. 2014. "From Multiculturalism to Post-Multiculturalism: Trends and Paradoxes." *Journal of Sociology* 50 (1): 51–64.

Griffith, Andrew. 2019. "How Does Ethnic Media Campaign Coverage Differ?" *Policy Options*, 2 October 2019. https://policyoptions.irpp.org/fr/magazines/october-2019/how-does-ethnic-media-campaign-coverage-differ/.

Gryzmala-Kazlowska, Aleksandra, and Jenny Phillimore. 2018. "Introduction. Rethinking Integration. New Perspectives on Adaptation and Settlement in the Era of Super-Diversity." *Journal of Ethnic and Migration Studies* 44 (2): 179–96.

Haas, Hein de, Stephen Castles, and Mark Miller. 2020. *The Age of Migration: International Population Movements in the Modern World*. 6th ed. London: Guilford Press.

Hayward, Mark. 2019. *Identity and Industry. Making Media Multicultural in Canada*. Montreal & Kingston: McGill-Queen's University Press.

Hiebert, Dan. 2016. *What's So Special about Canada? Understanding the Resilience of Immigration and Multiculturalism*. Migration Policy Institute, June 2015. https://www.migrationpolicy.org/research/whats-so-special-about-canada-understanding-resilience-immigration-and-multiculturalism.

Hollinger, David. 2006. *Postethnic America: Beyond Multiculturalism*. 10th anniversary ed. New York: Basic Books.

Husband, Charles. 2005. "Minority Ethnic Media as Communities of Practice: Professionalism and Identity Politics in Interaction." *Journal of Ethnic and Migration Studies* 31 (3): 461–79.

James, Carl, and Tana Turner. 2017. *Toward Race Equity in Education. The Schooling of Black Students in the Greater Toronto Area*. Toronto: York University, the Jean Augustine Chair in Education, Community & Diaspora. https://edu.yorku.ca/files/2017/04/Towards-Race-Equity-in-Education-April-2017.pdf.

Jeyasundarum, Brannavy. 2020. "What's Plaguing Toronto's Ethnic Press?" *The Local*, 23 November 2020. https://thelocal.to/whats-plaguing-torontos-ethnic-press/.

Karim, Karim H. 2002. *The Media of Diaspora: Mapping the Globe*. New York: Routledge.

Karim, Karim H., and Ahmed Al-Rawi, eds. 2018. *Diaspora and Media in Europe: Migration, Identity, and Integration*. Basingstoke: Palgrave Macmillan.

Khan, Salmaan. 2017. "Official Multiculturalism and the Promise of Equality." *Canada Watch* (Spring 2017): 11–12. https://robarts.info.yorku.ca/files/2012/02/CW-2017-Spring.pdf.

Kim, Amanda. 2020. "Ethnic Media Works to End the Infodemic." Blue Shield of California Foundation, 6 May 2020. https://blueshieldcafoundation.org/blog/ethnic-media-works-to-end-infodemic.

Kymlicka, Will. 2012. *Multiculturalism: Success, Failure, and the Future. Transatlantic Council on Migration*. Migration Policy Institute, February 2012. https://www.migrationpolicy.org/research/multiculturalism-success-failure-and-future.

– 2015. "Solidarity in Diverse Societies: Beyond Neoliberal Multiculturalism and Welfare Chauvinism." *Comparative Migration Studies* 3 (17): 1–17.

Latham, Robert. 2008. "Canadian Society Is Not Just Multicultural; It Is Multiversal." Research Snapshot. York University, Toronto. https://yorkspace.library.yorku.ca/xmlui/bitstream/handle/10315/29179/00110.pdf.

Li, Anita. 2019. "Canadian Media Lacks Nuance, Depth on Racial Issues." *Policy Options*, 10 September, 2019. https://policyoptions.irpp.org/magazines/september-2019/canadian-media-lacks-nuance-depth-on-racial-issues/.

Lindgren, April. 2011. "Front Page Challenge: A Case Study Examining What the Ethnic Media Promises and What It Delivers." *CERIS Working Paper Series* (82): 1–15.

Luo, Lin. 2016. "Digital Ethnic Media: Integrating Minorities and Connecting Diversities – Digital Diaspora, Virtual Diaspora Communities." Master's thesis, Lund University.

Mahtani, Minelle. 2002. "Representing Minorities: Canadian Media and Minority Identities." *Canadian Ethnic Studies* 33 (3): 99–131.

Malik, Kenan. 2012. "In Defence of Diversity." *The New Humanist*, 18 December 2012. http://www.eurozine.com.

– 2015. "The Failure of Multiculturalism. Community versus Society in

Europe." *Foreign Affairs*, March/April 2015. https://www.foreignaffairs.com/articles/western-europe/2015-02-18/failure-multiculturalism.

Mansouri, Fethi, Amanuel Elias, and Reem Sweid. 2017. *The Doing Diversity Project: Revitalising Multiculturalism through an Intercultural Lens and Deliberative Interventions*. Deakin University, Melbourne. https://centerforinterculturaldialogue.files.wordpress.com/2010/07/a017e-tddp_deakin_university_2017_digital_fa.pdf.

Marche, Stephen. 2016. "Canada in the Age of Trump." *The Walrus*, September 2016. https://thewalrus.ca/canada-in-the-age-of-donald-trump/.

– 2018. "An Apology for Multiculturalism." *Open Canada*, 13 August 2018. https://opencanada.org/apology-multiculturalism/.

Matejskova, Tatiana, and Marco Antonsich, eds. 2015. *Governing Through Diversity: Migration Societies in Post-Multiculturalist Times*. New York: Palgrave Macmillan.

Matsaganis, Matthew D., Sandra Ball-Rokeach, and Vikki S. Katz. 2010. *Understanding Ethnic Media: Producers, Consumers, and Societies*. Los Angeles: SAGE.

Matta, Baldev. 2019. "The Impact of Ethnic Media on the Well-Being and Integration of New Canadians." *Friends of Canadian Broadcasting*, 5 February 2019. https://legacy.friends.ca/explore/article/the-impact-of-ethnic-media-on-the-wellbeing-and-integration-of-new-canadians/.

Murray, Catherine. 2008. "Media Infrastructure for Multicultural Diversity." *Policy Options*, 1 April 2008. https://policyoptions.irpp.org/magazines/budget-2008/media-infrastructure-for-multicultural-diversity/.

NCM News Desk. 2020. "Analysis: How Ethnic Media is Covering the Pandemic." *New Canadian Media*, 10 May 2020. https://newcanadianmedia.ca/analysis-how-ethnic-media-is-covering-the-pandemic/.

– 2022. "Ethnic Media Provides Added Perspective on 'Freedom Convoy.'" *New Canadian Media*, 2 February 2022. https://newcanadianmedia.ca/ethnic-media-provides-nuanced-coverage-ignored-by-mainstream/.

Papoutsaki, Evangelia, and Elena Kolesova, eds. 2017. *Exploring the Role, Benefits, Challenges, and Potential of Ethnic Media in New Zealand*. Auckland: Unitec Press.

Perrigoe, Ross, and Mahmoud Eid. 2014. *Mission Invisible: Race, Religion, and News at the Dawn of the 9/11 Era*. Vancouver: UBC Press.

Pieterse, Jan Nederveen. 2007. "Global Multiculture, Flexible Acculturation." *Globalizations* 4 (1): 65–79.

Riggins, Stephen. 1992. *Ethnic Minority Media: An International Perspective*. Los Angeles: SAGE.
Ruble, Blair A. 2018. "Opportunity with Dignity: Lessons from Multiculturalism in Toronto." Wilson Center, 28 February 2018. https://www.wilsoncenter.org/article/opportunity-dignity-lessons-multiculturalism-toronto.
Saunders, Doug. 2013. "Immigrants' Children Find Multiculturalism Obsolete." *Globe and Mail*, 26 January 2013. https://www.theglobeandmail.com/opinion/doug-saunders-immigrants-children-find-multiculturalism-obsolete/article7870191/.
Spoonley, Paul, and Erin Tolley, eds. 2012. *Diverse Nations, Diverse Responses*. Montreal & Kingston: McGill-Queen's University Press.
Tasan-Kok, Tuna, Ronald Van Kempen, Mike Raco, and Gideon Bolt. 2014. "Towards Hyper-Diversified European Cities: A Critical Literature Review of Interculturalism." Utrecht University, Faculty of Geosciences. https://www.researchgate.net/publication/264001370_Towards_Hyper-Diversified_European_Cities_A_Critical_Literature_Review.
Todd, Douglas. 2019. "The Political Use and Misuse of Canada's Ethnic Media." *Vancouver Sun*, 7 July 2019. https://vancouversun.com/opinion/columnists/douglas-todd-the-political-use-and-misuse-of-canadas-ethnic-media.
Triandafyllidou, Anna, ed. 2017. *Multicultural Governance in a Mobile World*. Edinburgh: Edinburgh University Press.
Walane, Fayyez H. 2017. "Diversity: Rise of the Ethnic Media in Canada." *Canadian Newcomer Magazine*, 25 August 2017. http://www.cnmag.ca/diversity-rise-of-the-ethnic-media-in-canada/.
Werbner, Pnina. 2012. "Multiculturalism from Above and Below: Analyzing a Political Discourse." *Journal of Intercultural Studies* 33 (2): 197–209.
Wolters-Fredland, Benita. 2005. "We Shall Be Better Canadians by Being Conscious Jews: Multiculturalism and the Construction of Canadian Identity in the Toronto Jewish Folk Choir." *Intersections: Canadian Journal of Music* 25 (1–2): 187–209.
Yu, Sherry S. 2018a. *Diasporic Media beyond the Diaspora. Korean Media in Vancouver and Los Angeles*. Vancouver: UBC Press.
– 2018b. "The Commercialization of Journalism. Ethnic Media, News Production, and Business Strategies in the Digital Era." *Journalism Studies* 19 (16): 2433–50.

Yu, Sherry S., and Daniel Ahadi. 2010. "Promoting Civic Engagement through Ethnic Media." *Platform: Journal of Media and Communication* 2 (2): 54–71.

Yu, Sherry S., and Matthew D. Matsaganis, eds. 2019. *Ethnic Media in the Digital Age*, 1–9. New York: Routledge.

Yu, Sherry S., and Catherine A. Murray. 2007. "Ethnic Media under a Multicultural Policy: The Case of the Korean Media in British Columbia." *Canadian Ethnic Studies* 39 (3): 99–124.

Zapata-Barrero, Ricard. 2017. "Interculturalism in the Post-Multicultural Debate: A Defence." *Comparative Migration Studies* 5 (1): 1–23.

CHAPTER TWO

Researching Ethnic Media in Canada: Conceptual and Methodological Inquiries

Sherry S. Yu and Daniel Ahadi

INTRODUCTION

Scholars in the field of ethnic media research are challenged by several important questions that are central to the study of ethnic media since how we define, contextualize, and situate ethnic media has clear implications for the research process. For example, a researcher who defines ethnic media as primarily transnational media will face a different set of epistemological and methodological challenges than one who defines ethnic media as locally produced media. Similarly, different sets of research challenges emerge when researchers focus on analogue media versus digital media, print media versus broadcast media, and so forth. Likewise, how researchers situate ethnic media in the broader media system will also invite a set of questions to deal with. That is, are ethnic media part of the mainstream public sphere? Or are ethnic media independent of the mainstream public sphere and part of smaller "public sphericules" (Gitlin 1998, 173) challenging the mainstream public sphere as a counter-hegemonic force? With the growth of ethnic media, have they increased (ethnic) minority power? This chapter will address some of these ongoing debates and subsequent conceptual and methodological inquiries and provide some insights into ethnic media research in the digital age.

CONCEPTUAL INQUIRIES

Coining the terminology to define the field of ethnic media research is a complicated and nearly impossible task. In our search for Canadian ethnic media literature, we identified a body of academic sources in the form of books, book chapters, journal articles, policy reports, and reviews, which use varying definitions to describe what broadly has been referred to as ethnic media in communication and ethnic/diaspora studies. This section highlights some of the more commonly used terminologies, problematizing some while consenting to others, to provide an argument for why we have chosen "ethnic media" as the descriptor for this volume.

Defining Ethnic Media as a Research Subject

In the Canadian Multiculturalism Act (Government of Canada n.d.a) and the Official Languages Act (Government of Canada n.d.b), Canada's official languages are defined as English and French, while Indigenous languages are protected under the Indigenous Languages Act (Government of Canada n.d.c) to support the efforts of Indigenous peoples to reclaim, revitalize, maintain, and strengthen Indigenous cultures. Other settler languages, i.e., non-English and non-French languages, are referred to as third languages in Canadian cultural policy circles. Under the Broadcasting Act (Government of Canada n.d.d), both Indigenous and the third-language media sectors are referred to as minority languages (compared to the official English and French languages), and content production in these languages is safeguarded in the name of Canadian cultural diversity through representation in mainstream Canadian media (CRTC 2019). What differentiates the Canadian definition of ethnic media from others is its "official" exclusiveness for cultural and racial minorities. The Canadian Radio-television and Telecommunications Commission defines an ethnic program in the Ethnic Broadcasting Policy (CRTC 1999) as a program "in any language, that is specifically directed to any culturally or racially distinct group other than one that is Aboriginal Canadian or from France or the British Isles." CRTC excludes "Aboriginal Canadians" from here and governs Native broadcasting separately under the Native Broadcasting Policy (CRTC 1990).

Certainly, the minority–majority discourse as it is used in multicultural literature is, broadly speaking, flushed with flaws and controversy if considered within the context of the geographic concentration of ethnic populations. For example, in the city of Richmond, British Columbia, with a Chinese population of 53 per cent (Statistics Canada 2016), are Chinese media minority media? Added to this complexity for the Canadian context is the category of "visible minority" that in policy circles is code for anyone who does not look white: "persons, other than Aboriginal peoples, who are non-Caucasian in race or non-white in colour" (Statistics Canada n.d.). One of the issues with using "ethnic media" as a blanket label is that not all ethnic media are media by or for visible minority groups. For example, are Irish- or Scottish Gaelic–language media considered ethnic media? They are, if ethnic media are media for ethnic groups (Murray, Yu, and Ahadi 2007). What about South Asian media produced in English that are accessible for a broader audience? What is evidently important for the context of labelling media as ethnic is their focus on community-oriented news (not to be confused with local news), activities, current affairs, advertising, and so forth for the members of communities whose cultural and media needs are not met by the mainstream English- or French-language media. These communities have traditionally been defined as immigrant and visible minority communities in ethnic media literature (Ferrer and Retis 2019; Lee and Tse 1994; Matsaganis, Katz, and Ball-Rokeach 2010).

On the contrary, other terminologies such as diasporic or minority media (Siapera 2010) have been more reflective of the transnational nature and functionality of ethnic media. According to Karim (2002), "diasporic media" are media that originate in the country of origin and are transmitted to the diasporic communities across the globe. "Ethnic media," on the one hand, originate in the country of settlement. "Transnational media" as a category, while they can be diasporic or ethnic, has a broader definition: Gher and Bharthapudi (2004), for one, defined them as "communication, information or entertainment that crosses international borders without the regulatory constraints normally associated with electronic media." Thus, they are not ethnic per se but simply available for ethnic minorities. Naficy (2003), on the other hand, used diasporic media to refer to media for exiles, thus media that originate in the country of settlement, and transnational media to refer to media that originate in the country of origin. For example, much of the transnational and diasporic media that are consumed by the Iranian diaspora originates from Los Angeles or London. Acknowledging the complexity of such conceptualization, we invited our contributors to provide further conceptualization. In this volume, the term ethnic media embraces ethnic, diasporic, and transnational media that originate in either country of origin or settlement and are available to ethnic minorities in Canada.

Drawing a Boundary for Ethnic Media: Place and Space Questions

Ethnic media are physical entities, as in broadcasting and print publications, but are simultaneously and increasingly more digital entities, especially those that are transitioning to or natively digital. Thus, as much as the previous discussion of ethnic media being minority as opposed to majority, and local versus transnational, their presence in "place" (physical) versus "space" (digital) becomes an important conceptual inquiry for ethnic media research.

Ball-Rokeach, Kim, and Matei's (2001) Communication Infrastructure Theory illustrates how community organizations, ethnic media, and residents can collectively form a "storytelling network" to discuss various neighborhood issues, and if well connected to their city and national counterparts, can possibly serve as a civil society. At the centre of the "ethnic communication infrastructure" framework, there is the much-debated ability of media to foster collective consciousness, shared citizenship, and sense of belonging among populations of specific geographic entities (see, e.g., Benedict Anderson's *Imagined Communities*). For instance, what used to bond the Iranian community in Vancouver more than the language, ethnicity, or religion was their shared dissatisfaction with the political system back home (Ahadi 2016). The vast majority had fled Iran to escape the regime. Today, however, Iranians have a much more complex relationship with the regime and their country of origin. Many have, over the years, established financial and cultural ties with Iran – perhaps an unimaginable undertaking in the early years of settlement. Furthermore, diasporic communities, as they mature in their country of settlement, become highly diverse along cultural and socio-economic lines. The homeland or the country of origin, on one hand, and the culture developed in the new country of settlement, on the other, become entangled in a complex sense of being. That is, a sense of longing and nostalgic references to a past that no longer exists in the form they experienced prior to migration – which at best can be understood in terms of "imagined communities" in the words of Benedict Anderson (1991) – and a sense of longing for new membership in a new home as "Canadian."

Thus, ethnic communication infrastructure for an ethnic community cannot be considered to serve a homogeneous community. Especially since the refugee crisis in the aftermath of the various

Middle Eastern political liberation movements and conflicts in the 2010s, and the continued arrival of newcomers in immigrant-receiving countries such as Canada, the notion of a cohesive "we" has been subject to challenge in diasporic communities, as is also true broadly for historically culturally homogeneous countries. Arguably, this homogeneity has always been imagined and fictitious as intersectionality has consistently been part of the societal fabric, but hegemonically sidelined by the white dominant culture. Yet, the media as "symbolic mediators of identity" and belonging can assist in constructing a cohesive image of such communities for those who share similar imagination one way or another in the same physical "place" (Matsaganis and Ahadi 2018).

This focus on place puts an emphasis in ethnic media research on where these outlets are physically located. Changes in the ethnic composition of nation-states, and the flow of immigrants, global capital, and communication models, have shifted the geo-focus of struggles for social, political, cultural, and economic recognition from just the nation as a whole to the new frontiers of urban centres, or as Saskia Sassen (2018) argues, the "global city." Studies on global migration trends indicate that newcomers are more likely to settle in urban areas where communication infrastructure, commercial services, immigrant organizations, ethnic media, and so on are widely available for immigrant communities (Marques and Santos 2004; Sassen 2018). The city presents a far more concrete space for politics than the nation (Sassen 2018). Since nationally, politics need to operate within existing formal systems, whether the electoral political system or judiciary system, non-formal political actors like members of the diaspora who have not yet received permanent resident status or are relatively new to the formal political networks of national governments, are thereby more easily rendered invisible. The city is expected to accommodate a broad range of political activities and issues (e.g., gay rights, immigrant and refugee rights, rallies, gatherings, community centres).

As a consequence, much of local urban politics is concrete and enacted by people, rather than dependent on partisan, aligned, or formal bureaucratic processes of the nation-state. Informal economies, participation in local political institutions such as municipal boards, commissions, and councils, as well as cultural productions and self-expressions, are part of the so-called local, urban experience of being an immigrant (Marques and Santos 2004). According to Sassen (2005, 2018), global cities with their transnational and cosmopolitan flow of culture and economy have become venues for traditionally "unauthorized" segments of society to gain presence vis-à-vis institutions of power, and vis-à-vis each other. These unauthorized segments are those people who are disadvantaged and discriminated against because of their ethnicity, gender, or sexual orientation. This signals, as Sassen (2005, 92) argues, "the possibility of a new type of politics centred on new types of political actors."

Sassen's definition of global cities, however, has its own limitations. It predominantly focuses on cities that have historically served as sites of global flow of culture and capital. In her book, Sassen (2005) identifies specifically New York, London, and Tokyo, as well as several others as prominent global cities. However, there are also so-called "second tier cities" (Markusen, Lee, and DiGiovanna 1999, 2) to which Canadian cities belong (Cardoso and Meijers 2017), that attract thousands of new immigrants each year and are sites of a vibrant ethnic media landscape. Only recently have studies emerged on second-tier cities' ethnic media operations, such as Stockholm (Ahadi 2016), Auckland (McMillan and Barker 2021), and Vancouver and Los Angeles (Yu 2018).

Meanwhile, globalization and advancements in communication technologies have enabled new opportunities for diasporic communities to connect with their homeland through digital "space," for example, "digital ethnic media" (Ahmed and Veronis 2019, 99). When we refer to "the third-language media sector" in Canada, we often mean locally produced media for immigrant communities living in Canada, particularly in the context of the nation-state and nation-building. In other words, ethnic media are mainly third-language media, as in non-English and non-French, and because of this definition, we assume a Canadian production origin. This definition may have worked for a pre-digital age where legacy media like radio, television, and print dominated the ethnic media sector, and ethnic media were primarily consumed by first-generation immigrants. In our digital age, this definition is increasingly challenged by online ethnic media using websites, apps, social media, and streaming services as their dissemination platforms, and which are not primarily consumed by first-generation immigrants. The 1.5 and the second generation (and beyond) are actively producing and consuming media, especially in digital forms, that can be categorized as ethnic media since they are produced by a non-white

Canadian population, either in the two dominant languages or third languages. These media outlets provide the opportunity of a broader scope that includes media that may be available in both official languages, and can target communities beyond their respective ones, or originate online but from elsewhere. However, these media outlets cater primarily to ethnoracial communities in Canada. In short, digitization, transnationalization, and hybridity have complicated the ethnic media sector and the idea of an ethnic communication infrastructure, and subsequently, how we define these media practices.

METHODOLOGICAL INQUIRIES

Common areas of media research are institutions, audiences, and text (Bertrand and Hughes 2005). Ethnic media research is no exception. Much of the literature on Canadian ethnic media has concentrated on three areas of research: media consumption and audience research (e.g., Lee and Tse 1994), ethnic media production (e.g., Li 2015), and ethnic media content (e.g., Cheng 2005; Douai and Perry 2018). Central to critical media studies is the recognition of the relationship between production, the technical infrastructure, and the institutional structures that condition and shape the production, distribution, and consumption of ethnic media.

The diverse, complex, and layered diasporic identities and media strategies that contemporary researchers in the field constantly refer to (see, e.g., Georgiou 2003; Karim 2002), in our view, have to do with not only the variations in media consumption (e.g., the quantity and types of ethnic media outlets) but also journalistic practices and media representations and the consciousness these practices foster among users. In part, this reflects the approach ethnic media researchers have taken to media studies which focuses on how media technologies are appropriated and incorporated in everyday life in general, and how people think about the world through these media technologies (Silverstone, Hirsch, and Morley 1994).

In other words, ethnic media research looks at the content of these media technologies in terms of how they communicate belonging, country, home, and other immaterial aspects of diasporic life. The complexity is not simply defined by what types of media these communities consume on a day-to-day basis (satellite television, radio, print media, online sources, etc.) or whether the members of these communities identify themselves as "Canadian" "ethnic" or "ethnic-Canadian." Rather, the complexity becomes more interesting when we look beyond how producers encode media texts and how people decode them. Nick Couldry (2010) suggests that researchers should observe a range of contexts within which media practices take place. With a context-bound approach to media and audience studies, it becomes increasingly difficult to measure the degree to which ethnic media practices inhibit or promote civic and cultural adaptation. Rather, understanding civic and cultural adaptation comes down to examining who, under what conditions, and with which identity orientation consumes and engages with their media environment.

From this perspective, ethnic media should not be viewed through the lens of what Audrey Kobayashi (1993, 205) calls "red boot multiculturalism," that is, the financing of various cultural events such as festivals or art fairs for the sake of showcasing a multicultural façade. Rather, ethnic media should be concerned with how members of "ethnic groups" represent themselves via their content as politically engaged members of multiple communities, and in particular, the urban centres where they reside. This is based on the assumption that the aforementioned communication infrastructure, specifically ethnic communication infrastructure, shapes the potential for political action and civic engagement.

Given this context, there are added inquiries on the part of researchers to properly address complex layers of ethnic media production, consumption, and content. New conceptualizations and creative and innovative methods are suggested to deal with challenges for race-related research (Smets 2019 or see, e.g., Al-Rawi 2020; Kozar 2002). The next section discusses ongoing inquiries around commonly used methods as well as emerging methods for ethnic media that researchers have come to use and consider.

Inquiries for Commonly Used Methods

THE ETHNIC MEDIA SECTOR AS A RESEARCH SITE

The exploration of ethnic media institutions as businesses helps in understanding the political economy of the ethnic media sector. While the exploration of individual organizations offers qualitative information and contributes to enhancing an understanding of the overall landscape of the media sector, such efforts are not comparable to full-scale, nation-wide mapping if the purpose is indeed to obtain a full picture of the sector as a whole. This sector-wide information serves various purposes, not only for academic research, serving as a "population" for sampling, but also for ethnic media businesses to promote the marketability of the ethnic media sector within the media industry.

Mapping of the ethnic media sector has been undertaken sporadically in Canada: by academic institutions, such as the now-defunct BC Ethnic Media Directory by Simon Fraser University (part of the "Cultural Diversity and Ethnic Media in BC" study that the editors of this book, Daniel Ahadi and Sherry Yu, were involved in [Murray, Yu, and Ahadi 2007]) and the more recent Canadian Minority Media Database by the University of Alberta; by industry associations such as the Canadian Ethnic Media Association and National Ethnic Press and Media Council of Canada; and by commercial directories such as CARD Online (Yu 2016). However, these services pose some limitations in terms of comprehensiveness, public access, or sustainability, as they are often region- or media-type-specific or subscription-based (Yu 2016), or they become quickly obsolete once manual updating stops for various reasons, including lack of funding. Such variations and inconsistencies mean that these resources offer a different research site or populations of ethnic media as a sector within the media industry to researchers, depending on which directory they choose to use.

Given this situation, ethnic media research on media institutions tends to be qualitative and smaller in scale, focusing on a few media outlets (see, e.g., Baffoe 2012; Qiao 2013). This type of study may sound easier to conduct but faces its own challenges, that is, a significant level of prior "insider" knowledge about the community is needed to be able to locate media outlets worthy of research and provide a sound rationale for why they were chosen. This limitation (for "outsider" researchers) and privilege (for "insider" researchers) invites the question raised by Spivak (1987, 253) in reference to subaltern studies, asking whether "men [can] theorize feminism, can whites theorize racism, can the bourgeois theorize revolution and so on. It is when *only* the former groups theorize that the situation is politically intolerable." While resisting "elite methodology," Spivak (254) dismisses such in-group orientation, arguing that it "cannot be held as a theoretical presupposition either, for it predicates the possibility of knowledge on identity."

For ethnic media research, it is not too difficult to encounter studies done by researchers from the same ethnoracial community under investigation (see, in this volume, chapter 5 by Bukhari and chapter 12 by Bains). The same applies to audience and content research as discussed in the following sections, as it requires, especially the former, not only awareness but also actual practice of cultural sensitivity by researchers in their interaction with research subjects and the analysis of such interactions.

HUMAN RESEARCH AND ACCESS TO RESEARCH SUBJECTS

Quantitative research on ethnic (media) producers or audiences, especially research that is based on random sampling, is limited in academic research (see, e.g., Black and Leithner 1987, 1988) but more common in market research (such as Fairchild Television's "Canadian Chinese Media Monitor" 2007). Academic research tends to depend more on non-random, convenient sampling at specific locations. For example, Lee and Tse's study (1994) on "Hong Kong Immigrants to Canada" and their media consumption and the impact on acculturation used mall intercepts with over 900 respondents in Hong Kong and Vancouver. Chow's study (2018) on "Chinese-Canadian Adolescents" and the factors that influence acquisition and retention of heritage language and ethnic identity also used a specific location for sampling – over 500 surveys at heritage language schools in Calgary. Dali's (2005) study of Russian immigrants' use of Russian-language newspapers used posters in apartment buildings in North York, Toronto, to recruit fifty survey respondents. For qualitative research, dependency on snowball sampling is high, which as mentioned in the previous section, again requires in-depth prior knowledge about the community, especially around access for recruiting participants. Information available online (such as contact information) or via community organizations (Bukhari 2019) and professional networks (Veronis, Tabler, and Ahmed 2018) are some of the most common routes for snowball sampling for in-depth interviews and focus groups.

Human research further requires a particular set of cultural skills and sensitivities such as language and religion that enable researchers to build rapport and conduct fieldwork successfully. Indeed, many ethnic media studies have been conducted in the language of the ethnic community with an option of English offered to participants

(Li 2015; Lee and Tse 1994; in this volume, chapter 3 by Ng). Li's study (2015) of Chinese media producers provided participants with language options but the majority of interviews were conducted in Chinese.

Broadly speaking, insider knowledge and cultural skills and sensitivities are critical for any race-related research. Cornelius's (1982) study of undocumented immigrants suggested researchers build rapport with "microlevel social networks" (401) referring to "local notables" such as community organization leaders, merchants, teachers, and doctors (385). Studies also suggested considering participant-related factors that influence fieldwork such as sense of time, use of space, gendered relationships, and "economic structures" which participants are part of (401). Research on Pakistani Muslims in the UK (Zubair and Victor 2015), Kosovars in Switzerland (Cola and Brusa 2013), and undocumented immigrants in the United States (Cornelius 1982), for example, identified these culture or ethnicity/race-specific factors.

Race-related research equally suggests that researcher-related factors are significant, such as the role of interviewers, language of communication between interviewer and participants, and the interpretation of data (Cola and Brusa 2013). Interviews conducted by "outsider" interviewers, as opposed to "insider" interviewers, were found to show an us-and-them division to a certain extent (118). Nonetheless, it is also suggested that caution should be taken toward both "an essentialist manner (as if race can be boiled down to a simple equation of matching interviewer and interviewee race for maximum reliability)" and "a colorblind manner (as if race doesn't matter)" (O'Brien 2011, 90). The challenges of the former are noted to equally exist due to the heterogeneity of people within the same ethnoracial groups: socio-economic difference can deter the building of rapport even if the researcher and participants are from the same ethnoracial group.

Beyond such "intersectionality" or "superdiversity," ethnic media research also requires an understanding of heterogeneity resulting from "hybridity" and the "transnational or transdiasporic character" of group members and requires "a cosmopolitan framework and methodology" (Georgiou 2012 and Christensen 2012, cited in Smets 2019, 103). Audience research expands as the audience's use of cultural products expands in their forms and platforms. A reconceptualization of ethnic media is needed (as discussed in the previous section) as media production and consumption are considered in both the local and transnational sense: media that are locally grown versus media from home. A good example of media from home is the consumption of K-pop among hyphenated Korean Canadian youth as "a diasporic youth cultural practice" (Yoon 2019, 139). Digital, online, transnational, and private consumption of media content demonstrates a shift from previously analogue, locally accessible community media.

NEWS MONITORING AND NEWS DATABASES

Broadly, monitoring media text is one of the areas of race-related research studied solely or in triangulation with other methods (van Dijk 1991). Critical discourse analysis (CDA) is an example: it is "discourse analytical research that primarily studies the way social-power abuse and inequality are enacted, reproduced, legitimated, and resisted by text and talk in the social and political context" and has been widely used, particularly around class, gender, and race (van Dijk 2015, 466). Van Dijk's (1991) study of over 2,700 news articles in British newspapers showed the influence of media on the development of the majority's perception toward minorities. The use of particular structures and the relevant strategies related to meaning, style, and rhetoric assists the representation of minorities in a particular way.

Monitoring ethnic news content published by various forms of media – broadcasting, print, and digital in the form of text, audio converted into text, or visual – and multimodal analyses of this content is particularly important for two main reasons. First, it helps us understand not only what these media cover but also why they cover what they cover. These media tend to cover what mainstream media under- or misrepresent and amplify the voice of marginalized communities, or provide a "multilocal sense of belonging" connected to both the country of settlement and the country of origin (see, e.g., Cheng 2005, 142; Goodrum, Godo, and Hayter 2011; Yu and Ahadi 2010). Goodrum, Godo, and Hayter's (2011) comparative content analysis of coverage of China in the CBC, *Toronto Star*, and *Ming Pao* found a significant contrast: approximately 4 per cent versus 40 per cent coverage in mainstream media and Chinese-language media, respectively. Why ethnic media provide more coverage of the home country has been debated. Other than news of interest, one of the prominent factors is the political economy of ethnic media, resulting from limited resources for local production and a high dependency on imported news from the country of origin (Oh and Zhou 2012; Yu 2018).

Monitoring content also helps in exploring ethnic media more critically by challenging the assumption of pro-ethnic coverage in ethnic media and anti-ethnic coverage in mainstream media (Lindgren 2013; Oh and Zhou 2012). Lindgren's (2013) study of Korean, Russian, and Punjabi publications in the Greater Toronto Area, for example, found a lack of diversity, that is, a lack of coverage of other ethnic groups and even stereotyping of certain groups. Oh and Zhou's (2012) study of coverage of SARS in the *Toronto Star* and the *World Journal*, a Chinese-language newspaper, further found that both papers similarly used the responsibility frame, but the *World Journal* pointed at China or Chinese Canadians as responsible for the spread of SARS more so than the *Toronto Star.* As such, monitoring ethnic news content, and regular comparative studies of ethnic versus mainstream content or comparative studies across ethnic news content, are important to understand ethnic discourse not only as it is, but also to probe deeper nuances such as an ethnic media version of *othering*, a practice which has been discussed as though it belongs only to mainstream media.

However, whether there is a functioning news database to make this kind of research easier or even to advance it, is a question, especially for Canadian ethnic media research. ProQuest's Ethnic NewsWatch is a news database specific to "newspapers, magazines, and journals of the ethnic and minority press" containing over 340 publications, such as *Asian Week*, *Jewish Exponent*, and *El Nuevo Herald* (ProQuest n.d.). Certainly, its specific dedication to ethnic publications and the range of the collection are laudable. However, to conduct full-fledged research, especially Canadian ethnic media, it is far too limited. The number of Canadian ethnic newspapers and magazines (excluding "scholarly journals") included in the database is about ten publications, as of 2018. Thus, contrary to its intention to offer researchers "access to essential, often overlooked perspectives" (ProQuest n.d.), it ironically limits the opportunities to understand the representative discourse from ethnic media. The only available Canadian news database seems to be, as far as desk research for this chapter has found, Multicultural Canada (within SFU Digitized Newspapers and SFU Digitized Collections), which is useful for historical research.

The absence of comprehensive news databases of Canadian ethnic media makes it difficult to undertake comparative news monitoring and analysis. Researchers thus tend to select and/or sample from specific media outlets (see, e.g., Douai and Perry 2018; Lindgren 2013, 2015), rather than sampling from databases, such as ProQuest and LexisNexis, which are used for sampling mainstream news. Oh and Zhou's (2012) comparative content analysis of coverage of SARS mentioned above, for example, used LexisNexis to draw over 700 articles published in the *Toronto Star* but used the Toronto Reference Library to draw over 1,700 articles published in the *World Journal*.

The absence of comprehensive news databases, not to say the ones translated into English, further necessitates that researchers build a multilingual research team to be able to monitor publications from diverse minority-language communities. The above-mentioned study of Korean, Punjabi, and Russian newspapers (Lindgren 2015) was assisted by researchers from those linguistic groups to code the content. The authors' own "Cultural Diversity and Ethnic Media in BC" study (Murray, Yu, and Ahadi 2007) was also conducted with the assistance of two multilingual research teams, assigned to each phase of the study (media mapping and content analysis).

INQUIRIES FOR ETHNIC MEDIA RESEARCH 2.0

The multiplication of storytelling sites on social media platforms by and/or about ethnoracial minorities (e.g., Subtle Asian Traits [Facebook], nigahiga by Ryan Higa, and Superwoman by Lilly Singh [YouTube]) invite ethnic media researchers to a new subject of inquiry: are these ethnic media? As the author noted elsewhere (Yu 2020), the question comes from the overlap and simultaneous deviation from the widely used definition of ethnic media as media by and mainly for ethnic minorities (Matsaganis, Katz, and Ball-Rokeach 2010). These new initiatives are certainly by minorities but are not necessarily only for minorities. Due to the nature of social media and its wider accessibility, along with the involvement of hyphenated creators who represent multiple cultures, languages, ethnicities, races, and geographic associations in the productions, these "ethnic" but not entirely for "ethnic" initiatives are, in many cases, cross-culturally and transnationally available for all – whether the producers intended this or not. This parallel development of ethnic social media alongside legacy ethnic media confirms the usefulness of the notions of diaspora and hybridity in ethnic media research (Oh 2016; Smets 2019). In other words, the transnational nature of diasporic media use cannot be properly explained by hyper-local approaches taken by some ethnic media research undertakings and vice versa. Such complex media use and production of media content, especially by digital native and hybrid younger generations, requires more nuanced approaches to ethnic media audiences.

Nonetheless, the transnational and cross-cultural availability of these new initiatives can be only a technical possibility rather than an intention with an aim to facilitate cross-border or intercultural dialogue. Many are still developing with specific projects pursued for specific in-group issues, whether that be hyper-local ethnic issues or transnational diasporic issues (see, e.g., James's work [2019] on "Toronto Balkan Flood Relief"). However, given that online activism, propelled by the proliferation of social media platforms, is still relatively new, this area of inquiry, especially around cross-cultural/ethnic/racial collaboration, is worthy of continual monitoring. How far these initiatives extend interculturally and serve across, rather than only for individual communities, will be the focus of such monitoring.

Researching production, consumption, and content of ethnic social media further requires methodologies beyond the ones mentioned in the previous sections, although many studies, in fact, documented online activities. For race-related research in general, virtual ethnography is found to be useful as it shares the core of ethnography, that is, "the immersion of the researcher in the social or cultural situation, attempting to learn how life is lived there as opposed to the researcher approaching it with a particular preemptive research question(s) or assumption(s)," yet in the virtual space (Lenihan and Kelly-Holmes 2016, 256). For Canadian research specifically, studies on online diaspora include the aforementioned James's (2019) textual analysis of Facebook posts on "Toronto Balkan Flood Relief," a temporary site initiated by the Balkan diaspora in Toronto, along with interviews. The study observed how the site brought about offline activities that help share concerns within the local Balkan community and also mobilize aid for the home country. Al-Rawi's (2019) sentiment analysis of Facebook posts on "Arab Canadians," along with interviews, also observed discourse about Canada among current or prospective Arab Canadians and the influence of the Facebook administrator on the flow and direction of the discourse.

CONCLUSION

How ethnic media researchers define, contextualize, and situate ethnic media faces different conceptual and methodological challenges. The dynamic nature of ethnic media continually transforms what ethnic media are, by and for whom they exist, and how they are produced, distributed, and consumed. This nature simultaneously requires ethnic media researchers to seek new ways of looking at ethnic media, especially around their hybridity (not only producers and users but also the modes of production and consumption) due to multiple points of belonging and the question of place versus space as complicated in the digital age. What remains as a task is brainstorming ideas for a new conceptualization of ethnic (social) media and actively seeking innovative methodologies to study this trend. The new conceptualization does not intend to replace one side of the binary with the other (such as replacing analogue media with digital native media, or local with transnational), but rather acknowledges the heterogeneity of the ethnic media sector. The innovative methodologies will have to deal with this complexity, especially those of online undertakings. More importantly, it is encouraged for the ethnic media research community to pay attention to establishing research infrastructure that helps advance Canadian ethnic media research, such as regularly updated, open access ethnic media directories and ethnic news databases for large-scale, cross-ethnic quantitative and qualitative human research and news monitoring.

REFERENCES

Ahadi, Daniel. 2016. "Iranian Community Media in Stockholm: Locality, Transnationality, and Multicultural Adaptation." PhD diss., Simon Fraser University.

Ahmed, Rukhsana, and Luisa Veronis. 2019. "Digital Technology for Community Building: An Examination of Ethnic Media Consumption across Four Ethnocultural and Immigrant Groups in Ottawa, Canada." In *Ethnic Media in the Digital Age*, edited by Sherry S. Yu and Matthew D. Matsaganis, 97–110. London & New York: Routledge.

Al-Rawi, Ahmed. 2019. "Facebook and Virtual Nationhood: Social Media and the Arab Canadians Community." *AI & Society* 34 (3): 559–71.

– 2020. "Mobile News Apps as Sites of Transnational Ethnic

Mediascapes." *The Journal of International Communication* 26 (1): 73–91.

Anderson, Benedict. 1991. *Imagined Communities.* London: Verso.

Baffoe, Michael. 2012. "Projecting Their Own Images: The Role of the Black Ethnic Media in Reconstructing the Identities and Images of Ethnic Minorities in Canadian Society." *Journal of Alternative Perspectives in the Social Sciences* 5 (1): 28–52.

Ball-Rokeach, Sandra J., Yong-Chan Kim, and Sorin Matei. 2001. "Storytelling Neighborhood: Paths to Belonging in Diverse Urban Environments." *Communication Research* 28 (4): 392–428.

Bertrand, Ina, and Peter Hughes. 2005. *Media Research Methods: Audiences, Institutions, Texts.* New York: Palgrave Macmillan.

Black, Jerome H., and Christian Leithner. 1987. "Patterns of Ethnic Media Consumption: A Comparative Examination of Ethnic Groupings in Toronto." *Canadian Ethnic Studies* 19 (1): 21–39.

– 1988. "Immigrants and Political Involvement in Canada: The Role of the Ethnic Media." *Canadian Ethnic Studies* 20 (1): 1–20.

Bukhari, Syeda Nayab. 2019. "Ethnic Media as Alternative Media for South Asians in Metro Vancouver, Canada: Creating Knowledge, Engagement, Civic and Political Awareness." *Journal of Alternative & Community Media* 4 (3): 86–98.

Cardoso, Rodrigo V., and Evert J. Meijers. 2017. "Secondary Yet Metropolitan? The Challenges of Metropolitan Integration for Second-Tier Cities." *Planning Theory & Practice* 18 (4): 616–35.

Cheng, Hau Ling. 2005. "Constructing a Transnational, Multilocal Sense of Belonging: An Analysis of Ming Pao (West Canadian Edition)." *The Journal of Communication Inquiry* 29 (2): 141–59.

Chow, Henry P.H. 2018. "Heritage Language Learning and Ethnic Identity Maintenance among Chinese-Canadian Adolescents." *Journal of Identity & Migration Studies* 12 (1): 64–82, 169.

Cola, Marta, and Manuel Mauri Brusa. 2013. "Researching Ethnic Minority Groups as Audiences: Implementing Culturally Appropriate Research Strategies." In *Audience Research Methodologies*, edited by Geoffroy Patriarche, Helena Bilandzic, Jakob Linaa Jensen, and Jelena Jurišićpp, 119–36. New York: Routledge.

Couldry, Nick. 2010. *Why Voice Matters: Culture and Politics after Neoliberalism.* London: SAGE.

Cornelius, Wayne A. 1982. "Interviewing Undocumented Immigrants: Methodological Reflections based on Fieldwork in Mexico and the US." *International Migration Review* 16 (2): 378–411.

CRTC (Canadian Radio-television and Telecommunications Commission). 1990. "Native Broadcasting Policy." Public Notice 1990-89. Ottawa, ON: CRTC. https://crtc.gc.ca/eng/archive/1990/pb90-89.htm.
– 1999. "Ethnic Broadcasting Policy." Public Notice 1999-117. Ottawa, ON: CRTC. https://crtc.gc.ca/eng/archive/1999/pb99-117.htm.
– 2019. "Offering Cultural Diversity on TV and Radio." Ottawa, ON: CRTC. https://crtc.gc.ca/eng/info_sht/b308.htm.
Dali, Keren. 2005. "Russian-Language Periodicals in Toronto: Information Sources for Immigrants and Records for Documenting Community." *Slavic & East European Information Resources* 6 (1): 57–100.
Douai, Aziz, and Barbara Perry. 2018. "A Different Lens? How Ethnic Minority Media Cover Crime." *Canadian Journal of Criminology and Criminal Justice* 60 (1): 96–121.
Fairchild Television. 2007. "Ipsos Reid 2007 Canadian Chinese Media Monitor: Greater Vancouver Area." https://www.fairchildtv.com/english/ppt/ipsos_reid_2007_tor.pdf.
Ferrer, Alicia Ferrández, and Jessica Retis. 2019. "Ethnic Minority Media: Between Hegemony and Resistance." *Journal of Alternative & Community Media* 4 (3): 1–13.
Georgiou, Myria. 2003. "Consuming Ethnic Media, Constructing Ethnic Identities, Shaping Communities: The Case Study of Greek Cypriots in London." In *Race/Gender/Media: Considering Diversity Across Audiences, Content and Producers*, edited by R.A. Lind. Boston, MA: Allyn & Bacon.
Gher, Leo A., and Kiran Bharthapudi. 2004. "The Impact of Globalization and Transnational Media in Eastern Europe at the End of the 20th Century: An Attitudinal Study of Five Newly Independent States." *Global Media Journal* 3 (4): n.p.
Gitlin, Todd. (1998). "Public Sphere or Public Sphericules?" In *Media, Ritual and Identity*, edited by James Curran and Tamar Liebes, 168–74. London & New York: Routledge.
Goodrum, Abby A., Elizabeth Godo, and Alex Hayter. 2011. "Canadian Media Coverage of Chinese News: A Cross-Platform Comparison at the National, Local, and Hyper-Local Levels." *Chinese Journal of Communication* 4 (3): 311–30.
Government of Canada. n.d.a. "Canadian Multiculturalism Act. (R.S.C., 1985, c. 24 (4th Supp.))." Ottawa, ON: Justice Laws Website. https://laws-lois.justice.gc.ca/eng/acts/c-18.7/page-1.html.
– n.d.b. "Official Languages Act. (R.S.C., 1985, c. 31 (4th Supp.))." Ottawa, ON: Justice Laws Website. https://laws-lois.justice.gc.ca/eng/acts/o-3.01/.

– n.d.c. "Indigenous Languages Act. (S.C. 2019, c. 23)." Ottawa, ON: Justice Laws Website. https://laws-lois.justice.gc.ca/eng/acts/I-7.85/page-1.html.

– n.d.d. "Broadcasting Act. (S.C. 1991, c. 11)." Ottawa, ON: Justice Laws Website. https://laws-lois.justice.gc.ca/eng/acts/B-9.01/FullText.html.

James, Deborah. 2019. "Facebook for Community, Direct Action, and Archive: Diaspora Responses to the 2014 Floods in the Balkans." In *The Handbook of Diasporas, Media, and Culture*, edited by Jessica Retis and Rosa Tsagarousianou, 475–90. New Jersey: Wiley-Blackwell.

Karim, Karim H. 2002. "Public Sphere and Public Sphericules: Civic Discourse in Ethnic Media." In *Civic Discourse and Cultural Politics in Canada: A Cacophony of Voices*, edited by Sherry Devereaux Ferguson and Leslie Regan Shade, 203–42. Westport, CT: Ablex Publishing.

Kobayashi, Audrey. 1993. "Multiculturalism: Representing a Canadian Institution." In *Place/Culture/Representation*, edited by James Duncan and David Ley, 205–23. London: Routledge.

Kozar, Seana. 2002. "Leaves Gleaned from the Ten-Thousand-Dimensional Web in Heaven: Chinese On-Line Publications in Canada." *Journal of American Folklore* 115 (456): 129–53.

Lee, Wei-Na, and David K. Tse. 1994. "Changing Media Consumption in a New Home: Acculturation Patterns among Hong Kong Immigrants to Canada." *Journal of Advertising* 23 (1): 57–70.

Lenihan, Aoife, and Helen Kelly-Holmes. 2016. "Virtual Ethnography." In *Research Methods in Intercultural Communication: A Practical Guide*, edited by Zhua Hua, 255–67. New Jersey: Wiley-Blackwell.

Li, Xiaoping. 2015. "A Critical Examination of Chinese Language Media's Normative Goals and News Decisions." *Global Media Journal* 8 (2): 97–112.

Lindgren, April. 2013. "The Diverse City: Can You Read All about It in Ethnic Newspapers?" *Contemporary Readings in Law and Social Justice* 5 (2): 120–40.

– 2015. "Municipal Communication Strategies and Ethnic Media: A Settlement Service in Disguise." *Global Media Journal* 8 (2): 49–71.

Marques, M. Margarida, and Rui Santos. 2004. "Top-Down and Bottom-Up Reconsidered: The Dynamics of Immigrant Participation in Local Civil Society." In *Citizenship in European Cities: Immigrants, Local Politics and Integration Policies: Diversity and Convergence in European Cities*, edited by Karen Kraal, Steven Vertovec, and Rinus Penninx, 107–26. New York: Routledge.

Markusen, Ann R., Yung-Sook Lee, and Sean DiGiovanna. 1999. *Second Tier Cities*. Minneapolis: Minnesota University Press.

Matsaganis, Matthew, and Daniel Ahadi. 2017. "Ethnic Media and Acculturation." In *International Encyclopedia of Intercultural Communication,* edited by Young Yun Kim, 1–10. New Jersey: Wiley-Blackwell.

Matsaganis, Matthew D., Vikki S. Katz, and Sandra J. Ball-Rokeach. 2010. *Understanding Ethnic Media: Producers, Consumers, and Societies*. London: SAGE.

McMillan, Kate, and Fiona Barker. 2021. "'Ethnic' Media and Election Campaigns: Chinese and Indian Media in New Zealand's 2017 Election." *Australian Journal of Political Science* 56 (2): 1–19.

Murray, Catherine, Sherry S. Yu, and Daniel Ahadi. 2007. "Cultural Diversity and Ethnic Media in BC. A Report to the Canadian Heritage Western Regional Office." Centre for Policy Studies on Culture and Communities. Vancouver, BC: Simon Fraser University.

Naficy, Hamid. 2003. "Narrowcasting in Diaspora: Middle Eastern Television in Los Angeles." In *The Media of Diaspora*, edited by Karim H. Karim, 64–75. London & New York: Routledge.

O'Brien, Eileen. 2011. "The Transformation of the Role of 'Race' in the Qualitative Interview: Not if Race Matters, but How." In *Rethinking Race and Ethnicity in Research Methods*, edited by John H. Stanfield II, 67–94. London & New York: Routledge.

Oh, David C. 2016. "Reconsidering Ethnic Media Research: An Argument for a Diasporic Identity Framework." *Atlantic Journal of Communication* 24 (5): 264–75.

Oh, David C., and Wanfeng Zhou. 2012. "Framing SARS: A Case Study in Toronto of a Mainstream Newspaper and a Chinese Ethnic Newspaper." *Atlantic Journal of Communication* 20 (5): 261–73.

ProQuest. n.d. *ProQuest Ethnic NewsWatch*. https://about.proquest.com/en/products-services/ethnic_newswatch/.

Qiao, Stephen. 2013. "Chinese Canadian Publications from 1920s to 1980s: A Historic Perspective." Presentation at the Second Sino-American Academic Library Forum for Cooperation and Development, Lanzhou, China, July 2013.

Sassen, Saskia. 2005. "The Repositioning of Citizenship and Alienage: Emergent Subjects and Spaces for Politics." *Globalizations* 2 (1): 79–94.

– 2018. *Cities in a World Economy*. Thousand Oaks, CA: SAGE.

Siapera, Eugenia. 2010. *Cultural Diversity and Global Media: The Mediation of Difference*. West Sussex, UK: John Wiley & Sons.

Silverstone, Roger, Eric Hirsch, and David Morley. 1994. "Information and Communication Technologies and the Moral Economy of the Household." In *Consuming Technologies: Media and Information in Domestic Spaces,* edited by Roger Silverstone and Eric Hirsch, 15–31. London & New York: Routledge.

Smets, Kevin. 2019. "Doing Diasporic Media Research: Methodological Challenges and Innovations." In *The Handbook of Diasporas, Media, and Culture,* edited by Jessica Retis and Roza Tsagarousianou, 97–111. New Jersey: Wiley-Blackwell.

Spivak, Gayatri Chakravorty. 1987. *In Other Worlds: Essays in Cultural Politics*. New York: Methuen.

Statistics Canada. n.d. "Visible Minority of Person." Ottawa, ON: Statistics Canada. https://www23.statcan.gc.ca/imdb/p3Var.pl?Function=DEC&Id=45152.

– 2016. "Census Profile 2016: City of Richmond." Ottawa, ON: Statistics Canada. https://www12.statcan.gc.ca/census-recensement/2016/dp-pd/prof/details/page. cfm?Lang=E&Geo1=CSD&Code1=5915015&Geo2=PR&Code2=59&SearchText=Richmond&SearchType=Begins&SearchPR=01&B1=All&GeoLevel=PR&GeoCode=5915015&TABID=1&type=0.

van Dijk, Teun A. 1991. *Racism and the Press.* London: Routledge.

– 2015. "Critical Discourse Analysis." In *The Handbook of Discourse Analysis*, edited by Deborah Tannen, Heidi E. Hamilton, and Deborah Schiffrin. West Sussex, UK: John Wiley & Sons.

Veronis, Luisa, Zac Tabler, and Rukhsana Ahmed. 2018. "Syrian Refugee Youth Use Social Media: Building Transcultural Spaces and Connections for Resettlement in Ottawa, Canada." *Canadian Ethnic Studies* 50 (2): 79–99.

Yoon, Kyong. 2019. "Diasporic Youth Culture of K-pop." *Journal of Youth Studies* 22 (1): 138–52.

Yu, Sherry S. 2016. "Instrumentalization of Ethnic Media." *Canadian Journal of Communication* 41 (2): 343–51.

– 2018. *Diasporic Media Beyond the Diaspora: Korean Media in Vancouver and Los Angeles*. Vancouver: UBC Press.

– 2020. "Beyond the Third Space: New Communicative Space in the Making on YouTube." In *The SAGE Handbook of Media and Migration,* edited by Kevin Smets, Koen Leurs, Myria Georgiou, Saskia Witteborn, and Radhika Gajjala, 526–36. London: SAGE.

Yu, Sherry S., and Daniel Ahadi. 2010. "Promoting Civic Engagement through Ethnic Media." *Platform: Journal of Media and Communication* 2 (2): 54–71.

Zubair, Maria, and Christina Victor. 2015. "Exploring Gender, Age, Time and Space in Research with Older Pakistani Muslims in the United Kingdom: Formalised Research 'Ethics' and Performances of the Public/Private Divide in 'The Field.'" *Ageing & Society* 35 (5): 961–85.

CHAPTER THREE

Has Canadian Broadcasting and Multiculturalism Policy Supported Ethnic Broadcasting? The Case of Canadian Chinese-Language Television News

Elim Ng

INTRODUCTION

To what extent has Canadian policy fostered the flourishing of ethnic broadcasting?[1] Canadian regulation has been important in establishing ethnic broadcasting and continues to support its existence. However, interviews with Canadian Chinese-language television news (CCLTN) practitioners suggest that regulation does not incentivize the quality of content required to support the vision of multiculturalism assumed by CCLTN practitioners. Their thicker multiculturalism captures complex and organic processes that are part of Chinese-Canadian identity formation. Here, identities and communities become part of Canadian society through the use of their culture and traditions. Thus, thicker multiculturalism requires both immigrant adaptation and transnational connections. By contrast, a thinner multiculturalism demands that immigrants become part of Canadian society either without or with very minimal use of their culture and traditions (Mann 2016, 135). Given the difficulty of ethnic media market positions and the importance of multiculturalism in managing ethnocultural diversity, robust, forward-looking government interventions are needed. However, neoliberal policy trends and the thinning of official multiculturalism has permitted corporate divestment from ethnic broadcasting amidst a challenging business environment. Licensing and regulatory practices should require quality programming that speaks to the thick multiculturalism imagined by interviewees while also addressing the challenges and opportunities created by new technologies.

CCLTN refers to television programming that covers current events and information produced by Canadian corporations in Chinese languages for Chinese-speaking audiences in Canada. Chinese people comprise Canada's second largest visible minority, accounting for approximately 4.6 per cent of the Canadian population (Statistics Canada 2017a). I refer to corporations that produce CCLTN as CCLTN producers and the individuals working in this sector as CCLTN practitioners. CCLTN encompasses daily newscasts and magazine shows, usually in either Mandarin or Cantonese. Coverage includes stories about Chinese communities in Canada, Canadian national and local news, and international news with more focus on China, Hong Kong, and Taiwan. My argument draws on findings from my doctoral dissertation in which I used CCLTN as a case study to understand how minority media practitioners navigate overlapping governance claims of migrant sending and migrant receiving states (Ng 2019).

CASE BACKGROUND: CHINESE-LANGUAGE MEDIA IN CANADA

Chinese-language news media in Canada is available in all major formats including print, radio, and digital sources. Although Canadian owned and produced Chinese-language print media exists, the larger dailies import a significant portion of their content through partial foreign ownership, in the case of *Sing Tao*, or complete foreign ownership, in the case of *Ming Pao* (Ming Pao Canada 2021; Sing Tao Media Group Canada n.d.). Unlike print, radio must be licensed by the national government regulator, the Canadian Radio-television Telecommunications Commission (CRTC). Chinese-language radio programs may be played on multilingual stations while some outlets, like Fairchild Radio and *Sing Tao*'s A1 Chinese Radio, broadcast completely or predominantly in Chinese languages.

When this study began, there were three sources of CCLTN: OMNI TV, Global TV, and Fairchild Television. OMNI TV is owned by publicly traded Canadian telecommunications and media giant, Rogers Communications. OMNI must broadcast in at least twenty languages per month but focuses on a select number of languages for its daily original newscasts including Mandarin, Cantonese,

Filipino, and Punjabi (CRTC 2019; OMNI TV n.d.). Global Television is a Canadian English-language television network that produced an in-house Mandarin newscast between 2012 and 2016 consisting primarily of translated material (Quan 2011). Through subsidiaries and trusts, Global Television is owned by Shaw Communications, another major Canadian media and telecommunications corporation (CRTC 2016). Finally, Fairchild Television produces Talentvision and Fairchild Television – Mandarin and Cantonese channels that both produce daily original newscasts and reproductions of foreign news programs. Fairchild Media is majority owned by Chinese-Canadian businessman, Thomas Fung, and minority owned by TVB, a Hong Kong–based media firm (Fairchild Group n.d.; Joseph Chan).

CHINESE MIGRATION AND CHINESE COMMUNITIES IN CANADA

Large-scale Chinese migration to Canada began with migrant labourers in the mid-1800s and created one of the earliest and largest non-white immigrant groups in Canada. Intermittent economic recessions and racialized fears led to stereotypes about Chinese migrants outnumbering and corrupting white society (Li 1998, 29–37). In 1923, the Chinese Immigration Act effectively banned further Chinese migration until the law was repealed in 1947 (Chan 2014). Chinese immigrants did not arrive again in significant numbers until after immigration reforms in the 1960s. Initially, they came mainly from Taiwan, Hong Kong, and Southeast Asia, but then in the 1990s increasingly they came from the PRC, which now accounts for most Chinese immigration (Statistics Canada 2016).

Mandarin and Cantonese are the first and second most common mother tongues among Canadian immigrants at 7.9 and 7.7 per cent, respectively (Statistics Canada 2017b). Approximately 39.1 per cent of Chinese people in Canada speak Mandarin, and 36.9 per cent speak Cantonese (Statistics Canada 2017b). The remaining quarter speak other Chinese languages or no Chinese at all.[2] In terms of socio-economic status, Chinese people in Canada are more likely to hold university degrees than the general population, but they earn less than non-racialized groups, suggesting labour market inequity (Statistics Canada 2018). Compared with Black people and Latin Americans in Canada, however, the Chinese population face considerably less income disparity and are more likely to experience upward economic mobility by the second generation (Block, Galabuzi, and Tranjan 2019, 8–12).

The Canadian government has made efforts to recognize and include Chinese citizens in Canadian society, from restoring franchise in 1947 to a formal apology in 2011 for discriminatory immigration taxes. However, in moments of crisis or tension, racism against the Chinese in Canada resurfaces. In 1971, a *W5* documentary depicted Chinese students as a foreign invasion of Canadian university campuses (Hawthorn 2009). In the 1990s, the "monster house" controversy arose when Chinese homeowners moved into elite white neighbourhoods (Wang 1998); in the early mid-2000s, Chinese people were stigmatized over the SARS epidemic (D'Sa 2020), and in 2020, they were blamed for the COVID-19 pandemic. A 2020 Angus Reid Institute poll of Chinese people in Canada showed an increased experience of various forms of mistreatment as a result of the COVID-19 pandemic (Angus Reid 2020).

POLICY AREAS THAT GOVERN ETHNIC BROADCASTING

Canada governs ethnic broadcasting mainly through multiculturalism policy and broadcasting policy, both of which were shaped by massive postwar investments in state building projects. From the 1950s to the 1970s, key social security programs like the Canadian Pension Plan and universal healthcare were developed alongside national bilingualism, multiculturalism, and the CRTC (Armstrong 2010; Moscovitch 2015). Because civic identity, minority accommodation, and social security programs emerged as fused imperatives, it seemed appropriate for the government to intervene in the broadcasting system to support multiculturalism (Abu-Laban 2018). Over time, however, neoliberal governance trends combined with vacillating efforts to minimize multiculturalism and ethnocultural diversity have diminished government support for ethnic broadcasting (Ng 2019, 176–87).

CANADIAN MULTICULTURALISM POLICY

Multiculturalism became an official policy in Canada when the Pierre Trudeau government announced that Canada would practise "multiculturalism within a bilingual framework" in 1971 (Laselva

2014, 7–12). Although no universal definition of multiculturalism exists, a survey of parliamentary reports and academic literature suggests that there are four components in Canadian multiculturalism (Biles 2016, 11–12, 32–45; Dewing 2014, 2–3; Hansen 2016, 73–6; Canadian Heritage 2007, 2017, 2018, 2019; Citizenship and Immigration Canada 2008, 2009, 2010, 2011, 2012, 2013, 2014, 2015; Hou, Schellenberg, and Berry 2016). First, immigrant adaptation is the expectation that immigrants will adjust their behaviours and attachments to participate in Canada's mainstream social, political, and economic institutions. Second, cultural maintenance describes activities that keep cultural and linguistic traditions alive. Third, recognition means acknowledging minority achievements and contributions. And fourth, anti-discrimination is about fighting racism and ensuring that ethnocultural minorities are treated equitably.

These elements of multiculturalism outline essential terms and conditions for how ethnocultural minorities belong in Canada, though official practice and public comment have shaped their meaning and value over time. Bureaucrats have stressed the economic utility of immigration, and progressive detractors have argued that multiculturalism fails to truly respect minorities (Bissoondath 1998; Day 2016, 138–42). Moreover, all major political parties have engaged in the cynical use of multiculturalism and ethnocultural diversity during elections (Abu-Laban and Stasiulis 1992, 376). However, conservative parties have more consistently articulated and forwarded positions around fears that multiculturalism gives too much power to ethnocultural minorities and that multiculturalism, along with immigration, impedes the formation of a robust national identity (Gaucher 2020, 78–80, 93–4; Granatstein 1998; Winter 2015, 646–51). These criticisms have often led to policies that stressed immigrant adaptation as a replacement for, rather than companion to, other elements of multiculturalism (Blake 2013, 97–9; Dewing 2013, 2–3; Hansen 2016, 81–4). In practice, this treatment rejects ethnocultural pluralism in favor of ethnocentrism and strips multiculturalism down to the requirement that immigrants become more palatable to broader society (McCready 2012).

Conservative arguments reached the zenith of their influence under the Harper government (2006–2015). Controversial policies assumed problematic behavior in ethnocultural minorities and focused national identity on the military and the British Crown while bureaucratizing multiculturalism and the Charter (Blake

2013, 94–7; Dewing 2013, 2–3; Nieguth and Raney 2017, 102–5). The succeeding Liberal government has maintained a neoliberal approach that selects immigrants based on labour needs and treats multiculturalism largely as a set of symbolic exercises. Still, they reinstated pre-existing practices including modest funds for community initiatives supporting cultural maintenance and minority recognition, data collection and research on ethnocultural diversity, and international commitments to anti-racism (Canadian Heritage 2007, 2017, 2018, 2019 and Citizenship and Immigration Canada 2008, 2009, 2010, 2011, 2012, 2013, 2014, 2015).

Although some considered the 2016 Liberal election victory to be the public's affirmation of multiculturalism, the unfolding reality remains complex (Lawson 2015). Public opinion polling conducted since 2016 suggests that Canadians see multiculturalism as part of their national identity but may be less supportive of ethnocultural diversity and immigration than often assumed (Angus Reid Institute 2019; Reid 2016). Further, although right-wing populism is complicated with a spectrum of views, multiple sources of grievance, and a diversity of actors, ethnocentrism and anti-immigrant sentiment do find expression here (Erl 2021, 112–17). The relative success of the People's Party of Canada in 2021 and the Freedom Convoy protests of 2022 suggest that populist elements like these will stay in Canadian public life. While multiculturalism has remained part of Canadian national identity, pressure to minimize multiculturalism and ethnocultural diversity will likely continue.

CANADIAN BROADCASTING POLICY

Like multiculturalism, broadcasting policy is also connected to nation-building. When the government created the CRTC, the legislation stipulated that the broadcasting system would be "Canadian in content and character" (Broadcasting Act 1958 cited in Armstrong 2010, 31). The Royal Commission on Bilingualism and Biculturalism (RCBB) recommended support for multilingual broadcasting to recognize ethnocultural minorities (RCBB 1969). Further, the 1991 Broadcasting Act asserts that Canada's multicultural nature must be reflected in the Canadian broadcasting system (Government of Canada 2022). However, no specific mechanism for reflecting multiculturalism in Canadian broadcasting was outlined. Official bilingualism requires that the Canadian Broadcasting Corporation (CBC) provide French service, and the Aboriginal People's Television Network (APTN) partially meets Indigenous broadcasting needs (Government of Canada 2022; Roth 2005, 92). The CRTC only supports ethnic broadcasting through regulatory incentives and licensing for private corporations to provide these services (Salter and Odartey-Wellington 2008, 292–9). The result has been a reactive and experimental third-language broadcasting policy in which the commission responds to market and technological changes ad hoc.

By the 1980s, growing market demand and limited broadcast frequencies prompted the CRTC to address ethnic broadcasting systematically. In a landmark 1985 document, the government recognized support for ethnic broadcasting as a matter of following the Multiculturalism Act (CRTC 1985). Further, the commission indicated willingness to lower Canadian content quotas for ethnic broadcasters given their production capacity, but quotas were still required (CRTC 1985, 2009). When cable and satellite arrived in the 1980s and 1990s, ethnic broadcasters attempted to create channels that simply relayed foreign services. The commission's response was to approve them sparingly, asserting that non-Canadian specialty services should "contribute to, and not adversely affect the development of the Canadian broadcasting system" (CRTC 1983–1993 in CRTC 2004, para 2).

By the late 1980s, however, two interrelated changes began to diminish government support for ethnic broadcasting. First, successive Canadian governments from Mulroney (1984–1993) to the present embraced neoliberal policies that limited state intervention and relied on the market as an efficient and natural definer and distributor of value (Brodie 2007, 2014). Second, governments and media organizations have struggled to adapt to media shock, or "a series of overlapping and interrelated crises" characterized by the rapid onset of web-based content, globalization, and market concentration, among other issues (Taras 2015, 7–8).

In 2004, after receiving many requests and acknowledging the prevalence of pirated use, the CRTC reversed its position, so that foreign, third-language services were accepted as a rule rather than as an exception (CRTC 2004). Recognizing the intense competition this created for Canadian ethnic broadcasters, the CRTC identified five entities as "legacy" services with assigned market protections. These included mandatory carriage, which required distributors to carry legacy services, and buy-through, which required consumers to purchase legacy services when subscribing to a foreign service of the same language (CRTC 2004). As the following section will show, the CRTC's blend of neoliberal policy with nation-building goals, in this instance, has achieved mixed results.

METHODOLOGY

My analysis uses interviews conducted from 2013–2014 with participants from the three CCLTN producers of that time: OMNI TV, Fairchild Television, and Global Television. Interviewees included journalists, editors, regular guest contributors, management, those in advertising, and executives. Because of restructuring at OMNI during data collection, the study included both former and current employees. The study included twenty-two individuals; seventeen were Chinese and five were not. Among Chinese participants, nine spoke Cantonese, six spoke Mandarin, and one spoke both Cantonese and Mandarin. I conducted interviews mostly in English, though participants used Cantonese or Mandarin when this seemed appropriate to them. I recruited participants from information on channel websites and through snowball sampling. The participants were able to choose different levels of anonymity and even withdraw from the study up to one week after the interview. The first questions invited participants to discuss what they felt was important to the development of CCLTN, without mentioning government, to limit the possibility of overemphasizing the role of the state at the expense of other relevant factors. I analyzed the interviews thematically using an open coding protocol.[3]

INTERVIEW FINDINGS: REGARDING MULTICULTURALISM

Although participants did not comment at length on the merits of multiculturalism or analyze its components, they did speak extensively about what they believed to be the goals and value of their work and the needs of their audience. Here, they demonstrated insight into the experiences of immigration and settlement, on the one hand, and an evolving but important connection to their heritage and country of origin, on the other. Where official multiculturalism is increasingly thin and focused on immigrant adaptation, interviewees linked minority recognition, anti-discrimination, and evolving but ongoing homeland connections to immigrant adaptation. Taken together, their comments show an understanding that these elements work together to support the emergence of adaptive and integrated Chinese-Canadian identities and communities.

IMMIGRANT ADAPTATION

Interview participants repeatedly stressed that aiding immigrant adaptation is a key objective of CCLTN production and often justified their work in this way (Victor Ho; Norman Wong). Participants talked about teaching viewers "how to be Canadian" and even suggested that CCLTN can boost civic engagement (Susan Cheng; Madeline Ziniak). As one participant proposed, "Before, people probably don't care ... They don't want to vote. But now because the [Canadian] Chinese media is here to help them understand the election, the city, the province, then maybe people will want to vote. They will want to be involved" (Jenny Hu). In view of mainstream expectations about immigrant adaptation and corporate restructuring at the time, an element of self-justification must be accepted. However, multi-country studies have yielded significant evidence that minority media consumption does improve civic participation and awareness among immigrants (Annenberg School of Communication 2019; Matsaganis, Katz, and Ball-Rokeach 2010, 52–7, 181–5; Zhou, Chen, and Cai 2006, 51–5).

Participants also talked about the importance of providing information useful for daily life in Chinese languages. As one participant explained, "They [Chinese-Canadians] need to know what is going on [here]. It may be as simple of a thing like health and food security. If there's a food recall, then you want your viewer to know that, hey, you should not be buying this brand of strawberries because it's got salmonella" (Winnie Hwo). Another participant asserted that CCLTN is pertinent to life in Canada and cannot be replaced with foreign news services: "Local news contains local stories with local living. For example, the PRC government's news and programs won't teach you how to apply for child benefits in Canada or how to look for better school information in Vancouver" (V. Ho).

Further, mainstream newscasts can be challenging for some immigrants owing to the vocabulary and speaking speed. While policy has often stressed official language use in immigrant adaptation, interview participants emphasized that providing news and information in Cantonese or Mandarin helps new immigrants participate in Canadian society more fully and more quickly (S. Cheng; Jia Wang; M. Ziniak). Rather than choosing between official language competence or multilingualism, multilingual newscasts can be part of the immigrant adaptation process. As another participant explained, CCLTN provides information and context that gives Chinese immigrants "a common thing they can talk about with their neighbours" (W. Hwo). Further, research about minority media in North America confirms that Chinese-language news about the receiving state can help otherwise isolated immigrants become well-informed about their new surroundings (Zhou, Chen, and Cai 2006, 57–9).

Immigrant adaptation is a complex process that can be difficult to understand. Where the Canadian immigration system focuses on economic success, mainstream public conversations about immigrant adaptation have emphasized external signs of difference, such as religious dress or accented French or English (Montpetit 2017a; 2017b). By contrast, CCLTN practitioners discussed how news and information can build an internal sense of familiarity and belonging (W. Hwo; Gabriel Yu). "We want to give them something like what the mainstream media gives its audience ... Maybe not information that they need to know but [something that will] make them feel that they know the place. Sometimes, it makes you feel that you are isolated if you don't have the language ability and you don't know what's happening outside. But once you have a channel to see and you know what's happening every day ... Then you feel, oh, I belong here" (J. Hu).

Many CCLTN practitioners are, themselves, immigrants, and these comments reflect a belief that CCLTN supports an internal sense of familiarity that is necessary to substantive and observable signs of immigrant adaptations, such as civic participation and community involvement.

CULTURAL MAINTENANCE VERSUS TRANSNATIONAL CONNECTION AND HYBRIDITY

Although the RCBB thought multilingual broadcasting would be central to cultural maintenance, participants did not focus on teaching new generations Chinese languages. Rather, many described the value of their work in terms of both reflecting Chinese-Canadian emergent identities and facilitating evolving transnational connections to Chinese homelands (F. Qi; T. Ye).

Regarding the former, several participants asserted that Chinese-Canadians have their own stories and points of view, and these must be explored publicly (S. Cheng; M. Ziniak). One participant deliberated that "the exploration of what it means to be Chinese in Canada, and to understand how communities adapt and change, how they elect officials to public office, how they challenge themselves to raise money for charitable things ... we always felt that our role was to reflect those things" (Renato Zane). Another participant explained that mainstream newsrooms have often considered stories about Chinese communities to be too narrowly focused or too "ethnic" to put onto their broadcasts (M. Ziniak). The participant further explained, "I see a definitive need for editorial expression. It's not only that we're getting news in this language, but it's also that you're profiling success stories in your community. You're really drilling down in stories that traditional [mainstream] media can't cover" (M. Ziniak). Some participants also asserted that CCLTN viewers desire more attentive coverage of certain Canadian issues like immigration policy, discrimination, Sino-Canadian relations, and economic policy (F. Qi; S. Cheng).

Further, as new Canadian identities emerge, transnational connections persist but change as well. One participant explained that having family overseas necessitates foreign news briefings (F. Qi). Another explained the need for news about Hong Kong, Taiwan, and mainland China by describing a multifaceted attachment that cannot be erased: "Most of them continue to have a lot of connections back there, and this means they cannot totally ignore Hong Kong or those from the mainland can never ignore things happening in mainland China. Their daily lives or even their jobs may be directly or indirectly related to their hometown ... [They also have] emotional and communication needs ... I believe this is the major reason that Chinese radio and Chinese TV are so popular" (V. Ho).

Moreover, many participants claimed that mainstream news services do not give enough attention to Chinese homelands for CCLTN viewers (S. Cheng; T. Ye). Others complained that Western journalists unfamiliar with Chinese culture and history sometimes present stories framed by their own lack of context (F. Qi). Participants also cited media restrictions in the PRC and suggested that CCLTN can provide alternative coverage (S. Cheng; J. Jia; C. Mak). Official PRC policy treats media as an extension of the state – news media in China cannot contradict the Chinese government regarding a constantly evolving list of sensitive issues (Brady 2015). These have included the behaviour of top officials, air quality, Taiwan policy, archaeological findings, and the Tiananmen Square Incident (Jirik 2016, 3540; Wong 2008).

Due to the aforementioned constraints, participants asserted the importance of creating space for Chinese-Canadians to develop their own points of view (F. Qi). For them, this is part of the process of creating Chinese-Canadian identities, and reflects changing transnational connections. One participant declared that "we have to confront ourselves and figure out, we're not really Chinese or from Hong Kong only. We are Canadian. We're a blend" (R. Zane). Similarly, another participant described audience needs in this way: "The PRC also has their political agenda ... but we, the overseas Chinese community, have our own needs. And the media here has to consider these needs and fulfill them ... People here are not all PRC citizens. Many are citizens of Canada; they might come from HK, Taiwan, or mainland China. They are 'Canadian Chinese.' Therefore, these people will have different preferences" (V. Ho).

In the end, interview participants embraced neither a static preservation of cultural traditions nor the marginalization and hostility towards cultural maintenance articulated by some critics of multiculturalism. Rather, they described a community exercise in which hyphenated identities – inspired by evolving but ongoing connections to Chinese homelands and life in Canada – emerge and are facilitated by ethnic broadcasting.

MINORITY RECOGNITION, ANTI-DISCRIMINATION, AND RACISM

Participants also reflected on their experiences of racism, particularly with respect to what they encountered professionally. These experiences suggest that an approach to multiculturalism which stresses immigrant adaptation to the exclusion of minority recognition and support for cultural maintenance is incomplete. Indeed, some participants drew a strong connection between anti-discrimination and minority recognition.

In one instance, the lack of recognition was directly connected to discrimination when participants cited an attempt by corporate owners to pay employees working on ethnic broadcasts lower wages than those working on official language broadcasts (Caitlyn Kent;

F. Qi). Another participant suggested that not recognizing Chinese immigrant contributions has made Chinese minorities vulnerable to racial backlash from mainstream society. Referencing an English-language news article, she discussed the complaint that in the event of political upheaval in Hong Kong, repatriating immigrants and their relatives will overwhelm British Columbia's Lower Mainland (W. Hwo; T. Ye). This participant felt that such a characterization is only possible because Canadian society does not recognize how Chinese-Canadians have helped build up the Lower Mainland: "We built neighbourhoods here ... There was no Richmond when we came – so Richmond was built, Coquitlam was built ... a lot of neighbourhoods were built by Hong Kong money ... also don't forget the charity money for the Children's Hospital in BC. They actually have a separate Hong Kong Chinese donation drive evening ... The mainstream community just doesn't recognize these contributions, where all this money is coming from ... I think this needs to be recognized" (W. Hwo).

In a similarly pointed conversation, another participant discussed the controversy over the design of new money bills, in which the likeness of an Asian scientist had been rejected. In his words: "[A] recent example is the printing of money – the new money with an Asian scientist. The problem was not the process of consultation. The problem was the Bank of Canada accepted a racist opinion that Asian females are not representative enough of Canadians for the Canadian dollar" (G. Yu). He went on to assert that there is still a race problem in Canada because when an Asian person is rejected because she does not look Canadian enough, this affects all Asians, even those born and raised in Canada. These encounters with racism echo a history of discrimination motivated by the belief that Chinese people are too different to be part of Canadian society, and by the anxiety of being besieged by alien interlopers. As the original 1985 document notes, ethnic broadcasting has a role to play in combatting discrimination by providing diverse representations of ethnocultural minorities to themselves (Government of Canada 2022).

REGARDING CRTC REGULATION

Regulations and licences do not fall under the purview of most journalists and editors, and so participants who were administrators or executives tended to say more about government policy. However, over one-third of the participants commented on the CRTC and a quarter of participants talked about the business models of their corporate owners. The cancellation of OMNI newscasts up to and during the interviews raised sector-wide questions about why CCLTN work was so precarious as well as the role of business and government in CCLTN production.

When asked about what they saw as crucial to the development of CCLTN, participants typically first cited the growth of Chinese communities in Canada, but several also noted the importance of government support to CCLTN production (J. Chan; N. Wong). One participant explained: "For us, the saving grace was the CRTC regulation of Canadian content. It's cast in stone that these TV stations have to have Canadian content, and so, if you do not meet the requirements, you can lose your licence ... I think that has actually helped Chinese media, especially in broadcast, to hire a lot of young reporters ... If they don't meet the original Canadian content requirements, then the local newsrooms could become totally translated material and imported material from CCTV [and] Hong Kong TV" (W. Hwo).

Another participant, more aware of the government's shifting policy direction, commented on how deregulation could affect CCLTN in the future: "It's give and take ... they may take away the buy-through ... OK, we lost something, but will they give us back something? ... Harmonizing the licences could mean [that] we would be given the flexibility to lower our Canadian content ... but then what happens to the general Broadcasting Act? ... lowering Can Con means we'll be firing some people ... There will be less Canadian content contribution" (J. Chan). Here, neoliberal changes are experienced as a game of diminishing returns, though previous commitments to multiculturalism and nation-building provide ways of talking back.

Many interview participants complained that CRTC licensing had structured favouritism and unworkable business models into the CCLTN sector. The CRTC has been reluctant to grant multiple licences in a single third language because these markets are small and the licensees would likely fail. They would take up limited space on the radio spectrum and their failure would render CRTC commitment to ethnic broadcasting ineffectual. Fairchild TV was given legacy status to provide for Chinese speakers while the other legacy services provided for different groups. The licence for OMNI

TV, however, was created to accommodate many language groups with limited space on the radio spectrum. It also prevents them from developing programming that might compete with already specialized legacy services. One participant protested, "With twenty-two language markets, you need to find programs and pay for them, and then some of the markets are so small. They don't have the advertising potential, but you still need to serve them, because that is the CRTC requirement" (C. Mak). He went on to complain that the requirement to service twenty-two languages on linear television assumes that audiences will engage in outdated appointment viewing to watch programs in their own languages.

The value of supporting legacy broadcasters like Fairchild TV is further cast into question when they air reproductions that make extensive use of foreign content. Fairchild TV does produce original newscasts with in-house scripts, footage, and editorial control; however, reproductions of newscasts from China Global Television Network (CGTN), China's state-run TV network, uses both the footage and the accompanying scripts prepared by the Chinese government agency. The only difference is that a Fairchild TV desk and anchor are used to deliver the content (W. Hwo; F. Qi). The CRTC has aimed to protect the financial viability of ethnic broadcasting while trying to serve the largest number of language groups possible, but these efforts have not rewarded good journalistic practice and have created difficult market positions.

Finally, interview participants discussed the lack of commitment to ethnic broadcasting, not only from their corporate owners but also from the government, which they saw as being enablers of corporate divestment. Between 2013 and 2016, OMNI restructured its newsrooms several times, at one point cancelling third-language newscasts altogether (Houpt 2015). Many interview participants were affected and noted that amidst industry challenges, their corporate owners could easily abandon ethnic broadcasting in pursuit of other, more profitable opportunities (Wei Li; M. Ziniak). One participant stated: "They [OMNI's corporate leadership] are focusing on something else, not ethnic media. They are focusing on the market. They want to get more money. They're changing the whole direction. In the past, when Ted Rogers was the leader, he had that mentality to keep Rogers more diverse. And now, I think that Rogers Communications are focusing on something more mainstream" (G. Guo).

Taking their experiences into consideration, some subjects felt that the CRTC needs to require and incentivize corporations to invest in ethnic broadcasting (J. Hu; J. Wang). Another participant surmised that the commission seems to have lost focus and become complacent about the state of ethnic media in Canada: "I think [the] CRTC has kind of been too sleepy ... Chinese media is so critical for the multicultural fabric of our country ... are they really doing the job? And how well are they doing their job? I think if we leave these entities alone for too long, it's just human nature, they're bound to lose vision" (W. Hwo). For these and other participants, the CRTC needs to ensure that ethnic broadcasting not only exists but also fulfills its role as an essential contributor to Canadian multiculturalism (R. Zane; M. Ziniak).

CONCLUSION: POLICY AND LICENSING CONSIDERATIONS

These interview findings suggest that creating functional policy for ethnic broadcasting begins with acknowledging that ethnocultural minority identities and communities need to not only adapt to the immigrant culture but also be recognized as a minority group, protected against discrimination, and allowed to maintain evolving connections with their homeland. Ethnic programming that reflects these aspirations relies on original reporting in which distinct editorial expression, journalistic professionalism, and freedom from the political pressure of sending states are all a matter of course. Finally, corporate owners must fulfill their social obligations. Because ethnic media markets are small and only permit a limited number of providers, the ones that operate must support thick multiculturalism to justify government support.

In terms of regulating CCLTN, licensing needs to require that these standards are met by incentivizing ongoing investment into ethnic broadcasting and discouraging inadequate substitutes that have become too commonplace in CCLTN programming. Regarding local and national news about Canada, translated mainstream news segments should be differentiated from original content. Translated pieces do not typically include stories about Chinese people and communities in Canada because these are often considered too niche for official language news broadcasts. Moreover, reporting on how mainstream media covers an issue can be helpful, but ultimately, CCLTN practitioners need to do original reporting in order to explore what angles on a story speak to Chinese-Canadian audiences.

Regarding news and information about Chinese homelands, Canadian policy makers should neither ignore the context of the Chinese government's censorship policies nor neglect the PRC's interest in overseas Chinese communities. Rather, Canadian policy needs to support CCLTN in providing space for free and fair original reporting on homeland issues to aid the formation of Chinese-Canadian identities and attachments. Licensing should differentiate between original reporting and reproductions of foreign content. Reproductions should not count towards meeting licensing requirements, and clear labelling should inform the audience about the content.

The CRTC and the Canadian Broadcast Standards Council (CBSC) should work together to empower new immigrants and ethnocultural minorities as audience members. Language-appropriate education should include what constitutes professional journalistic practice in a liberal democracy, the unique social obligations of ethnic broadcasters given their regulatory supports, as well as how to appropriately access the mechanisms for complaints with broadcasters, the CRTC, and the CBSC. As misinformation and public mistrust have become social problems, the information needs of new immigrants and ethnocultural minorities – who are particularly exploitable because of language barriers and social marginalization – should be addressed (Ng 2021).

Finally, in view of the difficult business environment confronting CCLTN producers, policy makers need to consider the fate of ethnic broadcasting as the CRTC moves towards greater engagement with streaming services and other online platforms. Linear television is not an appropriate model for a single provider to service twenty-two languages in a calendar month. Criticisms about whether the government can or should attempt to regulate online services are substantive and cannot be avoided. However, the question of how to ensure the survival of ethnic broadcasting amidst massive changes in industry technology and viewing habits must be addressed.

NOTES

1 The terms "ethnic broadcasting" and "ethnic programming" problematically imply a strangeness that does not apply to French- or English-language media, but they are commonly used in policy and academic work.
2 No official count was taken of Chinese persons who do not speak any Chinese, but according to the author's calculations, they do exist. Please see "Proportion of Mother Tongue Responses for Various Regions in Canada," 2016 Census, Statistics Canada, 2017b, for a more complete breakdown.
3 Grounded theory techniques inspired the research design (groundedtheoryonline.org, 2021).

REFERENCES

Abu-Laban, Yasmeen. 2018. "Recognition, Re-distribution, and Solidarity: The Case of Multicultural Canada." In *Diversity and Contestations over Nationalism in Europe and Canada*, edited by John E. Fossum, Riva Kastoryano, and Birte Siim, 237–62. London: Palgrave Macmillan.

Abu-Laban, Yasmeen, and Daiva Stasiulis. 1992. "Ethnic Pluralism under Siege and Partisan Opposition to Multiculturalism." *Canadian Public Policy* 18 (4): 365–86.

Angus Reid Institute. 2019. "Immigration: Half Back Current Targets, but Colossal Misperceptions, Pushback over Refugees, Cloud Debate." *Angus Reid Institute,* 7 October, 2019. http://angusreid.org/election-2019-immigration/.

– 2020. "Blame, Bullying and Disrespect: Chinese Canadians Reveal Their Experiences with Racism during COVID-19." *Angus Reid Institute*, 22 June, 2020. http://angusreid.org/racism-chinese-canadians-covid19/.

Annenberg School for Communication. 2019. "Civic Engagement." *Metamorphosis Project*. http://www.metamorph.org/research_areas/civic_engagement/.

Armstrong, Robert. 2010. *Broadcasting Policy in Canada*. Toronto: University of Toronto Press.

Biles, John. 2016. "The Government of Canada's Multiculturalism Program: Key to Canada's Inclusion Reflex?" In *The Multiculturalism Question: Debating Identity in 21st Century Canada*, edited by Jack Jedwab, 11–52. Montreal & Kingston: McGill-Queen's University Press.

Bissoondath, Neil. 1998. "Multiculturalism." *New Internationalist*, 5 September 1998. https://newint.org/features/1998/09/05/multiculturalism.

Blake, Raymond. 2013. "New Dynamism? From Multiculturalism and Diversity History and Core Values." *British Journal of Canadian Studies* 26 (1): 79–95.

Block, Sheila, Grace-Edward Galabuzi, and Ricardo Tranjan. 2019. *Canada's Colour Coded Income Inequality*. Canadian Centre for Policy Alternatives. https://www.policyalternatives.ca/publications/reports/canadas-colour-coded-income-inequality.

Brady, Anne-Marie. 2015. "China's Foreign Propaganda Machine." *Journal of Democracy* 26 (4): 51–59.

Brodie, Janine. 2007. "Reforming Social Justice in Neoliberal Times." *Studies in Social Justice* 1 (2): 93–207.

– 2014. "Elusive Equalities and the Great Recession: Restoration, Retrenchment and Redistribution." *International Journal of Law in Context* 10 (4): 427–41.

Canadian Heritage. 2007. "*Promoting Integration: Annual Report on the Operation of the Canadian Multiculturalism Act 2006–2007*. Library and Archives Canada. https://epe.lac-bac.gc.ca/100/201/301/ar_multiculturalism_act/2006-2007.pdf

– 2017. *Multiculturalism From Now and Into the Future: Annual Report on the Operation of the Canadian Multiculturalism Act 2016–2017*. Library and Archives Canada. https://epe.lac-bac.gc.ca/100/201/301/ar_multiculturalism_act/CH31-1-2017-eng.pdf.

– 2018. *Strengthening Multiculturalism: Annual Report on the Operation of the Canadian Multiculturalism Act 2017–2018*. Library and Archives Canada. https://epe.lac-bac.gc.ca/100/201/301/ar_multiculturalism_act/CH31-1-2018-eng.pdf.

– 2019. *Respecting Diversity and Improving Responsiveness: Annual Report on the Operation of the Canadian Multiculturalism Act 2018–2019*. Library and Archives Canada: https://epe.lac-bac.gc.ca/100/201/301/ar_multiculturalism_act/CH31-1-2019-eng.pdf.

Chan, Arlene. 2014. *Righting Canada's Wrongs: The Chinese Head Tax and Anti-Chinese Immigration Policies in the Twentieth Century*. Toronto: James Lorimer & Company.

Citizenship and Immigration Canada. 2008. *Promoting Integration: Annual Report on the Operation of the Canadian Multiculturalism Act 2007–2008*. Library and Archives Canada. https://epe.lac-bac.gc.ca/100/201/301/ar_multiculturalism_act/2007-2008.pdf.

– 2009. *Promoting Integration: Annual Report on the Operation of the Canadian Multiculturalism Act 2008–2009*. Library and Archives Canada. https://epe.lac-bac.gc.ca/100/201/301/ar_multiculturalism_act/2008-2009.pdf.
– 2010. *Promoting Integration: Annual Report on the Operation of the Canadian Multiculturalism Act 2009–2010*. Library and Archives Canada. https://epe.lac-bac.gc.ca/100/201/301/ar_multiculturalism_act/2009-2010.pdf.
– 2011. *Promoting Integration: Annual Report on the Operation of the Canadian Multiculturalism Act 2010–2011*. Library and Archives Canada: https://epe.lac-bac.gc.ca/100/201/301/ar_multiculturalism_act/2010-2011.pdf.
– 2012. *Promoting Integration: Annual Report on the Operation of the Canadian Multiculturalism Act 2011–2012*. Library and Archives Canada: https://epe.lac-bac.gc.ca/100/201/301/ar_multiculturalism_act/2011-2012.pdf.
– 2013. *Promoting Integration: Annual Report on the Operation of the Canadian Multiculturalism Act 2012–2013*. Library and Archives Canada: https://epe.lac-bac.gc.ca/100/201/301/ar_multiculturalism_act/2013-2014.pdf.
– 2014. *Building on Diversity: Annual Report on the Operation of the Canadian Multiculturalism Act 2013–2014*. Library and Archives Canada https://epe.lac-bac.gc.ca/100/201/301/ar_multiculturalism_act/index.html.
– 2015. *Building a Diverse and Inclusive Society: Annual Report on the Operation of the Canadian Multiculturalism Act 2014–2015*. Library and Archives Canada. https://epe.lac-bac.gc.ca/100/201/301/ar_multiculturalism_act/2014-2015.pdf.
CRTC (Canadian Radio-television and Telecommunications Commission). 1985. "A Broadcasting Policy Reflecting Canada's Linguistic and Cultural Diversity." Public notice CRTC 1985–139. Ottawa, ON: Canadian Heritage. https://crtc.gc.ca/eng/archive/1985/PB85-139.htm.
– 2004a. "Approach to Assessing Requests to Add Non-Canadian Third-Language Television Services to the Lists of Eligible Satellite Services for Distribution on a Digital Basis." Broadcasting Public Notice CRTC 2004–96. Ottawa, ON: CRTC. https://crtc.gc.ca/eng/archive/2004/pb2004-96.htm.
– 2004b. "Improving the Diversity of Third-Language Television Services: A Revised Citizenship and Immigration Canada. 2008–2014. Annual Report on the Operation of the Canadian Multiculturalism Act."

Ottawa, ON: Library and Archives Canada. https://epe.lac-bac.gc.ca/100/201/301/ar_multiculturalism_act/index.html.
– 2016. "Various Television Services and Stations – Corporate Reorganization (Transfer of Shares)." Broadcasting Decision CRTC 2016–110. Ottawa, ON: CRTC. https://crtc.gc.ca/eng/archive/2016/2016-110.htm.
– 2019. "Licensing of a National, Multilingual Multi-Ethnic Discretionary Service." Broadcasting Decision CRTC 2019–172 and Broadcasting Order 2019–173. Ottawa, ON: CRTC. https://crtc.gc.ca/eng/archive/2019/2019-172.htm.
Day, Richard J.F. 2016. "(Never) Coming Out to Be Met? Liberal Multiculturalism and Its Radical Others." In *The Multiculturalism Question: Debating Identity in 21st Century Canada*, edited by Jack Jedwab, 127–48. Montreal & Kingston: McGill-Queen's University Press.
Dewing, M. 2014. *Background Paper: Canadian Broadcasting Policy*. Publication No. 2011-39-E. Ottawa, ON: Parliament of Canada. https://lop.parl.ca/sites/PublicWebsite/default/en_CA/Researchpublications/201139E.
D'Sa, Premila. 2020. "SARS-Fuelled Racism Scarred Chinese-Canadians. It's Happening Again with Coronavirus." *Huffington Post*, 30 January 2020. https://www.huffpost.com/archive/ca/entry/coronavirus-sars-racism-canada_ca_5e3241f6c5b611ac94cf4b36.
Erl, Chris. 2021. "The People and The Nation: The 'Thick' and the 'Thin' of Right-Wing Populism in Canada." *Social Science Quarterly* 102 (1): 107–24.
Fairchild Group. 2022. "Company Profile." https://www.fairchildgroup.com/index.php.
Gaucher, Megan. 2020. "Keeping Your Friends Close and Your Enemies Closer: Affective Constructions of 'Good' and 'Bad' Immigrants in Canadian Conservative Discourse." *Canadian Ethnic Studies* 52 (2): 79–82.
Granatstein, Jack L. 1998. *Who Killed Canadian History?* Toronto: HarperCollins Publishers.
Government of Canada. 2022. "Broadcasting Act. S.C. 1991. Consolidated Acts, c. 11." https://laws-lois.justice.gc.ca/eng/acts/b-9.01/.
Hansen, Randall. 2016. "Assimilation by Stealth: Why Canada's Multicultural Policy Is Really a Repackaged Integration Policy." In *The Multiculturalism Question: Debating Identity in 21st Century Canada*, edited by Jack Jedwab, 73–88. Montreal & Kingston: McGill-Queen's University Press.

Hawthorn, Tom. 2009. "Thirty Years Ago One Documentary Awoke a Silent Community." *The Globe and Mail*, 22 September 2009. https://www.theglobeandmail.com/news/british-columbia/thirty-years-ago-one-documentary-awoke-a-silent-community/article790434/.

Hou, Feng, Grant Schellenberg, and John Berry. 2016. *Patterns and Determinants of Immigrants' Sense of Belonging to Canada and their Source Country.* Ottawa, ON: Statistics Canada. https://www150.statcan.gc.ca/n1/pub/11f0019m/11f0019m2016383-eng.htm.

Houpt, Simon. 2015. "Rogers Cuts 110 Jobs, Ends All OMNI Newscasts." *The Globe and Mail*, 7 May 2015. https://www.theglobeandmail.com/report-on-business/rogers-to-cut-jobs-kill-all-omni-newscasts/article24306838/.

Jirik, John. 2016. "CCTV News and Soft Power." *International Journal of Communication* 10: 3536–53.

Laselva, Samuel. 2014. "Understanding Canada's Origins: Federalism, Multiculturalism, and the Will to Live Together." In *Canadian Politics*, 6th ed., edited by James Bickerton and Alain Gagnon, 3–20. Toronto: University of Toronto Press.

Lawson, G. 2015. "Trudeau's Canada, Again." *New York Times*, 8 December 2015. https://www.nytimes.com/2015/12/13/magazine/trudeaus-canada-again.html.

Li, Peter S. 1998. *The Chinese in Canada.* 2nd ed. Toronto: Oxford University Press.

Matsaganis, Matthew D., Vikki S. Katz, and Sandra J. Ball-Rokeach. 2010. *Understanding Ethnic Media: Producers, Consumers, and Societies.* Thousand Oaks, CA: SAGE.

Mann, Jatinder. 2016. "Review of *The Multiculturalism Question: Debating Identity in 21st Century Canada* ed by Jack Jedwa." *British Journal of Canadian Studies* 29, no. 1 (2016): 134–35.

McCready, L. 2012. "Militarization, Multiculturalism and Mythology: Canadian National Identity in a New Age of Empire." PhD diss., McMaster University.

Ming Pao Canada. 2021. "About Us." http://www.mingpaocanada.com/tor/cfm/intro_Eng.cfm.

Montpetit, Jonathan. 2017a. "Religious Garb OK for Cops, Judges, Says Bouchard-Taylor Report's Co-Author." *CBC*, 14 February 2017. https://www.cbc.ca/news/canada/montreal/charles-taylor-hijab-reasonable-accommodation-reversal-1.3982082.

– 2017b. "What We Can Learn from Hérouxville, the Quebec Town That

Became Shorthand for Intolerance." *CBC*, 27 January 2017. https://www.cbc.ca/news/canada/montreal/herouxville-quebec-reasonable-accommodation-1.3950390.

Moscovitch, Allan. 2015. "Welfare State." *The Canadian Encyclopedia*, 13 August 2015. https://www.thecanadianencyclopedia.ca/en/article/welfare-state.

Nieguth, Tim, and Tracey Raney. 2017. "Nation-Building and Canada's National Symbolic Order, 1993–2015." *Nations and Nationalisms* 23 (1): 87–108.

Ng, Edward. 2021. "COVID-19 Deaths among Immigrants: Evidence from the Early Months of The Pandemic." Ottawa, ON: Statistics Canada. 9 June 2021. https://www150.statcan.gc.ca/n1/pub/45-28-0001/2021001/article/00017-eng.htm.

Ng, Elim. 2019. "The Transnational Politics of Canadian, Chinese-Language Television News Production: Media, Immigration, and Foreign Policy." PhD diss., University of Alberta. https://doi.org/10.7939/r3-sjej-0868.

OMNI TV. n.d. "Schedule." https://www.omnitv.ca/ab/en/schedule/.

Reid, Angus. 2016. "Canadians Aren't as Accepting as We Think – And We Can't Ignore It." *CBC*, 4 October 2016. http://www.cbc.ca/news/canada/angus-reid-poll-canadian-values-immigration-1.3789223.

Roth, Lorna. 2005. *Something New in the Air: The Story of First Peoples Television Broadcasting in Canada.* Montreal & Kingston: McGill-Queen's University Press.

Royal Commission on Bilingualism and Biculturalism (RCBB), A. Davidson Dunton, Jean-Louis Gagnon, Clement Cormier, Royce Frith, Paul Lacoste, Gertrude Laing et al. 1969. "Report of the Royal Commission on Bilingualism and Biculturalism: The Cultural Contribution of Other Ethnic Groups." vol. 4. Ottawa, ON: Queen's Printer. http://publications.gc.ca/collections/collection_2014/bcp-pco/Z1-1963-1-5-4-1-eng.pdf.

Salter, Liora, and Felix Odartey-Wellington. 2008. *The CRTC and Broadcasting Regulation in Canada.* Toronto: Thomson Carswell.

Sing Tao Media Group. n.d. "Sing Tao Group Canada: Company Profile." http://eng.singtao.ca/.

Statistics Canada. 2016. "Table 5 – 98-400-X2016202 Admission Category and Applicant Type (7), Period of Immigration (7), Place of Birth (272), Age (12) and Sex (3) for the Immigrant Population Who Landed between 1980 and 2016, in Private Households"[Data Table]. Ottawa, ON: Statistics Canada. https://www12.statcan.gc.ca/census-

recensement/2016/dp-pd/dt-td/Rp-eng.cfm?LANG=E&APATH=3&DETAIL=0&DIM=0&FL=A&FREE=0&GC=0&GID=0&GK=0&GRP==110558&PRID=10&PTYPE=109445&S=0&SHOWALL=0&SUB=0&Temporal=2017&THEME=120&VID=0&VNAMEE=&VNAMEF=.
– 2017a. "Canada [Country] and Canada [Country]. Census Profile, 2016 Census." Catalogue no. 98-316-X2016001. [Data Table]. Ottawa, ON: Statistics Canada. https://www12.statcan.gc.ca/census-recensement/2016/dp-pd/prof/index.cfm?Lang=E.
– 2017b. "Proportion of Mother Tongue Responses for Various Regions in Canada, 2016 Census." [Data Visualization Tool]. Ottawa, ON: Statistics Canada. https://www12.statcan.gc.ca/census-recensement/2016/dp-pd/dv-vd/lang/index-eng.cfm#chrt-dt-tbl.
– 2018. "Table 63 – 98-400-X2016275 Visible Minority (15), Highest Certificate, Diploma or Degree (15), Generation Status (4), Age (9) and Sex (3) for the Population Aged 15 Years and Over in Private Households of Canada, Provinces and Territories and Census Metropolitan Areas, 2016 Census – 25% Sample Data" [Data Table]. Ottawa, ON: Statistics Canada. https://www150.statcan.gc.ca/n1/en/catalogue/98-400-X2016275.
Taras, D. 2015. *The Digital Mosaic: Media, Power, and Identity in Canada*. Toronto: University of Toronto Press.
Wang, Holman. 1998. "The Monster House Revisited: Race and Representations of Urban Change in Vancouver." Master's thesis, University of British Columbia. https://open.library.ubc.ca/cIRcle/collections/ubctheses/831/items/1.0088657.
Winter, Elke. 2015. "Rethinking Multiculturalism after Its 'Retreat': Lessons from Canada." *American Behavioral Scientist* 59 (6): 637–57.
Wong, Edward. 2008. "The Dead Tell a Tale China Doesn't Care to Listen To." *New York Times*, 18 November 2008. https://www.nytimes.com/2008/11/19/world/asia/19mummy.html.
Zhou, Min, Wenzhong Chen, and Guxuan Cai. 2006. "Chinese-Language Media and Immigrant Life in the United States and Canada." In *Media and the Chinese Diaspora: Community, Communications and Commerce*, edited by Wanning Sun, 42–74. New York: Routledge.

CHAPTER FOUR

Ethnic Media and Cultural Brokerage: An Overview from the Canadian Context

Mark Hayward

INTRODUCTION

The ethnic media sector in Canada is, and has been, a sector where private for-profit (although not always profitable) enterprises are the major players. In Canada, this arrangement originated in the 1950s when the government determined that the Canadian Broadcasting Corporation would provide programming in English and French with limited additional production in Indigenous languages (Hayward 2019). Subsequent revisions of Canadian media policy have placed an increased emphasis on diversity, but the industry remains dominated by organizations that depend upon revenue from advertising (and, to a lesser extent, paid access or subscription) to finance their operations. Accordingly, the individuals (and artifacts) that constitute the Canadian ethnic media sector are often engaged in a balancing act between their activities serving a community while navigating different cultural and linguistic contexts and the necessity of ensuring economic viability. Recognizing that these are not separate considerations, this chapter proposes brokerage as a framework for analyzing how the industrial practices of ethnic media in Canada are involved in processes of cultural and economic translation and calculation.

While the concept of translation, expanded to include a broader range of contextual factors, such as "cultural translation," has been used to explore some of these dynamics, this chapter explores what a deeper engagement with the concept of brokerage might contribute to the specific configuration of the relationship between the cultural, political, and economic aspects of ethnic media. The analysis of brokerage has a long history in anthropology and sociology although the concept is less frequently discussed in media and communication studies. Of particular relevance here are those studies in the social sciences focusing on the "cultural broker," understood as a social type whose function is to support translation across cultures and languages in ways that are often inseparable from the exchange of goods or services. However, the emphasis in this chapter is on brokerage rather than brokers, with the aim of shifting the focus from individuals to the distribution of brokerage activities across individuals, organizations, rules, and artifacts. A framework is proposed for how different types of brokerage might be used to describe and analyze the range of activities that constitute practices of cultural brokerage in the context of ethnic media. Three different types of brokerage common in media serving cultural and linguistic minorities are discussed: *representational* brokerage, *regulatory* brokerage, and *artifactual* brokerage. The first of these types of brokerage – representational brokerage – emphasizes those practices that are engaged in processes of translation such that they support the movement of cultural forms and their associated meanings across languages or cultural contexts. The second type of brokerage – regulatory brokerage – emphasizes those practices through which differences in law and regulation are navigated, negotiated, and even exploited as part of the distribution of media across legal jurisdictions. The third type of brokerage – artifactual brokerage – emphasizes how these practices of brokerage are embedded in artifacts and objects. The distinction between these three types of brokerage is heuristic rather than absolute since all three types intersect and overlap with each other, although here they will be discussed individually.

The following section outlines discussions on brokerage in the context of media and communication studies. It highlights how the term overlaps with, but is also distinct from, the kinds of practices that have been analyzed using the concept of cultural intermediaries. The following three sections provide overviews of each of the three types of cultural brokerage mentioned above, providing both expanded definitions and examples drawn from the history of minority media in Canada. The conclusion addresses how analyzing cultural brokerage in the context of ethnic media might contribute to a project of supporting both equity and diversity as an interrelated and mutually supportive political, social, and cultural project. Taking up an analysis of cultural brokerage in ethnic media in support of this egalitarian project is particularly important in the present moment given the growing role of algorithmic techniques for managing the flow of content across cultural and linguistic contexts. By taking up brokerage as a tool of critical analysis, it is possible to recognize and intervene in the processes by which these new technologies, and the institutional and discursive positions supporting their alignment with contemporary capitalism, threaten to foreclose social and cultural struggles for visibility and agency of historically marginalized groups and individuals.

LITERATURE REVIEW

Briefly looking back at the literature is helpful for understanding both the heterogeneity and unity of practices discussed in this chapter. At the same time, it is important to understand how the term can be differentiated from similar concepts more commonly used in media studies research, specifically that of the cultural intermediary.

In their widely read overview of the literature on brokerage in the social sciences, Stovel and Shaw (2012) note that "the crucial characteristics of brokers are that (a) they bridge a gap in social structure and (b) they help goods, information, opportunities flow across that gap" (141). The activities of cultural brokers fit within this definition, but with an emphasis on transactions involving the exchange of information and opportunities in the anthropological and sociological literature. The term originates in political anthropology where the cultural broker is typically discussed in relation to projects for national development and modernization. Mapped onto the conceptual frameworks of social theory from the mid-twentieth century that would also influence the study of communication (Shah 2011), both Wolf (1956) and Geertz (1960) analyze the cultural broker as a figure who mediates between local or traditional cultural and social forms and emergent national or global forms. Brokerage transits across and builds bridges between both cultural differences and geographic scales but is also embedded in a narrative of modernization and economic development. Drawing on this formulation of the concept, analyses of cultural brokerage have also been proposed to understand migration. Particular attention has been given to the translation work that supports the ability of recent migrants to interact with the broader (typically national) socio-cultural context to which they have relocated (Massey and Sánchez 2010).

However, the concept of the cultural broker has received comparatively little attention in media studies despite similar terms garnering more sustained consideration. The category of the "cultural intermediary" is taken up more widely by media studies and related fields to discuss and analyze various kinds of brokerage in the context of media industries (see Smith Maguire and Matthews 2014 for an overview of this research). This is representative of the enthusiasm with which the field of media studies has taken up Pierre Bourdieu's work on class and processes of cultural differentiation. For Bourdieu, cultural intermediaries are engaged in work that translates one type of capital into another; for example, cultural knowledge into economic value (Bourdieu 1984). The research on intermediaries in media and cultural studies emphasizes the contributions of the cultural intermediaries to the creation of meaning as part of processes of circulation, highlighting the extent to which the activities of intermediaries – even going so far as to include entire classes of workers such as those involved in marketing and promotion – go well beyond simple re-transmission (Du Gay 1997; Negus 1999; Nixon and Du Gay 2002).

While cultural intermediary is a concept that has proven useful for identifying and analyzing the types of labour and forms of self-perception that are common in different areas of the media and cultural industries, the term is less effective when it comes to describing the importance of intercultural negotiation that must be addressed when looking at media serving or representing cultural or linguistic minorities. As elaborated in Bourdieu, the cultural intermediary performs a translation role between different kinds of capital (cultural, social, or economic), but does so within a single cultural or linguistic context. For this reason, the concept of brokerage is better suited to describing the complex intercultural work embedded in many of the professional activities of individuals participating in ethnic media industries that are structured around navigating the relationship between majority and minority cultural and linguistic groups. An individual may act as both an intermediary and broker, yet the distinction is useful insofar as it contributes to a more nuanced description of the range of activities that take place in the ethnic media sector. It is a distinction that provides a more detailed understanding of how the activities of these individuals and organizations may differ in subtle, yet important ways, from similar practices in media contexts where ethnic or linguistic identity less explicitly inform organizational goals and the conceptualization of intended audiences.

There is some work that has taken up brokerage to analyze the transnational circulation of media and the intercultural aspects of this circulation. Importantly, a common theme across this literature, which distinguishes it from discussions of cultural brokerage in other areas of the social sciences, is the tendency to move across (if not explicitly collapse) the distinction between commercial and cultural brokerage. This distinction, while defining two categories whose relationship is complex and interdependent, is worth maintaining for how it draws attention to those activities which involve cultural and linguistic translation which sit in relation to, but cannot be made synonymous with, those practices whose primary function is the exchange of commodities. Braester's (2005) discussion of cultural brokerage in the context of Chinese cinema highlights how filmmakers work to mediate between the aesthetic prestige of cinema as a medium and cultural form, and the demands of the market. Robinson (2017), examining the organization and impact of Chinese-language film festivals in the United Kingdom, similarly highlights the imbrication of the cultural and economic elements of brokerage that takes place at such events. As he writes, "a cultural broker not only enables the movement of films across geographical and legal boundaries through their professional network of contacts, but also 'translates' this material – bridges the cultural and linguistic divisions that might otherwise render these films unfamiliar or incomprehensible" (Robinson 2017, 196). Similarly, Yue uses the concept of cultural broker to discuss the arc of Australian filmmaker and producer Pauline Chan (2018) by tracing her involvement with acting and directing, as well as her extensive involvement in the financial side of film distribution in the context of her diasporic identity. In each of these examples, the cultural brokerage makes possible the commercial exchange and, in doing so, highlights how cultural brokerage cannot be presumed to be a part of every commercial exchange.

Building on the above argument for attending to cultural brokerage, the remainder of the chapter further elaborates how cultural brokerage is woven into many of the practices that constitute ethnic media broadly defined. Each of the following sections provide an overview of a different type of cultural brokerage involving representations, objects, and laws. As noted above, these divisions are not meant to be absolute but are rather indicative of the range of activities and outcomes associated with cultural brokerage. Further, they introduce a thematic that is mostly absent from the literature of cultural brokerage in media and communication studies and is undertheorized in the broader literature on the term: technology. While many of the forms of cultural brokerage involve the exchange of objects, whether as commodities, gifts, or public goods, there is relatively little attention given to the place of technology and technical artifacts in these processes. This is a topic to which the chapter returns to in the conclusion through a discussion of cultural brokerage in the context of contemporary digital media. Attending to technologies of cultural brokerage is highlighted as one of the ways that the attention given to the means of communication in media studies might contribute to existing research on brokerage across the social sciences.

TYPES OF BROKERAGE: REPRESENTATIONAL BROKERAGE

Representational brokerage describes those practices that are engaged in processes of translation such that they support the circulation of cultural forms and their associated meanings across cultural contexts. Examples of representational brokerage are extensive and have been widely discussed by researchers examining the work of media producers and audiences. It involves those practices through which texts, genres, as well as modes of consumption (e.g., audience behaviours) navigate cultural or linguistic differences. It is the form of brokerage that most closely aligns with the common understanding of the term "translation," although recognizing that acts of translation should not be strictly limited to language and may include any system of meaning making. Consider, for example, Jackie Mittoo's recording of "Toronto Express" (1972), which repurposes the melody of Neil Young's "Ohio" and recontextualizes it in the context of the sonic and rhythmic forms of reggae. Mittoo does not make explicit the extent to which his version, which has no vocals, is intended to invoke the political themes of Young's lyrics about police violence against protesters at Kent State University in 1970. Similarly, there is no explicit explanation of the song's relationship to Mittoo's relocation to Toronto in 1969, a city in which Young lived for a period of time in the mid-1960s. Nonetheless, it is emblematic of Mittoo's broader cultural contributions to introducing and supporting the globalization of reggae music, initially in Jamaica, and later in Canada and the United Kingdom, in its borrowings from a song that would have been recently popular at the time of recording (Cyrus 2015).

A slightly different example of this process can be seen in the emergence and popular use of constructs like "continental" or "cosmopolitan" as a way of categorizing and presenting music that belonged to genres of popular music associated with European, but non-anglophone, contexts during the 1950s. Both terms are mobilized by record companies across the English-speaking world as a way of promoting recordings that evoked a sense of otherness in a way that could be aligned with popular ideas about European sophistication and permitted novel genres to be integrated within the existing map of hegemonic musical forms and their associated listening practices. In the United States, recordings of European-themed easy listening music, such as "Percy Faith Plays Continental Music" (1953), are promoted with the image of a globe-trotting romantic. Whiteoak (2007) documents the circulation of "continental music" in Australia, where it was used to describe a hodgepodge of global genres including Brazilian Samba, Italian popular music, and Latin American jazz, and notes its popular usage prior to the embrace of multiculturalist discourse in the 1970s. In Canada, prior to the licensing of multilingual broadcasters in the early 1960s, continental was introduced as a way of describing media that addressed (albeit indirectly) recent immigrants from Europe while remaining firmly grounded in the linguistic and cultural perspective of anglophone Canada (Stern 1955, 7).

Both of these aforementioned examples highlight how processes of translation must be understood in a more expansive manner that is not simply a self-contained process for the identification of equivalence between different cultural or linguistic codes. Mittoo's re-casting of Neil Young's composition participates in the practice of musical borrowing or "versioning" that characterizes how other genres of music have historically been incorporated into the musical culture of reggae. Similarly impacted by its time and context, the example of cosmopolitan music in the 1950s is significant for how it highlights the ways that representational brokerage can operate as a technique through which dominant cultural and economic interests can work to maintain control over cultural forms and their related economic interests. It is a reminder that the processes and practices contributing to the hybridization of textual elements are not ends in themselves but must be situated in relation to the broader processes of brokerage and exchange.

REGULATORY BROKERAGE

An important part of the context within which processes of representational brokerage takes place consists of the legal and regulatory systems. Regulatory brokerage entails the practices and processes through which the differences between these regulatory systems are navigated. For example, returning to the example of Mittoo's "Toronto Express," the decision to credit Mittoo as the only composer of the song is indicative of his contributions to the song but also likely an attempt to take advantage of the rights (and revenues) granted by intellectual property law. This example is not atypical as it is frequently the case that an analysis of practices of regulatory brokerage provide insight into the integration of practices of transnational and transcultural cultural brokerage with the structures of global trade. Broadly defined, it encompasses those practices or agreements that navigate the differences between laws and regulations across jurisdictions often. The offshoring of media production to jurisdictions with cheaper labour, or the relocation of manufacturing facilities or critical infrastructure to sites with reduced environmental protections, are two examples of how major media companies navigate between regulatory regimes with the aim of generating profit, also described as regulatory arbitrage (Fleischer 2010, 227). Indeed, regulatory brokerage has become a key characteristic of contemporary capitalism, taking on many forms across every sector of the economy.

Examples of regulatory brokerage are common across the history of the global distribution of audiovisual content. Given the dominant role played by cultural policies that often limited (whether intentionally or unintentionally) access to media produced in other parts of the world in the service of national culture, those engaged in regulatory brokerage have played a key role in supporting alternative distribution networks with the aim of making material accessible. In making sense of these practices, the distinction between formal and informal media economies is helpful for understanding the range of activities that are involved in regulatory brokerage. Lobato and Thomas explain this distinction and the interaction between the formal and informal stating: "Formal economies are industrially regulated. Informal economies operate without, or in partial articulation with, regulatory oversight. Neither zone can be fully understood without considering the other. Media history is a story of *interactions* between and across the formal and informal zones" (2018, 5).

Implicit in this distinction between formal and informal media economies is the relationship between regulatory regimes and territoriality, which is often in play when looking at ethnic media organizations that participate in the distribution of media across national borders. In Canada, the state has played a key role in structuring the parameters according to which many cultural brokers operate, whether through the establishment and enforcement of intellectual property law or other ways of regulating content. This has meant that the vast majority of industrial practices associated with ethnic media have also entailed some form of regulatory brokerage. The decision to support the creation of domestic broadcast services operating in non-official languages, beginning in the 1960s, derives both from the technical limitations of media distribution during much of the twentieth century that limited the spatial reach of media services as well as a desire to establish brokers, both culturally and commercially, who would be subject to Canadian legislative authority (see Hayward 2019 for a further discussion of the development of multilingual broadcasting during this period).

The broadcasting career of Johnny Lombardi, an important early multilingual broadcaster based in Toronto, provides a number of examples of regulatory brokerage. As noted above, Lombardi explicitly claimed the descriptor of continental rather than ethnic when describing the proposed service as a means of making his proposal more easily assimilable to the existing policy frameworks for Canadian media at that time. Lombardi also shifted the operation of his businesses following the introduction of Canadian content regulation. Bravo Records, a record label owned by Lombardi since his days as a radio host and concert promoter in the 1950s, shifted its operation from licensing music produced in Italy to the recording of Italian-language music in Canada. "I'm making my own Canadian content," Lombardi enthusiastically told a reporter in 1971 (quoted in Amatiello 2012). The importance of these state-sanctioned brokers continues with many broadcast services, including those that were established decades ago, functioning as redistribution platforms for multiple international services while also producing a smaller amount of domestically produced broadcast content.

At the same time, regulatory brokerage also highlights the fluid relationship between the distribution of media that adheres to regulatory norms across jurisdictions and those practices that operate in the space between jurisdictions. Historically, this contributed to the creation of informal networks for the quasi-legitimate distribution of music and audiovisual materials. These networks made possible the circulation of material that is not allowed to be distributed in Canada for reasons including censorship, intellectual property rights, as well as the limited service provided by licensed services (a by-product of the limited access to public broadcasting and private broadcast licences in a regulatory framework designed to support official bilingualism). Discussing the pirating of media from around the world via satellite in Canada, Taylor (2008) notes that consumers turn to satellite piracy since "there has been simply no legal way for various ethnic communities to access these channels" (98). In these cases, the decision to access pirated signals was a form of regulatory brokerage in which participation in the informal media economy is taken as a calculated risk in order to access content not otherwise available.

The emergence of digital media, despite the increased capacity for surveillance that networked media makes possible, further complicates the relationship between informal and formal media economies while preserving the key role for regulatory brokerage. Consider, for example, the importance of iRoko in the global distribution of Nigerian films. iRoko, which was founded in 2011 and has been operating as a standalone streaming service since 2013, holds a dominant position in the distribution of Nigerian films to many countries including Canada. The company's rapid growth has significantly transformed the political economy of film production in Nigeria, thanks to the company's role as the dominant digital distribution company for Nollywood film and has similarly disrupted and displaced the previously established informal distribution networks for physical copies (Haynes 2018). However, while being most active in Nigeria, its relationship to international intellectual property law is indicative of a more complex relationship to creativity, regulation, and location. Andrews (2020) notes that iRoko allows its producers to license their property in either the UK or the United States rather than Nigeria, in recognition of the stronger enforcement of intellectual property in those jurisdictions. This choice, preferred by both producers and iRoko (who often maintain an ownership stake in much of the content they distribute), is a clear example of regulatory brokerage where formal rather than informal networks are drawn upon to maintain legal and economic control. This, however, is not a universal arrangement since the success of many digital media companies, particularly video streaming platforms like YouTube, rely upon their capacity for operating between national regulatory regimes in a manner that permits the lax enforcement of intellectual property rights.

ARTIFACTUAL BROKERAGE

Attending to the historical impact of the shift from analogue to digital media that has taken place since the 1990s brings into focus the importance of artifactual brokerage. Artifactual brokerage describes how the circulation of media across different cultural and linguistic contexts is implicated in the design and use of material objects and infrastructural systems that make the circulation of media possible. It explores the central role non-human actors play in the networks that structure the operation of ethnic and minority media in Canada, whether in the form of infrastructure, technologies, or objects. Reading the history of ethnic media in Canada as a history of artifacts brings into focus how the potential for the distribution of information is shaped by the design, availability, and durability of material objects.

A widely experienced, but often overlooked example of artifactual brokerage is the continuing significance of global media formats, which illuminates the interaction between technical specifications, the global trade in media, and the political economy of communication. In its earliest forms, the establishment of media formats unique to particular global regions resulted from the adoption of different technical standards for broadcast television during the 1950s and 1960s. Tracing the global patterns of adoption highlights how the structures of political, cultural, and economic dependency affected the diffusion of technologies during the middle of the twentieth century. The adoption of formats followed the geopolitical contours of the period. The United States exerted its influence across the hemisphere resulting in the adoption of the standard established by the

US-based National Television Standard Committee (NTSC) across much of the Americas including Canada. Most of Europe, apart from France (having adopted another format known as SECAM), shared the Phase Alternating Line format (PAL) thanks in part to advocacy of the European Broadcasting Union. Parts of Africa and Asia adopted PAL following the lines of economic and political influence resulting from the history of European colonialism. Meanwhile, the Soviet Union and other Soviet-aligned countries across Europe and Asia adopted a standard that was derived from – but incompatible with – France's SECAM format known as NIIR, an abbreviation of Nautchno-Issledovateliskiy Institut Radio where the format was developed.

What previously impacted only national industrial policies and the global trade in audiovisual equipment developed into an organizing factor for the global distribution of audiovisual media for domestic use with the arrival of video cassette technology (commonly referred to as VHS or Video Home System), preventing recordings from different parts of the world being accessible in regions with different technical standards. In recounting this history, it is easy to emphasize only the perspective of major media producers and the consumption of mainstream media where these would have been minor concerns. Yet, it is not possible to extricate the international distribution of film and television that supported ethnic media in Canada from this history. In the Canadian context, these technological differences gave rise to a range of services who worked to navigate and circumvent these restrictions in order to provide access for marginalized minority audiences. Many of these brokers were small operations rather than major distributors, but their cumulative impact substantially structured the economy and phenomenology of film and television for minority communities. Sona HiFi (founded in 1978 and still in operation at the time of writing), for example, operated shops in both Toronto and Ottawa, and positioned itself as a distributor for equipment (especially video cassette recorders) that were capable of worldwide functionality. Other services were less visible, but not less important. Their services were discussed on multiple occasions in venues such as the "Videosyncracies" column in the *Toronto Star*, which provided information during the early years of home video. These discussions of format often invoke the importation of videotapes into Canada from other parts of the world including Asia and Europe by members of various migrant and diasporic communities (Levitch 1983a, Levitch 1983b).

An extension of the technical standards for television broadcast and analogue video recording continued with the introduction of the DVD format. While the DVD format was capable of being used across all technical specifications, the DVD consortium – the group tasked with establishing and maintaining standards for the format – adopted a system of region codes that limited interoperability across regions in response to lobbying by globally integrated media companies (Elkins 2016). The region code system, officially voluntary but effectively required due to its embrace by the major global film and television producers, allowed for media releases to be timed across global regions by creating a technical means for impeding distribution in particular markets. While the early history of video formats followed the contours of twentieth-century geopolitics and its imbrication with industrial policies globally, the DVD region code was more explicitly economic in its motivation, dividing and grouping markets by their comparative wealth and buying power (Elkins 2019). This allowed for the release of new material to be staged across the globe in a manner that allowed for greater profit to be extracted from richer markets while limiting the distribution of the same material in markets where prices and profits would be reduced. While there are many elements that might have been considered as part of the grouping of markets, the structure and enforcement of intellectual property was certainly a key factor with an emphasis on limiting the impact of media piracy.

Most recently, the discourse of ubiquity that has accompanied the rise of digital streaming may give the impression that the segmentation of the globe into markets by technical means is now a thing of the past. However, there are a number of ways in which user access to media via digital networks is aligned with various logics of partition in response to political or economic exigencies. The infrastructure that supports the downloading and streaming of media is located in the physical world, similarly, digital artifacts themselves have particular prescriptions about use and circulation embedded in their design that replicate the limits of duplication and playback that structured the flow of physical media in previous decades through code. There are a number of global players (Amazon Web Services, Google, Alibaba) whose operations span multiple jurisdictions even though their access to markets is conditioned by local, regional, and national service providers. The resulting system is less a global, digital internationalism than the inclusion of these companies in ecosystems that broker between technological capability, economic demand, and the requirements of national and regional regulatory systems (Elkins 2019b). It is the norm for major cloud services to limit access based upon location, operating in co-operation with various national authorities in the enforcement of intellectual property agreements or other arrangements regarding content access and censorship.

While some international services may be streamed directly by consumers, many international services work with partners based in Canada to provide digital services. For example, the Ethnic Channels Group, founded in 2004, has agreements with more than one hundred international services in more than twenty different languages to provide distribution support across North America, but also in Australia and the Middle East. The core of its business is to provide both technical support and regulatory advice for broadcasters looking to operate globally, although any global service traverses a series of markets with differing technical and political requirements. The activities of these companies are best viewed as being engaged in regulatory brokerage in contexts where the technical capacity of digital networks for geolocation and surveillance are being used to limit access in particular locations.

Alongside these companies involved in the brokerage of access to media for diasporic communities internationally, there have emerged a number of tools that make navigating the technical barriers to media access across regions possible. These tools fulfill many of the roles previously played by local media distributors converting across formats, and are examples of how artifacts (including tools) may serve to enact cultural brokerage. For example, virtual private network (VPN) clients allow users to circumvent access restrictions based on location derived from IP addresses. By allowing users to limit their exposure to the surveillance of governments or the aggressive protection of intellectual property rights, these clients (and infrastructure of associated proxy servers) permit the movement of media in and around barriers such as they exist in the digital context.

Global data service companies and VPNs are both, albeit in different ways, brokers, supporting the movement of media across cultural, linguistic, and regulatory contexts. The interaction between these artifactually embedded processes of control and the evasion of control, like the adaptation of earlier forms of media artifacts, is not unrelated to ethnicity although these technologies are not explicitly organized around ideas of identity and community. Rather, they highlight how many forms of identity and community traverse the economic and political borders these technologies work to enforce. This highlights how a comprehensive analysis of ethnic media must attend to the cultural, regulatory, and material aspects of contemporary culture and experience. Taking up this topic is an area where the traditions of media and communication theory might make significant contributions to broader discussions about brokerage across the social sciences, given its contributions to understanding the interaction between culture, social structure, and technology. Thus, it might be productive to return to the work of Innis or McLuhan to both draw upon their insights into the relationship between technology, subjectivity, and knowledge as well as draw out how their conceptualization of civilizational framing of media and culture might be expanded to engage with a more complex understanding of belonging and marginalization.

CONCLUSION: BROKERAGE AND DIGITAL MEDIA

Having provided a brief survey of three types of cultural brokerage and some examples, it is appropriate to reiterate that all three overlap with each other. It would be possible to return to the examples discussed, emphasizing different kinds of brokerage. However, the aim in providing a more refined analysis of brokerage is not only to provide tools for documenting the industrial practices specific to media serving cultural and linguistic minorities in Canada. In their survey of the literature on brokerage, Stovel and Shaw highlight how the role of the broker is both precarious and central by noting two interconnected aspects of the complex role they play: (1) that brokers often struggle to maintain relations of trust with the parties whose interactions they are supporting, and (2) that the broker can accrue significant power and influence given their importance to the movement of goods and information (151). Both of these aspects of the brokerage highlight how an analysis of brokerage is also a consideration of how power is distributed within a particular situation.

The history of ethnic media in Canada provides many examples where brokerage activities have been implicated in processes that have simultaneously provided recognition and marginalization. In these circumstances, it has often been the broker who has accrued power, wealth, and influence at the cost of more generally distributed benefits. The rise of contemporary data-driven media distribution did not disrupt this tradition, but rather displaced what were primarily treated as cultural, political, or economic matters onto the design and operationalization of new technologies and tools. By emphasizing the range of brokerage activities and how their interaction has supported, and continues to support, the existing industrial practices of minority media in Canada, it is possible to address how best to support the struggle to establish a more fully realized democratic media by means of, rather than in opposition to, cultural and linguistic differences.

REFERENCES

Amatiello, Michael. 2012. "CHIN Radio and Its Listeners: A Negotiation in the Post-War Commerce of Ethnicity." *Quaderni d'italianistica* 33 (1): 63–82.

Bourdieu, Pierre. 1984. *Distinction: A Social Critique of the Judgement of Taste*. Cambridge: Harvard University Press.

Braester, Yomi. 2005. "Chinese Cinema in the Age of Advertisement: The Filmmaker as a Cultural Broker." *The China Quarterly* 183: 549–64.

Cyrus, Karen A.E. 2015. "Jackie Mittoo at Home and Abroad: The Cultural and Musical Negotiations of a Jamaican Canadian." PhD diss., York University.

Du Gay, Paul, ed. 1997. *Production of Culture/Cultures of Production*. London: SAGE.

Elkins, Evan. 2016. "The DVD Region Code System: Standardizing Home Video's Disjunctive Global Flows." *International Journal of Cultural Studies* 19 (2): 225–40.

Fleischer, Victor. 2010. "Regulatory Arbitrage." *Texas Law Review* 89: 227–90.

Geertz, Clifford. 1960. "The Javanese Kijaji: The Changing Role of a Cultural Broker." *Comparative Studies in Society and History* 2 (2): 228–49.

Haynes, Jonathan. 2018. "Between the Informal Sector and Transnational Capitalism: Transformations of Nollywood." In *A Companion to African Cinema*, edited by Kenneth W. Harrow and Carmela Garritano, 244–68. London: Wiley.

Levitch, Gerald. 1983a. "Videosyncracies." *Toronto Star*, 30 July 1983, 71.

– 1983b. "Videosyncracies." *Toronto Star*, 19 November 1983, 18.
Lobato, Ramon, and Julian Thomas. 2018. *The Informal Media Economy*. London: Wiley.
Massey, Douglas, and Magaly Sánchez. 2010. *Brokered Boundaries: Immigrant Identity in Anti-Immigrant Times*. London: SAGE.
Negus, Keith. 1999. *Music Genres and Corporate Cultures*. London: Routledge.
Nixon, Sean, and Paul Du Gay. 2002. "Who Needs Cultural Intermediaries?" *Cultural Studies* 16 (4): 495–500.
Robinson, Luke. 2017. "Sole Traders, Cultural Brokers, and Chinese-Language Film Festivals in the United Kingdom: The London Taiwan Cinefest and the Chinese Visual Festival." In *Chinese Film Festivals*, edited by Chris Berry and Luke Robinson, 193–213. New York: Palgrave Macmillan.
Shah, Hemant. 2011. *The Production of Modernization: Daniel Lerner, Mass Media, and the Passing of Traditional Society*. Philadelphia: Temple University Press.
Smith Maguire, Jennifer, and Julian Matthews, eds. 2014. *The Cultural Intermediaries Reader*. London: SAGE.
Stern, Joe. 1955. "Private Broadcasters Speak in Many Tongues." *Canadian Broadcaster and Telescreen* 14 (16): 6–8.
Stovel, Katherine, and Lynette Shaw. 2012. "Brokerage." *Annual Review of Sociology* 38 (1): 139–58.
Taylor, Greg. 2008. "Grey to Black: Satellite Piracy in Canada." *Canadian Journal of Media Studies* 4 (1): 89–108.
Whiteoak, John. 2007. "Italo-Hispanic Popular Music in Melbourne before Multiculturalism." *Victorian Historical Journal* 78 (2): 228.
Wolf, Eric. 1956. "Aspects of Group Relations in a Complex Society: Mexico." *American Anthropologist* 58 (6): 1065–78.
Yue, Audrey. 2018. "The 'Diaspora Advantage' of Pauline Chan (1956–): From Multicultural Filmmaker to Cultural Broker." *Culture, Theory and Critique* 59 (2): 158–77.

PART TWO

Ethnic Media Practices: From the Analogue to the Digital

CHAPTER FIVE

Political Economy of Ethnic Journalism: Mapping the Terrain of South Asian Ethnic Media in British Columbia

Syeda Nayab Bukhari

INTRODUCTION

Ethnic media in the global north have grown exponentially over the last few decades (La Ferle and Morimoto 2009; Matsaganis, Katz, and Ball-Rokeach 2010; Shi 2009; Viswanath and Arora 2000). Deuze (2006, 262) notes "forty-five percent of all African American, Hispanic, Asian American, Native American and Arab American adults prefer ethnic television, radio or newspapers to their mainstream counterparts." Ethnic media are growing in Canada and other countries of the global north (Ahmed and Veronis 2020; Viswanath and Arora 2000); however, there is a lack of a centralized database or inclusive directory of all ethnic media operating in Canada. Despite occupying a significant place in the overall media landscape, it is difficult to accurately map its numbers, circulation, distribution, and ratings.

Ethnic media exist in different forms and at different levels, including analogue television, radio, print, and, recently, online/digital formats, such as social media and digital platforms (Matsaganis, Katz, and Ball-Rokeach 2010). Each type of media has advantages and disadvantages for its makers and users. Nonetheless, ethnic communities' media makers have ventured into all fields of media making (Georgiou 2013). There are two key factors for the growth of ethnic media in the global North. First, ethnic media provide a crucial alternative means of communication and representation in the public sphere to minority groups who are largely ignored or stereotyped in mainstream media (Yu and Ahadi 2010; Bukhari 2019; Cottle 2000; Cunningham 2001; Fleras 2009; Karim 2003; Mahtani and Dunn 2001). Second, ethnic media have established a media sector of their own within the media industry along with acquiring the status of a social institution due to the demands and opportunities generated by ethnic communities (Fleras 2009; Matsaganis, Katz, and Ball-Rokeach 2010). With the growth from analogue to digital/online media, a deeper look into the journey of ethnic media is required. This chapter focuses on South Asian ethnic media in Metro Vancouver and maps different types of media by exploring how content is developed and by whom, what types of media audiences use, how they engage with them, and at what levels of interest.

SOUTH ASIANS AND THE CURRENT ETHNIC MEDIA LANDSCAPE

The history of South Asian immigration to Canada dates back to the early 1900s (Nayar 2012) but remained low until the Canadian government's 1967 point-based immigration system opened the door to skilled immigrants from India, Pakistan, and other South Asian countries (Zaman and Bukhari 2013). South Asians currently comprise about 12 per cent of the population of Metro Vancouver, primarily concentrated in the cities of Surrey, representing 32 per cent of the population (Statistics Canada 2017a), and Abbotsford, representing 23 per cent of the population (City of Abbotsford 2014). Indians and Pakistanis make up the two largest and prominent groups, followed by a smaller number of Bangladeshis, Nepalis, and Sri Lankans (Statistics Canada 2017b; see figure 5.1). Indeed, their presence is felt in all walks of life; one can find many businesses owned and run by South Asians in these communities.

Like other immigrant groups, South Asians have many challenges in the nation-building discourse, which deemed them unfit to be included in the nation-building project of Canada that sought to make Canada a "white man's country" (Dua 2000, 109). As a result of racialized policies and perceptions, South Asians have encountered racism, discrimination, and hate crimes, frequently targeting their religions, cultural practices, and way of living in general (Rahim 2014; Zaman and Bukhari 2013). Inclusion and representation through all media and communication spaces reflects how well

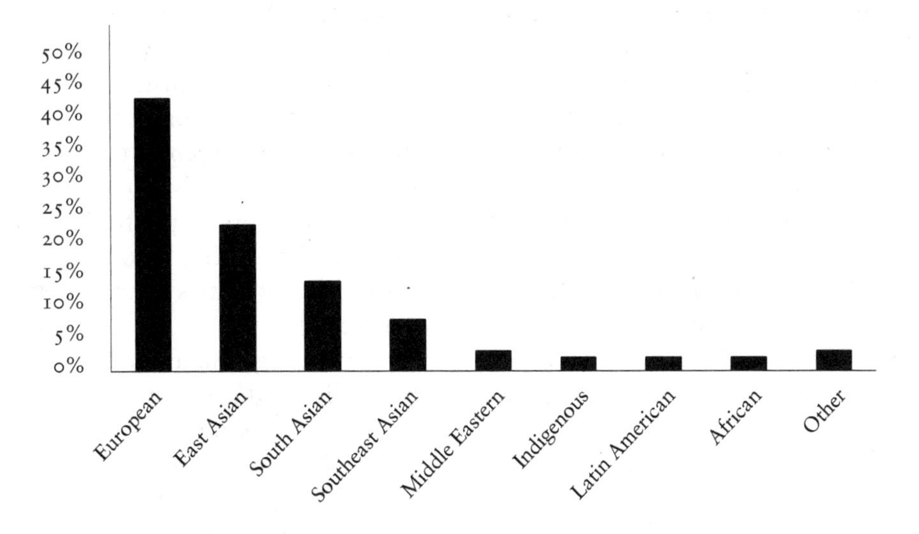

Figure 5.1: The demographic profile of Metro Vancouver (Statistics Canada 2021).

integrated a community is in the national framework of a country. Indeed, a 2005 study shows that immigrants consult various sources of information, including mainstream and ethnic media, to be able to quickly integrate into the system but do not find the desired content (Caidi and Allard 2005). There are two key reasons for this lack of serving the needs of immigrants by the mainstream media: First, mainstream media do not pay adequate attention to the issues of immigrants (Hill Collins 2009), thereby tacitly ignoring their existence within society. Second, mainstream media, particularly media with a conservative orientation, impose and promote a stereotyping of immigrants and diaspora communities which they might not identify with (Batziou 2011; Bukhari 2019; Jiwani 2006; La Ferle and Morimoto 2009; Mahtani and Dunn 2001).

Mainstream media deal with the issues of the mainstream, presented by the mainstream, and, for the mainstream, while the media and communication needs of ethnic communities are left for their own ethnic media to take care of (Mahtani 2001; Viswanath and Arora 2000). As a result, the concept of an alternative or ethnic media provides an opportunity for ethnic communities to create smaller but parallel systems of communications to meet their informational and communication needs (Matsaganis, Katz, and Ball-Rokeach 2010; Shi 2009; Yu 2012). Contrary to mainstream media, ethnic media are produced by ethnic media practitioners for their own communities (Matsaganis, Katz, and Ball-Rokeach 2010). Nevertheless, some of these media become a representative voice for their communities to mainstream society. Scholars argue that ethnic media, by opening alternative communication spaces, become de facto mainstream media specifically for ethnic minorities (Karim 2003; Matsaganis, Katz, and Ball-Rokeach 2010).

The growth of digital technologies for producing online media content has increased the outreach of the media producers. In fact, the "diversification of platforms creates opportunities for different voices within minorities to find expression" (Georgiou 2013, 97). With emerging technologies, ethnic media producers are utilizing these platforms as an opportunity for making and presenting their media content to a number of audiences. One of the salient features of digital media is the outreach that makes it possible for diaspora communities to receive and benefit from their globalized ethnic media (Yu and Matsaganis 2019). These media outlets may not hold the same significance for people living in their countries of origin (e.g., India, Pakistan), but they may present shared meanings for immigrants of these countries living around the world due to their common diasporic experiences. Using the lived experiences of media practitioners, as well as including audiences' voices, this chapter contributes to advancing existing knowledge about media uses, preferences, popularity, feedback mechanism, and the importance of various types of ethnic media of South Asians in Metro Vancouver.

METHODOLOGY

The qualitative data, conducted from fieldwork from 2013 to 2015, was collected through interviews, focus groups, and a research workshop, as well as drawing on secondary data (where available), and my personal experience as a South Asian woman, immigrant, and researcher. This study involved semi-structured interviews with thirteen (three women and ten men) media practitioners, including journalists, reporters, TV and radio anchorpersons, and media owners, identifying as Canadians of Bangladeshi, Indian, or Pakistani origin. All participants were working with different ethnic media outlets during the data collection period, some producing their own media content independently. A research workshop and four focus group discussions were conducted with fifty-two ethnic media audiences and key community representatives of South Asian communities, for a total of sixty-four study participants. Out of these participants, twenty-five were from the research workshop, twelve were from interviews, and twenty-seven were from focus groups.

The participants of the focus groups were mostly first-generation immigrants from Bangladesh, India, and Pakistan, with the exception of some who were born and raised in Canada. Snowball sampling was used for recruiting participants. As most South Asian media outlets are located mainly in the cities of Surrey and Burnaby within Metro Vancouver, British Columbia, this facilitated the recruitment of some of the most prominent, popular, and key position holders in the South Asian ethnic media and communities. All interviews, focus group discussions, and proceedings of the research workshop were audio recorded in accordance with the consent requirements of the Research Ethics Board of Simon Fraser University. The names given to the participants are pseudonyms and their organizations/media content cannot be mentioned in order to protect their identities. Semi-structured interview guides were used for interviews, focus group discussions, and the research workshop to obtain in-depth information.

FINDINGS

Ethnic Print Media: Maintaining Quality and Changing Technology

As of 2020, there are a couple of dozen South Asian ethnic weekly newspapers, bi-weekly journals, and monthly magazines published in Metro Vancouver. Most of these are published in Hindi, Punjabi, and Urdu languages. To attract readership, some publishers have begun publishing in English or bilingually. The interview with media practitioners revealed that print media are facing a difficult situation due to financial constraints and decreasing circulation. Despite this phenomenon, not unique to ethnic media, one can still find many forms of print publications, including weekly/bi-weekly newspapers and magazines such as the *Asian Journal*, the *Indo-Canadian Voice*, the *Link*, *Chardi Kala*, the *Miracle*, the *South Asian Post*, the *Urdu*

Journal, Darpan Magazine, and more, published in Metro Vancouver. Ahmed and Veronis (2020) published a report mapping South Asian media in different cities along with different ethnic media. Some ethnic media associations and networks claim to produce ethnic media directories; however, there is no comprehensive ethnic media list available or accessible in the public domain. Print media products in different languages are distributed at local ethnic grocery stores, Muslim mosques, Hindu temples, and Sikh gurudwaras around Metro Vancouver. For formal numbers, however, researchers must rely on the circulation and distribution numbers quoted by the ethnic print media sources (Oh and Zhou 2012, 265).

According to the interviews conducted with media practitioners, South Asian print media is more popular among seniors, particularly amongst first-generation immigrants. A large number of these senior immigrants consume print media due to their free time, the nature of their employment, retired/part-time employment status, language preference, personal interest, habits, and nostalgia. Zameer Ahmad, publisher of a newspaper in Vancouver for Pakistani-Canadians, explained that his paper is not only popular among seniors, but that content contributors also included senior members of his community: "The majority of my readers are seniors, although I go to youth events too, but I have more interaction with seniors due to my [own] age and also because the writers of my paper are mostly seniors. I also have some young writers, but they give little time. So, I do write extensively about seniors, their issues, and their experiences."

Aiming to promote the cultural connection of his readers, Ahmad noted that the senior content contributors of his paper had taken on the task of cultural transmission for their families and community at large. In contrast to the interest of seniors in reading and contributing to ethnic newspapers, a lack of interest among the community's youth was noted. Ethnic newspapers and journals, however, are considered a useful reference to find information about ethnic businesses and festivals, along with promoting items of interest for immigrants, such as air tickets: as Feroz, a middle-aged participant, notes: "With newspaper, the advantage is that if you miss news on the radio or TV, you can read it in the paper when you have free time. Then newspapers also provide useful information, like about community events, or even ads – like ads for travel agencies and competitive fares for India and Pakistan."

Print media seem to be struggling with financial sustainability, rapidly changing technology, and a lack of resources, such as professionally trained media personnel (Abernathy 2014). Ethnic media print journalists mostly used the term "one-man show" to describe their jobs as the majority of contributors (i.e., columnists) do not receive remuneration. Ethnic newspapers are also criticized for copying and pasting news from the country of origin's sources with little focus on the local news. According to Sandeep Singh, a media owner, most of these print media products are available free of cost and their expenses are met solely through advertising revenue. Hence, their value and quality are compromised: "We have weekly or monthly newspapers, and they are good for nothing … except for the front page, where you can find some local news, the rest is all copy and paste [from international newspapers]."

Singh was not the only one identifying a lack of financial resources as a factor affecting the quality of ethnic print media (Zhou 2009, 145). This was mentioned several times by others as the reason for copying most of their content and not having enough locally produced original stories. Elvis Lal, chief editor of a newspaper published in English, who develops his own reports and stories, considered this practice an unfair competition: "My biggest frustration with the ethnic media is that I try to be honest and do my own stories but I see all the other ethnic media just copying and pasting and I find it very unfair competition because if I tried the same thing, the mainstream media will come after me because I am very well known … I never do that kind of stuff, so that's a big frustration."

Interestingly, ethnic print media in English is perceived as having greater credibility and quality compared to ethnic language print media. Sunny, a participant, explained his preference for English print media, saying, "I think English ethnic papers are slightly different [better] as compared to other ethnic newspapers." Social class seems to play a role here, with participants who come from an educated class and are well-versed in English tending to express a preference for ethnic media published in English rather than in ethnic languages. Another reason for credibility could be linked with the wider readability of the English papers, making them accessible to mainstream readers as well.

Lal explains that his English-language paper is widely read by South Asian audiences as well as different governmental bodies, such as the Royal Canadian Mounted Police (RCMP), municipal government representatives, and mainstream media journalists. Owners of the Punjabi- and Urdu-language newspapers, on the other hand, had to take a proactive approach to engage these bodies by making extra effort to collaborate with them: "We want to collaborate with mainstream media, but we need community support for that. Mainstream media only comes to us once in a while when there is a major mishap in Pakistan like floods or earthquakes, otherwise they don't cover any local [community] issues. We invite them for many big events, but they never come. The reason is just that they are busy, or they don't have sufficient staff to cover [ethnic communities' events]" (Zameer Ahmad, publisher of a newspaper in Vancouver for Pakistani-Canadians).

Jabarjang Singh, working at a senior management level in a local ethnic media organization, claimed that "[w]ith the development of our ethnic media, the situation is changing now; with our greater understanding of languages and systems, English media now need us because we are the newsmakers now." Language could thus be facilitating and bridging the gap between the mainstream and ethnic population, yet it could also serve to hegemonize and solidify a class divide based on language politics.

The preference for English-language ethnic media could also be generational. In the case of South Asian ethnic media in Canada, increased use of English could conceivably expand audiences to include second- and third-generation South Asians. However, there were several problems identified on this front. For example, focus group participants argued that their children were not interested in analogue media, whether mainstream or ethnic because they would receive news more quickly and succinctly from social media. Rapid changes in technology, resources, or quality have brought media practitioners and readers across the board to an agreement that print media's future is uncertain. This may explain why focus group participants' narratives remained focused on radio rather than print media or even TV.

Ethnic Television: Narrowcasting versus Broadcasting

Currently, there are two ways to telecast ethnic programs on analogue TV. Some multicultural/community TV channels provide time slots for privately produced ethnic TV shows/content, and some mainstream media outlets have dedicated multicultural TV channels producing their own ethnic content. For example, Joy TV[1] and Shaw Multicultural Channel provide time slots to various ethnic communities to air their shows, while OMNI TV[2] presents in-house news and current affairs programs in different ethnic languages, such as for the Chinese and Punjabi populations in Vancouver, and Italian and Arabic populations in Montreal (Rogers 2020). These programs provide a vivid example of "narrowcasting."[3] Cunningham and Sinclair question the validity, purpose, and implicit aim of narrowcasting, arguing that there is an implicit oppositional notion inherent in the construction of mainstream broadcasting versus narrowcasting, whereby "[mainstream] broadcasting [acts] as the heartland of nation and family, and narrowcasting as the space of the migrant, the exile, the refugee" (Cunningham and Sinclair 2001, 44).

With limited resources, independent ethnic media cannot be compared with such mainstream media initiatives in terms of quality and quantity of coverage. As part of the resource-rich Rogers Media, a subsidiary of Canadian media giant Rogers Communications, the production quality of OMNI challenges ethnic media – an advantage of mainstream media's narrowcasting which has not been previously studied. The composition of the team which leads mainstream media narrowcasting can greatly affect how information and content is framed. For example, in the case of OMNI TV's Punjabi edition,[4] the majority of the team is based in Metro Vancouver and belongs to the Punjabi-Sikh South Asian community. According to a media practitioner's interview, they were able to engage better-qualified and more skilled journalists than could be acquired with less competitive compensation because OMNI could afford to pay market-based salaries. Additionally, OMNI could provide on-the-job training, which, again due to limited resources, was not ordinarily possible for most ethnic media outlets.

Presently, very little TV content is locally produced for analogue media by independent South Asian media producers. Instead, radio and print media continue to dominate. Audiences also did not show much interest in the few locally produced TV programs that did exist. Interviews revealed that some media practitioners were privately producing TV shows containing locally developed entertainment and information materials. However, these producers were struggling financially, grappling with the production and airtime costs associated with broadcasting on mainstream multicultural TV channels. Sandeep Singh, who was paying for airtime on a multicultural TV channel, admitted that he often felt trapped between the pressure to create quality programming and the struggle to sustain financial viability:

> Running a daily program on [a small community] channel is not easy … because we are competing with [national level] ethnic TV channels. Yet we were able to establish within six months; people started talking about us because my focus was to educate, inform, inspire, and empower the community and that's why I started bringing forward those issues, which matter … Now it's a daily program but I don't do daily recordings; I have the studio for one day from 9:00 a.m. till 5:00 p.m., we record for the whole week. There is so much pressure in a week, we sometimes do recordings for 7 or 8 shows.

Finding free time slots to screen locally produced ethnic content is not considered an easy task. Ethnic media producers describe the growth of locally produced ethnic TV programming as slow and expensive. The third, and relatively new way of broadcasting TV channels is offered through internet-based devices such as Jadoo TV, Shava, or IPTV, which emerged to serve the South Asian communities across Canada, the United States, and other immigrant host countries in the global north. These TV channels transmitted through internet-based devices can be watched on a regular TV and simultaneously on social media platforms such as Facebook Live. One such example is Canada One TV,[5] a Facebook TV channel that broadcasts shows produced in different cities of Canada for the Pakistani community living across the country. Given financial constraints, and increasing digital media popularity, the future of ethnic programming for analogue TV does not seem promising in the coming years. It will require vigilant research to follow up on this front.

Ethnic Radio: The Most Popular Medium

In contrast to print and TV, radio is the most popular media format among ethnic media practitioners as well as their audiences. Although the research sample included journalists producing TV shows and/or working in print journalism, many of them were additionally hosting radio shows, and radio remained the central point of discussion in interviews. This was also the case for focus groups with audiences. Most of the audiences also confirmed that they were active listeners of South Asian radio stations operating in Metro Vancouver. Seniors especially listened to different ethnic radio stations from early morning into the evening. Sujata, a senior focus group participant, said: "I wake up at five in the morning and then I turn on the radio; I listen to various religious programs and then I start my sewing work alongside … the radio." Perveen, another middle-aged focus group participant, shared her routine, saying, "I listen to a lot of radio but definitely when I am driving; I do enjoy radio, but I don't find time at home to listen to it." Radio programming allowed the audience to multitask, combining their radio consumption with tasks such as driving, cooking, or chores around the house.

Radio is also an affordable, easy-to-access, and interactive (live shows) medium for many audiences. When aired in ethnic languages, it connects people regardless of their literacy skills or knowledge base. The significance of community radio is greater than commercial radio, as it intends to inform, educate, and transform using the participatory community development model (Fox and Dutta 2019). Scholars theorizing alternative media emphasize the roles of community media in creating democratic spaces for pluralistic dialogues and encouraging the participation of laypersons in the form of active audiences and producers (Castells-Talens 2009; Rodríguez 2001), all roles that ethnic radio seems to embody.

Most ethnic radio stations in Metro Vancouver air hourly news bulletins, current affairs programs/talk shows, music, and entertainment shows, as well as live call-in shows on different topics. As with mainstream radio, these radio stations update their listeners regularly about weather, traffic, and other relevant news, such as currency exchange rates. Focus group participants confirmed listening to various radio stations during the day, which revealed their interest in and engagement with a variety of different program formats offered by different stations. Interestingly, while audiences confirmed listening to multiple radio stations, media practitioners did not follow the same pattern. Those who worked for a particular radio station rarely listened to other/competitor radio stations, either because of lack of time or interest. FM radio stations are more popular than AM stations, due to their better sound quality, as well as the fact that some playback devices, such as cellular phones, also have FM access but not AM. Nonetheless, different formats (e.g., live, solo, guest, and/or commentary shows), various schools of thoughts, and specific show hosts were some of the significant motivations for regularly tuning in to FM or AM radio stations.

Within the variety of programs, radio talk shows were the most popular segment, and this format seems to have a significant influence on the listeners, with shows related to social, political, and current affairs. As Satnam Singh, a media owner, explained: "If somebody wants to listen to songs or programs, they go online and watch it or go to iTunes and listen to latest songs. I consider that the role of the media are to present more community-based talk shows, which they cannot get on iTunes and elsewhere."

Talk shows specific to politics and current affairs are aired mostly in the morning hours and seem popular among listeners. The majority of the talk shows are call-in shows where listeners can get on the air and share their views (Nayar 2004). Amjad, a focus group participant, endorsed the media practitioners' viewpoints about talk shows: "I think the live talk shows with phone calls from audience are extraordinarily rich programs. These shows have a self-corrective mechanism; if someone is saying something wrong, some other person will call and correct them, stop them from spreading wrong information. That's the best thing! The programs include opinions from many people, and it feels like the community participates in such shows." Mukhtar Singh, another participant, confirmed the significance of radio, especially talk shows, but criticized the quality of some of these shows: "Radio is doing better than newspapers because the shows are current and they raise issues related to community, yet I would say that there is a dearth of trained journalists on radio. Often, they do not do their research and homework for their [talk] shows. It feels that they talk very superficially about several issues just to pass two hours of their show time." Narratives of the participants suggest that radio talk shows created active competition among radio practitioners and talk show hosts as they vied for their audience share. Perspectives shared by listeners and practitioners about these talk shows reveal multiple interrelated facts. First, the radio talk shows are popular for people with diverse backgrounds and have a considerable influence on audiences in terms of spreading information and knowledge about their areas of interest. Second, popular talk shows receive not only domestic phone calls but also international, giving ethnic radio a transnational edge by engaging people of the same ethnicity living around the world through live online broadcasting.[6] In the author's personal experience, people from India, the United States, and even Australia called in to Canadian live shows. One such example is Radio Hamsafar in Montreal, which is also aired online and is accessible via online applications. South Asian truck drivers based in American cities often called during the show to share their opinions about different issues. These issues are mostly connected to immigration, citizenship, and politics in these populations' countries of origin. These calls from around the world refer to the possibility and existence of a globalized ethnic media that is instrumental in identity formation based on solidarity, nostalgia, and interest about the country of origin, as well as shared diasporic experiences (Georgiou 2013). Lastly, talk show hosts realize their role and popularity in the ethnic media community, and immediate feedback through live phone calls from audience members keeps the pressure on the hosts to remain competitive and relevant for their audiences. With a profusion of ethnic radio outlets currently on the air through mobile applications, radio remains the most popular locally produced medium within the ethnic media spectrum for South Asians living in different cities of Canada.

Online or Digital Media: Opportunity or Liability?

In recent years, online ethnic media forums (e.g., YouTube, Facebook, Twitter, and Instagram), Internet-based broadcasting, and various streaming devices (e.g., Apple TV, Roku, Amazon Firestick, and unbranded Android) have become popular. Sher Singh, a media owner, was able to identify the shift: "Mainstream print media are also in trouble, even 100 and 150 years old mainstream print media are closing because of lack of revenue; no one prefers to read newspapers anymore, everything is on the Internet. The media that will survive now is Internet, TV, and ... radio."

At least four of the media practitioners interviewed for this chapter initiated their channels on different social media forums and had live talk shows. There are several reasons for this diversification, but flexibility, creativity, freedom of expression, conflicts with media management, and adventurism seem to be the most prominent reasons. Manpreet Kaur, a journalist hosting a popular talk show, maintained that "media owners like to stick to the more traditional business-oriented approach; they don't want to take risk[s] by changing the content which sells. People who have invested their money [in the ethnic media] think it [the change] will not be profitable; being creative and being a business owner could be two different things."

Kaur had resigned from a prominent radio channel and started a solo talk show on social media channels. Despite financial hardship as a result of investing personally in her program, the online platform provided her flexibility, creativity, freedom, and access to a large number of audiences. Another media practitioner, Shamim Akhtar, has been broadcasting a TV show on a multicultural TV channel in BC and some cities of Alberta for many years; however, recently he has also been using Internet TV and social media to air his show across Canada. Using these online platforms brings him a larger, pan-Canadian audience than airing it on a traditional TV channel.

Online and digital media provide an opportunity for increased interaction between media makers and their audiences (Yu and Matsaganis 2019). Programs aired on online media, especially social media forums, receive continuous audience feedback, often reflecting polarized positions. Media makers also have an option to engage directly with their public and make changes in their programming according to the feedback. Akhtar, producing a show from Vancouver, confirmed that he received most of his feedback from Ontario, especially from his target (and largest) audience in Toronto, where a large number of Pakistanis reside. He also added: "The online audience are more interactive and informed; they keep commenting on our shows using social media forums, while the audience watching the show on the traditional TV would call once in a while through a phone call ... online feedback also helps us in improving our program."

With fluid definitions of diaspora communities around the globe, "These ... particularistic media, such as ethnic and diasporic media; online transnational diasporic media; niche media in different platforms ... create spaces for minorities to shape the message, a sense of self and of community and thus advance a sense of security and inclusion" (Georgiou 2019, 97). Media practitioners, both seasoned and amateur, are cognizant of the fact that these platforms are becoming more popular. They agree that journalists' credibility and producing interesting content are significant factors in the potential to engage an online audience.

Ethnic media producers are increasing their online presence (Yu and Matsaganis 2019), yet how the audience of ethnic media, especially those resistant to new technologies, respond to these changes will determine how successful this shift could be. From the narratives of the participants, it seems that they are ready for the shift; some were already aficionados of online media originating in their countries of origins. One participant, Parveen, related her senior in-laws' habit of reading online newspapers published in India, adding, "I also read an Indian [English] newspaper online as per my childhood habit; it's updated online at 2 a.m. in the morning in India, so I must read it here as soon as it's updated there." Another participant, Shaam, an international student, also confirmed that he was using online media from India for information and entertainment.

Technological advancements, such as online and digital media help to deconstruct the hegemony of mainstream media and challenge the political economy of media. With the growing presence of ethnic media practitioners on digital platforms, there is an opportunity for occupying flexible, convenient, and safe communication spaces by producing genuine news and information of quality and interesting content based on audience feedback. These factors will be the leading bases for winning the audiences on online and digital media.

CONCLUSION

This chapter aims to provide an overview of existing ethnic media content, practices, and utility, including a discussion of how content is developed and by whom, what types of media audiences use, how they engage with them, and at what levels of interest. At the time of data collection, an array of ethnic media was being produced, including radio, TV, film, and online and print journalism. The data revealed that radio and online ethnic media in South Asian communities in BC were most popular and expanding exponentially, due to several factors including, but not limited to, demographic concentration in specific regions, a growing business community, flexibility, and a perception that these outlets were trustworthy platforms to start a public dialogue within and outside South Asian communities. Radio, specifically, was considered the favourite, as an accessible and inexpensive medium. Talk shows about local issues, politics, and immigrant/immigration-related policies and issues were the most popular among participants after entertainment content.

At the time of the study, ethnic print and analogue television were found to be struggling for survival due to a lack of overall audience interest, outreach, and competition from digital media. Many media owners were venturing into different types of media productions (e.g., print, TV, radio, and online) at the time, yet larger community groups in BC such as Punjabi-speaking Indo-Canadians dominated the ethnic media landscape, with the majority of ethnic media productions owned and presented by them. Since South Asian ethnic media are available in some of the major languages of South Asian countries such as Punjabi, Hindi, and Urdu, smaller South Asian communities remained underrepresented, without a voice in ethnic media.

First-generation immigrants and/or seniors constituted a large portion of ethnic audiences, with print media particularly more popular among seniors. Online or digital media seemed to take up communication space quickly, and most newspapers, radio channels, and TV programs are available online now. Media practitioners, especially those working solo, were producing proprietary content on social media platforms, thus attaining greater outreach and accessibility to global diasporas. The overall landscape of ethnic media is increasingly crowded and complex; the perception is that some mediums are dying out due to modern, faster, and more popular ways of accessing media content. However, analogue media is still relevant for some groups, more specifically, first-generation immigrants and seniors.

The data also reveal a clearly marked class divide, within and outside ethnic media, mostly influenced by language politics. The political economy of ethnic journalism as second-class journalism is evident by the narrowcasting, an imbalance in access to financial resources, and unfair competition; the nature of collaboration with English-speaking ethnic media reflects an indifference to third-language ethnic media. Nonetheless, with rapidly changing technologies, ease of accessibility, and greater outreach, media platforms are changing for everyone including globally ethnic and minority populations. Digitalization and technological advancement have revolutionized media making and consumption, and this has affected the existence of analogue media as well as the hegemony of mainstream media giants. This is a major disruptive shift with respect to how the political economy of media has conventionally been organized. These changes could lead to a gradual democratization of media in an organic way for all communities, irrespective of their location and demographics in the days to come.

NOTES

1 Joy TV's website states: "Joy TV serves Surrey & the Fraser Valley, Vancouver and Victoria, offering quality contemporary/classic entertainment and local information with a strong community focus, for a spiritually and culturally diverse audience of all ages" (Joy TV 2015).
2 OMNI TV's website states: "OMNI Television provides free over-the-air television service to ethnic communities in Toronto, London, Ottawa, Edmonton, Calgary, Vancouver, and Victoria. As an ethnic broadcaster, OMNI is committed to reflecting Canada's diversity through ethnocultural and third-language programming at a local, regional, and national level" (OMNI TV 2015).
3 Narrowcasting is defined as "special interest programming designed for niche audiences" (Chandler and Munday 2016, 290).
4 OMNI TV offers a Punjabi edition for different cities in Canada, for example, Toronto and Vancouver.
5 https://www.facebook.com/CANADAONETV.
6 Almost all ethnic radio stations in Metro Vancouver offer online streaming of their content through their websites.

REFERENCES

Abernathy, Penelope Muse. 2014. *Saving Community Journalism: The Path to Profitability*. Chapel Hill: University of North Carolina Press.

Ahmed, Rukhsana, and Luisa Veronis. 2020. "Creating In-Between Spaces through Diasporic and Mainstream Media Consumption: Ottawa, Canada." *The International Communication Gazette* 82 (3): 289–315.

Batziou, Athanasia. 2011. *Picturing Immigration: Photojournalistic Representation of Immigrants in Greek and Spanish Press*. Chicago: Intellect.

Bukhari, Syeda Nayab. 2019. "Ethnic Media as Alternative Media for South Asians in Metro Vancouver, Canada: Creating Knowledge, Engagement, Civic and Political Awareness." *Journal of Alternative & Community Media* 4 (3): 86–98.

Caidi, Nadia, and Danielle Allard. 2005. "Social Inclusion of Newcomers to Canada: An Information Problem?" *Library and Information Science Research* 27 (3): 302–24.

Castells-Talens, Antoni. 2009. "When Our Media Belong to the State:

Policy and Negotiations in Indigenous-Language Radio in Mexico." In *Making Our Media: Global Initiatives Toward a Democratic Public Sphere*, edited by Clemencia Rodriguez, Dorothy Kidd, and Laura Stein, 249–70. Cresskill, NJ: Hampton Press.

Chandler, Daniel, and Rod Munday. 2016. *A Dictionary of Media and Communication*. 2nd ed. Oxford: Oxford University Press.

City of Abbotsford. 2014. "2014 Demographic Profiles." https://www.abbotsford.ca/sites/default/files/2021-02/2014%20Abbotsford%20Summary%20Demographic%20Profile_spreads.pdf.

Cottle, Simon, ed. 2000. "A Rock and Hard Place: Making Ethnic Television." In *Ethnic Minorities and the Media: Changing Cultural Boundaries*, 100–17. Buckingham: Open University Press.

Cunningham, Stuart. 2001. "Popular Media as Public 'Sphericules' for Diasporic Communities." *International Journal of Cultural Studies* 4 (2):131–47.

Cunningham, Stuart, and John Sinclair, eds. 2001. *Floating Lives: The Media and Asian Diasporas*. Rowman & Littlefield Publishers.

Deuze, Mark. 2006. "Ethnic Media, Community Media and Participatory Culture." *Journalism* 7 (3): 262–80.

Dua, Enakshi. 2000. "The Hindu Woman's Question." *Canadian Woman Studies* 20 (2): 108–16.

Fleras, Augie. 2009. "Theorizing Multicultural Media as Social Capital: Crossing Borders, Constructing Buffers, Creating Bonds, Building Bridges." *Canadian Journal of Communication* 34 (4): 725–29.

Fox, Juliet, and Mohan J. Dutta. 2019. *Community Radio's Amplification of Communication for Social Change*. Cham: Springer International Publishing AG.

Georgiou, Myria. 2013. "Diaspora in the Digital Era: Minorities and Media Representation." *Journal on Ethnopolitics and Minority Issues in Europe* JEMIE 12 (4): 80–99.

Hill Collins, Patricia. 2009. *Another Kind of Public Education: Race, Schools, the Media, and Democratic Possibilities*. Boston: Beacon Press.

Jiwani, Yasmin. 2006. *Discourses of Denial: Mediations of Race, Gender, and Violence*. Vancouver: University of British Columbia Press.

Joy TV. n.d. "About Joy TV." https:/https://www.joytv.ca/about-joytv//www.joytv.ca/.

Karim, Karim H. 2003. *The Media of Diaspora*. New York: Routledge.

La Ferle, Carrie, and Mariko Morimoto. 2009. "The Impact of Life-Stage on Asian American Females' Ethnic Media Use, Ethnic Identification, and Attitudes Toward Ads." *Howard Journal of Communications* 20 (2): 147–66.

Mahtani, Minelle. 2001. "Representing Minorities: Canadian Media and Minority Identities." *Canadian Ethnic Studies Journal* 33 (3): 99–133.

Mahtani, Minelle, and Kevin Dunn. 2001. *Adjusting the Colour Bars: Media Representation of Ethnic Minorities under Australian and Canadian Multiculturalisms*. Burnaby, BC: Vancouver Centre of Excellence.

Matsaganis, Matthew D., Vikki S. Katz, and Sandra Ball-Rokeach. 2010. *Understanding Ethnic Media: Producers, Consumers, and Societies*. Thousand Oaks, CA: SAGE.

Nayar, Kamala Elizabeth. 2004. *The Sikh Diaspora in Vancouver: Three Generations Amid Tradition, Modernity and Multiculturalism*. Toronto: University of Toronto Press.

Oh, David, and Wanfeng Zhou. 2012. "Framing SARS: A Case Study in Toronto of a Mainstream Newspaper and a Chinese Ethnic Newspaper." *Atlantic Journal of Communication* 20 (5): 261–73.

OMNI TV. n.d. "Omni Advisory Council Mandate." http://www.omnitv.ca/on/en/omni-television-advisory-councils.

Rahim, Abdur. 2014. *Canadian Immigration and South Asian Immigrants*. Bloomington, IN: Author House.

Rogers. 2020. "OMNI Television Debuts National Daily Newscasts in Arabic and Filipino, Today." 1 September 2020. https://about.rogers.com/news-ideas/omni-television-debuts-national-daily-newscasts-in-arabic-and-filipino-today/.

Rodríguez, Clemencia. 2001. *Fissures in the Mediascape: An International Study of Citizens' Media*. New York: Hampton Press.

Shi, Yu. 2009. "Re-Evaluating the 'Alternative' Role of Ethnic Media in the US: The Case of Chinese-Language Press and Working-Class Women Readers." *Media, Culture & Society* 31 (4): 597–616.

Statistics Canada. 2017a. "Surrey, CY [Census Subdivision], British Columbia and British Columbia [Province] Census Profile, 2016 Census." Catalogue no. 98-316-X2016001. [Table]. Ottawa, ON: Statistics Canada. https://www12.statcan.gc.ca/census-recensement/2016/dp-pd/prof/index.cfm?Lang=E.

– 2017b. "Vancouver [Census Metropolitan Area], British Columbia and British Columbia [Province] Census Profile, 2016 Census." Catalogue no. 98-316-X2016001. [Table]. Ottawa, ON: Statistics Canada. https://www12.statcan.gc.ca/census-recensement/2016/dp-pd/prof/index.cfm?Lang=E.

Viswanath, K, and Pamela Arora. 2000. "Ethnic Media in the United States: An Essay on Their Role in Integration, Assimilation, and Social Control." *Mass Communication and Society* 3 (1): 39–56.

Yu, Sherry S. 2012. "Diasporic Media in Multicultural Cities: A Comparative Study on Korean Media in Vancouver and Los Angeles." PhD diss., Simon Fraser University.

Yu, Sherry S., and Daniel Ahadi. 2010. "Promoting Civic Engagement through Ethnic Media." *Platform: Journal of Media and Communication* 2 (2): 54–71.

Yu, Sherry S., and Matthew D. Matsaganis, eds. 2019. *Ethnic Media in the Digital Age*. New York: Routledge.

Zaman, Habiba, and Syeda Nayab Bukhari. 2013. "South Asian Skilled Immigrants in Greater Vancouver: Formal and Informal Sources of Support for Settlement." Working Paper Series. Metropolis British Columbia, Centre of Excellence for Research on Immigration and Diversity. https://canadacommons.ca/artifacts/1223431/south-asian-skilled-immigrants-in-greater-vancouver/1776507/.

Zhou, Min. 2009. *Contemporary Chinese America: Immigration, Ethnicity, and Community Transformation*. Philadelphia: Temple University Press.

CHAPTER SIX

Arab Canadian Media: Its History, Challenges, and News Coverage

Ahmed Al-Rawi

INTRODUCTION

Arab Canadians, regarded as a "visible minority" by the Canadian government, constitute a large ethnic group in Canada. Based on statistics drawn from the 2016 census, there were 429,975 Canadians who speak Arabic as their mother tongue, and it was the sixth largest immigrant language spoken. Currently, Arabs constitute about 1.4 per cent of the total Canadian population (Statistics Canada 2017; ODESI n.d.). This is a clear increase in population from an earlier census, where it was estimated that 348,000 Canadians of Arab descent resided in the country in 2001. This dramatic increase is due to the ongoing conflicts in the Middle East. Arabs in Montreal, for instance, are the second largest community after Blacks (19.7 per cent), constituting the second youngest visible minority group with a median age of 30.2, while the Arabic language is considered to be among the top ten foreign languages spoken in Canada by ethnic groups (Statistics Canada 2011). For several years, Arab Canadians have had the highest unemployment rate among all demographics in Canada, coming on top of other groups such as Indigenous and Black Canadians (Yarhi and Poulin 2022; Statistics Canada 2020).

Historically, Arab Canadians started immigrating to Canada in the late nineteenth century (Kidd 1991).[1] Numerous previous reports and studies mention, for example, that the first Arab Canadian was Ibrahim Abou Nader who originally came from Lebanon and landed in Montreal in 1882 (Abu-Laban 2008; Berthiaume, Corbo, and Montreuil 2014, 202, 217; Hourani and Shehadi 1992, 227).

However, a closer examination of the old Canadian censuses showed a different picture. While the 1871 census and all the earlier provincial ones did not offer any useful demographic details on the ethnic background and mother tongue of immigrants, these details became better reported in the following years. For example, the 1881 Canadian census revealed about six people whose mother tongue was Arabic. The Eastern Canadian census showed four Arabic-speaking persons coming from Egypt (n = 2), Algeria (n = 1), and Palestine (n = 1), while the Western and Territories Canadian census showed two persons originally from Syria and Algeria (ODESI n.d.). In addition, if one takes into account African immigration to Canada that preceded the 1880s, some of which might be from North Africa, Arabs' immigration to Canada might have started even earlier.

This chapter is divided into five sections, starting with an account of Arab media in Canada. It then discusses the first Arabic language newspaper, entitled *The Canadian Office*, and offers a review of Arab Canadian research as well as a broad discussion on the meaning of ethnic media to situate the study within a proper theoretical framework. Due to the growing number of Arab Canadian newspapers, this study is focused on conducting a textual analysis of one publication called *Hona London* (This is London هنا لندن), an Arab Canadian newspaper published in Ontario. Using a digital method called topic modelling, the study attempts to examine all the available ninety-six issues of the newspaper at the time the study was conducted in order to understand the salience of the topics.

OVERVIEW OF ARAB MEDIA IN CANADA

Regarding Arab Canadian media, there are tens of Arabic language outlets that are produced by Arab Canadians especially in Quebec and Ontario (RCI n.d.). These outlets include several newspapers, such as *Akhbar Al Arab*, which was established in 1976, along with *Al-Bilad*, *Al Mashriq wa Al Maghrib*, *Sada Al Mashriq*, *Al Rissalah*, and *Al Awsat*. In addition, the Canadian government previously ran an Arabic service on Radio Canada International and currently runs an Arabic website as part of its public diplomacy efforts targeting Arab audiences inside and outside Canada (Potter 2003, 54). Baha Abu-Laban (1980) mentioned that the main issues covered in the Arab Canadian media include the importance of maintaining the Arab identity and heritage, the Palestinian cause, and multiculturalism and integration into Canada.

It is important to note here that Arab Canadian media was highlighted in the Saudi Cables leaks posted by *WikiLeaks*. It was revealed that the Saudi embassy in Ottawa made regular over-payments to subscribe to the following newspapers: *Al-Muhajir*, *Al-Diplomacy Al-Dowali*, *Al-Rissala*, and *Al-Akhbar Al-Asiyawia*. In addition, one cable referred to the importance of countering anti-Saudi messages regularly found in the weekly newspaper *Al-Hayat Al-Arabia*, which is published in Toronto by the Shiite Al-Khoei Foundation. The same Saudi embassy cable mentioned supporting *Al-Bilad* and *Al-Mughtarib Al-Arabi* newspapers with $36,000 by subscribing for five years "provided that an annual assessment is made on the impact of this support on the newspapers' editorial stances and evaluating the benefits of continuing this support" (*WikiLeaks* 2011). The argument here is that these over-paid subscriptions were meant to influence the editorial decisions of these newspapers whose average annual regular subscription is around $150, exclusive of tax, based on several email inquiries by the author. However, Arab Canadian media are not the only ethnic media that regularly received direct or indirect support from foreign embassies; the Italian language publication *Corriere Canadese* once received a $2.8 million grant from the Italian embassy even though the funding ceased after 2010 (Boesvold 2010). Before the literature review, it is imperative to refer to the first Arab Canadian publication in the following section.

THE CANADIAN OFFICE OR المكتب الكندي

In this chapter, new evidence is presented regarding the first Arab Canadian newspaper that was published in Montreal in 1905 and ceased publication around 1910. It was known as *The Canadian Office – L'Office Canadien: Journal Commercial, Politique et Critique pour 4 Nations*, and this newspaper was originally published in four languages: Arabic, French, English, and Syriac (Al-Rawi 2015; The Canadian Newspaper Directory 1909; Dionne 1909, 233). Previous studies, however, inaccurately mentioned that the first Arab Canadian publication appeared in Montreal in 1908 under the title *Al Shehab* (The shooting star or الشهاب), which was published by a "young Syrian immigrant, Michael Zarbatany, who came to Canada at the age of 18 in 1902. In 1910, this bi-weekly newspaper ceased publication due to insufficient community support" (Abu-Laban, 1980, 151). In the same year, another newspaper entitled *Al*

Alamein (The two worlds or العالمين) appeared, which was "aimed at the first generation of migrants to arrive in Canada" (Asal 2016, 2012, 7).

Though there are only a few issues of *The Canadian Office* available, the following will summarize some main points regarding this newspaper. First, it was a Christian publication that covered news about sermons and clergy in different languages. Under the headline "A Question That Has a Prize," the newspaper ironically asks: "If the evils [in Ottoman's Turkey] were caused by the Armenians, why was Sultan Abudul Hamid II deposed?[2] If the harms were due to the [Ottoman] government, why were the Armenians hanged and why is Adana's[3] ruler still in power?" Second, the newspaper focused on gossip among the Arab community in Canada, often attacking religious figures for cynicism and irony. This is interesting because the beginning of Arab Canadian media imitates the features of yellow journalism. Third, the newspaper attempted to offer different information services that went beyond covering and commenting on news. For instance, the newspaper states on the cover page of one of the available issues (see figure 6.1) in non-standard Arabic language: "As the newspaper was established to faithfully cover the news and give real and accurate guidelines and since our pure objective is to offer our homeland fellows instructions and news and cover their conditions, positions, their trades, and ensure their fair treatment, we decided to devote an hour from eight to nine o'clock in the morning to offer advice to anyone seeking information about legal issues, Christian religious matters, and real estate inquiries including selling, buying, and renting properties."

Thus, the newspaper's perceived mission was not only covering news and focusing on Christian sermons, but it also extended to strengthening the ties with the Arab Canadian Christian community and offering them guidelines on how to better integrate into and function in Canadian culture. This seemed to be partly motivated by financial reasons as most of the news commentaries and general announcements in *The Canadian Office* included reminders and pleas to pay annual subscriptions to support the newspaper publication. *The Canadian Office* marked the beginning of Arab Canadian news media in Canada, a story that rapidly evolved in the following decades with the increasing number of immigrants. To better understand where Arab Canadian media and research are situated today, a literature review is provided in the following section.

L'OFFICE CANADIEN

THE CANADIAN OFFICE

Presenting to the public this edition, we desire to inform you of our reasons and of our program. Publishing this paper which will be a valueable means of advertising we want to render service to every body who may be in beed of advice, an information, tb those looking for a position oran employment, to those who possess the means of investment, for the selling of property, a farm or a mine.

We have also at the disposition of young men a place, an opportunity for marriage, i. e. for those who, isolated or prevented by timidity, look for a wife, a husband without any trouble they can enter into relation with the objectof their desire, thanks to the publication of our paper. The Canadian Office will be a general information office where you may obtain all you might need, servants, employees, work-men, drivers, chamber-maids, farmers.

THAT GOOD CLERGY

We have received a copy of a pamphlet written by a Catholic Priest of Montreal, the reading of which was enough to make one shiver from head to foot.

We have not the time to analize it but it is sufficient for the benefit of those who take interest in the misfortune of this world, to reprint the preface signed by the author, a foreign missionary in Montreal :

Figure 6.1 | Screenshot of the *The Canadian Office* newspaper's microfilm.

ARAB CANADIAN RESEARCH

In relation to the available literature on Arabs in Canada, it tends to exclude an examination of Arab Canadians' use of media by focusing instead on their historical, social, or cultural lives (Al-Rawi 2017a). For example, Baha Abu-Laban's canonical study *An Olive Branch on the Family Tree* (1980) offers a historical and cultural account of Arabs in North America but does not engage with issues of media consumption. Other studies that followed also did not engage in media use, including Tareq Ismael's edited works *Canadian Arab Relations* (1984) and *Canada and the Arab World* (1985); Abu-Laban's and Suleiman's *Arab Americans: Continuity and Change* (1989), alongside the works of Waugh and colleagues (1991), Ohan and Hayani (1993), and Michael Suleiman (1999). Further research focused on various aspects of Arab Canadians' lives, such as the issues of identity, education, multiculturalism, and acculturation, primarily through conducting interviews (Abu-Laban and Abu-Laban 1999a; Abu-Laban and Abu-Laban 1999b; Hayani

1999; Aboud 2002; Vallianatos and Raine 2007; Schoueri 2007; Eid 2007; McAndrew 2010; Sabra 2011; Tastsoglou and Petrinioti 2011; Rasmi 2012; Paterson and Hakim-Larson 2012; Rasmi, Chuang, and Safdar 2012; Hennebry and Momani 2013). Other works tackled the issue of politics and Arab Canadians (Abu-Laban 1988; Ismael 1985) or compared their social conditions to that of Arab Americans (Ismael 1976). A few other studies on Arab Canadians focused on specific nationalities, religious affiliations, or genders (Hamdan 2007; Lewis 2008). Other studies on the lives of Arab Canadians were limited to certain nationalities such as Sudanese Canadians (The Mosaic Institute 2010), Lebanese Canadians (Swan and Saba 1974; Tastsoglou and Petrinioti 2011), Syrian Christians (Marino 1994), or Palestinian Canadians (Zaidan 2011).

However, Arab Canadians' media use was not neglected in the late twentieth and early twenty-first century; in 1973, Asghar Fathi conducted a study on Lebanese Canadians' use of traditional media channels by interviewing fifty-one Muslim and twenty-two Christian Arab male immigrants living in a Canadian Prairie city. Fathi (1973) investigated their use of shortwave radio and found out that Muslim immigrants were less attracted to Western music and more tuned into transnational Arabic radio stations than their Christian counterparts. The trend of giving limited attention to the use of media outlets by Arab Canadians is also evident in more recent studies. For example, Abdulahad and colleagues (2009) conducted a survey to study the acculturation patterns of 153 Iraqi Canadians, focusing primarily on lifestyle and cultural adaptation. As such, there were only a few limited references to traditional media consumption. Further, Dalia Abdelhady (2011) conducted interviews with Lebanese immigrants living in the diaspora including Montreal, New York, and Paris to better understand how Lebanese immigrants defined their identities and kept the link with Lebanon. Abdelhady makes few references to the role of social media in maintaining the connection with Lebanon: "online media allows them to stay in contact with many friends and family members around the world. Exchanges of news, pictures, and conversations were conducted regularly, enabling my respondents to participate in cross-border networks and keep the homeland alive" (116).

Additionally, a comprehensive study examined the use of mainstream and ethnic media (TV, radio, newspapers, and online) in Canada by several immigrant groups (Afghan, West African, Arab, Caribbean,

Chinese, North Indian, Hispanic, Somali, Tamil, Portuguese, and Russian) in issues related to settlement (Karim, Eid, and Ebanda de B'béri 2007). Further, some studies focused on the role and nature of Canadian media productions on Arab Canadians which, in many cases, enhanced negative images by presenting them as "folk devils" (Ismael and Measor 2003; Perry and Poynting 2006; Burman 2006, 284; Poynting and Perry 2007; McClure 2012; Syed 2012).

The discussion of Arab Canadian research also often deals with the impact of 9/11 on their lived experiences as this event remains one of the most important turning points in the lives of Arab Canadians and Arab Americans alike. There have been numerous studies conducted on the discrimination or harassment faced by Muslim Canadians and in particular Arab Canadians, as well as the social and psychological changes that occurred in their lives after 9/11. In their study on Arab Canadians, Rousseau and colleagues (2011) found that Muslim Arab Canadians suffered more psychological tension and prejudice in comparison to Christian Arab Canadians. Other studies argued that the increased rate of prejudice and suspicion in North America was mostly based on their ethnic and religious backgrounds (Khouri 2003; Bahdi 2003; Khalema and Wannas-Jones 2003; Roach 2003; Helly 2004; Abu-Laban 2007; Henry and Tator 2006; Anderson 2008; Ameeriar 2012; Chongatera 2013; Amery 2013; Al-Rawi 2014). While most previous research focused on the issues of multiculturalism, radicalism, and terrorism-related issues, this study offers a more comprehensive picture of media coverage by Arab Canadians themselves, potentially filling a gap in ethnic Canadian scholarly literature.

THEORETICAL FRAMEWORK

Briefly reviewing the literature on ethnic media is relevant here as it points out two main trends: (1) the integrative approach, which states that ethnic media can help in integrating ethnic and minority groups into the mainstream culture in the way in which they help in fostering ethnic cohesion and cultural maintenance (Black and Leithner 1988a; Riggins 1992; Fleras and Kunz 2001; Matsaganis, Katz, and Ball-Rokeach 2010), and that they enhance the public sphere due to their role in encouraging debates on different issues that are relevant to ethnic groups (Husband 2005). And (2) the non-integrative approach, which claims that ethnic media can have a divisive role as it can result in further alienating minority groups from the mainstream culture (Turow 1997; Wilson, Gutierrez, and Chao 2003).

Whether integrative or not, it is important to study ethnic media because of its role and societal impact. In general, ethnic media can be a form of alternative media that are complementary to mainstream media since they are part of the convergence culture in what Sreberny calls "not only, but also" (2005). In other words, alternative media provide a complementary perspective to what is already covered in mainstream media. In this regard, alternative journalism attempts to change the hierarchy of access to news (Philo 2014) by focusing on the ethnic group rather than those who are powerful. This is achieved in the way that the different media platforms provide an outlet to voice the concerns and highlight the important issues relevant to specific groups (Franklin and Murphy 1998). Diasporic ethnic groups aim at reterritorializing and re-embedding their identities by consuming ethnic media: "Displaced from their homelands, they find ethnicity as the necessary place or space from which they can speak and counteract dominant discourses" (Karim 2007, 102).

Ethnic media generally provide the following services: providing basic information that is vital to civic engagement, preserving ethnic culture, uniting and strengthening the sense of community, and providing an alternative voice. Indeed, there needs to be more studies that investigate ethnic media in Canada (Black and Leithner 1988b; Ojo, 2006; Murray, Yu, and Ahadi 2007, 142), especially in relation to Arab Canadian media (Asal 2012). This chapter attempts to answer the following research question: What are the major topics that the Arab Canadian publication *Hona London* covered in its news coverage and commentary?

METHODOLOGY

To conduct this study, all ninety-six electronic issues of *Hona London* available from the newspaper's website (http://honalondon.ca/) were examined, and all pages were systematically analyzed using the convenience sampling technique, which does not rely on chance or probability in selecting its sample.[4] One of the main reasons behind choosing this newspaper is the fact that the Arabic text contained in the PDF files is readable, and all the issues published between May

2012 to May 2020 can be found on the website. Edited by Abdullah Al Farra, a former academic, the first issue of this monthly newspaper appeared on 18 May 2012, and it was still in circulation as of June 2020. The newspaper targets Arab Canadians in London and other surrounding cities in Ontario including Toronto. Its mission statement was highlighted in the newspaper's first issue:

> The goal of the newspaper is to become a message of peace and love for every Arab individual, for it will enhance the friendship and compassion ties among all the members of the Arab community wherever they are living. It also aims at highlighting the positive aspects of the Arab character by showcasing successful Arabs to be role models for our youth. The publication is also keen to see Arabs from all backgrounds can smoothly adapt with this beloved homeland, making everyone live in peace and security in Canada … The newspaper avoids all kinds of debates on sectarian, political, and religious differences … following the journalistic goal of respect, educate, and inform. (Al Farra 2012, 3)

As shown, in an effort to avoid any tension with the Arab community, the newspaper does not want to address serious divisive issues. There is a clear financial incentive for this, because such controversial topics might drive readers and, most importantly, advertisers away. Though it states that it is a non-profit publication, the high number of advertisements that appear in each issue indicates the pivotal role of advertising in sustaining the newspaper's publication.

Since the total number of the newspaper pages for all issues was 3,092, it became difficult to manually analyze the content. As a result, a digital method called topic modelling, using QDA Miner-WordStat 8, was used. Topic modelling is a machine learning technique that examines unstructured data to generate the salient topics. By relying on a certain algorithm, the topics are automatically identified based on their strength or prominence in the corpus, and the associated words and phrases with each topic are listed based on their co-occurrences. Given the space constraints in this chapter, the reader may refer to some of my previous publications that employed this digital approach, especially the use of proximity plots and topic modelling, to gain more background details (Al-Rawi 2017b, 2017c, 2019; Jiwani and Al-Rawi 2019).

Table 6.1 | Topic modelling of Hona London news coverage

No.	Topic	Keywords	Coherence	No.	Topic	Keywords	Coherence
1.	عبد الحفيظ شحبر	الحفيظ; شحبر; بلدة; عبد; عبد الحفيظ; عبد عمدة; الأستاذ; الحفيظ شحبر; السيد عبد;	0.385	9.	رئيس الوزراء جاستن ترودو	رئيس; ترودو; الوزراء; جاستن; جوستان; رئيس الوزراء; جاستن ترودو; جوستان ترودو; رئيس الحكومة; رئيس الوزراء الكندي; رئيس الحكومة الكندية; رئيس وزراء; جاستين ترودو;	0.313
2.	هيئة الإذاعة كندا الدولي	هيئة; الإذاعة; اردیو; الدولي; راديو; كندا; الكندية; كندا الدولي; هيئة الإذاعة; اردیو كندا; اردیو كندا الدولي; راديو كندا; راديو كندا الدولي; هيئة الإذاعة الكندية; هيئة الإذاعة الكندي; اردیو كندا الدولي اردیو; الصحافة الكندية;	0.375	10.	الشرق الأوسط	الشرق; الأوسط; الاوسط; المثال; سبيل; الشرق الأوسط; الشرق الاوسط; منطقة الشرق;	0.309
3.	محمد صلى الله عليه	صلى; وسلم; الله; عليه; النبي; الله عليه; صلى الله عليه; صلى الله عليه وسلم; رسول الله; القصد; والله; آب; وراء; الإقامة; الدائمة; واتس; والله من وراء; والله من وراء القصد;	0.371	11.	ا لو لا يا ت المتحدة	المتحدة; الولايات; الأمم; الولايات المتحدة; الأمم المتحدة;	0.305

No.	Topic	Keywords	Coherence	No.	Topic	Keywords	Coherence
4.	سوريا والعراق	واليمن; وليبيا; وسوريا; والعراق; ولبنان; سوريا والعراق;	0.363	12.	ياسر عرفات	ياسر; ياسر عرفات; عرفات;	0.296
5.	البنية التحتية	البنية التحتية; التحتية; البنية; حيز; التنفيذ; التواصل;	0.338	13.	السلطانة الأم	السلطانة; نوربانو; الأم; السلطانة الأم;	0.296
6.	منير القاسم	منير; القاسم; الدكتور; منير القاسم; الدكتور منير القاسم;	0.337	14.	فير و س كورونا	كورونا; فيروس; المستجد; بفيروس; فيروس كورونا; كورونا المستجد; بفيروس كورونا;	0.295
7.	الرئيس الأميركي دونالد ترامب	دونالد; ترامب; الرئيس; الأميركي; دونالد ترامب; الرئيس الأميركي; الرئيس الأميركي دونالد; الرئيس الأمريكي; الرئيس دونالد; الرئيس ترامب;	0.335	15.	اللّغة العربيّة	اللّغة; العربيّة	0.29
8.	باص النقل	باص; النقل; السريع; مشروع; باص النقل; باص النقل السريع; مشروع باص النقل السريع;	0.323	16.	الضفة الغربية قطاع غزة	الغربية; الضفة; غزة; قطاع; الضفة الغربية; قطاع غزة;	0.271

FINDINGS AND DISCUSSION

To answer the study's research question, table 6.1 shows the top sixteen topics in the Arabic news coverage of *Hona London*. These topics can be broadly categorized into the following: (1) Arab figures and Islam, (2) Arab countries and leaders, (3) Justin Trudeau and Canada, (4) Donald Trump and the USA, and (5) other. In this table, some of the general topics that refer to the newspaper's title and other promotional statements have been removed by the author because of their irrelevance.

The most prominent topic is related to references to Arab figures, especially Abdul Hafidh Shahbar (no. 1), the mayor of the Lebanese village Mdoukha, and the imam of the Islamic Centre in London, Munir Al Qassim (no. 6). Shahbar was highlighted in the news coverage because Mdoukha is regarded as London's twin city, and he was interviewed a few times to offer his insight about the importance of voting during the municipal election. Shahbar even expressed his candidate preferences about who he thought would best serve the interests of Arab Canadians in London, Ontario. The second Arab figure is Imam Al Qassim, who often highlights the importance of cultural integration and how Muslim Arab Canadians are part and parcel of the Canadian society. Other relevant but minor topics include "Muhammed peace be upon him" (no. 3), which is a common expression often used in religious contexts, and "Arabic language" (no. 15), a term often used as part of the interest in using and preserving the language. Though the newspaper is not a religious publication, it still uses some common religious expressions indicating its general conservative nature that aligns with the Arab culture in the Middle East. Such expressions are needed to better connect with readers, most of whom have recently immigrated to Canada. As shown, these topics are important because they provide evidence about the perceived role of *Hona London*, which aims at enhancing civic engagement, cultural preservation, and integration into Canada. This is reminiscent of the old concept of social responsibility of the press in general (Christians and Nordenstreng 2004) and the integrative function of ethnic media in particular (Deuze 2006).

The second topic category revolves around references to Arab countries and leaders. Here, we find that that the tenth topic pertains to the Middle East, and the fourth topic is about Iraq and Syria. Other associated words include Yemen, Lebanon, and Libya, all of which continue to witness armed conflicts, civil wars, and internal political upheavals. This is expected as these countries remain newsworthy and reflect the focus and concerns of Arab Canadian news editors of *Hona London*. In addition, and as Abu-Laban (1980) mentioned over four decades ago, another important topic is related to Palestine, for we find emphasis on Gaza and the West Bank (no. 16), and on the former Palestinian president, Yasser Arafat, being the only Arab leader on the list (no. 12). There is no doubt that Palestine and the Israeli–Palestinian conflict remain one of the most important discussion points for Arab Canadians (Abu-Laban and Bakan 2008; Al-Rawi 2019) and are also recurrent topics in the Arab media news coverage in the Middle East (Al-Rawi 2017b).

It is important to briefly mention the other topics that emerged from the analysis, including the topic of Canada, which is evident in references to Radio Canada International (no. 2), Justin Trudeau (no. 9), and public services like infrastructure (no. 5) and bus transportation (no. 8). These topics are meant to provide updates about various political and urban developments in Canada in general and in London in particular. Interestingly, the former Conservative prime minister, Stephen Harper, is not included in the top topics as there is preferential treatment to cover the news of Canada's Liberal leader, Trudeau. Upon examination of the proximity plot of the word "Canada" that statistically measures its association with other words, it was found that the words "immigration" and "permanent resident" were strongly connected. This close association shows that most of the news coverage and commentary on Canada does not only revolve around politics and development but also on the Canadian government's immigration and refugee settlement policies, an issue that is of utmost importance for the Arab Canadian community.

The topic of Donald Trump (no. 7) and the United States (no. 11) was further found to be prominent due to the political influence that the USA exerts in the Middle East and Canada. Finally, the "other" topic categories include coronavirus (no. 14) despite the fact that the COVID-19 pandemic is a relatively recent phenomenon. This indicates the intensity of the news coverage on the virus as a way to inform the Arab Canadian community about the symptoms and possible protection. The second minor topic is related to TV entertainment represented in Nurbanu Sultan (no. 13) which is a reference to *The Magnificent Century* Turkish TV show (*Sultan's*

Harem in Arabic) due to its wide popularity in the Arab world, especially during Ramadan (Yanardağoğlu and Karam 2013).

In summary, the major topics that *Hona London* covers include a mix of national, regional, and transnational geographical scopes. This is an important finding because it shows that the news readers, similar to other diasporic groups, consume news and commentaries that reflect their hybrid Arab and Canadian identities. Here, references to the readers' common Arabic language, Islamic religion, and original homelands are meant to maintain their cultural link, whereas discussion of Canadian national issues enhance civic engagement and cultural integration. In other words, *Hona London* and the majority of other Arab Canadian media outlets play an important symbolic role in the lives of Arab Canadians.

CONCLUSION

This chapter fills a gap in the literature on Arab Canadian media research and presents two main contributions. First, it offers new evidence on the first Arab Canadian publication, *The Canadian Office*, which first appeared in 1905. The origins of the newspaper were traced and the nature of its news coverage, which is partly characterized by its sensationalist nature, was reported. Second, the chapter empirically analyzes an Arab Canadian newspaper to understand the salient topics in its news coverage. The chapter explores all the news coverage of *Hona London* since it started publication in 2012. The digital method of topic modelling illustrates how some major issues are highlighted in the news coverage, especially the issues of Islam, Arab political leaders, Trudeau, and Trump in relation to the USA. As expected, the news coverage clearly attempts to bridge the information gaps with regard to news and events happening in Arab Canadians' original homelands and Canada. In many cases, the newspaper offers an important venue to facilitate civic engagement in terms of reporting on and discussing new immigration guidelines, voting issues, and understanding the legal rights of Arab Canadians. Some Canadian politicians also used the newspaper to promote their policies, especially before election times, while commercial advertisements from the Arab Canadian community cover the majority of the newspaper's pages, similar to other ethnic media publications. Since the focus is partly on community members and their news as well as ads, the newspaper indirectly creates imagined bonds among the community members. In other words, it functions as a symbolic bridge connecting citizens from this ethnic group and enhancing their connection to their host country, denoting its important role in the lives of Arab Canadians. There is also a clear emphasis on US politics due to Canada's geographical proximity with the United States, and this country's political as well as economic impact on Canada and the Middle East and North Africa (MENA) region.

For future research, it is important to interview Arab Canadian journalists to understand the challenges they face in their work and to examine other Arab Canadian media outlets to further explore the nature of their news coverage. Future Arab Canadian researchers and other interested scholars will find systematic digitized records of Arab Canadian newspapers useful since there are only a few sporadic attempts by some libraries in Canada such as collecting a few editions for a few months. This is especially useful considering that an increasing number of online and physical publications are disappearing. Hence, the systematic digital archiving of Arab Canadian press is crucial to preserve this important aspect of ethnic Canadian media.

NOTES

1 I would like to acknowledge the kind assistance I received from the librarians of Simon Fraser University, especially Sylvia Roberts, on the literature regarding the first Arab Canadian, and Sarah Zhang, for her guidance on exploring old Canadian censuses.
2 The Ottoman sultan was deposed on 27 April 1909.
3 Adana is a Turkish city that witnessed an Armenian massacre in April 1909.
4 I would like to thank Mr Abdelrahman Fakida, a graduate student at the School of Communication of Simon Fraser University, for his assistance in downloading the newspaper issues from the website.

REFERENCES

Abdelhady, Dalia. 2011. *The Lebanese Diaspora: The Arab Immigrant Experience in Montreal*. New York: New York University Press.
Abdulahad, Raika, Roger Delaney, and Keith Brownlee. 2009. "Valuing Interdependence: An Examination of Iraqi Canadian Acculturation." *International Social Work* 52 (6): 757–71.
Aboud, Brian. 2002. "The Arab Diaspora: Immigration History and the

Narratives of Presence, Australia, Canada and the USA." In *Arab Australians Today: Citizenship and Belonging*, edited by Ghassan Hage, 63–92. Melbourne: Melbourne University Press.

Abu-Laban, Baha. 1980. *An Olive Branch on the Family Tree: The Arabs in Canada*. Toronto: McClelland and Stewart.

– 1980. "Canadian Muslims: The Need for a New Survival Strategy." *Journal Institute of Muslim Minority Affairs* 2 (2): 98–109.

– 1988. "Arab-Canadians and the Arab-Israeli Conflict." *Arab Studies Quarterly* 10 (1): 104–26.

– 2008. "Arab Canadians." *The Canadian Encyclopedia*. 12 June 2008. https://www.thecanadianencyclopedia.ca/en/article/arabs.

Abu-Laban, Baha, and Sharon McIrvin Abu-Laban. 1999a. "Teens-Between: The Public and Private Spheres of Arab-Canadian Adolescents." In *Arabs in America: Building a New Future*, edited by Michael W. Suleiman, 113–28. Philadelphia: Temple University Press.

– 1999b. "Arab-Canadian Youth in Immigrant Family Life." In *Arabs in America: Building a New Future*, edited by Michael W. Suleiman, 140–55. Philadelphia: Temple University Press.

Abu-Laban, Baha, and Michael W. Suleiman, eds. 1989. *Arab Americans: Continuity and Change*. New York: Association of Arab American University Graduates.

Abu-Laban, Yasmeen. 2007. "History, Power, and Contradictions in a Liberal State." In *The Art of the State III: Belonging? Diversity, Recognition and Shared Citizenship in Canada*, edited by Keith Banting, Thomas J. Courchene, and F. Leslie Seidle, 95–104. Montreal: Institute for Research on Public Policy.

Abu-Laban, Yasmeen, and Abigail B. Bakan. 2008. "The Racial Contract: Israel/Palestine and Canada." *Social Identities* 14 (5): 637–60.

Al Farra, Abdullah. 2012. "Why This Newspaper…?" *Hona London*, 18 May 2012.

Al-Rawi, Ahmed. 2014. "The Representation of September 11th and American Islamophobia in Non-Western Cinema." *Media, War & Conflict* 7 (2): 152–64.

– 2015. "Mapping Arab Canadian Media: Historical and Critical Assessment." Intellectual and Artistic Contributions of Arab Canadians Symposium, sponsored by the Arab Canadian Research Group (ACANS), University of Ottawa, 25 September 2015.

– 2017a. "Facebook and Virtual Nationhood: Social Media and the Arab Canadians Community." *AI & Society* 34: 559–71.

– 2017b. "News Organizations 2.0: A Comparative Study of Twitter News." *Journalism Practice* 11 (6): 705–20.
– 2017c. "News Values on Social Media: News Organizations' Facebook Use." *Journalism* 18 (7): 871–89.
– 2019. "Gatekeeping Fake News Discourses on Mainstream Media versus Social Media." *Social Science Computer Review* 37 (6): 687–704.
Ameeriar, Lalaie. 2012. "The Gendered Suspect: Women at the Canada–US Border after September 11." *Journal of Asian American Studies* 15 (2): 171–95.
Amery, Zainab. 2013. "The Securitization and Racialization of Arabs in Canada's Immigration and Citizenship Policies." In *Targeted Transnationals: The State, the Media, and Arab Canadians*, edited by Jenna Hennebry and Bessma Momani, 32–53. Vancouver: UBC Press.
Anderson, Christopher G. 2008. "A Long-Standing Canadian Tradition: Citizenship Revocation and Second-Class Citizenship under the Liberals, 1993–2006." *Journal of Canadian Studies/Revue d'études canadiennes* 42 (3): 80–105.
Asal, Houda. 2012. "The Canadian Arab Press as Historical Source and Object of Study, from the Late 19th Century to the 1970s." *Canadian Journal of Media Studies* 10 (1): 1–27.
– 2016. *Se dire arabe au Canada: un siècle d'histoire migratoire.* Montreal: Les Presses de l'Université de Montréal.
Bahdi, Reem. 2003. "No Exit: Racial Profiling and Canada's War against Terrorism." *Osgoode Hall Law Journal* 41 (1–2): 293–316.
Berthiaume, Guy, Claude Corbo, and Sophie Montreuil. 2014. *Histoires d'immigrations au Québec.* Quebec City: Presses de l'Université du Québec.
Black, Jerome H., and Christian Leithner. 1988a. "Immigrants and Political Involvement in Canada: The Role of the Ethnic Media." *Canadian Ethnic Studies/Études éthniques au Canada* 20 (1): 1–20.
– 1988b. "Patterns of Ethnic Media Consumption: A Comparative Examination of Ethnic Groupings in Toronto." *Canadian Ethnic Studies/Études éthniques au Canada* 19 (1): 21–39.
Boesvold, Sarah. 2010. "Italian Newspaper's Funding Slashed by Government Sponsor." *Globe and Mail*, 23 March 2010. http://www.theglobeandmail.com/news/national/italian-newspapers-funding-slashed-by-government-sponsor/article4310768/.
Burman, Jenny. 2006. "Absence, 'Removal,' and Everyday Life in the Diasporic City." *Space and Culture* 9 (3): 279–93.

The Canadian Newspaper Directory. 1909. *The Canadian Newspaper Directory: A Complete List of the Newspapers and Periodicals Published in the Dominion of Canada and Newfoundland, with Full Particulars*. Montreal: A. McKim Advertising Agency.

Chongatera, Godfred. 2013. "Hate-Crime Victimization and Fear of Hate Crime among Racially Visible People in Canada: The Role of Income as a Mediating Factor." *Journal of Immigrant & Refugee Studies* 11 (1): 44–64.

Christians, Clifford, and Kaarle Nordenstreng. 2004. "Social Responsibility Worldwide." *Journal of Mass Media Ethics* 19 (1): 3–28.

Deuze, Mark. 2006. "Ethnic Media, Community Media and Participatory Culture." *Journalism* 7 (3): 262–80.

Dionne, M. 1909. *Proceedings and Transactions of the Royal Society of Canada*. 3rd series, vol. 2 (1908). Ottawa: James Hope & Son.

Eid, Paul. 2007. *Being Arab: Ethnic and Religious Identity Building among Second Generation Youth in Montreal*. Montreal & Kingston: McGill-Queen's University Press.

Fathi, Asghar. 1973. "Mass Media and a Moslem Immigrant Community in Canada." *Anthropologica* 15 (2): 201–30.

Fleras, Augie, and Jean Lock Kunz. 2001. *Media and Minorities: Representing Diversity in a Multicultural Canada*. Toronto: Thompson Publishing.

Franklin, Bob, and David Murphy. 1998. *Making the Local News: Local Journalism in Context*. London: Psychology Press.

Government of Canada. 2020. "#WelcomeRefugees: Canada Resettled Syrian Refugees." Ottawa, ON: Immigration, Refugees and Citizenship Canada. https://www.canada.ca/en/immigration-refugees-citizenship/services/refugees/welcome-syrian-refugees.html.

Hamdan, Amani. 2007. "Arab Muslim Women in Canada: The Untold Narratives." *Journal of Muslim Minority Affairs* 27 (1): 1–24.

Hayani, Ibrahim. 1999. "Arabs in Canada: Assimilation or Integration?" In *Arabs in America: Building a New Future*, edited by Michael W. Suleiman, 284–303. Philadelphia: Temple University Press.

Helly, Denise. 2004. "Are Muslims Discriminated against in Canada since September 2001?" *Canadian Ethnic Studies* 36 (1): 24–47.

Hennebry, Jenna, and Bessma Momani, eds. 2013. *Targeted Transnationals: The State, The Media, and Arab Canadians*. Vancouver: UBC Press.

Henry, Frances, and Carol Tator. 2006. *The Colour of Democracy: Racism in Canadian Society*. Toronto: Nelson Education.

Hona London. (This is London). 2022. http://honalondon.ca/news/issues.

Hourani, Albert H., and Nadim Shehadi, eds. 1992. *The Lebanese in the World: A Century of Emigration*. London: I.B. Tauris.

Husband, Charles. 2005. "Minority Ethnic Media as Communities of Practice: Professionalism and Identity Politics in Interaction." *Journal of Ethnic and Migration Studies* 31 (3): 461–79.

Ismael, T.Y. 1976. "The Arab Americans and the Middle East." *The Middle East Journal* 30 (3): 390–405.

– ed. 1984. *Canadian Arab Relations: Policy and Perspectives*. Ottawa: Jerusalem International Publishing House.

– ed. 1985. *Canada and the Arab World*. Alberta: University of Alberta Press.

Ismael, T.Y., and John Measor. 2003. "Racism and the North American Media Following 11 September: The Canadian Setting." *Arab Studies Quarterly* 25 (1–2): 101–36.

Jiwani, Yasmin, and Ahmed Al-Rawi. 2019. "Intersecting Violence: Representations of Somali Youth in the Canadian Press." *Journalism* 22 (7): 1757–74.

Karim, Karim H. 2007. "Nation and Diaspora: Rethinking Multiculturalism in a Transnational Context." *International Journal of Media & Cultural Politics* 2 (3): 267–82.

Karim, Karim H., Mahmoud Eid, and Boulou Ebanda de B'béri. 2007. "Settlement Programming through the Media." Settlement and Intergovernmental Affairs Directorate, Ontario Region, Citizenship and Immigration Canada, Government of Canada, Toronto, Ontario, Canada. http://atwork.settlement.org/downloads/atwork/Settlement_Programming_Through_Media1.pdf.

Khalema, Nene Ernest, and Julie Wannas-Jones. 2003. "Under the Prism of Suspicion: Minority Voices in Canada Post-September 11." *Journal of Muslim Minority Affairs* 23 (1): 25–39.

Khouri, Raja G. 2003. *Arabs in Canada: Post 9/11*. Toronto: Canadian Arab Foundation.

Kidd, J. 1991. "Arabs in Canada." *Archivist* 18 (2): 16–17.

Lewis, Nadia. 2008. "Iraqi Women, Identity, and Islam in Toronto: Reflections on a New Diaspora." *Canadian Ethnic Studies* 40 (3): 131–47.

Marino, N. 1994. "The Antiochian Orthodox Syrians of Montreal, 1905–1980: An Historical Study of Cultural and Social Change over Three Generations." PhD diss., Concordia University.

Matsaganis, Matthew D., Vikki S. Katz, and Sandra J. Ball-Rokeach.

2010. *Understanding Ethnic Media: Producers, Consumers, and Societies*. Thousand Oaks, CA: SAGE.

McAndrew, Marie. 2010. "The Muslim Community and Education in Quebec: Controversies and Mutual Adaptation." *Journal of International Migration and Integration/Revue de l'integration et de la migration internationale* 11 (1): 41–58.

McClure, Helen R. 2012. "The Crystallization of a Moral Panic: A Content Analysis of Anglophone Canadian Print Media Discourse on Arabs and Muslims Pre- and Post-9/11." PhD diss., American University, Washington, DC.

The Mosaic Institute. 2010. "Sudanese-Canadians and the Future of Sudan: Conference Report." Presentation at the Mosaic Institute Conference, sponsored by The Department of Foreign Affairs and International Trade and the Aurea Foundation, University of Winnipeg, 2 September 2010.

Murray, Catherine, Sherry S. Yu, and Daniel Ahadi. 2007. "Cultural Diversity and Ethnic Media in BC. A Report to the Canadian Heritage Western Regional Office." Centre for Policy Studies on Culture and Communities. Vancouver, BC: Simon Fraser University.

ODESI. (n.d.). Canadian Census. https://search1.odesi.ca/#/.

Ohan, Farid Emile, and Ibrahim Hayani. 1993. *The Arabs in Ontario: A Misunderstood Community*. Toronto: Near East Cultural and Educational Foundation of Canada.

Ojo, Tokunbo. 2006. "Ethnic Print Media in the Multicultural Nation of Canada." *Journalism* 7 (3): 343–61.

Paterson, Ashley D., and Julie Hakim-Larson. 2012. "Arab Youth in Canada: Acculturation, Enculturation, Social Support, and Life Satisfaction." *Journal of Multicultural Counseling and Development* 40 (4): 206–15.

Perry, Barbara, and Scott Poynting. 2006. "Inspiring Islamophobia: Media and State Targeting of Muslims in Canada since 9/11." TASA Conference, University of Western Australia and Murdoch University, 4–7 December 2006.

Philo, Greg. 2014. *The Glasgow Media Group Reader, Vol. II: Industry, Economy, War and Politics*. London: Routledge.

Potter, Evan H. 2003. "Canada and the New Public Diplomacy." *International Journal* 58 (1): 43–64.

Poynting, Scott, and Barbara Perry. 2007. "Climates of Hate: Media and State Inspired Victimisation of Muslims in Canada and Australia since 9/11." *Current Issues in Criminal Justice* 19 (2): 151–71.

Rasmi, Sarah. 2012. "Perceived Dyadic Cultural Discrepancies, Intergenerational Conflict, and Ethnocultural Identity Conflict in Arab Canadian Families." PhD diss., University of Guelph.

Rasmi, Sarah, Susan S. Chuang, and Saba Safdar. 2012. "The Relationship between Perceived Parental Rejection and Adjustment for Arab, Canadian, and Arab Canadian Youth." *Journal of Cross-Cultural Psychology* 43 (1): 84–90.

RCI. n.d. "Arab Press in Canada: A Message Not Given Its Due Right."

Riggins, Stephen H., ed. 1992. *Ethnic Minority Media: An International Perspective*. Thousand Oaks, CA: SAGE.

Roach, Kent. 2003. *September 11: Consequences for Canada*. Montreal & Kingston: McGill-Queen's University Press.

Rousseau, Cecile, Ghayda Hassan, Nicolas Moreau, and Brett D. Thombs. 2011. "Perceived Discrimination and its Association with Psychological Distress among Newly Arrived Immigrants before and after September 11, 2001." *American Journal of Public Health* 101 (5): 909–15.

Sabra, Samah. 2011. "Let's All Fit into This Multi-Culture Anyway: (Re) producing and Challenging Canadian National Identity." PhD diss., Carleton University.

Swan, Charles L., and Leila B. Saba. 1974. "The Migration of a Minority." In *Arabic Speaking Communities in American Cities*, edited by Barbara C. Aswad. Staten Island, NY: Center for Migration Studies of New York.

Schoueri, Nour. 2007. "Application of the Theory of Gender and Power to Relationships and Experiences among Middle Eastern and/or Arab Canadians." Master's thesis, University of Waterloo.

Sreberny, Annabelle. 2005. "'Not Only, but Also': Mixedness and Media." *Journal of Ethnic and Migration Studies* 31 (3): 443–59.

Statistics Canada. 2011. "Immigration and Ethnocultural Diversity in Canada: National Household Survey, 2011." Ottawa, ON: Statistics Canada. http://www12.statcan.gc.ca/nhs-enm/2011/as-sa/99-010-x/99-010-x2011001-eng.cfm.

– 2017. "Proportion of Mother Tongue Responses for Various Regions in Canada, 2016 Census." Ottawa, ON: Statistics Canada. http://www12.statcan.gc.ca/census-recensement/2016/dp-pd/dv-vd/lang/index-eng.cfm.

– 2020. "Labour Force Survey, September 20." Ottawa, ON: Statistics Canada. https://www150.statcan.gc.ca/n1/daily-quotidien/201009/dq201009a-eng.htm.

Suleiman, Michael W., ed. 1999. *Arabs in America: Building a New Future*. Philadelphia: Temple University Press.

Syed, Khalida. 2012. "Exotic/Other: Narratives of Muslims, the Role of Media and Popular Culture." *Cultural and Pedagogical Inquiry* 3 (2): 30–9.

Tastsoglou, Evangelia, and Sandy Petrinioti. 2011. "Multiculturalism as Part of the Lived Experience of the 'Second Generation'? Forging Identities by Lebanese-Origin Youth in Halifax." *Canadian Ethnic Studies* 43 (1): 175–96.

Turow, Joseph. 1997. *Breaking Up America: Advertisers and the New Media World.* Chicago: University of Chicago Press.

Vallianatos, Helen, and Kim Raine. 2007. "Reproducing Home: Arab Women's Experiences of Canada." *Al-Raida* 24 (116–17): 35–41.

Waugh, Earle H., Sharon McIrvin Abu-Laban, and Regula B. Qureshi, eds. 1991. *Muslim Families in North America.* Edmonton: University of Alberta.

WikiLeaks. 2011. "The Saudi Cables: Top Secret: The 24th Meeting Memorandum of the Networking Committee of External Media." *WikiLeaks.* https://wikileaks.org/saudi-cables/doc121795.html.

Wilson, Clint C., Felix Gutierrez, and Lena M. Chao. 2003. *Race, Sexism and the Media.* London: SAGE.

Yanardağoğlu, Eylem, and Imad N. Karam. 2013. "The Fever That Hit Arab Satellite Television: Audience Perceptions of Turkish TV Series." *Identities* 20 (5): 561–79.

Yarhi, Eli, and Jessica Poulin. 2022. "Unemployment in Canada." *The Canadian Encyclopedia,* 22 August 2022. https://www.thecanadianencyclopedia.ca/en/article/unemployment.

Zaidan, Esmat. 2011. "Mobility and Transnationalism: Travel Patterns and Identity among Palestinian Canadians." PhD diss., University of Waterloo.

CHAPTER SEVEN

Old and New Media of the Polish Diaspora in Canada

Szymon Zylinski

INTRODUCTION

The first Poles settled in Canada in the middle of the nineteenth century, but the largest immigration waves were caused by the world wars and oppressive communist systems in the second part of the twentieth century. In the years 1945–55, 600,000 Poles left Poland, and between 1956 and 1979, another 800,000 left (Kaczmarek 2012, 171). The last mobility – the so-called "Solidarity wave" – took place in the 1980s and was caused by a wave of strikes from Solidarity, an anti-bureaucratic social movement that aimed to advance workers' rights and social change (Pleskot 2015). During that decade, over one million Poles emigrated (Iglicka 2008, 4). In the second half of the 1990s, the number of Polish immigrants declined, and after Poland joined the European Union in 2004, it dropped significantly. As a result of EU support, the Polish economy improved, and it became a developed country in 2018 (FTSE Russell 2018). Economic or political emigration therefore diminished.

There are around one million Canadians that claim partial or full Polish ancestry, and almost 200,000 Canadians use Polish as their mother tongue (Statistics Canada 2016). Poles now live in all Canadian provinces. The biggest clusters can be found in Toronto and Mississauga (165,000), followed by Montreal (52,000), Edmonton (50,000), Vancouver (40,000), and Calgary (40,000). They are part of all occupational groups as defined by Statistics Canada (2016) and have had their representatives in the Canadian Parliament (Ministerstwo Spraw Zagranicznych, Ministry of Foreign Affairs, 2013). Between the years 1867 and 2017, there were twenty-one members of the Canadian Parliament of Polish Heritage, with the most prominent being Stanley Haidasz, Wladyslaw Lizon, and Tom Kmiec (Parliament of Canada n.d.).

Poles in Canada have also created various media outlets that, for decades, have provided information and a sense of belonging to the Polish diasporic communities in Canada. However, with the advent of the Internet, traditional media outlets such as newspapers, TV, and radio have lost their most important role – that of the news provider – because the news can now be accessed in Canada from online platforms that are based in Poland. Such a paradigm shift may undermine the purpose of traditional Polish-Canadian media, and most of them have resorted to publishing ads of local businesses with occasional journalistic articles. The situation worsened further when media houses, due to the requirements of new media platforms, were forced to direct some of their output to social media (Bivens 2008). The generational shift also plays a big role in dispersing information, where both media houses and readers are hesitant in adopting new means of communication. This paper aims to map the online presence of Polish diasporic media in Canada and present modes of operation of traditional diasporic media in a new media landscape.

DIASPORIC AND POLISH DIASPORIC DISCOURSE

Ethnic media are perceived "as the media that are produced by and for migrants and deal with issues that are of specific interest for the members of diasporic communities" (Bozdag, Hepp, and Suna 2012, 97). Their roles are to manufacture "culturally relevant and locally vital information to immigrants in the host society" (Yin 2015, 3); to guide newcomers in a new environment (Ogunyemi 2012); to strengthen an individual connection with oneself and deepen a sense of belonging (Georgiou 2006); to create an atmosphere for introspective communication (Bozdag, Hepp, and Suna 2012), and eventually to "(re-)create home" (Karim 2003, 10). Ahadi (2016) argues that diasporic "communication infrastructure provides an important social, cultural, economic, and political support network that can help community members to build a sense of belonging to the larger society" (1). Yu (2015) adds that "ethnic media take charge in cross-ethnic and cross-cultural partnerships that effectively benefit all" (138), and Al-Rawi (2018) mentions the ethnicization process as a crucial one in mobility. Participation in mobility transforms the definition of home and nation, and representatives of the exiled communities often shift to being more ethnic that they used to be when residing in their country of origin (hooks 2009).

The overarching theoretical framework in ethnic media research concerns the functionality of ethnic media. What role do they play in society? Instrumental (informative) or symbolic (identity orientation) (Matsaganis and Ahadi 2017)? There are two main perspectives on ethnic media: integrative and non-integrative. Integrative says that ethnic media introduce host society rules and regulations to the newcomer; non-integrative maintains the opposite, that ethnic media enclose immigrants with group-centred communication, and limit information from and about the new country (Black and Leithner 1988). A third perspective holds that diasporic media engage in geo-ethnic storytelling to provide "culturally relevant and locally vital information to immigrants in the host society" (Lin and Song 2006, 364).

Discussing modern ethnic media has to touch upon advertising that has eroded editorial and news content in the rapidly changing newspaper industry (Cottle 2000, 2). Global processes reconfigured the strategic goals and market potential of key media players that were forced to adapt to new modes of communication (Herman and McChesney 1997). The focus solely on advertising, as can be seen in the Polish diasporic press, is damaging to the content of periodicals that drift from news-providing platforms to bulletins full of ads with sensational form. Tabloidization of media, understood as a decline in journalistic standards, has been lamented for a long time (Bird 2009). This dubious trend is responsible for the erosion of media content and serves a certain agenda, which most often is of monetary value (Herman and Chomsky 2002).

Financial scarcity was one of the factors that caused Poles to leave their country, and another was political persecution. Each emigration wave has different motivations that drove Poles to leave the motherland during World War II and the Solidarity movement in the 1980s. Consequently, the aims of Polish communities and their media were different. Polish periodicals were an important element of social, cultural, and political life in Canada and elsewhere outside Poland. However, the Polish diaspora is not strong in terms of human resources and has neither created resilient groups, such as influential organizations (e.g., lobbying groups) nor does it have media representation appropriate to its size in Canadian political or cultural life (Ministerstwo Spraw Zagranicznych 2013). In addition, research on the Polish immigration issues is rather modest (Bajor 2009; Kaczmarek 2012).

Many researchers have focused on Polish diasporas around the world (Sandberg 1974; Kubiak and Pilch 1976; Sekowska 1994) and explored their media (Ruta 2010; Kaczmarek 2012), especially the ones in the United States (Piatkowska-Stepaniuk 2010; Leonowicz-Bukala 2012). Polish communities in Canada have also been researched (Turek, 1967; Grabowski 1975; Radecki 1979; Avery and Fedorowicz 1982; Reczynska 1996; Slany 2002; Lustanski 2009), but when it comes to Polish media in Canada, they were usually discussed as part of a bigger project about the Polish diasporic community in general (Kowalik 1976; Kristjanson and Bashuk 1974; Paczkowski 1977). There have been very few papers that consider Polish diasporic media in Canada as the sole subject focus.

One of the earliest examples is a monograph by Turek (1962), in which he presented the short history of Polish Canadian media, such as *Zwiazkowiec* (The Alliancer) or *Czas* (Time), discussed Polish-Canadian periodicals, and provided a bibliography. Turek also began academic research on the Polish diaspora in Canada at the University of Toronto and there created the Canadian Polish Research Institute in 1956 (2020). Lesniczak (2016) divided his analysis of Polish media in Canada into three parts: before World War II, in the years 1939–89, and after political reforms in 1989. He provided a short description of a few chosen periodicals and admitted that the multicultural policy of Canada enabled Polish immigrants to keep their traditions and culture. Stepaniuk's (2005) paper entitled "The Polish-Canadian Press: Historical Overview" is the only one written in English. Besides an account of press titles, it points the reader to the collection of Polish-Canadian press at the Library and Archives of Canada, which includes most of the Polish titles published in Canada. None of the aforementioned research examines new media, and this chapter therefore fills this research gap.

METHODOLOGY

To map the online presence of Polish diasporic media in Canada, this research had to first assess the exact number of active Polish media outlets in Canadian provinces and territories. The data on Polish organizations and centres were outdated (Canadian Polish

Congress 2022; Polish Alliance of Canada 2021; Polish Canadians 2021), and therefore Google was used to create a list of all active Polish media (30) in Canada. The keywords used were: Polish words for Polish Canadian media; Polish media in Canada; media for Poles in Canada, etc. The mapping period was January 2019. During interviews and electronic communication, media personnel were consulted about the content of their media.

Only the most representative cases (highest circulation among other diasporic titles, listenership, impact on local community) were analyzed in terms of content, and only currently active media titles were taken into consideration. As part of the study, eleven media representatives (journalists, radio DJs, editors) were also interviewed in person, in Polish. Recorded semi-structured interviews, each ranging from thirty to sixty minutes, took place in the Greater Toronto Area in February 2019, and in the Greater Vancouver Area from September to November 2019. Interviewees' names and sexes were randomized. During the coding process, each interviewee was assigned a Polish-sounding pseudonym using an online software name-generator (Losownik n.d.). The women to men ratio was kept. It is worth noting that online media are plentiful; however, they often lack regularity. Many of them had periods of activity, and then seem to have been abandoned.

Based on the previous discussion, this study proposes to answer the following research questions: How are Polish diasporic media represented online? Do Polish diasporic media help to integrate into Canadian society? What role do Polish diasporic media play in Canadian society?

TRADITIONAL POLISH DIASPORIC MEDIA LANDSCAPE

As of March 2020, there are twenty-five traditional media outlets of the Polish diaspora in Canada: sixteen in Ontario, four in British Columbia, two in Alberta and Quebec, and one in Manitoba (see table 7.1 for more details). There are thirteen newspapers (weeklies, bi-weeklies, and monthlies), eleven radio stations, and one TV station, all of which were confirmed by the interviewees. All titles are owned by private individuals and are run on a for-profit basis.

Some of the media have a long and complicated history of ownership. For example, monthly periodical *Fakty-Czas* goes back to

Table 7.1 | Presence of Polish traditional media on new media platforms

Medium	Website	Facebook	YouTube	Twitter	Other
Fakty-Czas	x	-	-	-	-
Glos Polski	x	-	-	-	-
Goniec	x	x	x	x	-
Monitor	-	-	-	-	-
Nowy Przeglad	x	-	-	-	-
Polish Canadian Trucker	-	-	-	-	issuu.com
Przeglad	x	x	-	-	-
Puls	-	-	-	-	issuu.com
Wiadomosci	x	x	-	-	-
Zycie	x	x	-	-	-
Radio 7	x	-	-	-	-
Radio Polonia	x	-	-	-	-
Radio Puls	-	-	-	-	-
Radio Rodzina	x	x	-	-	-
Radio Bis	x	-	-	-	-
Polish Credit Union TV	x	-	x	-	-
Głos Polonii	x	-	-	-	issuu.com
Radio IKS	x	x	-	-	soundcloud.com
Radio Mega	-	x	-	-	-
Radio Miks	-	-	-	-	-
Panorama Polska	x	-	-	-	-
Polskie RadioRadio Edmonton	x	-	-	-	-
Panorama	x	x	-	-	-
Radio Polonia	x	x	-	-	-
Radio Polonia Half na pol	-	x	-	x	-

Source: Observational data from author's fieldwork.

1914 when *Czas* started being published in Winnipeg (Fakty Inc. 2017). Others are relatively new constructs like *Glos Polonii* from Vancouver, with the first issue published in 2016 (Pipala 2016). Newspapers are currently distributed free of charge, except for *Goniec* which costs two Canadian dollars, and rely on advertisements from local businesses and services, such as Polish stores, car dealerships, immigration lawyers, etc. The advertisements dwarf the articles, which are quite often poor quality. Some newspaper producers are against such practices, for example, Aleksandra, a Polish paper owner, who states: "Those are not newspapers! For me this is not a newspaper, it's the expanded advertising flyer."

Interestingly, local Canadian content, even concerning Polish diaspora, is in the minority compared to news from Poland. Such focus on the information from the country of origin has been established by other studies (Yu and Murray 2007; Matsaganis, Katz, and Ball-Rokeach 2005). Kacper, a journalist, divulged that for his periodical, most articles are commissioned from journalists based in Poland. Moreover, the texts they send in have already been published in the Polish press, so they are essentially just reprinted with an editorial adjustment for the diasporic reader.

Newspapers are quite often produced by a small number of personnel and are often operated by one person (for example, *Goniec*, *Glos Polonii*). Some media have decided to cooperate and merge under one title (for example, *Radio Puls* and *Puls* periodical) or to share common identification (like the weekly *Zycie* and *Radio 7* or *Radio Polonia* and the associated magazine *Panorama*). Such consolidation helps to share advertisement revenue and audience.

When considering Polish radio stations, it appears they are simply radio programs that are broadcasted on multilingual, ethnic, community stations. For example, both *Radio Mega* and *Radio Miks* from Vancouver are hourly programs broadcasted on Co-operative Radio, CFRO, 100.5 FM. *Radio IKS* also broadcasts once a week on the Red FM station and *Radio Polonia* from Montreal broadcasts on CFMB 1280 AM.

The only diasporic television channel, Polish Credit Union TV, was founded in 1988, and is broadcasted on CHIN network, City TV (program 7, channel 57), every Saturday for sixty minutes. They claim that they reach over 300,000 people in Canada, and in the Rochester, Buffalo, and Detroit regions of the United States (St Stanislaus–St Casimir's Polish Parishes Credit Union Limited n.d.).

Figure 7.1 | Example of advertisement on ethnic media website.

Whereas diasporic media comment on and cite Canadian media, Canadian media rarely report on Poland. It only happens when something of great importance happens, such as the Smolensk tragedy, where the Polish president and members of the parliament died in a plane crash (CTV News Toronto 2010), or when Polish citizen Robert Dziekanski was killed during an arrest at the Vancouver International Airport (Foulds 2019). Such events are rare, and the Polish diaspora generally only appears in Canadian media during traditional celebrations. On those occasions, one may see the Canadian policy of multiculturalism in action. Abu-Laban and Gabriel (2002) describe such a trend as "selling diversity," where women and men of various ethnic backgrounds are transformed into trade-enhancing commodities.

Maciej, a journalist from Vancouver, praises the aforementioned policy; however, he admits that quite often, it is pushed to the extreme. He provides an example of an event in Vancouver called

"Polish Days," during which an African band also takes the stage "that doesn't have anything in common with Polish ones ... but when Canada, which is a multicultural country, looks at it, it approves it and provides funding." Such support mechanisms have their equivalent in media, occasionally providing multiethnic content, yet all interviewees confirmed lack of any government funding. Critical multiculturalism scholars call such an attitude "3S" (saris, samosas, and steel drums), a mocking reference to government officials fulfilling their agenda by having ethnic elements present, without much deeper meaning (Yuk 2011). Such government policies and actions Kobayashi (1993) calls "red boot" multiculturalism.

MAPPING ONLINE PRESENCE

Of the ethnic media outlets researched, nineteen out of twenty-five have a website, while the rest exist only in the print form; seven out of nineteen are not regularly updated and play the role of an online business card, only containing information about the medium, address, and corresponding graphics. Websites seem to be incomplete or not properly functional. For example, social media icons and links from the "In the print" section of the *Fakty* website do not lead anywhere (Fakty Inc. 2017). The majority of online content lacks modern, clean, simple design. The websites are full of display-type advertisements that are crammed on the page and overwhelm the viewer. The layout resembles printed brochures, where it is evident that texts exist only to sell ads. They take over the main page, pushing all other information aside (see figure 7.1). Titles that upload content regularly are *Bejsment*, *Goniec*, *Glos Polonii*, *Panorama*, *Przeglad*, and *Zycie*. *Goniec* is the only periodical that is present on Facebook, Twitter, and YouTube.

Facebook is the most popular social media platform for Polish ethnic media, with ten out of twenty-five media outlets present. However, their posts typically gather only a few likes and sometimes none. It seems that Facebook is treated as a tool to redirect traffic to websites. In some cases, posts are just copied and pasted from the paper version of the periodical without any comment or adjustment to online content production rules. Eryk Glowacki, from one of the newspapers, admits that Facebook is a double-edged sword that damages the Internet version of his paper because it keeps the traffic, and therefore advertisement revenue, to itself. Another media representative, Maciej Michalak, says that the press is in decline; in his opinion, it is not worthwhile to invest in new media because readers of his periodical are mostly elderly people who are not enthusiasts of the Internet and prefer to get their information in a printed form. Interestingly, not all media personnel share his opinion; for example, *Gazeta Gazeta* ceased to print paper copies in February 2019 and moved its operation entirely to the web. Such a move was forced by the rising cost of print and the visible potential of online readership.

Radio Polonia from Montreal also grasps connected communication. It is the only Polish radio program in Canada whose website features current news and an archive since 2017 (Radio Polonia n.d.). Moreover, it started to publish its own monthly magazine, *Panorama*, the first issue of which was printed in November 2019. It caters to readers from Quebec but cooperates with Polish diasporas from around the world (Szara and Leszczewicz 2019). It is the only periodical whose digital version is hosted on the home website. Other titles (*Głos Polonii* and *Puls*) use Issuu.com as a platform to distribute their digital copies. It is difficult to quantify the number of people accessing the digital versions of those periodicals and their engagement with the content. On the contrary, easily quantifiable is the Polish Credit Union TV; although they maintain that they reach hundreds of thousands of people with their traditional content on television, their YouTube channel has only 1,250 subscribers, and views of each of their uploads are below 100 (Polish Credit Union TV n.d.).

MODES OF ONLINE CONTENT DISTRIBUTION

Wiadomosci is the weekly publication from Mississauga with the highest printed number and Bejsment.com is its website. *Wiadomosci* has a circulation of 14,000 copies per week, with 60 to 116 pages, bound, and is distributed in Mississauga and the Greater Toronto Area. In the digital format, one can only see the front pages of the printed periodical, order classifieds, and buy ads. *Bejsment* has a modern one-page layout design with the text to ads proportion of around 50 per cent, which seems high, but is still less than other Polish ethnic media websites that serve as advertising hubs. Bejsment.com is updated several times a day and features local news that concerns the diasporic community. However, avid readers often point out in the comment section that the editor draws content from mainstream media outlets such as *The Globe and Mail*, *National Post*, *Toronto Star*, etc. User Rahuciachu comments on the text published on Bejsment.com: "Johny, why are you pissed off at the editors, they only copy/paste from Canucks' papers, portals and so on. Nothing original, so how can there be anything original?" *Bejsment* also has many subsections, such as Poles and Canada, advice from Granny Jelonka, and obituaries, to name just a few. They play a community consolidation role, where readers can educate themselves and keep in touch with other members of the community.

The Facebook page of *Wiadomosci/Bejsment* regularly publishes links to articles first printed in the paper version before posting them on their website. Interestingly, these are just links without any additional information about the content. It seems that this form of new media communication is necessary, although, editors do not engage with sporadic comments under the posts. As of March 2020, the page was followed by 1,820 individuals, but each post gathers only a few likes, mostly below ten. This conversion rate is very low compared to the potential reach and circulation of *Wiadomosci* among the Polish community. Eryk from the newspaper office says that "Facebook is like a double-edged sword. Sometimes, I have a feeling it brings damage to the Internet newspaper. Beforehand, when Facebook wasn't around, people entered our website to read. When Facebook became popular, some people only click on links there, and that's it. They don't visit websites, and it's a great loss." The traffic stays within social media and is not used by the media houses to generate revenue from ads. Perhaps the lack of knowledge on how to utilize Facebook's potential or the reluctance to study new communication techniques are to blame.

The first issue of *Glos Polonii* from Vancouver was published on 1 September 2016 and coincided with the termination of another ethnic newspaper, *Takie Zycie*, in British Columbia. In the first issue, the editor-in-chief wrote that "for sure we will shun from politics in a typical Polish style" (Pipała 2016); however, in later issues, biased politics played a crucial role in each copy. The left-of-centre sympathy of this title is evident because it critiques right-wing parties and therefore recreates the political-media situation in Poland, where media are partisan.

Each issue of *Glos Polonii* has approximately twenty-four to twenty-eight pages, mostly in black and white with a few colour pages. The local reporting is poor, with only a few entries that discuss events in British Columbia and Canada, more generally. Most of the content is written by journalists based in Poland. This paper does not have any social media presence, and its online platform takes the form of a website, where some articles from the paper version are uploaded. Advertisements take up a quarter of the website body and are packed on the right-hand side in the form of a rolling display. *Glos Polonii* has an archive of all published issues of the paper version in the Issuu.com repository (Issuu n.d.).

Goniec has a peculiar history because it was initially a paid newspaper that evolved into free distribution, but now costs two Canadian dollars, including HST. This right-wing paper is the only one among Polish diasporic media in Canada that has a presence across many social media channels: Facebook (2,270 likes), YouTube (2,230 subscribers), and Twitter (147 followers). Its website is a modern one-page design, with a few display advertisements that do not obstruct text. However, after clicking on an article, the content is displayed and is accompanied by a block of advertisements.

Goniec, similar to *Wiadomosci*, publishes links to articles on Facebook without any comment or introduction. Such content gathers very poor feedback, with its likes oscillating below ten for most posts. However, its YouTube presence, since 2012, features regularly uploaded videos with content ranging from interviews with diaspora representatives, right-wing Polish politicians visiting North America, to commentary from Editor-in-Chief and owner Andrzej Kumor. Videos typically gather 200 to 300 views with less than five comments. The Twitter account seems to be the weakest of its social media channels; Tweets to its 147 followers include links to the articles published on the website Goniec.net, and they are introduced with a short description.

Gazeta, also called *Gazeta Gazeta*, was created by the Solidarity wave emigrants in the 1980s and played an important role in the assimilation of Poles in Canadian society. Its editors, for instance, praised the multicultural policy of their new homeland. As one of the first diasporic periodicals, it turned digital in 2003. Both versions were published until February 2019 when it became cost-ineffective to publish a print version, especially given that *Gazeta* focuses on professional journalism and not on selling advertising space (*Gazeta* 2015). Since then, it has only been available online and the newest articles are distributed in a newsletter format that are sent out regularly. Its current format is reminiscent of a left-wing information portal that promotes multicultural values.

DISCUSSION AND CONCLUSION

Ethnic media are indispensable among the diasporas, and the traditional ones played important roles in the Polish community. With the introduction of new forms of communication, it is expected that they embark on social media platforms and continue to carry their mission (or to make a profit, as it seems to be the driving force behind most Polish diasporic media in Canada). Yet, old media do not embark on new media platforms, and if they do, they do not use their full potential. This means that the Polish diaspora is not represented well on newer platforms. Facebook is the most utilized platform, while Twitter and YouTube are marginally utilized. Interestingly, there is no evidence of Instagram usage by the media outlets.

Polish diasporic media are both integrative and non-integrative. Some titles carry on the multicultural Canadian ethos, reporting on the matter, while others are focused on nationalistic content (as in the case of *Goniec*). The second approach is less common; it shows that Poles, even living in a very progressive Canadian environment, still cling to their motherland that is cultivated by the currently ruling party in Poland. Most journalists and media personnel in Polish diasporic media are not trained professionals, and their work falls under the community media paradigm.

Due to the lack of implementation of new media strategies, the audiences' engagement is rather low because there is no space to voice their opinion, concerns, and views. Of course, there are Facebook fan pages, but not all articles are published there because they take traffic from websites that are highly saturated with ads. Interviewed owners of Polish diasporic media view social media as unwanted but necessary streams of content dissemination. On the other hand, audiences find it easier to access content on social media, however, they do not engage with it often. It is worth noting that the comments are aligned with the political scope of the diasporic title.

As polarization among the titles and the audiences could be seen quite well, Polish diasporic media in Canada play a crucial role in informing about any events or gatherings that are celebrated, irrespective of political views. Especially, traditional customs are a strong pull for Canadian Poles that miss them in the multicultural northern American culture. The media quite often are initiators of those celebrations, which are then abundantly described and narrated.

Generally, the media analyzed here do not play an instrumental or symbolic role in the community; however, as discussed above, there are some exceptions. Representatives of media outlets say they focus on local news, but in reality, they focus on local advertising, which can play a connective and symbolic role. Most of its traditional journalistic content space is now needed to provide advertising space, and their online presence is forced by global communication development in the form of social media. Nonetheless, there is no all-Canada Polish medium, neither traditional nor online. Only Ontario, British Columbia, Alberta, Quebec, and Manitoba have some kind of Polish ethnic media, whereas only Ontario has a thriving market and competition among the titles.

The best websites that provide information on the Polish diaspora are *Bejsment* and *Goniec* from Ontario, where the competition is fierce, and the diasporic population is the biggest. Undoubtedly, *Goniec* seems to be the most news media-savvy. However, its communication role for the local Polish diaspora is highly questionable. This is firstly because of its ring-wing bias, and secondly, because it has been accused of anti-Semitism. B'nai Brith Canada, the section of the oldest Jewish organizations in the world committed to combatting anti-Semitism, has blamed *Goniec* for hateful material (B'nai B'rith Canada 2019). This Jewish organization filed complaints to the appropriate Canadian police forces (Blackwell 2020) and controversial texts were removed from the online platform.

The Polish diaspora in Canada is diverse in terms of political views. As it has become less popular due to the lack of new immigration waves, new generations have begun to blend into Canadian society, quite often forgetting about their roots. These new generations are not active consumers of diasporic media and prefer gathering information at the source, from Polish media in Poland through online access.

ACKNOWLEDGMENTS

This publication was written as a result of my stay as a visiting scholar in the School of Communication at Simon Fraser University, Vancouver, Canada, co-financed by the European Union under the

European Social Fund (Operational Program Knowledge Education Development), and carried out in the Development Program at the University of Warmia and Mazury in Olsztyn (POWR.03.05. 00-00-Z310/17). I would also like to thank the staff at Simon Fraser University's School of Communication for providing me with academic opportunities, and Dr Daniel Ahadi, who was my host during my visit, for his guidance.

REFERENCES

Abu-Laban, Yasmeen, and Christina Gabriel. 2002. *Selling Diversity: Immigration, Multiculturalism, Employment Equity and Globalization.* Toronto: Broadview Press.

Ahadi, Daniel. 2016. "Iranian Community Media in Stockholm: Locality, Transnationality, and Multicultural Adaptation." PhD diss., Simon Fraser University.

Al-Rawi, Ahmed. 2018. "Regional Television and Collective Ethnic Identity: Investigating the SNS Outlets of Arab TV Shows." *Social Media + Society* 4 (3): 1–16.

Avery, Donald H., and J.K. Fedorowicz. 1982. *The Poles in Canada.* Ottawa, ON: Canadian Historical Association.

B'nai B'rith Canada. 2019. "'Jews Are Spying on You,' Ontario Polish Newspaper Claims." 15 August 2019. https://www.bnaibrith.ca/_jews_are_spying_on_you_ontario_polish_newspaper_claims?.

Bajor, Agnieszka. 2009. "Jan Kowalik – badacz i bibliograf prasy polonijnej" (Jak Kowalik – researcher and bibliographer of Polish diasporic press). In *Kultura ksiazki i prasy polonijnej: Dziedzictwo narodowe i swiatowe* (The culture of Polish press and books), edited by Maria Kalczynska, Danuta Sieradzka, and Zdzislaw Malecki, 145–57. Katowice: Wydawnictwo Uniwersytetu Slaskiego.

Bird, Elizabeth. 2009. "Tabloidization: What Is It, and Does It Really Matter?" In *The Changing Faces of Journalism: Tabloidization, Technology and Truthiness,* edited by Barbie Zelizer, 40–50. New York: Routledge.

Bivens, Rena K. 2008. "The Internet, Mobile Phones and Blogging." *Journalism Practice* 2 (1): 113–29.

Black, Jerome H., and Christian Leithner. 1988. "Immigrants and Political Involvement in Canada: The Role of the Ethnic Media." *Canadian Ethnic Studies* 20 (1): 1–20.

Blackwell, Tom. 2020. "Canadian Polish-Language Newspaper Blames

COVID-19 on Jews in Anti-Semitic Tirade." *National Post*, 7 August 2020. https://nationalpost.com/news/canada/newspaper-tied-to-government-funded-polish-group-blames-covid-19-on-jews-in-anti-semitic-tirade.

Bozdag, Cigdem, Andreas Hepp, and Laura Suna. 2012. "Diasporic Media as the 'Focus' of Communicative Networking Among Migrants." In *Mediating Cultural Diversity in a Globalized Public Space*, edited by Isabelle Rigoni and Eugénie Saitta, 96–115. London: Palgrave Macmillan.

Canadian Polish Congress. 2022. "Polish Media in Canada." https://kpk.org/polishmediaincanada.

Canadian Polish Research Institute. 2018. "Prezesi." 18 January 2018. http://www.canadianpolishinstitute.org/board/presidents-pl.html.

Cottle, Simon. 2000. *Ethnic Minorities and the Media: Changing Cultural Boundaries*. Buckingham: Open University Press.

CTV News Toronto. 2010. "Canada Grieves with Poland, Harper Tells Memorial." 15 April 2010. https://toronto.ctvnews.ca/canada-grieves-with-poland-harper-tells-memorial-1.502881.

Fakty Inc. 2017. "Fakty." (Facts). http://www.fakty.ca/index.html#.

– 2017. "Stanisław Stolarczyk." http://www.fakty.ca/onas.html.

Foulds, Christopher. 2019. "Mother of Robert Dziekanski, Taser Victim, Dies in Poland." *Province*, 28 November 2019. https://theprovince.com/news/local-news/mother-of-robert-dziekanski-taser-victim-dies-in-poland.

FTSE Russell. 2018. "Poland: The Journey to Developed Market Status." https://content.ftserussell.com/sites/default/files/research/poland---the-journey-to-developed-market-status_final.pdf.

Gazeta. 2015. https://gazetagazeta.com/o-nas/.

Georgiou, Myria. 2006. *Diaspora, Identity and the Media: Diasporic Transnationalism and Mediated Spatialities*. New York: Hampton Press.

Grabowski, Yvonne. 1975. "Language in Contact: Polish and English." In *Sounds Canadian: Languages and Cultures in Multi-Ethnic Society*, edited by Paul M. Migus, 59–68. Toronto: P. Martin Associates.

Herman, Edward S., and Robert W. McChesney. 1997. *The Global Media: The New Missionaries of Corporate Capitalism*. New York: Bloomsbury Academic Press.

Herman, Edward S., and Noam Chomsky. 2002. *Manufacturing Consent*. New York: Pantheon Books.

hooks, bell. 2009. *Belonging: A Culture of Place*. New York: Routledge.

Iglicka, Krystyna. (2008). "Migration Movements from and into Poland in the Light of East-West European Migration." *International Migration* 39 (1): 3–32.

Issuu. n.d. "Rekacja." https://issuu.com/rekacja.

Kaczmarek, Marlena. 2012. "Geneza i rozwój prasy polonijnej oraz emigracyjnej" (The genesis and development of Polish immigration press). *Rocznik prasoznawczy* (Yearly press journal) 6: 171–90.

Karim, Karim H., ed. 2003. "Mapping the Diasporic Mediascapes." In *The Media of Diaspora: Mapping the Globe*, 1–18. New York: Routledge.

Kobayashi, Audrey. 1993. "Multiculturalism: Representing a Canadian Institution." In *Place/Culture/Representation*, edited by James S. Duncan and David Ley, 205–31. New York: Routledge.

Kowalik, Jan. 1976. *Bibliografia Czasopism Polskich Wydanych Poza Granicami Kraju od Wrzesnia 1939 Roku* (Bibliography of Polish press printed outside the country since September 1939). Lublin: Katolicki Uniwersytet Lubelski (Catholic University of Lublin).

Kristjanson, Wilhelm, and Bashuk Natalia. 1974. *The Multilingual Press in Manitoba.* Winnipeg: Canada Press Club.

Kubiak, Hieronim, and Andrzej Pilch. 1976. *Stan i potrzeby badan nad zbiorowościami polonijnymi* (Condition and needs for research on Polish minority groups). Wroclaw: Zakład Narodowy im. Ossolińskich.

Leonowicz-Bukala, Iwona. 2012. "Media polonijne w USA" (Polish diasporic media in USA). *Komunikacja Spoleczna. Czasopismo elektroniczne* (Social communication. online journal) (4): 41–69.

Lesniczak, Rafal. 2016. "Polonijne media w Kanadzie – historia i terazniejszosc" (Polish diasporic media in Canada – history and present day). In *Polonia kanadyjska Przeszlosc i terazniejszosc* (Polish Canadian diaspora), edited by Waldemar Glinski, 183–97. Warsaw: Wydawnictwo Naukowe UKSW.

Lin, Wan-Ying, and Hayeon Song. 2006. "Geo-Ethnic Storytelling: An Examination of Ethnic Media Content in Contemporary Immigrant Communities." *Journalism* 7 (3): 362–88.

Losownik. n.d. http://losownik.pl/imie/losuj/name-surname.

Lustanski, Joanna. 2009. "Polish Canadians and Polish Immigrants in Canada: Self-Identity and Language Attitude." *International Journal of the Sociology of Language* (199): 39–61.

Matsaganis, Matthew D., and Daniel Ahadi. 2017. "Ethnic Media and Acculturation." In *The International Encyclopedia of Intercultural*

Communication, edited by Young Yun Kim, 1–10. West Sussex: Wiley-Blackwell.

Matsaganis, Matthew D., Vikki S. Katz, and Sandra Ball-Rokeach. 2010. *Understanding Ethnic Media: Producers, Consumers, and Societies*. Thousand Oaks, CA: SAGE.

Ministerstwo Spraw Zagranicznych (Ministry of Foreign Affairs). 2013. *Raport o sytuacji Polonii i Polaków za granicą 2012* (Report on Polish diaspora and Poles abroad 2012). Warsaw: Ministerstwo Spraw Zagranicznych.

Ogunyemi, Ola. 2012. *What Newspapers, Films, and Television Do Africans Living in Britain See and Read: The Media of African Diaspora*. New York: Edwin Mellen Press.

Paczkowski, Andrzej. 1977. *Prasa Polonijna w Latach 1870–1939: Zarys Problematyki* (Polish diasporic press in years 1870–1939). Warsaw: Biblioteka Narodowa.

Parliament of Canada. n.d. Library of Parliament. https://lop.parl.ca/sites/PublicWebsite/default/en_CA/.

Piatkowska-Stepaniuk, Wieslawa. 2010. "Idee i rola nowojorskiej prasy polonijnej" (Ideas and role of Polish diasporic press from New York). In *Polonijny Nowy Jork* (Polish New York). Opole: Wydawnictwo Swietego Krzyza.

Pipala, Krzysztof. 2016. "Witamy. Szansa na Sukces" (Welcome. A chance for success). *Glos Polonii* (The voice of Polish diaspora), 1, 2.

Pleskot, Patryk. 2015. "Polish Political Emigration in the 1980s: Current Research, Perspectives, and Challenges." *Polish American Studies* 72 (2): 49–64.

Polish Alliance of Canada. 2021. "Polskie Media w Kanadzie." http://www.polishalliance.ca/polish-media-in-canada?id=131.

Polish Canadians. 2021. "Polskie Media." http://polishcanadians.ca/?page_id=65&lang=pl.

Polish Credit Union TV. n.d. YouTube channel. https://www.youtube.com/channel/UC9VrJzXWqwH6JQpV4J7_OPA.

Radecki, Henry. 1979. *Ethnic Organizational Dynamics: The Polish Group in Canada*. Waterloo: Wilfrid Laurier University Press.

Radio Polonia. n.d. "Archiwum Audycji" (Broadcast archives). http://www.radiopolonia.org/archiwum.htm.

Reczynska, Anna. 1996. *For Bread and a Better Future: Emigration from Poland to Canada, 1918–1939*. Toronto: Multicultural Historical Society of Ontario.

Ruta, Przemysław. 2010. "Prasa dla Polaków w Irlandii" (Press for

Poles in Ireland). *Rocznik Prasoznawczy* (Annual press journal) (4): 85–94.

Sandberg, Neil C. 1974. *Ethnic Identity and Assimilation: The Polish-American Community; Case Study of Metropolitan Los Angeles.* Westport: Praeger Publishers Inc.

Sekowska, Elżbieta. 1994. *Jezyk zbiorowosci polonijnych w krajach anglojęzycznych: Zagadnienia leksykalno-slowotworcze* (The Polish language in English-speaking countries. Lexical and morphological issues). Warsaw: Warsaw University Press.

Slany, Krystyna. 2002. "Imigracja polska w Kanadzie w dekadzie lat dziewięćdziesiątych" (Polish immigrants to Canada in the nineties of the twentieth century). In *Emigracja z Polski po 1989 roku* (Migration from Poland after 1989), edited by Klimaszewski Boleslaw, 151–75. Krakow: Grell.

St. Stanislaus-St. Casimir's Polish Parishes Credit Union Limited. n.d. "Polish Credit Union TV." https://www.polcu.com/Personal/InOurCommunity/PolishCreditUnionTV/.

Statistics Canada. 2016. "2016 Census Program Content Test: Design and Results." Ottawa, ON: Statistics Canada. https://www12.statcan.gc.ca/census-recensement/2016/consultation/92-140/92-140-x2016001-eng.cfm.

Stepaniuk, Violette. 2005. "The Polish-Canadian Press: Historical Overview." Library and Archives Canada. https://www.collectionscanada.gc.ca/obj/005007/f2/005007-205-e.pdf.

Szara, Bozena, and Andrzej Leszczewicz. 2019. "Od redaktora" (From the editor). *Panorama: Magazyn Radia Polonia* (Panorama: magazine of *Radio Polonia*) 1: 3.

Turek, Wiktor. 1962. *Polish-Language Press in Canada: Its History and a Bibliographical List.* Toronto: Polish Alliance Press.

– 1967. *Poles in Manitoba.* Toronto: Polish Research Institute in Canada.

Yin, Hang. 2015. "Chinese-Language Cyberspace, Homeland Media and Ethnic Media: A Contested Space for Being Chinese." *New Media & Society* 17 (4): 556–72.

Yu, Sherry S. 2015. "The Inevitably Dialectic Nature of Ethnic Media." *Global Media Journal, Canadian Edition* 8 (2): 133–40.

Yu, Sherry S., and Catherine A. Murray. 2007. "Ethnic Media under a Multicultural Policy: The Case of the Korean Media in British Columbia." *Canadian Ethnic Studies* 39 (3): 99–124.

Yuk, Joowon. 2011. "The Multiculturalism Backlash: European Discourses, Policies and Practices." *Cultural Trends* 20 (3–4): 337–340.

CHAPTER EIGHT

Italian Canadian Media: From Representation to Integration

Daniela Sanzone and Angelo Principe

INTRODUCTION

Historically, Italians in Canada have been quite active in the media context. The earliest record of Italian media is *L'Italo Canadese*, with its first issue published in Montreal on 15 March 1894 (see figure 8.1). The experience of Italian Canadian journalism can be summarized into several stages, which followed the community's progression in survival and integration into their new country while still being involved in Italian politics and affairs. The first stage lasted from 1894 until 1915 (*L'Italo Canadese*), while the second stage began in 1916 with the weekly magazine *L'Italia*, followed in 1923 by *Le Fiamme d'Italia*, an openly fascist journal, until 1940. The third stage was begun in 1941 by the historian Antonino Spada of the Montreal-based *Il Giornale Italo-Canadese,* which evolved into *Il Cittadino Canadese* the following year. *Il Cittadino Canadese* is the oldest newspaper in the Italian language still published as a weekly tabloid. These three stages are connected to as many periods of Italy's political and institutional life: first, Liberal Italy, 1861–1914; second, from the year Italy entered the Great War until the Fascist dictatorship, 1915–1939; and third, from Italy entering World War II in 1940 to the present (Principe 2009).

An important stage could be added, from the 1980s to 2020s, considering the main shift of media attention from politics in the native land to politics and economics in Canada. Through content analysis of thirty-eight Italian Canadian media (see table 8.1), the findings of this study illustrate that Italians have used the press mainly for economic

Table 8.1 | List of Italian media in Canada, 1894 to present

Name	Dates	Region
L'Italo Canadese	1894–1915	Montreal
Corriere del Canada	1896	Montreal
La Tribuna Canadiana	1898–1924	Toronto
Lo Stendardo	1898	Toronto
La Patria Italiana	1903	Montreal
L'Italia	1916–1923	Montreal
Le Fiamme d'Italia	1929	Montreal
Itala Gente	1923	Montreal
L'Araldo	1923	
Risveglio		
Il Giornale ItaloCanadese, later *Il Cittadino Canadese*	1940–Present	Montreal
Il Grido della Stirpe	1929	Montreal
Corriere Italiano	1929	Montreal
Il Bollettino Italo-Canadese	1929–1941	Toronto
L'Italia	1929	
L'Eco Italo-Canadese	1936–1938	Vancouver
L'Emigrato	1931–1932	Toronto
Il Progresso Italo-Canadese	1931–1932	
Il Messaggero Italo-Canadese	1933–1934	Toronto
La Voce Operaia	1933–1935	Toronto
Il Lavoratore	1935–1938	Toronto
La Voce degli Italo-Canadesi	1938–1940	Toronto
La Verità	1948	
Canadian Lakehead Herald	1930s	Fort William, Port Arthur
Corriere Canadese	1953–Present	Toronto
Panorama	1954	
CHIN Radio	1966	Toronto
Channel 47 – CFMT-OMNI TV	1979–Present	Toronto, Montreal, Vancouver
Vice Versa	1982	Online in the 1990s
Lo Specchio	1984–Present	Greater Toronto Area
Telelatino TLN	1984–Present	Greater Toronto Area
Eyetalian	1993	
Il Postino	2000–Present	Ottawa
PanoramItalia	2002–Present	Toronto
Accenti	2003–Present	Montreal
Panorama ItalianCanadian	2004–Present	Greater Toronto Area

development and socio-political representation. It also emerges that at the beginning of the twentieth century, newspapers were created predominantly for advertising products, services, and job offers within the Italian community. Between the two wars and into the 1970s, Italians living in Canada used the press mostly to participate in the Italian political arena overseas. Italian Canadian media supported the polarized political debates inside the community, for example, about fascist and communist activities in Italy. From the 1980s, interviews with Italian Canadian journalists show that the main objective of the Italian diaspora has been to gain socio-political representation and greater economic power in Canada.

Italian Canadians are, in the 2020s, integrated socially, politically, and economically in Canadian society. Italian Canadians historically have been deeply involved with ethnic media, which may have contributed to the inclusion of this ethnic group. However, following the most recent changes in immigration and technologies in the global society, the existing ethnic media structure may not be the right tool to support the integration anymore, and ethnic media may be reconsidered. "Ethnic" journalists may find a new role, more integrated in the mainstream Canadian fabric, including the journalism society, for a better, less stereotyped, and more inclusive representation of all communities.

LITERATURE REVIEW

Yu and Matsaganis (2019) underline that "[p]ositive minority journalism has historically been an important function of ethnic media." However, they add that many ethnic media producers "have to struggle with a tension between performing as advocates for their audiences, as well as conforming to the standard of objectivity of mainstream journalism" (185). While recognizing that the ethnic media sector is undergoing the same tremendous changes as the mainstream media industry, Yu and Matsaganis point out that "ethnic media will continue to play an important role within ethnic communities, both established and emerging" (183). They also emphasize that ethnic media are often considered "to offer second-class journalism, attributed mainly to the lack of sociocultural and financial resources. Therefore, ethnic media news content is treated "as a kind of journalism that has its own league rather than journalism for all" (Husband 2005; Matsaganis and Katz 2014; Yu 2017; Yu and Matsaganis 2019, 185).

Anno I NUMERO PROGRAMMA 2 CTS. MONTREAL, 15 MARZO 1894

L'ITALO CANADESE

ESCE OGNI SABATO

PRIMO, ED UNICO GIORNALE PER GL'INTERESSI ITALIANI NEL CANADA

PIETRO CATELLI, Proprietario. (PATRIA E RELIGIONE.) UFFICIO PROVVISORIO 40 JACQUES-CARTIER

ABBONAMENTO:

Un Anno - - - -	$2.00
Sei Mesi - - - -	1.25
Tre Mesi - - - -	75

Pagamento anticipato.

AVVISI:

Prima inserzione, la linea, 10c. Seguenti 5c

L'Italo Canadese est l'unique journal italien imprimé en Canada, et représente les intérêts de plus de dix milles Italiens.

En conséquence est le meilleur agent d'annonces.

Avis aux annonceurs.

The Italo Canadese is the only Italian journal printed in Canada. It represents the interests of more than ten thousand Italians and is the best advertising medium.

PARVA FAVILLA

Orgogliosi e felici del successo col quale fu accolto il nostro programma e per soddisfare le replicate richieste di avvisi ed abbonamenti che ci pervennero non solo da Montreal, ma da tutte le città Canadesi, ove risiede emigrazione italiana, noi pubblichiamo oggi il primo numero-saggio dell' Italo Canadese.

Se è *parva favilla* grande siamo sicuri sarà l'incendio; se il giornale oggi comincia, con sole quattro pagini, fra pochi mesi, confidiamo di raddoppiarle; perchè non vi sarà italiano che rifiuterà d'ajutare l'impresa patriottica, disinteressata che abbiamo intrapreso.

L'Italo Canadese si presenta con una tiratura da uguagliare molti periodici settimanali inglesi e francesi e offre vantaggi seriamente commerciali a tutti coloro che avranno l'avviso nelle sue colonne, estendendo i suoi abbonati e lettori negli Stati Uniti e in Italia.

La più grande varietà d'articoli *Coloniali*, *Sociali*, *Politici*, non che una nutrita *Cronaca* dalle principale città Canadesi e dall' Italia, renderanno, speriamo, il giornale utile ad ogni classe di cittadini.

Il nostro romanzo:

"*La via dell' Abisso*" di grande attualità, di alto e commovente interesse, vede la prima volta la luce nelle colonne dei giornali.

Unendo all' utile il dilettevole non mancheranno nell' *Italo Canadese. Sciarade, Rebus* a premio.

E da ultimo riserviamo ai nostri gentili abbonati prima della fine del 1894 un "*Grande premio sorpresa*".

Confidando adunque nel patriottismo degli' Italiani, nella generosità di quanti amano gl' italiani, l'Italo Canadese comincerà le sue publicazioni settimanali il 1o Aprile p. v.

P. Catelli

PARLIAMOCI CHIARO

Nati per un solo scopo, soldati sotto una sola bandiera colla lealtà, colla franchezza della coscienza onesta, noi ci presentiamo oggi ai lettori. Parliamoci dunque chiaro col cuore sulle labbra, colle mani nelle mani.

Il nostro scopo è la prosperità, la pace, l'unione delle colonie canadesi; sulla nostra bandiera sta scritto: rispetto, amore alla patria e alla religione in cui siamo nati.

E'inutile dunque che attorno a noi i rospi velenosi vomitino bava, e inutile che ci gridino voi siete di un tale o di un tale altro partito. Fango, parliamoci chiaro, una volta per sempre, non ne raccoglieremo. Alle calunnie alle insinuozioni degli invidiosi noi, risponderemo sempre con i fatti. Il giornale non è soltanto un foglio di carta stampata su cui pochi possono esprimere le proprie idee: dietro a questo foglio di carta vi è una legione di amici fedeli, influenti s mpie pronti a fare il bene per il bene e anche il bene per il male.

Temprati alla lotta della vita civile, non indietreggieremo tanto facilmente il giorno del combattimento. Questo modesto periodico apre le sue colonne a coloro che soffrono, a coloro che sperano. Esso sarà l'avvocato difensore dei nostri interessi, il padre affezzionato che non negherà mai un aiuto, un consiglio, il fratello amoroso che piangerà dei vostri dolori, gioirà dei vostri successi

Agli amici non domandiamo che la continuazione della calda simpatia che oggi ci addita la via faticosa da percorrere, agli indifferenti la fede nel nostro avvenire; ai nemici... Ma ne abbiamo noi dei nemici?

No— perchè chi è italiano di mente e di cuore, chi non ha negato la madre che lo ho allattato; la chiesa che lo ho battezzato, non può odiare la missione di pace e di fratellanza che si impone di compiere l'Italo Canadese. No, non abbiamo nemici, perchè chi lo fosse o mostrerebbe di seguire abbietti sentimenti personali, o negherebbe di essere italiano.

Ed è perciò che con la sicurezza di serbarsi giusti con tutti, veri con tutti, imparziali con tutti, l'Italo Canadese sipresenta a voi, o fratelli italiani, e stringendovi in un grande amplesso di pace, intuona col poeta il canto:

"Siam tutti fratelli
Dall' alpi al Libeo."

IN GIRO PER IL MONDO

A New York c'è una classe di giovani che è conosciuta sotto il nome di Veneri assassine.

Nelle tane di Bowery e di Chatham esse accalappiano i merli, li spogliano di ogni loro avère e, dato il caso, li accoppano anche come tanti agnelli.

Esse, le Veneri assassine, popolano taverne ove si beve birra cattiva, si ascolta pessima musica e si ha la compagnia disgustosa della più lurida gentaglia della città e dei sobborghi.

Sere sono un italiano, certo Franci, uscito di casa con 500 dollari in tasca, fu visto entrare in una di quelle taverne, forse per bere un sorso di birra, poichè era onesto, tranquillo, morigerato. Le Veneri assassine lo ubbriacarono, lo derubarono e, forse, lo ammazzarono, poichè egli non fu più visto uscire.

***

A proposito di bestie.

La più grande macelleria del mondo è quella del signor Swift di Chicago.

Nel 1885 nella macelleria del signor Swift si sono ammazzati 429 483 buoi, quasi un mezzo milione.

Il signor Swift è un *yankee* magro e secco, ha 47 anni.

Nel 1876 aveva una piccola bottega, dove vendevasi la carne al dettaglio. A Chicago incominciò a trattare grossi affari per forniture degli Stati vicini.

Ora uccide circa 14000 capi di bestiame al giorno. I la 1500 impiegati sotto la direzione di un gerente pagato 45 mila lire all'anno.

Cosa curiosissima: un sol macellaio basta per l'uccisione dei 1400 buoi, coll'aiuto di un enormo martello meccanico che li colpisce sul cranio.

***

Un prete greco, di Temesvar, desiderando prender moglie, per fare più in fretta fece inserire il seguente annunzio sui giornali:

"Un giovane parroco greco, di 28 anni, con 2000 fiorini di stipendio, desidera sposare una signorina benestante d'anni 30. Rivolgersi ecc."

Sciarada

Dagli ebrei fu il *primier* venerato,
All'amante il *final* non è grato,
Se sei scaltro, il *total* t'è svelato.

La più elegante edizione del "Guerrier meschino" sarà estratta a sorte fra i spiggatori della precedente Sciarada.

BENVENUTO (1)

Se io non dovessi scrivere nella lingua di Tasso e di Dante sarei stato incapace di sciogliere un lungo canto per dare il benvenuto ed a ugurare lunga e prospera vita al primo giornale italiano che nasce nel n ostro paese. La lingua italiana è una musica ed io che amo la musica alla follia mi sono innamorato di cosi bella lingua, come l'allievo si entusiasma per il virtuoso. Questi italiani me l'avevano sempre dipinti intrattabili, di difficile conversare. Eppure ogni volta che io ebbi dei rapporti con i figli della superba Italia non incontrai in loro che delicatezza, cortesia ed affabilità. Fu nel luglio del 1890 che comprai la prima grammatica italiana. Villeggiovo in campagna ed ero venuto in città per affari. Traversando la strada S. Giacomo fui fermato da un individuo che mi dimandò gentilmento in italiano. Signore conoscete voi dove sta la posta? questa parola, posta, mi fece indovinare cio che egli desiderava e accennai colla mano l'edificio in questione. Prima di ritornare alla campagna passai alla libreria Beauchemin e comprai una grammatica italiana. Ed oggi prendo un vero piacere a leggere i capolavori di cui è cosi ricca questa lingua.

Benvenuto dunque all' Italo Canadese e possa avere fra gli stessi Canadesi tanti assidui lettori per arrivare al patriottico scopo che si propone.

Germain Beaulieu.

THE BELT LINE R. R.

The Belt Line R. R. Cy è la compagnia, che tra poco si accingerà alla costruzione della Ferrovia, che circonderà tutta l'Isola di Montreal con un tracciato di 75 miglia. Il consiglio Direttivo è composto di tutti uomini, i quali per la loro posizione finanziaria e sociale garantiscono la riuscita. Siamo lieti poter notare tra essi il nostro amico C. H. Catelli, la cui reputazione—fatta di operosità, di integrità ed intelligenza—è abbastanza conosciuta. Sia pei vantaggi che questa novella intrapresa arrecherà agli interessi del pubblico, sia per l'importanza del pro-

(1) E' con vero piacere che pubblichiamo questo articolo di un giovine e noto scrittore canadese che conosce a perfezione la nostra lingua e che è animato da sintimenti di alta simpatia per noi

Figure 8.1 | Copy of *L'Italo Canadese* published in Montreal on 15 March 1894. This weekly was published every Saturday and offered six pages in tabloid format. It was mostly composed of business advertising and services for Italian Canadians. The first issue contained forty-four advertisements, thirteen of which were for Italian businesses.

As Karim (1998) outlines, ethnic media have helped members of minorities integrate into the larger society, and at the same time have contributed to ethnic cohesion and cultural maintenance. In some cases, Karim states, aside from making the "host society" less fearsome and more suitable to many, ethnic media have also facilitated a better self-understanding of the new homeland. Raboy (1990) argues that in Canada, while the state supports multicultural and multiracial services, "minority group media" have played a significant role in "defining just what it means to be Canadian." By their efforts "for recognition of their interests against the dominance of a one-dimensional Canada ... they have maintained the Canadian difference against the overwhelming forces of continental integration in North America" (8). However, this significant contribution was never officially acknowledged, and, although Canada has been the first country to give official status to a minority group – the French – it then disregarded the broader diversity of its people (Karim 2002). In the context of governmental regulation, Yu (2016) finds that the Canadian Ethnic Broadcasting Policy gives minorities the ability to speak to their own communities, but not to other ethnic communities or the majority communities. This leads to a one-way form of communication, where minority viewers have access to majority news, but not vice versa.

The supporting role of ethnic media for integration has been stated on the homepage of the National Ethnic Press and Media Council of Canada, which began exercising its influence in the late 1990s. However, being rarely able to contribute to the integration of their community, or to form a critical mass to influence the political agenda in their new country, has been a common critique of most ethnic media publications (Viswanath and Arora 2000; Browne 2005; Murray, Yu, and Ahadi 2007; Siapera 2010; Lindgren 2011, 2013). Lindgren, with Murray, Yu, and Ahadi (2007), argues that more content analysis of ethnic media production is needed to verify whether they really help integration and understanding of the new country. She emphasizes that the message produced by ethnic media in North America frequently reflects stereotypical identities, rather than the diversity intrinsic of each community. Moreover, ethnic media are rarely able to function as alternative media; to the contrary, they often corroborate the dominant ideology about immigration. With Kymlicka (2008) and Mahtani (2008), Lindgren asks for a better understanding of the news media structures in ethnic communities and the role they play in the integration process for newcomers (2013).

The literature is ambivalent on the general level of support that ethnic media brings to the social integration of their community into mainstream Canadian life. This historical review finds that Italian Canadian media have served early and twentieth century immigrants with basic but significant support to an easier life in Canada.

ITALIANS IN CANADA

Between 1876 and 1976, more than 26 million Italians left their country, temporarily or permanently (Iacovetta 1992). Although Italians arrived in Canada much earlier (Woodsworth 1909, 131; Richard 1992, 59), it was only after 1951 that Canada became a popular destination for mass immigration: "Between 1946 and 1976, more than four hundred forty thousand Italians arrived in Canada, of whom a majority settled in the three major cities of Toronto, Montreal, and Vancouver" (Iacovetta 1991, 51). The reasons can be related to the fact that immediate postwar immigration was primarily linked to men who came to Canada from Italy looking for work. In the following years, however, more than 90 per cent of the immigrants came as part of a family sponsorship program (Iacovetta 1991). Prior to 1991, Italians were the largest share of immigrants to Canada, and up to 2011, in the Greater Toronto Area (GTA), the Italian language represented the most common spoken mother tongue (Statistics Canada 2012). As of the 2016 Census (Statistics Canada 2016a, b), almost 1.6 million Canadian residents stated they had Italian ancestry. Since the first important wave of immigration, at the beginning of the twentieth century, newcomers from Italy came together in subgroups based on regional dialects, creating colonies, associations, patron saints' celebrations, and parishes for every city or village of their country of origin (Ramirez 1989, 9). Historically, and to some extent in modern times, Italy has been characterized by its diversified land, where cities and towns have spoken distinct dialects that enhanced their unique literature, cuisine, and culture. Italians reconstructed this fragmentation throughout most of Canada (DeMaria Harney 1998), although in Toronto they also identify as "an Italian community" (Zucchi 1988, 5). Indeed, although Italians perceived their geographical representation as important and often spoke only their regional dialect, this factor does not seem to have impacted the media production, which was always written and spoken in standard Italian, at least in the intentions.

METHODOLOGY

This work is based on Principe's past research and Sanzone's recent research and interviews, as well as Sanzone's experience as a professional ethnic media journalist in Toronto. Her work connected her with the local ethnic and mainstream journalism communities in Toronto and Ontario between 2001 and 2012. Over more than sixty years, Principe has assembled an archive of original copies of Italian Canadian media, which he donated to York University in 2018. This unique collection is the invaluable source for an historical account: over fifty Italian Canadian publications, which were issued over two centuries in various formats including bulletins, daily newspapers, illustrated magazines, and political and cultural periodicals, have been published in Toronto, Ottawa, Montreal, Winnipeg, and Vancouver (see table 8.1). The findings derive from content analysis of thirty-six publications, which include original newspapers obtained from personal collections, online archives, and websites, as well as from Italian, Canadian, and American public libraries and the Canadian National Archives. Although certain other newspapers have been referenced in studies and by other media outlets, they have not been found. The content analysis of the collected Italian Canadian publications has been related to the major historical events in Italy and Canada that form the background of much publishing to explore the motivations and objectives that directed the evolution of the Italian media in Canada. In addition to reviewing the news content, the study analyzed interviews and numerous personal conversations with journalists and members of the Italian community in both Canada and the US.[1] In particular, fifteen interviews were conducted between September and December 2019 by Sanzone in the form of semi-structured elicitation surveys of Italian Canadian journalists and producers operating in Toronto between the 1980s and the 2010s. The interviews have received ethics review and approval by the Human Participants Review Sub-Committee, York University's Ethics Review Board, are considered to conform to the standards of the Canadian Tri-Council Research Ethics guidelines, and are strictly anonymous. These in-depth interviews with open-ended questions were carried out in English[2] and the findings are summarized below in the section devoted to the ethnic journalism experience and grouped in narrative common themes. Narrative inquiry helped elicit professional and personal aspects of journalistic practices in Italian Canadian ethnic media, including journalistic values used to deliver representations of the community, and the journalists' views of ethnic media and their role.

MAIN FINDINGS: THE EARLY DAYS

Between the end of the nineteenth and the beginning of the twentieth century, Italian immigration to Canada was not very high. Those who arrived were mostly uneducated and destitute (De Stefani 1914), and many were therefore unable to read or afford newspapers. Despite these conditions, Pietro Catelli started *L'Italo Canadese*, which was in circulation for at least two years (see figure 8.1). *L'Italo Canadese* offered six pages in tabloid format and was primarily composed of business advertising and services for Italian Canadians. The first issue contained forty-four advertisements, thirteen of which were for Italian businesses. Two mentioned an employment agency that Catelli was opening for new immigrants, and one promised free letter-writing services, which suggests a high level of illiteracy at the time. The newspaper also published a note in English and in French: "*L'Italo Canadese* is the unique Italian newspaper published in Canada and it represents the interest of more than ten thousand Italians. Consequently, it is the best publicity agent" (15 March 1894; see figure 8.1). *L'Italo Canadese* was also recognized by the Italian consulate as an important pillar of the community, suggesting a good relationship between the publisher and the Italian diplomats representing the Italian government. On 7 July 1894, the journal printed, "Signor C. Mariotti, the Italian Consul in Montreal, as the gentleman and patriot that he is, neglects nothing to encourage the movement of progress, regeneration and inspiration that, after a few months, is felt in our Colony,"[3] and followed with the consul's congratulations to the editor. In the same issue, *L'Italo Canadese* published an article about socialism and anarchism entitled "The Revolution." It was signed by Saey, the Conservative Catholic editor-publisher of the paper, who wrote: "This troubling monster which frightens Europe has now reached with the name of Socialism and Anarchy such paroxysm, which is the most ardent question of the day. Pious writers and unbelievers, sectarian principles, inexperienced peoples [of Europe] all in competition made this problem unsolvable which is an effect of the intellectual emancipator experiment voted by Emilio Soffi, Agostino Depretis as progress, lowering thrones and altars and upsetting any order in the civil society."[4] In the 14 July 1894 issue, *L'Italo Canadese* published a photograph of the Italian prime minister, the Honorable Crispi, and a long article praising him and his successful political career, confirming its interest in Italian politics.[5]

In Montreal, there were also two competing weeklies, *Corriere del Canada*, founded by L. Nobile in 1896, and *La Patria Italiana*, founded by Bernardino di Francesco in 1903 (Briani 1977). By 1904, two well-known Italian travel agents in Montreal, Antonio Cordasco and Alberto Dini, acquired the two newspapers and used the publications mostly as advertising bulletins for their businesses. In Toronto, the first Italian newspaper was *Lo Stendardo*, published in 1898 (Principe 1999). Years later, in 1924, Henry Corti (whose real name was Enrico Corticelli),[6] owner and editor-in-chief of *La Tribuna Canadiana*, wrote that his weekly publication had been published for sixteen years, and claimed that over that period, various other new publications did not survive for long. Little is found about the "various publications" mentioned by Corti. Even *La Tribuna Canadiana* was not regularly published, other than during the municipal, provincial, and federal elections, since it was financed by the Conservative Party of Canada (Principe 2009). After the elections, it was published "when possible,"[7] which suggests it had mainly political objectives in Canada. However, having connections within the Conservative Party, Corti used the newspaper to support those Italians who wanted to bring their family members to Canada, and he was well remunerated for these services.[8] For *La Tribuna Canadiana*, Principe located two issues, dated 31 August 1918 and 11 November 1924.[9] The November issue commemorated the Italian victory in the Great War; its twenty pages include news, photographs, and information regarding the two "tag days" held in Toronto in 1917 and 1918 to collect money for the Italian Red Cross. This issue is also a source of information about Toronto's Italians because it lists those involved in some commercial, industrial, artistic, or professional activities, with short notes about their respective activities. Italian Canadian media, at the beginning of the twentieth century, continued to devote large proportions of content to major contemporary European issues directly affecting Italy, in particular, the political struggle between fascists, communists, royalists, and other Italian and European movements.

In the 1920s, Italians in Canada produced a substantial number of publications. Until 1923, the four Italian-language newspapers – in Montreal, the weeklies *L'Araldo* and *L'Italia* and the monthly *Itala Gente*, and in Toronto, *La Tribuna Canadiana*[10] – all supported the "Patrio" (patriotic) government, regardless of which party or person was in power. In fact, they were in favour of fascist politicians, even of Mussolini, who was not yet the leader of the Fascist Party but the prime minister appointed by the king. Some Italians who defined themselves as fascists in Canada were dissatisfied with what they considered the "lukewarm" way the Italian Canadian press treated fascism and Mussolini (Principe 1999). In 1929, there were *Le Fiamme d'Italia*, *Il Grido della Stirpe*, *L'Italia*, and *Corriere Italiano* among others (Flames of Italy, The cry of the ancestry, Italy, and Italian courier) (Principe 2003).

The Italian debate against fascist racial policy was going on in other parts of Canada as well. In Montreal, the creation of the first Fascist Club provoked one of several breakups of immigrant associations and news media. In reaction, some newspapers during this period were collocated on opposite sides of the political spectrum, such as *L'Araldo* and *Il Risveglio*, with the latter mentioned by Spada (1969) in his book, although no copies have been found.[11] In Toronto, anti-fascists produced five newspapers of various socially oriented values: the Catholic *L'Emigrato*, the conservative *Il Messaggero Italo-Canadese*, the socialist *La Voce Operaia*, the communist *Il Lavoratore*, and *La Voce degli Italo-Canadesi*. The industrial and agricultural workers of Fort William and Port Arthur, Ontario, published the rather singular *Canadian Lakehead Herald* in three languages: English, Ukrainian, and Italian (Principe 1982). The first issue of the anti-fascist weekly *L'Emigrato* appeared on 30 December 1931 in Toronto and ended its publication in the summer of 1932, at the same time as *Il Progresso Italo-Canadese*. The struggle against fascism in Canada was taken over in 1933 by *Il Messaggero Italo-Canadese* (Principe 1999).

The first issue of *Il Bollettino Italo-Canadese*, which was "welcomed by many people in the community," was published in Toronto on 20 September 1929, not long after the Lateran Treaty with the Vatican. Its first editorial, entitled "Il Giornale di Tutti," reads: "*Il*

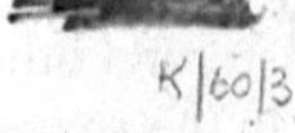

K|60|3

LA VOCE OPERAIA

PERIODICO ANTIFASCISTA

- 3 Cent. La Copia -

Anno 1° No. 9. TORONTO, SABATO, 18 NOVEMBRE 1933. 251 Campbell Ave

CONTRO LA GUERRA, CONTRO IL FASCISMO

Il veterano delle unioni Inglesi TOM MANN delegato alla Convenzione Internazionale contro la guerra a New York, parla applauditissimo a 3,500 persone alla Massey Hall.

Toronto 11 Nov. Alla Massey Hall ha avuto luogo un comizio contro la guerra e contro il fascismo, sotto gli auspici della C. L. D. L.

Finiti i brevi discorsi degli oratori locali Anna Buller dopo d'aver fatto appello per una colletta volontaria che frutto' 313 dollari e 80 cent., presenta l'oratore principale della serata Tom Mann un veterano del movimento radicale inglese di 77 anni ma ancora vispo pieno di coraggio e di entusiasmo.

La sala era gremita al punto che [illegible] a casa perche' non c'erano piu' posti. I Presenti come un sol uomo si alzano tutti in piedi e dopo parecchi minuti di applausi spontanei e fragorosi, intonano l'Internazionale.

Nel discorso di circa un'ora e mezza, il vecchio lottatore ha denunziato tutte le forme di repressione a cui il proletariato internazionale e' soggetto, ha illustrato in modo inequivocabile come gli interessi della classe capitalista conducono inesorabilmente alla guerra, che per essere combattuta con spreco di vite umane e di ricchezze, dal proletariato che dalla guerra non ha nulla da guadagnare ma tutto da perdere, ha esortato i lavoratori ad organizzarsi politicamente, ed a combattere il pericolo di una nuova guerra.

Per la pace [illegible] il fascismo, strumento della reazione capitalista.

Terminati i [illegible] applausi che han salutato la fine del discorso Anna Buller domanda insistentemente che, in ottemperanza alle regole dei proprietari della sala, si cantasse "God save the King" gli astanti hanno intonato l'Internazionale. Il comizio si e' sciolto alle ore 11.30

Italiani, prendete atto!

Quando gli antifascisti hanno detto che i consolati fascisti all'estero sono [illegible] agenzie di spionaggio e di propaganda fascista, molti hanno detto che si esagerava. Ebbene quelli Italiani che ancora non credevano a cio' ora sono serviti.

Nella recente visita a Toronto del Console Generale fascista in Ottawa, in un discorso, fra l'altro ha detto: "Io e il cav. Ambrosi mio collega, siamo, prima di tutto dei consoli fascisti. Non ammettiamo transazioni con la nostra coscienza fascista, non scendiamo a compromessi con coloro [illegible] restato nel campo contrario .... non e' umanamente possibile ammettere che esistano degli italiani avversari del regime in buona fede. Se essi esistono, e se persistono nell'errore, bisogna dire che siano schiavi dell'ignoranza, e vanno inquadrati fra i nemici della patria.

A buon intenditor ....

Non vi e' via di mezzo; o si e' schiavi dell'ignoranza o si e' nemici della Patria.

Solo i fascisti sono intelligenti e patrioti. Non e' la prima volta che sentiamo dire queste bestialita' dai fascisti. Ne hanno detto delle peggiori. Vogliamo solo richiamare l'attenzione di quegli italiani che ancora non sono diventati delle pecore e dei servi, di rivendicare all'antifascismo l'onore di essere ancora nella trincea opposta, prima di tutto, in nome dello spirito umano calpestato dal fascismo, in nome della liberta' di pensiero e di azione sociale soffocata, in nome di tutte le vittime della barbarie fascista, in nome di un grande popolo ridotto alla piu' degradante abbiezione morale e materiale, perche' la fame in Italia non batte solo al tugurio operaio, ma ha invaso anche il ceto medio, e professionale, e non sono rari i casi di suicidi e di ladrocini di pane e sacchi di patate da parte di professionisti.

Noi siamo i difensori del popolo italiano oppresso dal fascismo che nessuna agenzia fascista potra' ingannare con le storielle e le frottole. La verita' e' che il fascismo ha fatto dell'Italia un cimitero vivente sotto tutti i rapporti, e solo la plutocrazia e i gerarchi hanno risolto il *loro* problema. Ma come tutte le cose, anche la menzogna e la scelleratezza hanno un limite, e se a questo non siamo ancora arrivati, ci si arrivera' certamente. Cosi' scomparira' la tirannia con i suoi [illegible].

Italiani prendetene atto.

Il fascismo vi vuole tutti asserviti al suo carro sottomessi. Non vuole che siate degli uomini pensanti, ma del gregge da comandare e da sfruttare.

Coloro che ancora credevano essere possibile per amor patrio una qualsiasi convivenza con coloro che abusivamente rappresentano l'Italia, sono finalmente disillusi.

"La patria non si nega ma si conquista", vi gridano per solleticarvi nel vostro intimo attaccamento alla terra che vi diede i natali. Ed e' vero. Essi l'hanno conquistata la patria, se l'hanno tolta e l'hanno messa a disposizione dei forcaioli come gli Agnelli, i Perroni, i Pirelli ecc. che coi gerarchi ne hanno fatto scempio.

La patria e' un'astrazione. Al disopra di questo mito vi e' il popolo che ogni uomo onesto e libero e' chiamato ad esaltare e difendere. Non vi e' altra via: o di qua' o di la della trincea.

Nemici d'Italia noi? Mai.
Antifascisti? Sempre.

ZETA

Lo sciopero dei sarti

Toronto, 16 Nov.

I sarti impegnati nello sciopero con la Ontario Boy's Wear da oltre due settimane, malgrado la polizia abbia istituito un sistema "per mantenere l'ordine" che non e' affatto imparziale, ma in aperta simpatia con i padroni, (per parte nostra, nessuna meraviglia) lo spirito, la determinazione di lotta fino alla vittoria e' negli operai piu' vivo che mai.

Tutte le mattine alle ore 6.30 gli operai quasi al completo sono invariabilmente a picchettare fuori della fabbrica per indurre qualche crumiro ad abbandonare il lavoro.

Verso le 9 ant. si recano alla sede dell'organizzazione A. C. W. of A. 248 Spadina Ave. dove o[illegible] della stessa, trovano di che far colazione e riscaldarsi con una buona tazza di caffe' quindi hanno le loro riunioni affollate, animate, incoraggiate dalla solidarieta' degli operai organizzati nell'Amalgamated.

Infatti, oltre ad essere aiutati nel picchettare la fabbrica, oltre al vitto per la giornata, servito nei locali dell'Amalgamated, gli scioperanti ricevono un sussidio settimanale di 4 dollari per i celibi e di 6 dollari per i coniugati.

Durante queste due settimane si e' avuto 10 arresti, alcuni perche' ingombravano il "traffico" dei crumiri, si capisce, due ragazze perche' non potendo parlare in

(continua in 6 pagina)

Figure 8.2 | Copy of *La Voce Operaia*, 18 November 1933.

Bollettino Italo-Canadese has no links with political parties, associations or groups of people: it is for the Italians, or better, for the emigrants. We seize every opportunity to assert our 'Italianness' (Italianità) in this foreign land but it is our resolution to cooperate with local authorities in order that our countrymen know the laws governing this country. And that people of other nationalities will firmly understand that Italians have been, are, and will always be bearers of civilization, wherever they settle."[12]

In the 1930s, though, *Il Bollettino Italo-Canadese* switched to pro–Italian government fascist content (Principe 1999). Such issues were not nearly as present in Canadian media at the time. However, the *Toronto Daily Star* editorial of 26 September 1938 mentions local Italian propaganda, quoting the Italian writer Ignazio Silone's book *Fontamara* in its article "Who They Are" referring to fascists as "men in black shirts. They had come at night; otherwise they couldn't have the pluck. Most of them stank of wine ... They were of the type who does not like hard work."[13]

The socialist biweekly *La Voce Operaia* (1933–1935) was in circulation for months when *Il Messaggero Italo-Canadese* ended its publication (Principe 2009; see figure 8.2).[14] The first issue of *La Voce Operaia* appeared in July 1933. The editors were militant workers, all members of the "Circolo Mazzini" which was open to all anti-fascists including communists. Their weekly *La Voce Operaia* attacked fascism publishing news and presented facts about Italy that otherwise would never be known by Italian Canadians. *La Voce Operaia* came to an end when the communist group withdrew its participation. The communist group's decision to end their support was a result of the Communist Party of Canada's (CPC) choice to publish its own Italian newspaper, the biweekly *Il Lavoratore*, which began in 1935 and ceased publication three years later.[15] After this experience, leaving aside the communists, Italian anti-fascists found their longed for unity and published *La Voce degli Italo-Canadesi.* The leaflet, introducing the new weekly, was signed by several well-known Italian Canadians, among them, Dr Agrò of Hamilton, Spada and Vigilante of Montreal, and Di Giulio and Palermo of Toronto. The editors of *La Voce degli Italo-Canadesi* made clear the Italian Canadian democratic identity of the newspaper, pointing out that *La Voce* followed Garibaldi's and Mazzini's tradition of the *Risorgimento* and the ideals of William Lyon Mackenzie and Louis J. Papineau, leaders of the Canadian Rebellion of 1837–38.

Interestingly, these references show that Italians may have felt a part of Canadian history, and therefore they are a sign of integration. After 1939, when Hitler and Stalin secretly split Poland among themselves and Germany triggered World War II, the anti-fascist *La Voce degli Italo-Canadesi* ended its publication with the 30 April 1940 issue. In 1940, when Mussolini's Italy entered the war with Hitler's Nazi Germany, more than 600 Italian men, and several women, believed to be involved with fascism were interned in the Kingston Penitentiary. The fascist newspapers closed soon after, although fascists interned at Petawawa continued to create rough, handwritten copies of *Il Bollettino*.[16] As long as the internees believed that Mussolini would win the war, a certain Perilli continued to publish it in the concentration camp. Putting together information heard from the guards and from a small shortwave radio he kept hidden, "writing with a pen, Perilli would put together two or three copies of *Il Bollettino* and internees would read them and pass them along to others."[17]

FROM THE 1950S TO THE 1970S

There was less Italian Canadian publishing during and after World War II. One exception has been the publication of *La Verità*, a self-defined anti-communist weekly, which started in 1948 (Canadian Citizenship Branch 1949, 19). In 1953, *Corriere Canadese*, still published today, was established in Toronto by the twenty-year-old Daniel (Dan) Andrew Iannuzzi, Jr. Iannuzzi created Daisons Publications Ltd, with five weeklies published over time: *Corriere Canadese*, *Corriere Sportivo*, *Corriere del Quebec*, *Corriere del Niagara*, and *Teledomenica*.[18] Iannuzzi was also the founder of the Ethnic Press Association of Ontario. In 1990, *Corriere Canadese* became a daily, publishing from Monday to Friday. In 1954, about a year after the first publication of *Corriere Canadese*, Luigi Petrucci began the weekly *Panorama*. Both weeklies defined themselves as independent, anti-communist, and supporters of Democrazia Cristiana (at the time, the centre Christian Democratic Party of Italy). In the Canadian context and in those years, however, while *Corriere Canadese* supported the Conservative Party, *Panorama* was for the Liberal Party. Italian newspapers historically have been affiliated to political parties or specific political ideologies, and therefore connected to a "Polarized Pluralist Model ... characterized by a high level of politicization" (Hallin and Mancini 2004, 298). In Canada, for decades, there has been no difference. *Corriere Canadese* reached the less objective political point when, in 1960, during the Italian government led by Prime Minister Tambroni, the Italian Police fired during a demonstration, killing eleven people and wounding several hundreds. As a consequence of that tragedy, Tambroni was forced to resign but, according to *Corriere Canadese*, he "had made a real service to democracy" (30 July 1960). However, in the 1970s, *Corriere Canadese* took the lead in some initiatives that positively impacted the Italians in Canada. Two initiatives of a particular interest in this context are: (1) the campaign to abolish the "Vocational Schools" and (2) the support given to the movement to introduce classes of Italian language in secondary schools, in the public, and Catholic boards. Vocational schools were created as a means to familiarize teenagers with the workforce. These schools became, however, places steering Canadians of Italian origin into manual work, discouraging access to higher education. Italian activists, with the support of *Corriere Canadese*, made the community aware of these issues and together, they stood firmly against this trend. The community resistance induced the school authorities to reform the system (Federation of Italian-Canadian Associations and Clubs 1973).

These above-mentioned examples show how the newspaper shifted its main attention from issues in Italy to issues in Canada. On 11 April 1980, several women called in to talk about domestic violence and abuse by their husbands during Father Pollo's *Parliamone insieme* (Let's talk about it together) program on CHIN Radio. This opened up a window on how Italian Canadian media could be used to highlight issues happening in Canada.

1980S AND ONWARD

By the 1980s, the Italian community had become one of the most numerous and best integrated in Canada. The same general business model, based on community advertising, supported many local ethnic media businesses. The Italian Canadian community fostered Italian-language independent media in print, on the radio, and on airwaves and cable TV, and sponsored large cultural events. In 1999, the federal government officially started regulating ethnic news media, developing a specific regulation, the Ethnic Broadcasting Policy, implemented by the Canadian Radio-television and Telecommunications Commission (CRTC 1999). This was done in the national interest to help newcomers integrate and ensure that national news was available in the languages of the most numerous communities in each province or municipality.

At the beginning of the 1980s, the characteristics of Italian immigration to Canada started to change. While earlier immigration from Italy, like from many countries, mostly comprised blue collar and field workers, including illiterate adults and families, recent immigration now consists mainly of educated single professionals or academic students who are used to travelling and are at least familiar with English (Sanzone 2015). The material life of media publications changed as well. Many news organizations created in the late twentieth century, like CHIN Radio, CFMT-TV (later renamed OMNI Television), Telelatino Network (TLN), and the *Lo Specchio* weekly publication, are still currently active and their material is archived in collections, libraries, and digitally.

In the 1980s and 1990s, Italians were still operating in the Ontario media industry. Emilio Mascia owned TLN, Johnny Lombardi owned CHIN Radio, Iannuzzi owned *Corriere Canadese* and CFMT-TV, and Sergio Tagliavini and Giovanna Tozzi published *Lo Specchio*. Many private conversations and interviews with journalists from the community, collected by Sanzone as a journalist, show that there was an opportunity in these years to create a large Italian media pole which could have consolidated the political and social power of Italians in Ontario and influenced Canadian politics. However, according to the interviews, this opportunity was lost because of the lack of professional figures in the Italian Canadian media world and the rivalry among the broadcasting players. As a result, CFMT-TV was sold to Rogers, a Canadian company, in 1986.[19] In 1992, a group of approximately fifty Italian Canadian journalists formed an organization, the Associazione dei Giornalisti Italo-Canadesi (AGIC), with the objective of promoting initiatives aimed at improving the professional journalistic activity in Ontario. The president of the association, which lasted until the end of the 1990s, was Angelo Persichilli.[20] In the 1990s, Italians produced a smaller number of newspapers, and the media outlets tended to be less political. Starting in those years, Italian Canadian media started to embrace North American journalistic values. Even if two magazines, *Vice Versa* and *Eyetalian*, were involved in the political and cultural debate, their style and level of content were comparable for the first time to respected mainstream Canadian publications, such as *Maclean's*.[21] The trilingual *Vice Versa*, founded in 1982, went online in the 1990s. The quarterly magazine *Eyetalian* was launched in 1993 by Nick Bianchi, Teresa Tiano, and Pino Esposito (Servello 2012). Its name is meant to suggest "self-examination by Italians living within an English milieu" (6). It is aimed at the second and younger generations of Italian Canadians, by reporting on controversial topics in the community, reclaiming the "ethnicist" connotations of the colloquial word "eyetalian" and the challenges of dual cultural identities (Danesi 1994). The magazine encountered commercial difficulty, leaned towards a general lifestyle magazine format, and concluded its publication in 1998. *Il Postino*, published in Ottawa in 2000 by a young group of Italian Canadians in Ottawa, conveyed the history of the Italian community in the capital of Canada. It is still being published online at https://ilpostinocanada.com/.

As the millennium ended, the landscape of news media changed internationally, impacted by the web and new technologies, and new corporate business models in the media. In Canada, media and broadcasting corporations became the main players in the news economy. Ethnic media became part of local and community news channels and business markets, mandated by the government to be available to everyone in a given broadcasting region. In this context, ethnic news has been recognized as necessary to newcomers as well as all Canadians (Mathani 2008). In 2002, *PanoramItalia* magazine was founded in Montreal by publisher Antonio Zara. It is currently published bimonthly in two different editions, in Montreal and in the GTA, with the objective of unifying Italian Canadians and rekindling their "connection to their Italian heritage, while also presenting the beauty and diversity of Italian culture to all Italophiles."[22] In 2003, Domenic Cusmano and Licia Canton founded *Accenti*, which today has an online-only format. In 2004, Enzo Di Mauro and Roberto Bandiera started the magazine *Panorama ItalianCanadian*, distributed in the GTA and in digital format until 2020.

THE ETHNIC JOURNALISM EXPERIENCE

The stories assembled from the comments of the Italian Canadian journalists interviewed by Sanzone are grouped here in several narrative themes that give voice to their experiences using the everyday language of their professional activities and community interactions. These journalists worked in Italian Canadian ethnic media, print, radio, and TV, between the 1980s and the 2010s.

A common theme is the desire that journalism produced by ethnic media and journalists becomes much more widely accessible to all Canadians, since Canada has become a diverse society and citizens should know each other better in order to better live together. However, these stories point out that the quality of current ethnic representations in both ethnic and mainstream news media has improved but remains a work in progress because of the lack of funding and the low regard for ethnic journalism. Despite the changes in the media world, these narratives suggest that ethnic media are stereotypically perceived as less prestigious or professional than journalism practiced in the mainstream media organizations. Therefore, their level of content is not expected or required to be comparable to the mainstream one.

These narratives also suggest several barriers to a diversity of journalistic styles and voices in the ethnic communities. First, there is the critique that ethnic journalism cannot be entirely separated from advocacy (Husband 2005; Yu and Matsaganis 2019). However, these professionals work and expect to be perceived as journalists, not just advocates of their communities. A second barrier stems from the monolingualism of mainstream news journalists. The business model suggested by federal policy requires ethnic television channels to schedule at least 60 per cent ethnic programming each month (each week for radio). In particular, the CRTC regulates that 50 per cent of all programming broadcast by ethnic stations be third-language programming – that is, any languages other than English and French – or in Indigenous languages to reflect Canada's linguistic diversity (CRTC 1999).

According to the narratives, broadcasting news in third languages prevents the possibility that ethnic voices are heard by other ethnic communities, including the mainstream. Another theme recalls the challenges of immigration and the ensuing social diversity, pointing to both the divisions within ethnic communities, as well as the similarities across ethnic groups. The assembled stories show that ethnic journalists feel equipped to bring a lot of value to the journalistic profession. Most of them believe their lived experience includes being cultural translators or interpreters across and between diverse communities, living next to and within each other, and this bridging work could facilitate a richer and more realistic view of both national and world affairs. Ethnic journalists ensure that they can help connect newsrooms around the world and reduce the impact of fake news and mass events on social media. They also aim to improve representation and reduce bias, and, as quoted by one interviewee: "Help understand the complexity of a society that is not homogeneous." By their focus on local news, ethnic journalists articulate a more nuanced point of view on diversity in many settings that can be, as another interviewee pointed out, "an effective tool for ensuring there are strategies in place to understand diversity." The collected stories suggest that mainstream journalism in Toronto could benefit from more intercultural understanding through international journalistic perspectives. Another Italian Canadian journalist recommended that "ethnic journalism and mainstream journalism should integrate their universes and work together for a better comprehension of the complexity of reality."

Finally, another narrative theme points to the changes, over decades, of the business models common in journalism. As the Italian community became more affluent and integrated in the Canadian economy, between the 1980s and the 1990s, Italian media businesses flourished, with several newspapers, radio, and TV stations that were run by, and employed, ethnic journalists and staff. As the whole media industry became more corporate in the 2000s, Italian Canadian journalists believed their trade followed mainstream journalism, becoming mostly, if not only, "a vehicle for advertising, an empty shell," as another interviewee said. In fact, the assembled narratives from the interviews of Italian Canadian journalists tell that they view positively the role of their media for fair representation and social integration. At the same time, they saw their ethnic peers working in a journalistic market that intersects only rarely with the mainstream North American journalism community and feel that the value of their Italian Canadian journalistic perspective is still not fully supported, recognized, or integrated in Canadian journalism. The collected narratives suggest that in the corporate era, ethnic media budgets allowed for much less production value and virtually no interaction with the mainstream news media industry.

DISCUSSION AND CONCLUSION

In the twenty-first century, a multiplicity of ethnic communities is a normal part of Canadian life, where different cultures coexist, interact, and blend. This review of Italian ethnic media suggests that historically, it helped Italians integrate into Canada. However, since the beginning of the new millennium, Italian Canadian media face the same hardships as mainstream media in trying to compete with digital and social media, building the trust of their audiences, and finding consumers among the new generations living in more integrated and diverse cultural communities. Immigration profiles and global economic relations are changing the demographics of immigration. In particular, the most recent waves of Italian immigration in Canada, along the lines of the general immigration trends in Canada, are more educated, familiar with English and North American culture and business communities, and more interested in global affairs. Overall, the Canadian population is more diverse than ever, and more connected to the world than it has ever been.

Ethnic media remain important to support newcomer communities in living beside the various ethnic communities in Canada and also play a new role today. Traditionally, Italian Canadian media started and often functioned without professional journalists, and their content was not conceived for the benefit of mainstream Canadian news culture, which, at the same time, was not ready for that kind of integration. Publications were started and supported by the few literate and business-oriented members of the immigrant communities. Topics focused primarily on political affairs happening in Italy and financial profit in Canada. However, the stories assembled from the interviews with professional Italian Canadian journalists show that what is needed today is a fully integrated news journalism reflecting the sensibilities of diverse ethnic communities living in Canada. In this vision, ethnic news reflects the diverse composition of Canadian society, and requires professional journalists who are able to integrate North American reporting values and culture, reflecting historical Canadian standards, with perspectives and approaches common outside North America. In fact, local Canadian ethnic perspectives on Canadian and world news are not reported outside of local ethnic news. The narrative suggests that the current level of diversity in mainstream news perspectives is not conducive to a deeper understanding of local diverse communities as well as global affairs.

In the historical relationship between Italian Canadian media and mainstream media, the ethnic distinctions have become much smaller than in earlier periods. Mainstream media may come to integrate professional journalists that can do more than speak several languages, and do not qualify by simply belonging to an ethnic group. What increasingly matters is articulating the Canadian experience of living in more than one ethnic life, and including mainstream Canadian culture. This lived experience would support the creation of media that are able to tell stories and mediate transparently relevant conversations across cultural differences to all Canadians.

Ethnic journalists can be cultural translators and interpreters across and between diverse communities living next to and within each other. The world is increasingly complex and diverse, and journalists who know more than one culture, not just different languages, can contribute to facilitate a richer and more realistic view of national and world affairs. Being competent to monitor the Canadian circulation of international and digital information, which is indispensable in a globalized world, they can reduce the impact of fake news and explain mass events on social media. They can ask for and provide richer material for public education and intermediate stories across different cultures. They can finally leave behind the "ethnic" label, as it no longer corresponds to a society in which most people belong to several traditional cultures as well as many new ones.

ACKNOWLEDGMENTS

We would like to thank Cătălin Ivan for his great support and editing. Thank you to the Italian Chamber of Commerce for the book *Yesterday, Today and Tomorrow* published by Mansfield Press Inc. on this topic.

NOTES

1 Principe often recorded his conversations dedicated to collecting Italian Canadian media.

2 These interviews are part of work conducted by Sanzone for her ongoing PhD dissertation.

3 "Signor C. Mariotti Console d'Italia a Montreal, da quel gentiluomo e patriota che è, nulla tralascia per presiedere il movimento di progresso, il soffio rigeneratore che spira da pochi mesi nella nostra Colonia."

4 Agostino Depretis (1813–1887) was prime minister of Italy for several mandates.

5 Francesco Crispi (1818–1901) was the first prime minister from Southern Italy, a prominent figure of the Risorgimento, and a monarchist who cultivated friendship with Germany in foreign policy.
6 We do not know why Corticelli used a pseudonym; however, at the time it was quite common for Italians to anglicize their given names to avoid racial prejudice.
7 *La Tribuna Canadiana*, 31 August 1918.
8 Principe obtained this information after speaking to several older Italians during the research for his PhD dissertation (2019).
9 The 31 August 1918 issue of *La Tribuna Canadiana* has survived thanks to Giambattista Grittani, who kept a copy since it contained an article commemorating his "hero" brother, Leonardo, who died fighting in the Great War.
10 McLaren (1973) lists four mastheads for the same magazine: *La Tribuna Canadese*, *La Tribuna del Canada*, *La Tribuna Canadiana*, and *La Tribuna Canadese.*
11 See *Il Cittadino Canadese* (special issue for its fiftieth anniversary), no. 52, 27 October 1993, 25.
12 *Bollettino Italo-Canadese*, 20 September 1929. In Principe (1999, 85–6).
13 See the editorial "Who They Are" in the *Toronto Daily Star*, 26 September 1938.
14 The Italian Section 253 of the Amalgamated Clothing Workers of America, the Italian section of the Independent Labour Party, the Female Circle Anita Garibaldi, and the Italian group of the United Workers of America were collaborating with the Circolo Mazzini for the publication of *La Voce Operaia*. See figure 8.2 for a copy of the publication.
15 *Il Lavoratore* (17 September 1938) published the following announcement: "The Delegates at the Lavoratore Conference of September 4, considering the financial difficulties (which became more and more exacerbated, because of the industrial crisis and the poor organization indispensable for sustaining and developing a workers' journal such as ours) have decided to suspend the publication of *Il Lavoratore.*"
16 Two former internees, Ruggero Bacci and Francesco Frediani, told Principe this in an interview.
17 The quote is part of a long interview Principe had with both Bacci and Frediani, at Frediani's home; the interview is recorded on tape and it is stored in Principe's archive.
18 *Corriere Canadese*, 22 and 29 November 2004, and *Tandem*, 28 November 2004.

19 History of Canadian Broadcasting, https://www.broadcasting-history.ca/listing_and_histories/television/cfmt-dt.
20 Angelo Persichilli, a well-known journalist, worked at CFMT, *Corriere Canadese*, and the *Toronto Star*. In 2011, he became the director of communication in Prime Minister Stephen Harper's office.
21 This emerged from private conversations that Sanzone had with former Italian Canadian journalist Corrado Paina, who worked for CFMT, and is currently the director of the Italian Chamber of Commerce in Toronto.
22 https://www.panoramitalia.com/.

REFERENCES

Briani, Vittorio. 1977. *La Stampa Italiana All'estero Dalle Origini Ai Nostri Giorni*. Roma: Istituto poligrafico dello stato.
Browne, Donald R. 2005. *Ethnic Minorities, Electronic Media and the Public Sphere: A Comparative Approach*. Creskill, NJ: Hampton Press.
Canadian Citizenship Branch, Research Division. 1949. "Italians in Canada." RG 131, file 18885, 11. Secretary of State, PAC, Immigration Branch.
Corriere Canadese. 1960. "Comunisti sono andati per suonare e sono stati suonati" (Communists went to beat and were beaten). 30 July 1960.
CRTC (Canadian Radio-television and Telecommunications Commission). 1999. "Ethnic Broadcasting Policy." Ottawa, ON: CRTC. https://crtc.gc.ca/eng/archive/1999/PB99-117.HTM.
Danesi, Marcel. 1994. "Hurtin' Words." *Eyetalian* (Summer 1994).
De Stefani, Carlo. 1914. *Il Canada e l'emigrazione italiana*. Firenze: Tipografia Ricci.
DeMaria Harney, Nicholas. 1998. *Eh, Paesan! Being Italian in Toronto*, edited by Robert D. Sider. Toronto: University of Toronto Press.
Federation of Italian-Canadian Associations and Clubs. 1973. "Immigrant Children and Vocational Schools." Toronto: Toronto Board of Education, Special Committee on Vocational Schools.
Hallin, Daniel C., and Paolo Mancini. 2004. *Comparing Media Systems: Three Models of Media and Politics*. Cambridge: Cambridge University Press.
Husband, Charles. 2005. "Minority Ethnic Media as Communities of Practice: Professionalism and Identity Politics in Interaction." *Journal of Ethnic and Migration Studies* 31 (3).
Iacovetta, Franca. 1991. "Ordering in Bulk: Canada's Postwar Immigration Policy and the Recruitment of Contract Workers from Italy." *Journal of American Ethnic History* 11 (1): 50–80.
– 1992. *Such Hardworking People: Italian Immigrants in Postwar*

Toronto. Montreal & Kingston: McGill-Queen's University Press.

Karim, Karim H. 1998. "From Ethnic Media to Global Media: Transnational Communication Networks among Diasporic Communities." International Comparative Research Group, Strategic Research and Analysis, Canadian Heritage.

– 2002. "Public Sphere and Public Sphericules: Civic Discourse in Ethnic Media." In *Civic Discourse and Cultural Politics in Canada*, edited by Sherry Devereaux Ferguson and Leslie Regan Shade, 230–42. Westport, CT: Ablex.

Kymlicka, Will. 2008. *The Current State of Multiculturalism in Canada and Research Themes on Canadian Multiculturalism, 2008–2010*. Ottawa, ON: Citizenship and Immigration Canada.

Lindgren, April. 2011. "Front Page Challenge: A Case Study Examining What the Ethnic Media Promises and What It Delivers." CERIS *Working Paper Series* (82): 1–15.

– 2013. "The Diverse City: Can You Read All about It in Ethnic Newspapers?" CERIS *Working Paper Series* (95): 1–22.

McLaren, Duncan. 1973. *Ontario Ethno-Cultural Newspapers, 1935–1972*. Toronto: University of Toronto Press.

Mahtani, Minelle. 2008. "Racializing the Audience: Immigrant Perceptions of Mainstream Canadian English Language TV News." *Canadian Journal of Communication* 33 (4): 639–60.

Matsaganis, Matthew D., and Vikki S. Katz. 2014. "How Ethnic Media Producers Constitute Their Communities of Practice: An Ecological Approach." *Journalism: Theory, Practice and Criticism* 15 (7): 926–44.

Murray, Catherine A., Sherry S. Yu, and Daniel Ahadi. 2007. "Cultural Diversity and Ethnic Media in BC. A Report to the Canadian Heritage Western Regional Office." Centre for Policy Studies on Culture and Communities. Vancouver, BC: Simon Fraser University.

Principe, Angelo. 1982. "The Multicultural Press." *Poliphony, Bulletin of the Multicultural History Society of Ontario* 4 (1): 94–98.

– 1999. *The Darkest Side of the Fascist Years: The Italian-Canadian Press, 1920–1942*. Toronto & Buffalo, New York: Guernica.

– 2003. "I Fasci in Canada." In *II fascismo e gli emigrati: La parabola dei Fasci italiani all'estero (1920–1943)*, edited by Emilio Franzina and Matteo Sanfilippo, 101–13. Rome-Bari: Laterza.

– 2009. "Un Secolo e Più Di Stampa Italo-Canadese: 1894–2000." *Studi Di Emigrazione/Migration Studies* XLVI (175).

– 2019. "Italian-Canadian Newspapers: 1894–2015." Unpublished manuscript.

Raboy, Marc. 1990. *From Cultural Diversity to Social Equality: The Democratic Trials of Canadian Broadcasting*. NHK (Japan Broadcasting Corporation).

Ramirez, Bruno. 1989. *The Italians in Canada*. Ottawa, ON: Canadian Historical Association.

Roth, Lorna. 2005. *Something New in the Air: The Story of First Peoples Television Broadcasting in Canada*. Montreal & Kingston: McGill-Queen's University Press.

Sanzone, Daniela. 2015. "From Mass Immigration to Professional Workers: A Portrait of the Present Italian 'Comunità.'" *Italian Canadiana* 26–29 (1): 31–52.

Servello, Domenico. 2012. "Manage, Negotiate, and Challenge Identities: Young Italian-Canadian Identities from the Eyetalian Perspective." *Quaderni d'italianistica* 33 (1): 83–108.

Siapera, Eugenia. 2010. *Cultural Diversity and Global Media: The Mediation of Difference*. West Sussex: John Wiley & Sons.

Spada, V. Antonino. 1969. *The Italians in Canada*. Canada Ethnica, VI. Ottawa & Montréal: Riviera Printers and Publishers Inc.

Statistics Canada. 2012. "Visual Census – Language, Toronto, 2011 Census." Ottawa, ON: Statistics Canada. http://www12.statcan.gc.ca/census-recensement/2011/dp-pd/vc-rv/index.cfm?Lang=ENG&TOPIC_ID=4&GEOCODE=535.

– 2016a. "2016 Census." Ottawa, ON: Statistics Canada. https://www12.statcan.gc.ca/census-recensement/2016/dp-pd/index-eng.cfm.

– 2016b. "Linguistic Diversity and Multilingualism in Canadian Homes, 2016 Census." Ottawa, ON: Statistics Canada. https://www12.statcan.gc.ca/census-recensement/2016/as-sa/98-200-x/2016010/98-200-x2016010-eng.cfm.

Viswanath, K., and Pamela Arora. 2000. "Ethnic Media in the United States: An Essay on Their Role in Integration, Assimilation, and Social Control." *Mass Communication and Society* 3 (1): 39–56.

Yu, Sherry S. 2016. "Ethnic Media Moving Beyond Boundaries." In *The Routledge Companion to Media and Race*, edited by Christopher P. Campbell, 160–72. New York: Routledge.

– 2017. "Ethnic Media as Communities of Practice: The Cultural and Institutional Identities." *Journalism* 18 (10): 1309–26.

Yu, Sherry S., and Matthew D. Matsaganis, eds. 2019. *Ethnic Media in the Digital Age*. New York: Routledge.

Zucchi, John E. 1988. *Italians in Toronto: Development of a National Identity, 1875–1935*. Montreal & Kingston: McGill-Queen's University Press.

CHAPTER NINE

Moviegoing in Stereoscope: Film Advertising in Diasporic Communities in Urban Canada

Paul S. Moore and Jessica L. Whitehead

INTRODUCTION

A curious new phenomenon began in 1953 in Toronto. Buried deep in the small print of daily mainstream newspapers, film advertising began to include Italian titles for films at several outlying neighbourhood movie theatres.[1] Larger versions of these movie ads soon began to appear in the city's brand new Italian-language community newspaper, *Corriere Canadese*, like a magnified version of the miniscule film titles in the daily press. A parallel process happened with a few German film titles in mainstream movie listings concurrent with relatively large ads in Toronto's German-language newspaper. Within a few years by the end of the 1950s, films imported from Athens were advertised weekly in Montreal's Greek-language newspaper, and movies imported from Hong Kong and Singapore were advertised in Vancouver's Chinese-language newspaper. In the late 1960s, dedicated Chinese cinemas began advertising in Toronto's Chinese-language daily paper, *Shing Wah*. Then, in the 1970s, Indian films began to get regular advertising from dedicated Bollywood cinemas in Toronto's South Asian community newspapers. However, ads for diasporic films tell only half the story. Mainstream cinema chains, conversely, began to advertise their Hollywood movies in many of the same diasporic newspapers, with everything but the movie title translated into Polish, Spanish, Portuguese, Ukrainian, and other languages. This side of the equation, however, seems only to have happened in newspapers in European languages. There was a stark difference for racialized communities, with a near total lack of translated, mainstream movie advertising in newspapers serving Chinese, Indian, and other Asian ethnic communities.

This chapter explores how the diasporic press in Canada promoted what we will call a "stereoscopic" mixture of moviegoing for many European ethnic communities by promoting diasporic popular culture alongside translated ads for mainstream movies. Unlike the "accented" and "fragmented and self-reflexive strategies" of diasporic filmmakers (Naficy 2001, 88), we cannot assert that individuals or audiences developed a critical awareness out of their twinned experiences of moviegoing. We are merely describing the discourse collectively constituted by advertising both diasporic and Hollywood movies alongside each other. For new immigrants from Europe in the 1950s and 1960s, we propose this bi-cultural address served as an unofficial form of multiculturalism, years before official multiculturalism mirrored the mix of official languages and "mother tongues" in the public sphere. And yet, in the domain of movie ads, at least, this twinned invitation to either enjoy your ethnic enclave or go downtown to join the mass audience was not extended across the colour line to racialized ethnicities in Chinese-, Gujarati-, Korean-, Urdu-, or other Asian-language newspapers. This initial research only documents the content of movie advertising in two ethnic newspapers – the Italian-language *Corriere Canadese*, from 1954 to 1974, and the Chinese-language *Shing Wah*, from 1967 to 1987 – one on either side of the colour line, taking shape on either end of the timeline of official multiculturalism. Our research highlights historical differences between these two communities and how they fit into the larger film industry in Canada. The empirical observation of a racialized difference is simple and stark. The outcome is nonetheless surprising, raising questions our study cannot yet answer: Why did mainstream cinema companies in Toronto continue to advertise in Italian in *Corriere Canadese* into the 1980s while never starting to advertise in Chinese in *Shing Wah*? Even as thousands of Chinese-speaking immigrants settled in the city? Even as the number of Chinese cinemas grew, which was clear evidence for the existence of an audience? Even after official multiculturalism tacitly encouraged greater diversity in ethnic outreach? Indeed, the very opposite happened in the 1970s, when some Chinese movie theatres occasionally undertook extra effort and expense to advertise in English in mainstream newspapers.

THE STEREOSCOPIC IMAGINATION OF CANADIAN MULTICULTURALISM

Our review uses film advertising as a partial, quotidian archive of diasporic media in Toronto. Our approach is situated in a cultural studies paradigm of post-structural actor-networks where the imaginations of modernity are structured for reading publics through cultures of remediation and circulation (Latour 2005; Lee and LiPuma 2002). This framework has primarily been applied to global, digital cultures (Bolter and Grusin 1999; Gaonkar and Povinelli 2003). We adopt it here to a survey of twentieth-century print advertising addressed to prospective diasporic audiences. In this advertising, ethnic and immigrant communities were addressed as both diasporic enclaves and an important part of the mass public for Hollywood films. We call this dual address "moviegoing in stereoscope" to signal the unique sociological position of a "stereoscopic imagination" (Paravantes 2017, 213). We adapt this idea for a diasporic media public to propose a type of dual consciousness, both integrated into the normative dominant culture and also a subculture apart, uniquely able to read across the two domains (Meer 2010; Moreiras 1999). Summarizing the emergent literature on "cultures of circulation," Straw explains that "the encounters in question are not simply those between cultural objects and their consumers, but just as importantly, those by which cultural objects join up with each other and position people in new relationships" (2017, 428).

In our case of European-language ethnic enclave audiences in urban Canada, the result is a bi-cameral mediascape: local and doubly global, yet parochial and doubly commercial. Note we did not simply adopt DuBois's (1903) terminology of "double consciousness" for this dual social perspective to respect how that concept addressed the particularities of the racial divide in the post-emancipation United States. Instead, the bi-cultural address of moviegoing in stereoscope is a mass cultural appeal to commercial entertainment, which recognizes how diasporic popular movies were themselves modeled on genres and norms largely shared with Hollywood movies. The conception of double consciousness is similar in some respects, insofar as African-Americans are self-aware of a "dreadful objectivity, which follows from being both inside and outside the West," because of "the inescapable pluralities involved in the movements of Black peoples" across the spectrum of white ideals and cultural experience (Gilroy 1993, 30, citing Wright 1953; see also Collins 1986). But the action of the colour line is to exclude and deny rather than invite and extend. The African-American experience of Black silent movie audiences has been critically cast as a matter of "laughing at themselves" (Stewart 2005, 93). This important addition of an element of amusement and popular culture, however, does not transform the fact of racialized segregation into a welcome inclusion in the mass public.

Multiculturalism in Canada was a political response to the bilingualism of French and English that signalled the influence of waves of post–World War II European immigrants (Iacovetta 1991; Troper 1993). Since the adoption of multicultural policy, critical examinations of its roots and its construction by policy makers have exposed its function as a mechanism to create groups of "others" (Thobani 2007; Winter 2015). The specific notion of a "mosaic" of multiculturalism was largely an earlier establishment's reaction to distance Canada from the American "melting pot" by turning instead to classification into groups or types (Day 2000, 146–50). Porter (1965) recast the mosaic as vertical, to signify its entrenched hierarchy of inequalities (see also Fleras 2014). For media industries, existing market frameworks largely facilitated entrepreneurs to develop commercial multicultural and ethnic media in Canada, funded by advertising (Hayward 2019; Yu 2010). An important question is the integrating role of diasporic media (Conway 2017; Karim 2003; Yu 2018). This concern has already been addressed for the contemporary context of digital media, circulating globally online (Abada, Hou, and Ram 2009; Shaw 2007; Yu and Matsaganis 2018). We look instead at the history of diasporic media in Canada, and our narrow focus on film advertising permits a comparative breadth across a wide time span and multiple communities (Berger 2020).

For this preliminary comparison of diasporic media in Canada across a racialized colour line, we consider movie advertising in two ethnic newspapers: one Italian-language before official multiculturalism, and the other Chinese-language after the launch of inclusive policies. Newspapers are generally esteemed for their journalism and defined as an institution central to the democratic public sphere and political discourse, but they are also commercial objects (Gans 2003). Advertising may be a secondary pillar in the minds of publishers and readers alike, but its social role can be considered core to the cultural functioning of newspapers as maps or menus for consumption and leisure (Heinze 1990). In our previous work, movie advertising in newspapers has been positioned as central to the social constitution of empirical audiences into a mass public for cinema (Moore 2019; Whitehead and Moore 2021). A particular audience is part of a reading public, an imaginary community implicitly connecting similar cultural groups, places, and practices through the continual circulation of texts such as newspapers and their advertising (Anderson 1991; Warner 2002). Publicity is a mechanism whereby "empirically disparate and socially diverse audiences could come to treat moviegoing as something done collectively" (Moore 2012, 382). This is the theoretical premise that permits us to focus on newspaper ads as a residual trace of the conditions for immigrants' settlement and cultural integration, because they effectively create an informal archive of ephemeral everyday practices. In short, it matters which theatres and movies are advertised to readers of diasporic newspapers. Whatever the reason some theatres are present, and others absent, the collection of those purchasing ads helps constitute the geographic, cultural, and linguistic scope of the diasporic media public. Our synopsis of which theatres advertised to readers of diasporic newspapers provides a simple measure of intercultural engagement, or instead can help discern the existence of a self-enclosed ethnic enclave. There may be unknown reasons for structural patterns of what appears and what is absent – subsidies, profit margins, or sales managers' biases – but the empirical observation of the pattern is an important first step.

METHODOLOGY

Our analysis is based primarily upon a comprehensive survey of twenty years of cinema advertising in two Toronto ethnic newspapers during the emergence of diasporic moviegoing in their respective communities. We turn first to film ads of all types in the Italian-language *Corriere Canadese* in the years 1954 to 1974 when Italian movie theatres first opened and then proliferated across the city and into the suburbs. We then look at the Chinese-language *Shing Wah*, focusing on the years 1967 to 1987, when new, dedicated Chinese cinemas started in business and flourished. Chosen to heighten contrasts, these two cases represent the largest European-language community in Toronto before official multiculturalism, and the largest Asian-language community after official multiculturalism. Our review of *Corriere Canadese* depended upon microfilmed copies available at the Toronto Reference Library. We analyzed weekly cinema advertising for this entire period, which was primarily printed in the *Illustrato* edition when the newspaper expanded upon its initial weekly edition. Our review of film advertising in *Shing Wah* depended upon digitized copies from the Multicultural History Society of Ontario, available online through Simon Fraser University's hosting of the Multicultural Canada project. Although the paper was daily, we quickly confirmed cinema advertising changed only weekly, and therefore collected only a weekly sample for analysis. Further, we include brief descriptive accounts of a few selected cinemas and entrepreneurs of central importance, whose stories were reported informally by reporters in the same newspapers where their advertising appeared, and occasionally also in Toronto's mainstream press. Ultimately, we analyze diasporic filmgoing as a way to expose a racial divide within diasporic media in Canada. Based on these two cases, it seems possible that European diasporic advertising in the 1950s set a paradigm for a multicultural mediascape that was not matched in later racialized diasporic advertising in the 1970s, even after formal government policy encouraged pluralistic Canadian citizenship.

MAIN FINDINGS: *CORRIERE CANADESE* (1954–74)

The *Corriere Canadese* was started in 1954 by an Italian-Canadian businessman from Montreal, Dan Iannuzzi. Several earlier Italian newspapers were published in Toronto, as early as 1898, but all Italian-language publications were banned when Italy entered the war in 1940, both anti-fascist and conservative perspectives (Principe 1999).[2] Many Italian-born Canadians were interned as enemy aliens under the Defence of Canada Act (Whitehead 2018). The end of these wartime measures was followed by significant postwar immigration of labourers from Italy (Zucchi 1990). Italian-identified community groups and businesses proliferated in the early 1950s, providing advertising clients for a new paper, the *Corriere*, including five cinemas that had recently switched to Italian films. The Studio and Pylon were located on College Street in Toronto's Little Italy, just west of downtown; the Continental and Major were located on St Clair Avenue, northwest of downtown in an emerging ethnic enclave, the Corso Italia; one downtown theatre, the Savoy, was playing a mix of European art films and regularly advertised when its current feature was Italian. Three of these theatres (the Studio, Pylon, and Continental) were owned by brothers Lionel and Bob Lester, who shifted their long-standing family business towards an audience of new immigrants from Italy (Allen 1961).

When the Lesters first opened the Studio in 1951, they tried to attract an art house crowd in addition to the Italian-Canadian immigrant audience. Initially playing a variety of European films, they branded the place as a cosmopolitan hub for cinephiles from across the city and especially the nearby University of Toronto (Thomson 1951). The school's student newspaper, *The Varsity*, often had ads for the theatre and also reviewed its films in its "Critic in the Dark" column (Clinton 1953). However, the Lesters shifted quickly to cater to the primary audience of Italian immigrants; by the late 1950s, the campus paper reported that the Studio had shifted its programming to play ordinary Italian films, no longer subtitled, and only rarely the art cinema of interest to the film society at the university. This shift to screening popular Italian films spotlighted how art cinema proved to be unprofitable in Toronto (Wilson 1958). An exception occurred in January 1959, when the Pylon showed Fellini's *I Vitelloni* with English subtitles, which was reported with excitement in *The Varsity* (Wilson 1959). And yet, Lionel Lester was reported as saying 99 per cent of their audience was Italian with almost none from the university crowd (*Toronto Star* 1959).

Lester's failure to make art house cinema a profitable model coincided with a new group of Italian-Canadian business owners who started their own theatres and distribution companies in Canada, circumnavigating expensive New York distributors by importing their films directly from Italy. Rocco Mastrangelo was prominent among this group of Italian immigrants, arriving in Toronto in 1957. In the 1960s, he purchased the Pylon from the Lester brothers (still around in 2022 as the Royal), operated the Radio City off St Clair Avenue, and started the Radio City Film Exchange (Whitehead and Moore 2021). While the Lesters were the first to shift focus to imported Italian films, Rocco Mastrangelo was a pioneer for being himself part of the Italian diaspora. He also ran the Vogue in suburban Port Credit and operated a distribution office in Montreal. Mastrangelo and other Italian theatre owners catered to the popular tastes of their communities in procuring films directly from Italy, such as "spaghetti" westerns, comedies, and erotic films, almost none of which were subtitled.

Figure 9.1 | As part of its thriving Italian-language subsidiary, Famous Players renovated and twinned the St Clair in 1974. Notice the dubbed version of *The Exorcist* among imported Italian coming attractions, some of which may have been distributed in Canada by Rocco Mastrangelo, and thus archived at the University of Toronto Media Commons. *Corriere Canadese*, 10 August 1974, 10.

These expanding ventures are reflected in their movie advertising. The earliest film ads in the *Corriere Canadese* were fairly simplistic text without illustrations, on a page of film news from both Hollywood and Italy. By the 1970s, the paper's movie publicity had grown to cover several illustrated pages. The column of ads was titled by the newspaper as *I programmi dei Cinema Italiani Preferiti: Un lembo di su olo italiano in Canada*: "Favuorite Italian cinema programs: a strip of Italian soil in Canada" (*Corriere Canadese* 1972).

Italian theatres were not the only places to appeal to the Italian immigrant audience; mainstream theatres also advertised their Hollywood movies in the *Corriere Canadese*. First-run downtown movie palaces such as the Odeon and the Imperial theatres advertised their premiere Hollywood movies, translating local information into Italian while keeping the movie advertising in its original English. Similarly, highbrow plays at the Royal Alexandra and events such as the ballet and opera also advertised directly to Italian readers in the *Corriere Canadese* by translating their advertising into Italian. The newspaper also had surprisingly large ads, translated into Italian, for the risqué entertainment at burlesque shows downtown at the Casino, Lux, and Victory theatres. Although these shows were also advertised in the mainstream press, their relatively large size and prominence in the *Corriere Canadese* is notable. Mainstream advertising in Italian newspapers became commonplace for many kinds of products but especially for movies. By the late 1950s, all three of Toronto's mainstream chains – Famous Players, 20th Century, and Odeon – advertised in the Italian newspapers with partially translated copy from their mass circulation displays. Similar Hollywood movie advertising appeared in translation in Greek, Ukrainian, and Portuguese newspapers, among others, and continued in the *Corriere Canadese* into the late 1980s. The widespread adoption of translated mainstream movie ads demonstrates the importance of the buying power of Italian and other European immigrant communities to the movie business in Toronto. With the introduction of television in the 1950s, theatre attendance in Canada was consistently declining; outreach to include these new diasporic communities was a way to garner a new base of consumers. Using the ethnic press to attract an audience for mainstream movies demonstrates the film business's latent recognition of what became codified as multiculturalism even before official policy existed.

Famous Players Canadian Theatres, a subsidiary of Hollywood's Paramount Pictures, later became a major part of the Italian film scene, taking direct control of the Lesters' remaining theatres in the 1960s (Whitehead and Moore 2021). The chain also switched its St Clair theatre, a large cinema in the Corso Italia, to films from Italy, and arranged to show Italian-dubbed Hollywood features from Paramount and other studios. The dubbed version of *The Godfather*, renamed *Il Padrino*, had its North American premiere at the St Clair in 1972 to much fanfare in *Corriere Canadese* with pages of advertising and articles (Ciolfi 1972). The St Clair was profitable enough for Famous Players to renovate and divide the theatre into a dual screen multiplex in 1974, making "*il primo 'twin cinema' italiano al mondo*" (see figure 9.1). The St Clair twin theatre played the next Oscar winners for Best Picture in their Italian-dubbed versions: Paul Newman and Robert Redford in *La Stangata*, and *Il Padrino Parte II*. The Italian version of Paramount's *Serpico*, starring Al Pacino, was advertised as having simultaneous world premieres in Toronto and Milan. None of these dubbed Italian versions were advertised in the mainstream press. Many Italian theatres in Toronto went beyond films and regularly presented live acts from Italy. Mastrangelo arranged a live satellite television feed at the Radio City and St Clair for a 1976 World Cup elimination game. Over 2,000 people packed the theatres to watch Italy's victory, "as if everyone was actually in Rome watching the game live" (Graham 1976). The longevity and popularity of Italian theatres in Toronto demonstrates how Italian immigrants were a major subculture that maintained cultural ties and language through popular culture. The Italian community's vibrant cinema culture also demonstrates how mainstream business embraced diasporic media in European immigrant communities earlier than mandated by official multiculturalism.

SHING WAH (1967 TO 1987)

Chinese-language periodicals in Canada date to at least the early twentieth century, as early as 1903 in Victoria, British Columbia (Zhao 2017). In Vancouver, the long-standing daily newspaper, *Chinese Times* (大漢公報), was established in 1906, initially under other titles, and was published until 1992. Toronto's Chinese community was established just as early as the ones in Vancouver and Victoria, although relatively smaller, with a high proportion relocating from British Columbia (Chan 2011, 59–60; Lam 1980; Oh 2016). According to the Simon Fraser University description of the online version, Toronto's *Shing Wah Yat Po* (醒華日報) began in 1916 as a daily newspaper and was published until 1990. The paper had direct links to the Chinese Nationalist League or Kuomintang. By the mid-1950s, Chinese films were regularly screened in both Toronto and Vancouver, in both cases playing only weekly or occasionally in downtown theatres located close to each city's Chinatown neighbourhoods. Exhibitions of Chinese films in Toronto were only occasional in the 1950s, sponsored by the Culture and Film Club of the Chinese Community Centre of Ontario (安省中華總會館). Many film screenings were given at the Casino, a burlesque on Queen Street near Bay Street in the immigrant-associated Ward, an area that was primarily Chinese businesses in these years (Lorinc, McClelland, and Scheinberg 2015). Although many other ads in *Shing Wah* would include a business name, address, and telephone number in English, the Community Centre's film screenings were advertised entirely in Chinese writing, with even the name of the theatre spelled only phonetically (加仙那戲院). In these years, the imported films were usually two or more years old, such as *The Cruel Murder of the Concubine* (1950), which played in Toronto in June 1954. It is interesting to note that the Casino advertised prominently at the time in the *Corriere Canadese* and other European-language newspapers, but the theatre was not a client of *Shing Wah*, despite our findings that the Chinese community used it as a regular location to show its imported movies.

Daily advertising for at least two movie theatres dedicating several days or the entire week to Chinese-language films had started by the end of 1967 in *Shing Wah* in Toronto. The time coincides, of course, with policy changes to combat the most egregious forms of systemic racism in immigration, leading up to the articulation of official multiculturalism as a political strategy (Day 2000; Walcott 2014). Our survey of advertising indicates that the first dedicated Chinese cinema in Toronto was the Wing-Va Theatre (永華戲院), an older, small theatre at 344 College Street just west of Spadina Avenue. The Wing-Va had been named the Melody since 1953, when it focused on German and other European films. New owners, Dave Chow and his father, incorporated the Wing-Va in December 1967; the English name was a phonetic version of the phrase "eternal China." Chow's early ads in *Shing Wah* kept the melody motif from the earlier theatre name by adding a staff of musical notes next to the theatre name, above the address. One early show was a benefit performance by a Chinese-Canadian music group before the film *A Gifted Scholar and a Beautiful Maid*.

Our survey of advertising found the Elektra Theatre (伊力特戲院) also began advertising Chinese films by December 1969, operating in a theatre that had most recently shown Greek movies at 360 College Street immediately next to the Wing-Va. Later renamed the Lido, its earliest ads boasted the best seats, best colour and image on its screen, and best sound system for a Canadian premiere of a new Chinese film with English subtitles. We also found that another former Greek cinema, the Ellas, on Queen Street East at Broadview, had started playing Chinese films in 1972, soon renamed the China Cinema. At various times in the 1970s, several other old theatres became venues for Chinese movies, advertising only in Chinese papers such as *Shing Wah*, some located outside Chinese-identified neighbourhoods. An especially prominent Chinese cinema in Toronto was the Pagoda Theatre (金都戲院), formerly the LaSalle Theatre at 526 Dundas Street West at Spadina Avenue. Owned and managed by husband and wife Gee and Mei Lem, immigrants from Canton, advance notices of their new business began in *Shing Wah* late in October 1970. "Please pay attention for the opening screening date," noted the first ads, giving the new theatre's name only in its Chinese characters, but the address in English (*Shing Wah* 1970).

Just a few months after opening, the Lems took the unusual step of advertising the Pagoda's popular Chinese movies in English in the *Toronto Star. The Grand Passion* was "an unforgettable picture [that] portrays the Chinese swordsmanship [and] patriotism during the Tartars invasion in the 12th century … Color with Full English Subtitles. Adult Entertainment. An 'Experience' for Everyone!" (*Toronto Star* 1971a). *Escorts Over Tiger Hills* was "another thrilling, spectacular sword-fighting film [set] during the Sung Dynasty in China … Color with Full English Subtitles" (*Toronto Star* 1971b). For their first anniversary in November 1971, the Lems brought a live-action troupe of acrobats to perform martial arts in person at the Pagoda, an unusual event of enough interest to the general public to get a lengthy article in the *Star*: "Some of the action will be live this weekend at the Pagoda Theatre, the Toronto temple to Chinese sword-fighting movies … [At] the Wing-Va, on College St. … movies appeal mainly to older members of the Chinese community and many of them have no subtitles. Only the Pagoda, with posters in Chinatown restaurants and occasional advertisements in English-language papers, tries to appeal to non-Chinese moviegoers. 'Quite a few of them come,' says Mrs. Lem. 'They like the fighting'" (Stoffman 1971).

If Italian films in Toronto in the 1950s were clearly a long-distance outlet for a diasporic popular culture, Chinese movies in the 1970s were also a global cultural force in their own right. Shaw Theatres were already a major theatre chain based in Singapore with studio production facilities in Hong Kong. Brothers Run Run and Run Me Shaw were occasionally noted as Asian film tycoons in news stories in the 1950s, many years before they opened their first North American theatre in Vancouver in October 1971 (*Chinese Times* 1971; *Vancouver Sun* 1971; see also *Chinatown News* 1965; Fu 2008; Po-Yin Chung 2007). For the independent owners of Toronto's early Chinese theatres, booking a Shaw Brothers film was a significant milestone, reported as part of a larger *Toronto Star* article. "The Shaw Bros. movies are reportedly the best being made in Hong

Kong but none of them has yet played Toronto ... After half a year of negotiations, the Wing-Va has booked a Shaw Bros. movie called *The Twelve Medallions*." (Stoffman 1971). We found ads where the Shaw-scope logo was prominently displayed, actually replacing Wing-Va as the theatre name, although we found it took until 1978 for Toronto to have a formal branch of Shaw Cinemas, when the Lido (Elektra) became directly owned by the global corporation.

A Toronto branch of another pan-Pacific chain, Golden Harvest Theatres (嘉禾劇院), opened in 1976 in the former Victory Theatre, right on the corner of Spadina and Dundas. Like the Shaw chain, Golden Harvest had also first opened in Vancouver in 1974 to anchor a Canadian branch for their global expansion (Walsh 1974; see also Fan 2010; Fore 1994). Two years later, they expanded to Toronto right in the heart of Chinatown, later building a brand new cinema in 1986 in the basement of a new office and condominium building at 186 Spadina Avenue (O'Reilly 1984). By this time in the 1980s, another large, brand new purpose-built Chinese cinema had already opened. The Far East Cinema (遠東劇院) was an entirely new kind of business venture, a modern, purpose-built cinema at 270 Spadina. Its opening was advertised late in 1984 with illustrations of the new building that hint at the later development of the adjoining Dragon City Mall, which rebuilt the entire southwest corner of Spadina and Dundas.

MOVIEGOING IN STEREOSCOPE? ONLY ON ONE SIDE OF A RACIALIZED COLOUR LINE

Diasporic movie theatres occasionally attracted the attention of journalists in Toronto's mainstream press. Fascinated by an emerging urban diversity, news stories could show a picture of a marquee giving a movie title in Greek or German to show cultural changes to the city resulting from immigration. In 1966, for example, a *Toronto Star* reporter took a "tour of the ethnic movie circuit," carefully noting differences from mainstream cinemas in terms of who made up the audience, how they behaved, and what was sold at the snack bar. He wrote:

> For an English-speaking Torontonian, most of these theatres offer an atmosphere with a charming touch of old Europe – or some interesting signs of U.S. razzmatazz, European style ... For pure volubility, nothing can touch Friday and Saturday

> night audiences – they're comprised mainly of men: men of all sizes, shapes and ages ... If they don't like what's happening on screen, they talk back to it ... Let a gorgeous female appear, or some hint of sexy action, and the ululations rise in choruses ... The theatres themselves, most of which are owned by individuals, cannot afford to advertise in the English newspapers, in the hope that they might draw a slightly wider audience. So, English-speaking filmgoers, unless they are in the habit of scanning the Italian paper *Corriere Illustrato*, are bound to miss much film fare. (Zeldin 1966)

At this point, in 1966, all of the references were to European-language movies. Just a year later, the reporter might also have attended the first of the city's Chinese cinemas. Remarkably, for our purposes, the cost and logistics of newspaper advertising were cited as the main barrier to the general public taking interest in attending these diasporic movie theatres. Recall, on the other hand, how some of the early managers of Chinese cinemas found the money to advertise their subtitled films in the mainstream daily press in the early 1970s, despite the high cost and logistics. Of course, they had a popular commodity in the craze for kung fu movies. And yet, even when mainstream cinemas played the latest Bruce Lee martial arts hits, downtown movie palaces did not create Chinese-language translations of their English advertising for the readers of Toronto's Chinese newspapers.

Indeed, when Bruce Lee films became big mainstream hits in 1973, Clyde Gilmour's review in the *Star* was patronizing, not even mentioning the star by name: "One of the surprise box-office hits of the year is *5 Fingers of Death* ... An 'eastern' rather than a western, this Chinese film blandly borrows from the well-worn traditions of Hollywood's ritualistic cowboy stories" (Gilmour 1973). Recall the stark contrast from the 1950s, when highbrow Italian art films found the intrigued attention of cinephiles from the University Film Club, reported with enthusiasm in *The Varsity*. Further, the cost of attracting a multicultural audience to Chinese theatres fell to their owners, even for Bruce Lee films. For example, the Pagoda cashed in on Lee's fame with the general public, advertising an older, subtitled film in English in the *Star*: "Starts tomorrow, Canadian premiere. After *The Big Boss*, Bruce Lee comes again in another thriller, *Fist of Fury*. Box-Record Breaker of All Kung-Fu Movies. No One Can Afford to

樂都戲院
金都戲院
LIDO THEATRE
362 COLLEGE STREET, TORONTO
PAGODA THEATER
DUNDAS ST. W., TORONTO
STARTS TOMORROW CANADIAN PREMIERE
after "THE BIG BOSS"
BRUCE LEE comes again in another thriller
fist of fury
A Box-Record Breaker of All Kung-Fu Movies
No One Can Afford To Miss It
COLOR WITH ENGLISH SUBTITLES
Adult Entertainment
ADULTS: $2.75 CHILDREN $1.00
added attraction: 'FUNG FUNG'

Figure 9.2 | The Pagoda and Lido Theatres sometimes advertised in English to the general public, here riding the popularity of Bruce Lee's kung fu stardom. Ad for *Fist of Fury* at the Lido and Pagoda Theatres, *Toronto Star*, 30 July 1973, 36.

Miss it" (*Toronto Star* 1973). The crossover appeal of kung fu movies, and Bruce Lee in particular, briefly upended the relation between mainstream and diasporic cinema (see figure 9.2). The situation was entirely different from the way mainstream movie ads were translated into Italian and other European languages and printed in

Table 9.1 | Moviegoing in stereoscope: differences between movie ads in the Italian and Chinese ethnic press in Toronto

Moviegoing in stereoscope?	Movie ads in *Corriere* (1954 to 1974)	Movie ads in *Shing Wah* (1967 to 1987)
Diasporic cinema	Continually imported films, often without English subtitles	Continually imported films, usually with English subtitles
Mainstream movies	First-run film ads in translation; also Italian-dubbed versions of Hollywood films	Absent, even as popular Chinese films are advertised in English in mainstream newspapers

European-language diasporic newspapers. Immigrant communities in the 1950s and 1960s were addressed in their diasporic languages to enjoy both Hollywood movies downtown and films from their homelands in ethnic enclave theatres, but Chinese audiences were not addressed in this same stereoscopic way. Mainstream cinema chains never placed ads in Asian-language newspapers. Instead, during moments of popular Asian cinema, it was, paradoxically, the mainstream, mass public who had the option of moviegoing in stereoscope, watching dubbed Bruce Lee hits downtown while Chinese theatres invited them to also come watch subtitled versions of his earlier films in Chinatown.

CONCLUSION

It is evident from our analysis of the advertising content that there was a clear difference in how the mainstream industry reached out to address the Italian and Chinese populations (see table 9.1). The Italian case demonstrates a community that was quickly embraced by the local branch of the film industry. The Italian circuit was dedicated to the popular Italian audience, rarely subtitling the films exhibited at theatres. This circuit had close connections with the largest film chain in Canada, Famous Players, which operated the

Italian language St Clair theatre in Toronto, and also played Italian-language films without subtitles at many of their other theatres across the country in addition to exhibiting dubbed Paramount features in Toronto. From almost the beginning of Italian-language films, mainstream chains like Famous Players, 20th Century, and Odeon all published translated ads in the *Corriere Canadese*. While Chinese theatres attempted to draw mainstream audiences with subtitled films, Italian theatres in Toronto rarely attempted to attract a non-Italian crowd. Despite greater awareness of popular Chinese movies, the diasporic audience and exoticized difference from the mainstream still sustained journalistic forays into immigrant theatres in the 1970s and beyond, now for Chinese theatres. In 1976, for example, the *Toronto Star* reported:

> Perhaps the subtitles are in fractured English, but the movies shown at Toronto's four Chinese movie theatres provide a unique window on one of the world's oldest cultures ... "Maybe it's old-fashioned," said John Lai, the operator of the China Cinema on Queen St. E., "but in Chinese movies they tell people how to judge right from wrong. People are told how to be good to their family." ... According to Lai, many Chinese immigrants bring their children to the historical and mythological dramas "so they will learn about the way of life." (Jones 1976)

This colloquial explanation of what made a Chinese movie culture distinct hints toward the kind of research necessary to explain the empirical differences in how movie ads appeared in Italian and Chinese newspapers in Toronto. Further research may help track and trace the history behind this racialized division, such as qualitative interviews and archival investigations behind the scenes of advertising translation services, movie business agents, and circulation managers selling ads in diasporic community newspapers. Having documented the differences as they appeared in advertising, at present, we can only observe the apparent divide across a racialized colour line, and speculate on the reasons behind it. Nonetheless, this contribution to a history of diasporic media in Canada demonstrates an example of a racial divide. Diasporic communities were treated differently by the movie industry, and this racial divide also extended to the distinct ways ethnic cinemas appealed to some in the general public. Whereas cinephiles of European art films sought out Italian films, these theatres rarely advertised in English to the mainstream, even when playing dubbed Hollywood blockbusters. On the other hand, some Chinese cinemas advertised to the general public in English when playing subtitled action-fighting films. Our analysis of film advertising demonstrates how these communities created their own distinctive media spaces, audiences, and circuits of distribution.

ACKNOWLEDGMENTS

Several graduate students at Toronto Metropolitan University provided research assistance: Meng Jian, Vy Tran, Aaron Demeter, and Neboja Stulic. Special thanks are owed to Meng Jian for translating a selection of ads from Chinese-language newspapers. This research was supported by Insight Grants from the Social Sciences and Humanities Research Council of Canada and a postdoctoral fellowship from the Faculty of Arts and Science at the University of Toronto.

NOTES

1 Two early examples when Italian films were advertised only in small print for neighbourhood audiences: *Buon Giorno, Elefante!*, at the Pylon, *Toronto Star*, 9 September 1953, 15; double-bill of *Pagliacci* and *Paisan*, at the Major St Clair, *Toronto Star*, 2 November 1953, 36.

2 Although occasional films were specially imported from Italy before World War II, only a limited number of Toronto's early Italian newspapers have survived, making it difficult to confirm film advertising before the 1950s.

REFERENCES

Abada, Teresa, Feng Hou, and Bali Ram. 2009. "Ethnic Differences in Educational Attainment among the Children of Canadian Immigrants." *Canadian Journal of Sociology* 34 (1): 1–28.

Allen, Harry, Jr. 1961. "Canadian Highlights." *Motion Picture Exhibitor*, 8 February 1961, 15.

Anderson, Benedict. 1991. *Imagined Communities: Reflections on the Origins and Spread of Nationalism*, rev. ed. New York: Verso.

Berger, Stefan. 2020. "Comparative and Transnational History." In *Writing History: Theory and Practice*, 3rd ed., edited by Stefan Berger, Heiko Feldner, and Kevin Passmore, 292–316. London: Bloomsbury.

Bolter, Jay David, and Richard A. Grusin. 1999. *Remediation: Understanding New Media*. Cambridge: MIT Press.

Chan, Arlene. 2011. *The Chinese in Toronto from 1878*. Toronto: Dundurn Press.

Chinatown News (Vancouver). 1965. "Run Run Shaw: Film Mogul." 18 December 1965, 8–11.

Chinese Times (Vancouver). 1971. *Shaw Theatre* advertising, 27 October 1971, 2.

Ciolfi, Ranato. 1972. "Grande successo al St. Clair di 'Godfather' in italiano." *Corriere Canadese*, 23 October 1972, 6.

Clinton, Germaine. 1953. "Critic in the Dark." *The Varsity*, 23 November 1953, 5.

Collins, Patricia Hill. 1986. "Learning from the Outsider Within: The Sociological Significance of Black Feminist Thought." *Social Problems* 33 (6): 14–32.

Conway, Kyle. 2017. "The Meanings of 'Multicultural' in Canada's 1991 Broadcasting Act." *Canadian Journal of Communication* 42 (5): 785–804.

Corriere Canadese (Toronto). 1972. "I programmi dei cinema italiani perferiti." 10 March 1972, 10.

Day, Richard. 2000. *Multiculturalism and the History of Canadian Diversity*. Toronto: University of Toronto Press.

DuBois, W.E.B. 2009 [1903]. *The Souls of Black Folk*, edited by Brent Hayes Edwards. New York: Oxford University Press.

Fan, Victor. 2010. "New York Chinatown Theatres under the Hong Kong Circuit System." *Film History* 22 (1): 108–26.

Fleras, Augie. 2014. *Racisms in a Multicultural Canada: Paradoxes, Politics and Resistance*. Waterloo, ON: Wilfrid Laurier University Press.

Fore, Steve. 1994. "Golden Harvest Films and the Hong Kong Movie Industry in the Realm of Globalization." *Velvet Light Trap* 34: 40–58.

Fu, Poshek, ed. 2008. *China Forever: The Shaw Brothers and Diasporic Cinema*. Urbana: University of Illinois Press.

Gans, Herbert J. 2003. *Democracy and the News*. New York: Oxford University Press.

Gaonkar, Dilip P., and Elizabeth A. Povinelli. 2003. "Technologies of Public Forms: Circulation, Transfiguration, Recognition." *Public Culture* 15 (3): 385–97.

Gilmour, Clive. 1973. "Five Fingers of Death." *Toronto Star*, 24 April 1973, 34.

Gilroy, Paul. 1993. *The Black Atlantic: Modernity and Double Consciousness*. Cambridge: Harvard University Press.

Graham, Bob. 1976. "Metro Italians Cheer Soccer Win." *Toronto Star*, 17 November 1976, C2.
Hayward, Mark. 2019. *Identity and Industry: Making Media Multicultural in Canada*. Montreal & Kingston: McGill-Queen's University Press.
Heinze, Andrew R. 1990. *Adapting to Abundance: Jewish Immigrants, Mass Consumption and the Search for American Identity*. New York: Columbia University Press.
Iacovetta, Franca. 1991. "Ordering in Bulk: Canada's Postwar Immigration Policy and the Recruitment of Contract Workers from Italy." *Journal of American Ethnic History* 11 (1): 50–80.
Jones, Frank. 1976. "Up Front: The Good Guy Always Wins in Chinese Films." *Toronto Star,* 26 March 1976, A1, A4.
Karim, Karim H. 2003. *The Media of Diaspora: Mapping the Globe*. New York: Routledge.
Lam, Lawrence. 1980. "The Role of Ethnic Media for Immigrants: A Case Study of Immigrants and Their Media in Toronto." *Canadian Ethnic Studies* 12 (1): 74–92.
Latour, Bruno. 2005. *Reassembling the Social: An Introduction to Actor-Network-Theory*. New York: Oxford University Press.
Lee, Benjamin, and Edward LiPuma. 2002. "Cultures of Circulation: The Imaginations of Modernity." *Public Culture* 14 (1): 191–213.
Lorinc, John, Michael McClelland, and Ellen Scheinberg, eds. 2015. *The Ward: The Life and Loss of Toronto's First Immigrant Neighbourhood*. Toronto: Coach House.
Meer, Nasar. 2010. *Citizenship, Identity and the Politics of Multiculturalism: The Rise of Muslim Consciousness*. London: Palgrave Macmillan.
Moore, Paul S. 2012. "Advance Newspaper Publicity for the Vitascope and the Mass Address of Cinema's Reading Public." In *Companion to Early Cinema*, edited by André Gaudreault, Nicolas Dulac, and Santiago Hidalgo, 381–97. Malden, MA: Wiley-Blackwell.
– 2019. "'It Pays to Plan 'Em': The Newspaper Movie Directory and the Paternal Logic of Mass Consumption." In *Companion to New Cinema History,* edited by Daniel Biltereyst, Philippe Meers, and Richard Maltby, 365–77. New York: Routledge.
Moreiras, Alberto. 1999. "Hybridity and Double Consciousness." *Cultural Studies* 13 (3): 373–407.
Naficy, Hamid. 2001. *An Accented Cinema: Exilic and Diasporic Filmmaking*. Princeton: Princeton University Press.

Oh, David C. 2016. "Reconsidering Ethnic Media Research: An Argument for a Diasporic Identity Framework." *Atlantic Journal of Communication* 24 (5): 264–75.

O'Reilly, Karen. 1984. "King's Court Condominiums are in the Heart of Chinatown." *Globe and Mail*, 2 June 1984, H4.

Paravantes, Andrew. 2017. "Review of *Utopian Moments: Reading Utopian Texts*, Aviles and Davis, eds." *Utopian Studies* 28 (1): 209–13.

Po-Yin Chung, Stephanie. 2007. "Moguls of the Chinese Cinema: The Story of the Shaw Brothers in Shanghai, Hong Kong and Singapore, 1924–2002." *Modern Asian Studies* 41 (4): 665–82.

Porter, John. 1965. *The Vertical Mosaic: An Analysis of Social Class and Power in Canada*. Toronto: University of Toronto Press.

Principe, Angelo. 1999. *The Darkest Side of the Fascist Years: The Italian-Canadian Press, 1920–1942*. Buffalo: Guernica.

Shaw, Deborah, ed. 2007. *Contemporary Latin American Cinema: Breaking into the Global Market*. Lanham, MD: Rowman & Littlefield.

Shing Wah (Toronto). 1967. Wing-Va Theatre advertising. 27 November 1967, 4.

– 1970. Pagoda Theatre advertising. 23 October 1970, 2.

Stewart, Jacqueline Najuma. 2005. *Migrating to the Movies: Cinema and Black Urban Modernity*. Berkeley: University of California Press.

Stoffman, Daniel. 1971. "It's the Real Thing at Chinese Swordfighting Movie House." *Toronto Star*, 19 November 1971, 32.

Straw, Will. 2017. "Circulation." In *A Companion to Critical and Cultural Theory*, edited by Imre Szeman, Sarah Blacker, and Justin Sully, 423–33. New York: John Wiley & Sons.

Thobani, Sunera. 2007. *Exalted Subjects: Studies in the Making of Race and Nation in Canada*. Toronto: University of Toronto Press.

Thomson, Hugh. 1951. "The Studio Opens Doors." *Toronto Star*, 6 October 1951, 12.

Toronto Star. 1959. "Newcomers Invest in Foreign Movies." 4 July 1959, 3.

– 1971a. Pagoda Theatre advertising. 8 April 1971, 38.

– 1971b. Pagoda Theatre advertising. 21 May 1971, 30.

– 1973. Pagoda and Lido Theatres' advertising. 30 June 1973, 36.

Troper, Harold. 1993. "Canada's Immigration Policy since 1945." *International Journal* 48 (2): 255–81.

Vancouver Sun. 1971. Shaw Theatre advertising. 27 October 1971, 23.

Walcott, Rinaldo. 2014. "The Book of Others (Book IV): Canadian Multiculturalism, the State and Its Political Legacies." *Canadian Ethnic Studies* 46 (2): 127–32.

Walsh, Michael. 1974. "Chinese Theatres Set to do Battle Here." *Vancouver Province*, 7 December 1974, 51.

Warner, Michael. 2002. *Publics and Counterpublics*. New York: Zone Books.

Whitehead, Jessica L. 2018. "The Italian-Canadian Internment: The Case of the Mascioli Brothers of Timmins, Ontario." *Italian Canadiana* 32: 101–19.

Whitehead, Jessica L., and Paul S. Moore. 2021. "*Cinema Paradiso*: Toronto's Italian Language Cinemas and Distribution Networks." In *Italian Americans On Screen*, edited by Ryan Calabretta-Sajder and Alan J. Gravano, 183–211. Lanham, MD: Lexington Books.

Wilson, Warren. 1958. "Worth Watching." *The Varsity*, 4 March 1958, 5.

– 1959. "I Vetelloni." *The Varsity*, 9 January 1959, 5.

Winter, Elke. 2015. "A Canadian Anomaly? The Social Construction of Multicultural National Identity." In *Revisiting Multiculturalism in Canada*, edited by Lloyd Wong and Shibao Guo, 51–68. Boston: Sense Publishers.

Wright, Richard. 1953. *The Outsider*. New York: Harper and Row.

Yu, Sherry S. 2010. *Mapping Canadian Diasporic Media: The Existence and Significance of Communicative Spaces for Overseas Canadians*. Vancouver: Asia Pacific Foundation of Canada.

– 2018. *Diasporic Media Beyond the Diaspora: Korean Media in Vancouver and Los Angeles*. Vancouver: University of British Columbia Press.

Yu, Sherry S., and Matthew D. Matsaganis, eds. 2018. *Ethnic Media in the Digital Age*. New York: Routledge.

Zeldin, Arthur. 1966. "Let's Go Down to the Old 'Nabe' Tonight." *Toronto Star*, 23 July 1966, 18.

Zhao, Qinyu. 2017. "Chinese Media in Canada: An Exploratory Study of Orient Star Media's Cross-Media Publishing." PhD diss., Simon Fraser University.

Zucchi, John E. 1990. *Italians in Toronto: Development of a National Identity, 1875–1935*. Montreal & Kingston: McGill-Queen's University Press.

CHAPTER TEN

Communal Authority and Communicational Autonomy: Print and Digital Media of South Asian Ismaili Muslims in Canada

Karim H. Karim

INTRODUCTION

The Canadian community (*jamat*) of Nizari Ismaili Muslims (henceforth, Ismailis) is characterized, on the one hand, by participation within a tightly knit communal institutional structure and, on the other, a vibrant engagement within the national public sphere. Ismaili media promote and celebrate engagement with the larger society. Some individuals from this relatively small immigrant group have achieved national significance in politics, government, civil society, the judiciary, journalism, academia, arts, business, and other professions (Karim 2011; 2021). Interaction with Canadian society is matched by strong attachment to the transnational Ismaili community; this is particularly true of its South Asian or Khoja members (Magout 2019) who form the vast majority of Canadian Ismailis. This ethno-religious community's analogue publications saw an initial period of free expression and critique of leadership before they were reined in. However, since the mid-1990s, the Internet has enabled individuals to establish autonomous media that have unsettled institutional control.

Capital intensive print media that are able to reach community members *en masse* are no longer necessary to challenge authorities discursively. Digital systems have facilitated "increasingly open contests over the authoritative use of the symbolic language of

Islam" (Eickleman and Anderson 2003, 1) in many Muslim settings. Several diasporas engage in internal discussions and debates, some of which are quite fractious (Karim and Al-Rawi 2018). Communal leadership's monopoly over authoritative interpretations has been diminished with autonomous individuals' and groups' ability to offer alternative views through online platforms.

This chapter is placed within contexts of Ismaili leadership, organizations, and tradition, which are necessary for a nuanced understanding of the social environment in which the community's media operate. Heidi Campbell, a prominent scholar of religious media, states:

> The question of authority in religious engagement online involves investigating multiple layers of authority. It is not enough to say that the Internet transforms or challenges traditional authority; rather, researchers must identify what specific form of authority is being affected. Is it the power position of traditional authority leaders? Is it the established systems by which policy decisions are made and information is passed on to community members? Is it the corporate ideology of the community? Or is it the role and interpretation of the official rhetoric and teaching? Studying authority online involves identifying these multiple layers in order to discover whether it is religious roles, systems, beliefs, or sources that are being affected. (2007, 1044)

Khoja Ismaili media have been shaped by specific positioning vis-à-vis the religious leadership (Imam), systems (councils), Ismaili beliefs, and the sources of official rhetoric and teaching. Recognizing the particular aspects of hierarchy that non-hegemonic discourses are challenging and what kinds of traditional authority are *not* being challenged provides insight into the particular nature of the community's discursive dynamics. Additionally, identifying the diversity among non-institutional voices helps to situate their relative positions. This chapter conducts an overview of Ismaili Canadian media's operation in the last half-century. It examines communal authority, transnational and national linkages, and the Khojas' Satpanth tradition (which is elaborated upon below), all of which provide necessary background for reviewing the ethno-religious community's media dynamics.

METHODOLOGY

Access to Ismaili institutional archives is difficult, and it is not clear whether the community's early publications (which are not available in public collections) have been preserved. This discussion on Ismaili Canadian media is based on the author's personal, incomplete collection of print materials from 1975 to 2019 as well as a three decades-long examination of the community's major Internet-based organs. The media's characteristics, editorial positioning, and constraints on free expression were studied. Contents were also scrutinized for information about the founding and other aspects of certain print media, of which only certain issues were available.

A survey of Ismaili online media administrators provided information about the nature of outlets, reasons for establishment, and relationships with communal institutions. Eleven major institutional and autonomous Ismaili digital media consented to complete a questionnaire. Thirty-one open-ended questions inquired about the objectives, establishment, and naming of the respective medium; individuals or organizations involved; work required; preferences and advantages of digital platforms; sources of content; criteria for inclusion and categorization of material; feedback mechanisms and kinds of user responses; and views on media technologies in Islamic/Ismaili contexts. Nine completed questionnaires were received by email from the primary founders and operators of the media, and two were conducted in person. The survey gave the respondents the option of maintaining anonymity, which most of them exercised. Findings of the survey are provided later in this chapter's section on digital media.

COMMUNICATIVE AUTHORITY

The hegemony of Ismaili institutions has been of significance in shaping the community's media content. This transnational Shia Muslim community is led by a hereditary imam, the Aga Khan, who traces his lineage to the Prophet Muhammad. Over the last century, the group's leadership has developed a form of communal self-governance that has Western organizational features, including a constitution. National and regional councils comprise boards for religious matters, economics, education, health, social welfare, youth, and sports. The imam appoints their officials (who work without pay) and maintains authority over the transnational community through them. (The Aga Khan Development Network is a separate, non-denominational institutional structure that the imam also heads.) Various global aspects of administration are conducted from the imam's secretariat in France (Aiglemont), a Seat of the Imamat in Portugal, and the Institute of Ismaili Studies in Britain.

The first clause of the Ismaili Constitution states that the "Imam has inherent right and absolute and unfettered power and authority over and in respect of all religious and Jamati matters of the Ismailis" (Aga Khan 1998, 9). Communication matters appear in other clauses:

- 5.6 (i) names the councils' aims and objectives to publicize information about Ismaili institutions' contribution to global development;
- 8.4 (d) enables the Ismaili Tariqah and Religious Education Board (ITREB) to publish materials on Islam and the Ismaili Tariqah;
- 14.1 (c) prescribes disciplinary action against an Ismaili who "prints, publishes, or circulates any material … purporting to be in the name of or relating to" the imam or an Ismaili institution.

Ismailis' esoteric leanings, historical persecution by other groups (Virani 2007), and current minority status in every country where they live have determined the top-down approach to communal media. This transnational group's members remain vulnerable to attack from militant groups (BBC 2015; Haider 2017). Anti-Ismaili polemics from hostile sources appear from time to time in print and on Internet-based media (e.g., Lalani 2021 and "r/ExIsmailis" on Reddit) and the concern is that unguarded comments in Ismaili outlets will lead to further marginalization and violence against community members.

TRANSNATIONAL AND CANADIAN

The Ismaili community's transnationalism substantially influences its media. Estimates of the global, multi-ethnic Ismaili population vary widely, with the realistic number being around three million (Magout 2019). Places of worship (*jamatkhanas*) have been established in most places with sizable *jamats*. The largest concentrations of Indigenous Ismailis are in Afghanistan, Pakistan, India, Syria, Tajikistan, Iran, and China. Their diasporas reside in North America, Europe, Africa, the Middle East, Southeast Asia, and Australasia. The economically and politically dominant Khoja Ismailis originate from western regions of South Asia. (Other Khojas adhere to Twelver Shia and Sunni persuasions of Islam.) Indian Ismailis have been residing in Africa since at least the 1830s.

At around 100,000 people, Canada has one of the largest diasporic Ismaili populations (Grantham 2018; Mohamed 2017). Husain Rahim, thought to be the first Ismaili in Canada, arrived in Vancouver in 1910 from India and became prominent in the 1914 *Komagata Maru* standoff with the government (Ismailimail 2014). The next record is not until four decades later when two brothers from Pakistan came to eastern Canada in the early 1950s as students and eventually settled in Ottawa (Karim 2011). Ismaili immigration rose significantly and communities were formed in the 1960s, when Canada's race-based restrictions were lifted. The expulsion of Ugandan Asians in 1972 led to notable growth. A large group of refugees arrived from Afghanistan in the 1990s. Other community members include those with Iranian, Syrian, Tajik, (Indigenous) African, and Euro-Canadian backgrounds. The bulk of the community has migrated to Canada from African countries, being largely of Khoja background. At least two generations of Ismailis from immigrant families have been born in Canada. The largest *jamats* are in Toronto and Vancouver, with substantial presence also in Calgary, Edmonton, Montreal, and Ottawa (Karim 2021). Community members draw upon "their religious tradition as well as modernity to shape new forms of organization" (Ross-Sheriff and Nanji 1991, 102).

TRADITION

Ismaili media contents reflect the group's complex historical, socio-cultural, and religious dynamics. Prior to the twentieth century, there was little contact between various regions of the transnational group. Therefore, despite a common adherence to the hereditary imam (who himself was often inaccessible), differences in religious practices took shape between them over time. Certain pre-Islamic Persian conceptions, commemorations, and rituals appear in Iranian, Afghan, and Pamir (Tajik) communities' traditions (Elnazarov 2014). The Khoja Satpanth tradition in India developed in a multi-religious milieu in which followers of Islam and Indic faiths engaged with each other, producing hybrid religious understandings and practices (Khan 2004). The sub-continent's pluralistic socio-religious milieu, existing simultaneously and in tension with exclusionary orthodoxies, have fostered fluid identities and organic expressions that cross boundaries and share the symbolism of interacting faiths. A central part of Satpanth's religious rituals is the recitation of *ginans*, a large lyrical body composed between the thirteenth and the nineteenth centuries in northwestern Indian languages. These hymns are akin to devotional songs produced by other South Asian Muslims, Sikhs, and Hindus, but they reflect specifically Ismaili theology. *Ginans* are a cherished heritage among Khojas in Canada and are recited daily in *jamatkhanas*, in addition to Arabic ritual prayers.

However, the Satpanth tradition exists in a state of stress due to internal Ismaili dynamics as well as broader religio-political tensions of the last century. The partition of India and formation of Pakistan as a Muslim homeland in 1947 produced a strong tendency towards notions of religious essentialization. As religious identities have hardened, *ginanic* content is sharply criticized by doctrinaire Muslims as being Hindu. Such perceptions do not take into account either the religious hybridity of the context in which the hymns were composed nor the esoteric approach of the discourses that are primarily given to seeking universal spiritual truths. Khojas residing in Pakistan, where Islamists have become influential, have come under intense pressure to defend Satpanth's Islamic validity (Khan 2004).

Khojas have a hegemonic position in the global Ismaili community and make up around three-quarters of the group's Canadian population (Karim 2021). However, apparently acting under pressure from doctrinaire Muslim views, the community's global institutions have felt it necessary to embark upon what Michel Boivin remarks is "the withdrawal of the Ginans as a normative source" (2010, 47). Ismaili leadership has been in a long process of Arabizing and Persianizing the Khojas' traditions. This appears particularly paradoxical given Khojas' hegemonic position and the contemporary Ismaili institutional emphasis on pluralism (Dharamsi and Mitha 2019). Contemporary endeavours to engage actively with other Muslims, who may not always be sympathetic to broader religious pluralism, leads to the sidelining of aspects of Ismaili heritage that appear inconvenient and troublesome for the communal hierarchy's "outreach" activities. Official institutional media rarely mention the Khoja tradition; however, some autonomous Khoja media are dedicating considerable digital space to Satpanth, as will be discussed later.

MAIN FINDINGS

Print Media

Ismaili Canadian media organs had come into existence by the 1970s, which appears to have been a decade of substantial growth, aspiration, and creative effervescence in the community. One only has to look back to the early twentieth century to Ismaili print media of Africa and South Asia to find a similarly lively literary culture of autonomous commentary (Bhamani circa 1975). The *jamat*'s councils in Canada were in the phase of formation and individual members were taken with ideas such as the freedoms of expression and the press in their new country of settlement. Ismaili media, which were primarily in print at this time, were mainly produced under the aegis of the institutions established by the Imam. As will be discussed below, early publications did exhibit some editorial tendency towards criticism, but were brought to heel by institutional leadership – underlining the councils' authority over the community's members. An exception was a pamphlet series titled *Do You Know?* produced independently in the 1980s by Akbarally Maherally, a former community official who had become sharply critical of all of the elements in Campbell's analytical framework: institutional roles, systems, beliefs, and sources (2007). Otherwise, it was unusual in this period for autonomous individuals to publish material for the communal readership. Even those Khojas working for ethnic newspapers (e.g., *Rainbow World* and *Community Digest*, both in Vancouver) for the broader South Asian communities viewed their endeavours as being distinct from institutionally produced Ismaili media.

The 1970s and early 1980s were a time of attrition regarding the independence of the community's publications, which were in the forms of newsletters, magazines, pamphlets, souvenir booklets, directories, religious texts, and recorded tape cassettes and vinyl records. They were largely in English with occasional materials in Gujarati and French. In contrast to the national and transnational consolidation that was to take place later, enterprising individual committees of the Ismaili council were able to publish periodicals in this period. The role of university students is particularly noteworthy. The *jamat*'s institutions have generally managed over the years to assert authority over student associations, the only Ismaili organizations with elected officers, and prevent published critique of the community's leadership. However, the early period appears to have manifested a certain freedom of speech.

The Vancouver-based *Forum* of the Ismaili Youth Organization was one of the community's earliest publications, appearing in 1972. The "Editorial Comment" in the March 1975 edition noted that it was the magazine's third year and also saw itself as fulfilling the "Imam's wishes for a regular Ismaili publication" (Ismaili Youth Organization 1975) in Canada. Its contents, including a variety of topics such as religious festivals, the community's history, economic opportunities in Canada, and the country's immigration policy, indicate that it served the *jamat* at large rather than just the youth. The *Ismaili Mirror* of Pakistan (Editor 1973) mentioned a Toronto "Ismaili Newsletter"/"News Bulletin" inaugurated in December 1972; however, further information about it could not be located.

Student bodies in Alberta were active publishers in the late 1970s and early 1980s. A 1981 newsletter of Calgary's Ismaili Students' Organization, called *Chhapo* ("Newspaper"), referred to an upcoming vote on whether the body's magazine, *Focus*, should continue. (The latter was not available for examination.) This matter had arisen "due to a conflict with Ismailia Constitution which prohibits any publication that does not have prior approval" (Member for Education 1981, 3). The alternative was to "join the [Ismaili council] Publication Committee in their endeavour to put out a magazine for the whole Jamat" (4). It noted that Edmonton's Aga Khan Ismailia Students' Association (AISA) had decided to keep publishing its *Echo* magazine, which seems to have been founded in the late 1970s. The latter's July 1981 edition had an eclectic selection of articles on secular and religious topics, including one in Gujarati. The most intriguing items were a letter to the editor from a first-year student criticizing the association itself (Somani 1981), demonstrating the openness of the publication, and a feature piece on "Community-Administration Interface" (Fatoo 1981) in a democratic society, which raised thought-provoking issues regarding the freedom of speech in community contexts. In this, AISA challenged, in Campbell's terms, "the corporate ideology of the community" and "the established systems by which policy decisions are made and information is passed on to community members" (Campbell 2007, 1044).

The first issue of *Ismosaic*, a magazine produced centrally by the Western Canadian Ismaili council, was published in July 1976 in Vancouver. Its name illustrated an engagement with the Canadian government's then relatively new multiculturalism policy and the recently arrived Ismailis' place in larger society. This was very much in line with the community's leadership which encouraged integration into the new country of settlement (Karim 2021). The editorial stated: "'ISMOSAIC' means the culture, role and pattern of life of Ismailis as an integral part of the Canadian mosaic ... the objectives of this magazine are to attempt to reflect the various interlocking and overlapping aspects of Ismailis in a Canadian context – their economic, cultural and social aspects and their role as Canadian citizens." It also said that the magazine was meant to serve Ismailis in western Canada but expressed consternation that "the response from Edmonton, Calgary and Winnipeg has not been encouraging" (Editorial Board 1976, 1). Even such mild criticism of other Ismaili institutions by a *jamati* organ is unthinkable under the later tight editorial controls. The major eastern Canadian counterpart of this largely secular publication was *Ontario Ismaili*, which seems to have begun appearing in 1977.

The Ismailia Association for Canada, the council's branch responsible for administering religious matters, initiated several specifically religious magazines in the second half of the 1970s. These included a national periodical called *Hikmat* and the regional counterparts *Winnipeg Ismaili Newsletter*, *Calgary Crescent*, *Al-Akhbar* (Vancouver), *Al-Risalah* (Montreal), *Al-Kawkab* and *Chandraat Bulletin* (Edmonton), and *Al-Ismaili* (Toronto). Whereas they operated within the institutional system, their relative autonomy and dynamism stands in contrast to subsequent controls of the national and transnational communication hierarchies that eventually disbanded them.

Although Ismailia Association's national magazine, *Hikmat*, was similar to the transnational community's religious periodicals like *Africa Ismaili* (Kenya) and *Ilm* (UK), it was initially conceptualized as a forum for critical discussion. The first issue's "Letter from the Publisher" made "a public commitment to truth" and assured its readers that "if we feel that an article is honest in its presentation of facts, and that the criticism of us or any other Jamati organization is constructive and well-directed, then *we will guarantee publication of the article solely on its literary merits*" (H.H. The Aga Khan Shia Imami Ismailia Association 1976, 5). This "Letter" and the editorial both questioned the supposed infallibility of council administrators, thus clearly challenging established systems and corporate ideology. The masthead listed PhD student Aminmohamed Hassanali Amershi as the "Editor-in-Chief." However, his name did not appear in the following editions and the idea of criticizing the council leadership was not broached again, indicating that there had been an adverse reaction from the institutional hierarchy to the magazine's initial editorial policy.

It seems that the window of self-critique in the immigrant group engaging with the Canadian socio-political milieu closed as the community's organizational structure affirmed control over its media. In 1977, the Imam established the Institute of Ismaili Studies (IIS) in London, UK, as an important node in the transnational community's institutional structure. *Jamati* religious publications around the world were required to submit material to the IIS for vetting by the mid-1980s. *Hikmat*, whose issues became less regular in the mid-1980s, was also restructured, but this turned out to be a temporary measure. Religious publications in various countries were instructed to cease in 1992 as the IIS became the primary and global institution for issuing materials on the Ismaili faith. Whereas the latter has published numerous academic books as well as curricular materials for the transnational community, it has yet to publish a periodical specifically for the *jamat*'s consumption.

With the growing consolidation of Ismaili media, the activities of the imam, his family, and the non-denominational Aga Khan institutions became the focus of the secular community publications from the 1980s. The editorial of the inaugural Navroz (March) 1981 issue of *The Canadian Ismaili* started with a confession of sorts: "Just before we went to press someone asked us, 'Where is the Canadian part of your publication?'" (Bharmal 1981, 2). Local content like events and achievements of the community in Canada did grow in later editions, but transnational material about the Imam and his global institutions generally remained dominant. There was a name change in 1992, which reflected the integration of the periodical into the global Ismaili infrastructure: "Starting with this issue, we will be using our new name – the ISMAILI, CANADA – instead of the now-familiar CANADIAN ISMAILI ... the new name is part of an international standardization of the names of other *jamati* magazines" (Ismail 1992, 2).

As Aiglemont's communications department became more active, it sent an increasing amount of material for publication in nationally based periodicals. Consequently, some issues were overwhelmed by international content at the expense of news about local *jamats*. *The Ismaili, Canada* began producing digital editions in 2015. The magazine had published three times a year for a long time, to coincide with major Ismaili festivals, but it has been producing one annual issue since 2018. *Al-Akhbar*, a print weekly newsletter, emerged in the 1990s to keep the larger *jamats* informed about institutional committees' activities, with separate editions being produced by regional councils and distributed in *jamatkhanas* on Friday, the Muslim holy day. Occasional souvenirs of the Imam's jubilees and other major communal events also continue to appear in print.

Digital Media

Ismaili Canadians turned to nascent Internet-based media in the early 1990s. The first non-institutional listserv appeared in 1994, followed soon by websites (Mawani 2003). Some council and non-denominational Aga Khan institutions also began to make their presence online in the mid-1990s. In a speech to the 1996 Commonwealth Press Union Conference, the Ismaili imam agreed that the new media held potential but also expressed reservations: "If new technology can break down walls which have isolated whole communities from progress and enlightenment, that same technology can also remove the barriers to less welcome change. The communications revolution is a two-edged sword, opening exciting doors to the future, yes, but also threatening venerable cultures and traditional values" (Aga Khan 1996).

Whereas the print newsletter *Al Akhbar*'s British Columbia version appeared online in 1993, emergence of other regional editions seems to have had been delayed by concerns about the Internet's two-edged nature. (Prompted by the COVID-19 restrictions on religious gatherings where the print media were distributed, digital issues were produced from March 2020 onward.) The IIS, the transnational community's central research and teaching institution, did not have an online presence until 2000. TheIsmaili.org, the community's official website, was founded in 2007; it now also disseminates information using other platforms such as Facebook, Twitter, Instagram, and SoundCloud.

The vast majority of Ismaili digital media, however, are operated by autonomous individuals or groups. One of the earliest, "the ISN (Ismaili Social Network), run by two dissident Ismailis, dealt primarily with theological and doctrinal issues. Ummah-net and Ilmnet, based in the United States and Canada, respectively, tended to attract university students and young professionals and dealt with a wider range of issues." The community's institutions were wary of the Internet "because they provided a forum for unmediated discussions and access to unauthenticated versions of the firmans, or private guidance of the Imam to the community" (Mawani 2003, 44).

Ismaili cyberspace is now filled with content on multiple platforms produced by non-institutional operators. The most popular autonomous outlets are oriented largely towards religion, culture, and institutional and individual Ismaili achievements; others cater to business, professions, networking, matchmaking, LGBTQ+ issues, parody, and humour. Amaana (http://www.amaana.org/), Ismaili Gnosis (https://ismailignosis.com/), Ismailimail (https://ismailimail.blog/), Ismaili.net (http://ismaili.net/), NanoWisdoms (http://www.nanowisdoms.org/nwblog/), and Simerg (https://simerg.com/) are among those that have heavy transnational traffic of over hundreds of thousands of hits yearly.

Operators of eleven major Ismaili outlets were interviewed on an anonymous basis. Those among them who run non-institutional media stated that they spend hundreds of hours annually in service of sharing information about the faith's traditions and contemporary events without pay or carrying advertisements on their sites. Unlike the community's early print media producers, they are not students and are generally not directly critical of the religious leadership, systems, beliefs, or sources of official rhetoric and teaching. One autonomous website founder says that existence of these media do not contravene the Ismaili Constitution, stating that the imam had instructed the Canadian council's president in 2013 that "the institutions should work with these private Ismaili media publishers on a 'basis of trust.'" The website founder saw this statement by the imam as instructing the communal institutions to show "confidence, respect, and trust in the private Ismaili media publishers" (Ignition Interview 2018). However, the official institutions' media guidelines do not permit them to mention autonomous Ismaili media, or provide links to them even when borrowing content from them verbatim (Virani 2021), thus raising issues of journalism ethics including plagiarism.

The earliest non-institutional Ismaili websites were established in 1993: FIELD (First Ismaili Electronic Library and Database, later renamed Ismaili.net) and Amaana. Ismaili.net's objectives are "to protect and save the Ismaili Heritage ... [and] to bring life to the Ismaili Studies and interaction between Ismailis and their faith today." Amaana was founded because "there was a lack of well-written and official websites on the Ismaili faith." They have been popular among their audiences: Ismaili.net reported 177 million hits in fifteen years and half a million Facebook followers. The objective of Ismailimail, founded in 2006, was to "gather and categorize all the past, present and future openly available news, articles, pictures, videos, and everything related to Ismaili Muslims and the community, for easy search and reference." Its popularity is evidenced in obtaining "11 million marks in less than 9 years."

The founder of Simerg, established in 2009, said that "religious [print] publications had ceased in 1992; all of a sudden these magazines were abandoned. TheIsmaili.org was the only forum, but it was primarily secular. I thought to myself that here's an opportunity to contribute religious and spiritual understanding of our faith, which had collapsed." There was disappointment, even after institutional websites were established, as Amaana's operator noted: "In the year 2000, IIS.ac.uk was launched and I considered giving up the intense personal effort and financed by me, but many readers pleaded [with] me not to as they said that the IIS website does not fulfill the needs that my website was providing like devotional pages on Imamat Day, Navroz and the Imam's Birthday as well as Muslim and Ismaili holy days and their significance and so I carried on. Thereafter *the-Ismaili.org* ... has not fulfilled this need as the navigation does not allow easy access to detailed descriptions."

Ismaili Gnosis's founder described other problems and lamented the absence of attention to esoteric knowledge, which the Ismaili branch of Islam holds to be particularly important:

> The *Ismaili Gnosis Facebook* forum was created first in 2007. Its creation actually follows from our participation in prior mediums – the *ILMnet listserv* and the *Ismailism Yahoo Group* run by Jim Davis. In 2005 we created a Yahoo email list called

> *IsmailiYouth*, which was active for a couple of years with moderate participation. However, in 2006, Ismailis started having theological discussions in several *FB* groups such as *Ismaili Students Everywhere*. One of the issues that came up was that several non-Ismailis with anti-Ismaili agendas would join these discussions, hijack them and blitz the forums with anti-Ismaili messages attacking the Ismaili Imamat and the Jamat. As a result, many unsuspecting Ismailis were misled and left confused theologically about their faith. At the same time, the official programs and institutions of the Ismaili community in North America (and probably worldwide) are totally lacking in spaces for esoteric discussion and intellectual engagement with its religious beliefs and doctrines.

Apart from material related to religion, autonomous media operators also feel that certain cultural aspects of the history of Ismailis are also not addressed by institutional media. Established in 2015, KhojaWiki states: "the wonderful 700-year migratory history of the Khojas should not be allowed to die, even as our elders pass away. Our response is KhojaWiki.org – a not-for-profit collaborative effort to systematically record living people's stories about their own experiences and their recollection of the stories of their parents and other ancestors, in their own words, using the power of the Internet" (n.d).

Contributors are populating KhojaWiki with content on culture, history, places of diasporic settlement, and biographies (including those of non-Ismaili Khojas). Its founder states that it is an "authentic source of contemporary Khoja history and tradition." The above reasons for the founding of autonomous media all refer to dissatisfaction with established systems of communal information.

Ismaili communal institutions have not given a high priority to the collection, study, and archiving of certain aspects of the transnational community's heritage. Whereas considerable research has been conducted on the early periods of the Arab, Persian, and Central Asian sections of the community, the history of Khoja Ismailis remains neglected by comparison. This appears particularly counterintuitive since it is individuals from this branch who currently predominate in the global and Canadian leadership of Ismaili institutions. On the other side, the majority of the founders/operators of autonomous digital media are also of Khoja background.

The IIS's website is widely viewed as the primary institutional vehicle carrying materials on the multi-ethnic Ismaili community's history and tradition. According to the institute's communications manager, "We generally create content on the basis of what various [IIS] academics are doing in terms of lectures and conferences as well as publications of books and articles." The reliance on the IIS scholars' research has produced a predominance of material on non-Khoja Ismaili history on its website. There appears to be a contradiction about what is considered important in Ismaili tradition and what is actually being studied and disseminated. The communications manager's response to the survey's question "What are your views about the use of contemporary media technology in relation to the long Islamic/Ismaili tradition?" is noteworthy: "It is important to reach out to audiences using the digital medium to enhance their knowledge and understanding of traditions. Access to *ginans* or other devotional literature online for example, is very important in keeping these traditions alive and accessible to a wider range of audiences." However, in reality, the IIS's website has very little material on *ginans*. The centralized religious educational system also gives less importance to what it terms "devotional literature" than what *jamati* adherents appear to want.

Several autonomous digital media have sought to fill the gap. Ismaili.net provides extensive text and audio databases of *ginans* as well as *qasidas* (lyrical poems) from other Ismaili traditions. A University of Saskatchewan Ismaili scholar has developed Ginan Central, a large searchable textual and audio database of *ginans*. Here, the product of a "mainstream" scholarly endeavour shares ground with ethno-religious media to serve the needs of a Canadian community and its transnational counterparts. Ismaili.net, Ismailimail, Amaana, and Simerg also contain numerous materials related to Satpanth. This large and growing body of online content on a significant Ismaili tradition is illustrative of how autonomous digital media have provided an important means for a discourse that provides alternatives to the "corporate ideology" and "official rhetoric and teaching" (Campbell 2007) regarding the community's heritage.

DISCUSSION

This chapter applies Campbell's framework (2007) to analyze Ismaili Canadians' print and digital productions relating to the Imam's religious role, the council system, Ismaili traditions, and sources of official rhetoric and teaching. Unlike specifically anti-Ismaili sources, it is rare for Ismaili media to challenge the Imam because the community's identity centers on his religious status and *jamati* membership requires formal allegiance to him. Maherally's print materials and Lalani's YouTube videos are rare examples of direct defiance of the religious leader from what were initially internal communal positions. Given the placement of most Ismaili print publications within the ambit of the administrative structure, it has been possible for communal institutions to impose authority on them.

The advent of the Internet has, however, considerably shifted the terrain. It has enabled autonomy in Ismaili production of media materials that directly or indirectly critique systems, corporate ideology, and sources of official rhetoric and teaching. However, despite this newfound autonomy, practising Ismailis generally do not criticize the imam's discourse. Nevertheless, indirect challenges to the imam do occur, such as in the closed Facebook discussion group "Ismailis for Social Justice," where participants may counter his conservative views on meritocracy. In such instances, other participants may respond with arguments favouring the imam. Other relatively non-confrontational discussion groups include "r/Ismaili" and "r/Ismailis" on Reddit. However, the platform's "r/ExIsmailis" is consistently oppositional.

As "official" organs of the community, the institutional media claim to be authoritative and are often seen as such by most adherents. However, the official communal media's guidelines do not permit them to mention or provide links to autonomous Ismaili media. On the other hand, the latter also position themselves as authoritative sources in providing access to resources related to the community's traditions, which are otherwise difficult to obtain. Some survey responses indicate discontent with official websites' lack of material on the community's religious resources. Autonomous operators have populated their own media with such content, stating that this is the primary reason for establishing their outlets and spending an enormous amount of their time and energy. The approach of most sites, so far, has not been to articulate critique of official sites but instead to present the material which they believe that the community desires. This includes aspects of the Khoja Satpanth tradition including large collections of *ginans* along with *qasidas* (poetry) of other Ismaili traditions.

CONCLUSION

There were some unexpected developments prompted in 2020 by the COVID-19 lockdowns, whose in-depth examination is beyond this chapter's scope. The weekly Al-Akhbar e-newsletter temporarily changed to a daily medium, providing information related to the pandemic as well as links to webinars on a wide variety of topics, including religion. It became a primary communal link in the absence of physical gatherings in *jamatkhanas*. Friday evenings became a time for disseminating an hour-long program that frequently featured community leaders, particularly the president of the national Ismaili council. A streaming service called The Ismaili TV was inaugurated on 24 April 2020, providing programs transnationally. Unprecedented use of online media occurred when the imam himself began sending occasional formal written messages in multiple languages via TheIsmaili.org (Aga Khan 2020). Telephone-based programming was also provided, especially for seniors lacking access to the Internet. The use of Gujarati, which has been disappearing from other forms of Ismaili communications, and occasional mentions of Satpanth-related information were notable.

In this reinforced online presence was a vigorous affirmation of Ismaili institutional media's authority. The hesitancy in engaging with the Internet expressed in the 1990s seems to have dissipated. Campbell (2007) states that a negotiating process takes place in the ways that technology uses are justified in contexts of religious community. It is also noteworthy that certain autonomous media representatives are occasionally invited by Ismaili institutions to cover major public events involving the Aga Khan as members of the press. The community's official structures seem to be acknowledging the relevance of autonomous media in the Ismaili Canadian mediascape.

REFERENCES

Aga Khan. 1996. "Keynote Address." Speech presented at the Commonwealth Press Union Conference, Cape Town, South Africa. http://www.nanowisdoms.org/nwblog/5137/.

– 1998. The Constitution of the Shia Imami Ismaili Muslims. n.p.

– 2020. "Message from Mawlana Hazar Imam." *Ismaili*. https://the.ismaili/global/news/imamat-news/message-mawlana-hazar-imam.

BBC. 2015. "Pakistan Gunmen Kill 45 on Karachi Ismaili Shia Bus." *BBC News*, 13 May 2015. http://www.bbc.com/news/world-asia-32717321.

Bhamani, A.N. Ca. 1975. "Ismaili Journalism as I See It." *Africa Ismaili: A Collection of Articles of Permanent Value* 10: 32–5.

Bharmal, A.N. Navroz 1981. "Editorial." *The Canadian Ismaili*, 2.

Boivin, Michel. 2010. "Ginans and the Management of the Religious Heritage of the Ismaili Khojas in Sindh." In *Ginans – Texts and Contexts: Essays on Ismaili Hymns from South Asia in Honour of Zawahir Moir*, edited by Tazim R. Kassam and Francoise Mallison, 25–53. New Delhi: Primus.

Campbell, Heidi. 2007. "Who's Got the Power? Religious Authority and the Internet." *Journal of Computer-Mediated Communication* 12 (3): 1043–62.

Dharamsi, Karim, and Farouk Mitha. 2019. "His Highness Prince Karim Aga Khan: Affective Pluralism, Social Change, and the Nonviolent Civil Reshaping of the Public Square." In *Contemporary Icons of Nonviolence*, edited by Anna Hamling, 186–202. Newcastle upon Tyne, UK: Cambridge Scholars.

Editor. 1973. "Toronto 'Ismaili Newsletter.'" *Ismaili Mirror*, April 1973, 18.

Editorial Board. 1976. "Editorial." *Ismosaic* 1, no. 1 (July): 1.

Eickelman, Dale F., and Jon W. Anderson. 2003. *New Media in the Muslim World*. Bloomington: Indiana University Press.

Elnazarov, Hakim. 2014. "The Luminous Lamp." In *The Study of Shi'i Islam*, edited by Farhad Daftary and Gurdofarid Miskinzoda, 529–41. London: IB Tauris.

Fatoo, H. 1981. "Community-Administration Interface." *Echo* 4 (1): 23–27.

Grantham, Barbara. 2018. "Ismaili Community Shows What Happens When Canada Shelters Good People from the Storm." *Province*, 5 May 2018. https://theprovince.com/opinion/op-ed/barbara-grantham-ismaili-community-shows-what-happens-when-canada-shelters-good-people-from-the-storm.

Haider, Otared. 2017. "Syrian Ismailis and the Arab Spring." In *Middle Eastern Minorities and the Arab Spring*, edited by K. Scott Parker and Tony E. Nasrallah, 147–74. Piscataway, NJ: Gorgias Press.

His Highness the Aga Khan Shia Imami Ismailia Association. 1976. "Letter from the Publisher." *Hikmat* 1 (1): 5.

– 1980. "Observation and Comments on Our Modern Ginanic Literature." Paper presented at the International Ismailia Association

Review Meeting, Nairobi, Kenya. http://www.ismaili.net/heritage/node/31647.
Ignition Interview. 2018. "Pulling Back the Curtain on Ismaili Digest & Ismaili Ignition." *Ismaili Digest*, 10 June 2020. https://ismailidigest.org/2018/06/10/pulling-back-the-curtain-on-ismaili-digest-ismaili-ignition-a-team-interview/.
Ismail, K. 1992. "1992: A Historic Year." *The Ismaili Canada* 6 (2): 2.
Ismaili Youth Organization. March 1975. "Editorial Comment." *Forum*. n.p.
Ismailimail. 2014. "Was Husain Rahim the First Ismaili to Settle in Canada?" *Ismailimail*, 25 December 2014. https://ismailimail.blog/2014/12/25/was-husain-rahim-the-first-ismaili-to-settle-in-canada/.
Karim, Karim H. 2011. "At the Interstices of Tradition, Modernity and Postmodernity: Ismaili Engagements with Contemporary Canadian Society." In *A Modern History of the Ismailis*, edited by Farhad Daftary, 265–94. London: IB Tauris.
– 2021. "Khoja Ismailis in Canada and the United States." *Oxford Research Encyclopedia of Islam in North America*. Oxford: Oxford University Press.
Karim, Karim H., and Ahmed Al-Rawi, eds. 2018. *Diaspora and Media in Europe: Migration, Identity, and Integration*. London: Palgrave Macmillan.
Khan, Dominique-Sila. 2004. *Crossing the Threshold: Understanding Religious Identities in South Asia*. London: IB Tauris.
KhojaWiki. n.d. https://khojawiki.org/Main_Page.
Lalani, Salim. 2021. "God and Money," YouTube video, https://www.youtube.com/watch?v=mHZmxkodtAg.
Magout, Mohammad. 2019. "Transnationalizing Multiple Secularities: A Comparative Study of the Global Ismaili Community." *Historical Social Research* 44 (3): 150–79.
Mawani, Rizwan. 2003. "The Nizari Ismaili Community and the Internet." *ISIM Newsletter* 12: 44.
Member for Education, Ismaili Students Organization. 1981. "Member for Education." Chhapo, 4–6.
Mohamed, Rahim. 2017. "A Brief History of the Ismailis in Canada." Policy Options. 8 March 2017. https://policyoptions.irpp.org/magazines/march-2017/a-brief-history-of-the-ismailis-in-canada/.
Reddit. n.d. "r/ExIsmailis." https://www.reddit.com/r/ExIsmailis/.
Ross-Sherriff, Fariyal, and Azim Nanji. 1991. "Islamic Identity, Family and Community: The Case of the Nizari Ismaili Muslims." In *Muslim*

Families in North America, edited by Earle H. Waugh, Sharon Abu-Laban, and Regula Qureshi. Edmonton: University of Alberta.

Simon Fraser University Library. 2012. "Husain Rahim (1865–1937)." *Komagata Maru: Continuing the Journey*. http://komagatamarujourney.ca/node/14693.

Somani, A. 1981. "Letters." *Echo* 4 (1): 4.

Virani, A. 2021. "In Memoriam Bio." Email, 19 March 2021.

Virani, Shafique. 2007. *The Ismailis in the Middle Ages: A History of Survival, a Search for Salvation*. New York: Oxford University Press.

PART THREE

Ethnic Media and Integration: Identity, Citizenship, and Civic Engagement

CHAPTER ELEVEN

Rungh: The Many Colours of a Pan-Ethnoracial Medium

Yasmin Jiwani and Marie Bernard-Brind'Amour

INTRODUCTION

The term *ethnic media* has generally been used to refer to the media of a specific, identifiable ethnic group whose ethnicity is homogeneous, albeit fractured by class and religion. Communication theorist Karim H. Karim (2012) argues that ethnic media constitute a form of alternative media. What defines ethnic media as "ethnic" is the standpoint of those making the media, those consuming it, and how ethnicity is defined in the larger societal context. In this chapter, we examine *Rungh*, a magazine that was launched in 1992, originally as the *South Asian Quarterly of Culture, Comment and Criticism* in Vancouver, Canada, that is best defined as a pan-ethnic alternative media. Further, *Rungh* employs advocacy journalism, supporting an alternative activist viewpoint to the mainstream media's "so-called objective" journalism (Berney and Robie 2008, 1). This chapter traces *Rungh*'s inception and development, focusing on the organization's evolution from a South Asian quarterly to a multifaceted pan-ethnoracial medium. It outlines the fiscal challenges that forced the organization to deploy a mediatized tactical intervention in order to survive and to broaden its perspective, so as to encompass an anti-racist, critical artistic framework that centres indigeneity in the Canadian context and underscores the struggles of self-representation. In doing so, *Rungh* embodies a pan-ethnoracial identity, drawing together artists, cultural workers, writers, and poets to provide a voice to the racially marginalized and thereby mounting a challenge to the white settler hegemonic forces inherent in Canadian society.

METHODOLOGICAL APPROACH

In analyzing *Rungh*, we employ a critical cultural studies approach (Hall 1992; Kellner 1995; Williams 1977), which utilizes a historical and contextual examination of *Rungh* magazine, with particular attention to the conditions that gave rise to it, the internal issues that the co-founders experienced, and the evolution of the magazine over time. In doing so, we undertook a critical examination of archived issues of the magazine on both the Simon Fraser University and *Rungh* websites, focusing on the range of articles and perspectives that were included, as well as the politics that informed them. Additionally, we studied contemporaneous news articles and Statistics Canada reports through online archives to situate the beginning of *Rungh* within the economic, political, and social context for South Asians in Canada. We also relied on the personal experiences and insights of one of the authors of this chapter (Yasmin Jiwani), who was actively involved in the Vancouver cultural arts scene at the time that *Rungh* was created and who also contributed to its early issues. To complement the analysis, we conducted semi-structured interviews with two of the magazine's co-founders, Zool Suleman and Sherazad Jamal. These interviews utilized a feminist conversation approach (see Hesse-Biber and Leavy 2007) in order to generate an insightful exchange between the interviewees and ourselves as the interviewers. They were recorded on Zoom with the consent of the participants. Both interviewees were then provided with a copy of the written analysis and were solicited for their feedback and consent.

MAIN FINDINGS

Rungh *Magazine: Birth and Evolution*

The late 1970s to the early 1990s were tumultuous times in many respects. Issues of race and representation were at the forefront, inspiring and instigating numerous challenges to the dominance of whiteness in the cultural and academic sectors of different nations (Hall, Critcher, Jefferson, Clarke, and Roberts 1978; Hall 1982; Said 1978). In Canada, the shockwaves of resistance to white hegemony were felt immediately in the cultural sector. The 1989 In Visible Colours Film and Video Festival in Vancouver was a vibrant contestation of white dominance and control of the film and video sectors. The festival, a brainchild of the co-organizers Zainub Verjee, who was with Women in Focus (a feminist video collective), and Lorraine Chan, who was with the National Film Board, brought together women of colour and Indigenous women from over seventy different countries, screening their works and simultaneously implementing an educational program in schools.

However, even prior to In Visible Colours, the Vancouver scene was a vibrant milieu of alternative media from marginalized racialized communities, which included such publications as *Ankur*, a South Asian quarterly, *Aquelarre*, a Latinx publication, and the spirited *Kinesis*, a feminist daily which had already evinced internal challenges to white feminist hegemony and was subsequently headed by Fatima Jaffer, the first woman of colour to be its editor. Following In Visible Colours, Vancouver witnessed a plethora of anti-racist gatherings, such as *Yellow Peril: Reconsidered* (a film, video, and photo exhibition in 1990), "The Appropriate Voice" (the 1992 Writers' Union of Canada conference), "Race and the Body Politic" (an artist residency at the Banff Centre in 1992),[1] and "It's a Cultural Thing" (the 1993 Association of National Non-Profit Artists Centres conference) (Lai 2014).

Monika Gagnon points out in *Other Conundrums* that these gatherings reflected an "impatience with the very terms of current arrangements" that developed from the "constraints of politeness and educating allies in the struggle" (2000, 53). Participants sought affirmation and empowerment in a space where they could be free to exchange without the daily constraints imposed on them in spaces that did not center people of colour. A different space was therefore necessary. Though these cross-racial alliances and race-focused events caused controversy in the press, in academic and policy circles, the "Writing Thru Race" conference held in Vancouver in 1994 created unprecedented debate on the matter due to the exclusivity of its daytime events for Indigenous writers and writers of colour, and again galvanized the resistance to white racist power structures. The anger even made its way to the House of Commons and raised questions of reverse-racism and the place of identity politics in Canada.[2]

Vancouver and Toronto were landscapes of resistance from the margins. In Toronto, the Desh Pardesh festival featuring South Asian artists of colour was central, and alternative publications such as *Diva: A Quarterly Journal of South Asian Women* and the *Toronto*

South Asian Review were thriving. Other alternative publications were increasingly focusing on representations of race, gender, and sexuality, as for example, *Parallelogramme*, *The Independent Eye*, and *Fuse Magazine*. This was the broader cultural milieu in which *Rungh* was born. Its mandate was created by both founders, as their joint contribution to the growing landscape of resistance. In retrospect, both co-founders noted in their last editorial in volume 3, issue 4, 1997, that "*Rungh* started as an idea. In the first editorial we stated that *Rungh* was about documenting and creating 'documents'; it was about dialogues, activism and creating a forum for discussion; finally, *Rungh* was about defining and challenging definitions. East-Indian. Paki. Indo-Canadian. Curryeater. These were the terms used to describe us South Asians." *Rungh*'s focus on South Asian realities clearly took its colour from the race politics that were rampant throughout the country, and most especially in British Columbia, the home province of Vancouver, where *Rungh* was born. In the section below, we highlight the broader context within the province and the country at large that contributed to the conditions which influenced *Rungh*'s emergence in 1991.

Demographic Changes and Economic Realities

The 1990s signalled rapid changes in immigration with a significant increase in the immigration of South Asians to Canada, many settling in British Columbia. Between 1981 and 2001, the number of South Asians in Canada more than tripled from 223,000 to 917,000 (Tran, Kaddatz, and Allard 2005). South Asians made up 1.2 per cent of the total Canadian population in 1991 (Raza 2012). In BC, 11 per cent of the population had Asian ancestry, with 3 per cent specifically reporting East Indian (read South Asian) as their only ethnic origin (Statistics Canada 1994). Vancouver specifically was the centre of recent immigration from Asia to Canada.

As visible minorities, South Asians were more concentrated in the lower-paid job sector, or the secondary market (Raza 2012). Immigrants who arrived after 1982 earned significantly less than their white counterparts (with a proportional income of 0.81 to 1 compared to non-visible minorities), not accounting for gender, age, and ability. An even greater disadvantage for newer immigrants was their lack of social networks, which resulted in a low social capital and little information about jobs or connections within companies. Reduced networking opportunities and exclusion from informal systems often blocked upward mobility within industries. This institutionalized racism was accompanied by explicit acts of racist violence.

Racism in the 1990s

The increased immigration of South Asians to Vancouver as early as the 1970s provoked a substantial degree of racism, "ranging from racist signs and bumper stickers to acts of vandalism, assaults on individuals, and [...] minor riots" (Johnston 1984, 21). *Rungh* co-founder Sherazad Jamal, an Ismaili Muslim South Asian Canadian, recalls:

> When we immigrated in the 70s, racism was more in-your-face. We were called various names on the playground. There was name-calling, we were harassed and people would throw rocks at you, intimidate you, beat you up ... and when they found out where you lived they would come throw things at your house. The people in authority didn't really know how to deal with it. They would tell the victim of the abuse to go and explain themselves to the abuser. "Just come to some understanding!" But that was the recipe for more abuse. (Sherazad Jamal, interview by author, 3 June 2020)

Racism against South Asian immigrants had long historical roots (Buchignani, Indra, and Srivastava 1985). An article from the *Vancouver Sun*, published in January 1992, succinctly captures the paradoxical sentiments that were being expressed; namely, that while racism was a growing reality, the issue was one of a cultural difference. The Economic Council of Canada argued that "federal funding should be diverted away from specific ethnic activities and groups, and towards improving race relations instead" (Griffin 1990).

Representational Violence

As expected, the racism that South Asians and other racialized minorities experienced was not confined to daily acts but also mediated through the mainstream media (Bannerji 1986; Jiwani 1992a). South Asian communities were depicted as being ultra-patriarchal, highly traditional, and married to archaic customs that they had brought with them when they immigrated to Canada. Critical in this discourse was the racist sexism which portrayed South Asian women as helpless victims of cultural norms, and South Asian men as monolithic, aggressive, sexist, and unpolished men (Griffin 1990; Thobani 1992). These stereotypes are similar to those ascribed to Muslim men, but with little acknowledgement of the significant difference within the South Asian diaspora.

In the cultural realm, several articles also criticized the lack of South Asian representation on television and in the art world. Even specifically ethnic TV stations such as Cathay International Television, Inc., underrepresented the South Asian community, according to a CRTC ruling (Canadian Press 1988). In December 1991, Ann Rosenberg writing for the *Vancouver Sun* specifically addressed the lack of South Asian representation in the art world when the Artists' Coalition for Local Colour opened a discussion with the Vancouver Art Gallery (VAG), after initially boycotting it. About ninety people, including fifteen curators from public galleries, gathered to discuss charges against the gallery in its handling of the exhibition *Fabled Territories* featuring the art of a dozen South Asian artists living in Britain. South Asian artists especially felt that local galleries had to make significant changes in order to adequately work with and highlight artists from their community. As Jiwani (1992b, 14) observed: "Located outside the pale of legitimized, institutional structures, these groups provide a valuable contribution to the otherwise monocultural landscape of the Canadian arts world. They draw attention to the inequities of mainstream arts institutions."

Rungh: *Reflecting Local Needs and Building International Links*

While the landscape in which *Rungh* was born was rife with a variety of alternative media, the specific needs of a subaltern South Asian population were not being met. For instance, ethnic newspapers such as the *Link*, *Chardi Kala*, and many others addressed the needs of specific linguistic and cultural subpopulations within the larger South Asian diaspora. Others, such as *Sanvad*, while critical, did not seem to go far enough to cover the cultural terrain and the nuances of generational sensibilities that characterized the wider South Asian diaspora. Moreover, many of the existing media did not cover events and issues within the art world, nor did they stray far from the heterosexual norms of the larger community. *Rungh*, as a South Asian publication, emerged to serve as a vehicle of expression for South Asian artists and cultural workers. It heralded the beginning of a new kind of alternative publication – polished, artistic, regular, and high-end as compared to the occasional publications and low-end production value of the other alternative publications emerging from the racialized margins. More than that, *Rungh* exhibited writings about film, food, poetry, and art – cultural works that spanned an entire continuum of artistic creations by South Asian writers and artists. As *Rungh* co-founder Sherazad Jamal puts it:

> We were looking not just to represent words – we were trying to represent art ... The Punjabi version of *Ankur* already existed, and there were also community newspapers like *Link*. Then, there were parallels like *Rice Paper*, and Paul Wong's "Yellow Peril." Video Inn had their own in-house magazine that they started to represent race initiatives in their magazine as white allies. The *Toronto South Asian Review* was a literary journal so again, it was primarily words. There was nothing like what *Rungh* was doing on an art and intellectual level. That was our audience. (Sherazad Jamal, interview by author, 3 June 2020)

Rungh, which means "colour" in Gujarat, Hindi, Punjabi, Farsi, and other languages, was created as a space for marginalized communities to discuss their experiences and opinions, as well as to share their art (see figure 11.1). In a climate where the increasing presence of visible minorities was causing tensions to rise, artists of colour were faced with challenges both in their daily lives and in the art world that confined them within forced narratives. *Rungh* was an opportunity to challenge these narratives while reshaping the Canadian cultural landscape. It documented the historical changes that were bringing the South Asian community closer together, starting with the first issue which included documentation on Desh Pardesh, a Toronto conference that represented a "benchmark for the South Asian cultural community in Canada" (Jamal and Suleman 1992). This "multi-disciplinary arts festival" sought to highlight "underrepresented and marginalized voices within the South Asian diasporic community" (SAVAC 2022). Like Desh Pardesh, *Rungh* challenged stale labels, addressing racism in cultural spheres, the war on women, and "the complex convergence of race, homophobia and AIDS" (Jamal and Suleman 1992). While the Desh Pardesh festival was a linchpin at the national level, *Rungh* was also influenced by events occurring in the South Asian diaspora in the UK, and the diasporic media within those communities, as, for example, the UK South Asian publication, *Bazaar Magazine* (Sherazad Jamal, interview by author, 3 June 2020).

From its beginnings, *Rungh* was intersectional. It tasked itself with maintaining community in the face of change and uncertainty, all the while empowering those on the margins of the margins. However, diasporic ethnic media like *Rungh* provided a community space that complemented existing media in South Asians' countries of origins while providing a distinctly different medium that reflected life in Canada (Rigoni and Saitta 2012). It did not ignore mainstream Canadian mass media but interacted with it critically. This is precisely the role of diasporic media, including videos, television, cinema, music, and internet spaces: to negotiate new cultural identities while challenging the ways in which communities are represented by the mass media (Cunningham 2001). In its print iteration, *Rungh*'s circulation was approximately 500–750 copies, reaching a wide community with common interests.

As a "space for self-reflexive discourse" for the community, *Rungh* also served as a hub of communicative networking among cultural players (Rigoni and Saitta 2012), allowing South Asian individuals to make up for some of the lack of social capital that contributed to the economic disadvantages and discrimination they faced (Raza 2012). As a successful minority diasporic medium, the magazine and events articulated resistance towards the universalistic ideologies of Canada (Georgiou 2013), especially the discourse leaning towards assimilation.

Starting with a target audience of the South Asian cultural community, *Rungh* loosened its "ethnic press" label in 1998 and featured more content about film and short fiction from other racialized communities. Today, *Rungh* continues to focus on art and activism within and outside the art world, but with a broader emphasis on work by Indigenous, Black, and People of Colour artists (The Cultch 2018). As Zool Suleman, one of *Rungh*'s founders put it, "*Rungh* was inspired by an absence of voices in Canada's cultural landscape. These voices today are referred to as IBPOC (Indigenous, Black, and People of Colour) – this term, also, does not do justice to the range of absences which exist" (The Cultch 2018).

Figure 11.1 | Vol. 1, issue 1 of *Rungh*.

Several aspects of *Rungh* deserve further mention here. First, it responded to a growing audience with specific needs within the South Asian diaspora. Second, it mirrored other initiatives that were taking place both nationally and internationally, demonstrating how ethno mediascapes transcend borders and boundaries (Appadurai 1990).

Third, what defined *Rungh* as different, aside from its content, was its look. While Zool Suleman focused on actualizing the editorial vision in word, co-founder Sherazad Jamal's focus was on doing the same visually. Her goal was to develop a considered aesthetic for the magazine that visually described the diasporic experience of the South Asian community. She worked with her own design and advisory team, composed of South Asian visual artist Amir Ali Alibhai, and Caucasian graphic designers Dugg Simpson and David Lauleinen of Eyebyte Design. Their working partnership became a site in which the ideals of creating spaces where voices of colour were given primacy with white ally support were put into practice. Hence, *Rungh* embraced a strategic essentialism (Spivak 1988).

In the Interstices of All That Is Alternative: Locating Rungh *in the Landscape of Alternative Media*

In his seminal work on alternative media, John Downing reminds us that the problematic category of "alternative" always presupposes something it is alternative to (Downing, Villarreal Ford, Gil, and Stein 2001). The question then becomes one of ferreting out what the alternative is in a world that seems to be full of alternatives (even within what is generally referred to as the mainstream). Indeed, the debate over the definition of alternative media has preoccupied much of the early literature. Clemencia Rodríguez (2001) defines it as citizens' media, astutely pointing out that previous definitions of what constitutes alternative in alternative media tended to deploy binary structures predicated on essentialist notions of power, as in small media versus big media, capitalist versus socialist, etc. Carpentier (2011) and others have referred to alternative media as participatory media, fracturing the lines between producers and consumers.

However, rather than debating the issue, we adhere to a definition of alternative media as media which are critical of power structures and hegemonic blocs. Such a definition fits the *Rungh* magazine model best. Rather than relying on small-scale and simple production values, *Rungh* embraces a more polished look. Moreover, where small-scale and participatory media tend to be horizontal in organization, *Rungh* is more of a collective structured on hierarchical principles, headed previously by the two co-founders with an advisory group, and now spearheaded by one of the original founders with assistance from an advisory group and a structured board of directors. Here, Marisol Sandoval and Christian Fuch's (2010) definition best captures the complexity of *Rungh*; instead of focusing solely on the processes of production or the commodified final product, *Rungh*'s alternativeness stems from the perspectives it offers, the writers and artists it features, and its alliances with other marginalized groups. It is the critique articulated in this media that makes it an alternative media.

Rungh's critique of dominant societal standards and exclusionary politics is premised on a celebration of difference that is not simply a cosmetic performance of difference but rather one anchored in the complexity and contradictoriness of difference; in other words, a critique that is levelled at hegemonic power within and outside of marginalized communities. This is most apparent in its critical coverage of artistic productions and its giving voice to those who are on the interstices of the margins. In this way, *Rungh* stands in opposition to the mainstream ethnic newspapers of the time, as, for example, the *Link*, which represented the voice of the South Asian communities as a whole, but often incorporated a very mainstream orientation focusing on consumer behaviour and an apolitical stance, much like the Latino press in the USA during the early 1980s (Downing 1992). However, in the latter case, as Downing observes, the Latino media assumed a more assimilationist stance and were, consequently, less empowering for the marginalized communities they served. *Rungh*'s alternative and critical politics were front and center, posted on the masthead which described it as "an interdisciplinary magazine committed to the exploration of traditional and contemporary South Asian cultural production and its contexts."

Nancy Fraser's concept of a subaltern counterpublic is especially applicable to *Rungh*, given its peripheral status on the margins of the larger South Asian communities. As Fraser defines it, subaltern counterpublics are "parallel discursive arenas where members of subordinated social groups invent and circulate counterdiscourses, which in turn permit them to formulate oppositional interpretations of their identities, interests, and needs" (1992). Hence, if the diasporic South Asian public sphere can be regarded as a counterpublic, *Rungh* would constitute a subaltern counterpublic, dealing with such taboo topics as sexuality, contesting traditions, and asserting a full recognition of citizenship rights. An examination of *Rungh*'s various issues reveals its status as a subaltern medium reaching subaltern audiences: for instance, volume 3, issue 2 examined South

Asian identity in contemporary alternative film and video, issue 3 considered "queering" the diaspora, issue 4 focused on immigration and citizenship rights, and subsequent issues dealt with eating disorders, food, and antiracism.

Changes and Survival

It is fair to say that the systemic choices of funders to underfund *Rungh* played a significant role in the decision to pass on the editorship of the magazine in 1997. As Sherazad Jamal recalls, one of the issues that was endemic was the struggle for funding and resources to make the *Rungh* project sustainable. Through 1998, Jamal continued her work as art director and production, distribution, and event coordinator, until the new Gill editorial team took over management and production of *Rungh* in 1998 to 1999. As she described it, being an unpaid worker and stay-at-home mom came with all the judgments and expectations of those roles, both inside and outside the home.

As an independent lawyer, Zool Suleman's office was often the site where discussions, tactical interventions, and other activist endeavours were funnelled, adding to the already existing stresses of paid and unpaid activist work. As a result of these internal and external issues, the task of editing and producing the magazine was passed on to a series of guest editors. Jamal remarked that had adequate funding been available to sustain the *Rungh* project, it is likely that this decision would not have been made.

From 1998 to 2000, *Rungh* continued its tradition of providing critical commentary, pushing the boundaries of normative values both within and outside the South Asian diaspora. However, the transition to a series of guest editors also reflected a change. Taking the helm, guest editors Ashok Mathur and Sourayan Mookerjea stated in a *Rungh* editorial:

> One of our concerns was that, as soon as we broach the subject of anti-racism, we necessarily move beyond what might be thought of as an exclusively "South Asian" issue. How then, do we address anti-racism adequately but still maintain some sort of connection to South Asian arts and culture?
>
> What we decided upon was a blend of materials originating from a relatively wider spectrum of contributors. (vol. 4, issues 1 and 2)

Figure 11.2 | *Rungh*'s "Temptation Issue."

Volume 4 of *Rungh* then shifted to a critical examination of anti-racism pedagogy from a wider perspective (see figure 11.2). It marked a pivotal point in the transition of the magazine from a strictly South Asian focus to one that embraced a more inclusive critique of racism from across the spectrum of racialized communities and interrogating race essentialism. It was at that point that the original founders, Jamal and Suleman, left the magazine. The issues that followed this juncture were headed by a new editorial team consisting of Prem Gill, Jarnail Gill, Sharan Gill, Jagdeesh Mann, and Harry Sadhra.

The 1999 issue, under the editorial eye of Prem Gill, Jarnail Gill, and Sharan Gill, reflected yet another shift. The cover, for example, featured a deliberately provocative cover of an apparently naked (though only visible from shoulders up), visually eye-catching young South Asian woman, licking a piece of fruit. Titled the "Temptation Issue," the contents focused on films, but the theme of tempting sexuality was evident in the visuals included throughout the magazine. Writing about the magazine in 1999, the *Vancouver Sun* reporter Marke Andrews (1999) observed, "It's safe to say that *Rungh* is making the transition from essay forum to pop-culture clarion in such a way as to not lose its reader base. Despite the come-on cover and the added colour on its pages, *Rungh* still manages to 'promote dialogue, document events and challenge definitions.'"

The "Temptation Issue" marked a playful way to subvert common stereotypes of South Asian women as passive victims of an oppressive cultural order. However, in so doing, the issue also reflects the same patriarchal objectification of women as that pervading dominant and mainstream media.

By late 1999, after two publications in which the Gill editorial group had put forth their renewed vision replete with a new logo and feel, *Rungh* ceased publication. In part, this was due to the constant and endemic pressure of finding funding that would support their efforts and provide stability to the organization. The Canadian government had provided core funding to several of the larger arts establishments, but *Rungh* was not one of them. It remained on the margins as a marginal publication serving a marginalized population. Without an advertising base, the magazine depended on grants for its survival. At five dollars a copy, it was hard-pressed to accumulate enough of a profit margin to keep going.

Revival through Remembrance

In 2004 and 2005, *Rungh* re-emerged from its period of dormancy, not to continue its publication but to keep the cultural memory of its short life intact. Suleman retrieved the physical archives from the

Gills, re-registered the *Rungh* Society, and Jamal secured funding to digitize its archive of previous issues in an "in process" website. This was the first step in mediatization as a tactic of survival.

Rungh relaunched in September 2017 at the Primary Colours/ Couleurs primaires gathering on Lekwungen territories near Victoria, British Columbia. The choice of this gathering as the site signalled *Rungh*'s reinterpretation and shift to centre Indigenous artists, placing the "I for Indigenous" first in IBPOC (Indigenous, Black, and People of Colour) to reflect current discussions in the Canadian art world. This gathering also mirrored *Rungh*'s covering of Desh Pardesh in its first issue in 1992, which then signalled a focus on South Asian artists. As well, it was reminiscent of *Rungh*'s shift in focus in the "Anti-Racism Issue" (vol. 4, issues 1–2) with the editors Ashok Mathur and Sourayan Mookerjea, which reflected a wider spectrum of contributors. By 2017, the tone of discourse in the art world and beyond had changed to give attention to Indigenous issues, and *Rungh* became part of the push to view the art world through an Indigenous lens rather than the currently dominant white point of view.

In addition to the shifting discourse of the art world to focus on Indigenous issues, a Canada 150 grant from the BC Museums Association, of which *Rungh* is still part, helped set the relaunch in motion. Canada's 150th brought up several discussions on Indigenous issues outside of the art world spurred in part by the publication of the Truth and Reconciliation Commission's Report and the ensuing changes at the Canada Council. *Rungh*'s changes in partnership and involvement with Primary Colours reflected this reality.

At *Rungh*'s relaunch celebration party, numerous artists and contributors spoke about what the magazine represented for them in the 1990s. Suleman, for his part as a co-founder, spoke about *Rungh*'s mission and its evolution from a largely South Asian magazine to one that is more inclusive of differences, as previously mentioned. As he put it:

> People always said to me, "What's *Rungh* about? Is it a South Asian project? Is it for brown people?" and my reply always back is that "*Rungh* means colour." We've changed our tagline. It is true that we're rooted in South Asian histories and that we have a space from which we emanate. But this space is inclusive, this space is trying to not totalize everything, but trying to engage with things and have these conversations. We're in

> the middle of a significant, and I hope continuous Indigenous moment in this country. And I think we need to honour that, not as a moment, but as a future and a present. And *Rungh* wants to be a part of that conversation too. And in that conversation we also have to deal with: the settlers have arrived here, all the immigrants arrived here, the refugees arrived here, many by choice, many not by choice. And those conversations need to be included as well. (*Rungh* Communications 2018)

This is not to say that *Rungh* completely shifted away from its South Asian focus in 2017. As reported in an article on "Centering Indigenous Art Practices" in an online issue of *Rungh* (2019), the gathering titled "Redness: Blackness: Thinking," led by Rinaldo Walcott and David Garneau, was also pivotal in shifting *Rungh*'s focus. The gathering discussed the issues related to the terms "Black," "Indigenous," and "People of Colour" that can act as destructive "silos" and lead to "false binaries and hierarchies" (Creighton-Kelly, Trépanier, and Suleman 2019). The conversation with Suleman, Creighton-Kelly, and Trépanier underscored the importance of challenging these issues through rejecting binaries and creating spaces in which all artists of colour, whether addressing "Asian-ness or blackness, or brownness or Latin-ness," can express themselves outside of the dominant white lens.

Mediatization as a Strategy of Survival

A major aspect of tactical mediatization is the incorporation of new media into an organization's "mandate and system of values" (Sawchuk 2013, 47) while "maintaining prior practices of communication" (56) that the group has adopted through years of democratic conversation and group decision-making. Today, *Rungh* embraces a two-pronged approach that reflects tactical mediatization: it adopts various ways of maintaining and sharing its archive while also creating new forms of media to bring *Rungh* into the present day and keep it in tune with current political questions. To preserve its archives, *Rungh* has created partnerships with Simon Fraser University's library in order to digitize its previous and current issues. It has also formed a partnership with Artexte Information Centre, an artist-run "library, research centre and exhibition space for contemporary art" in Montreal (Artexte 2020). Suleman has sought to

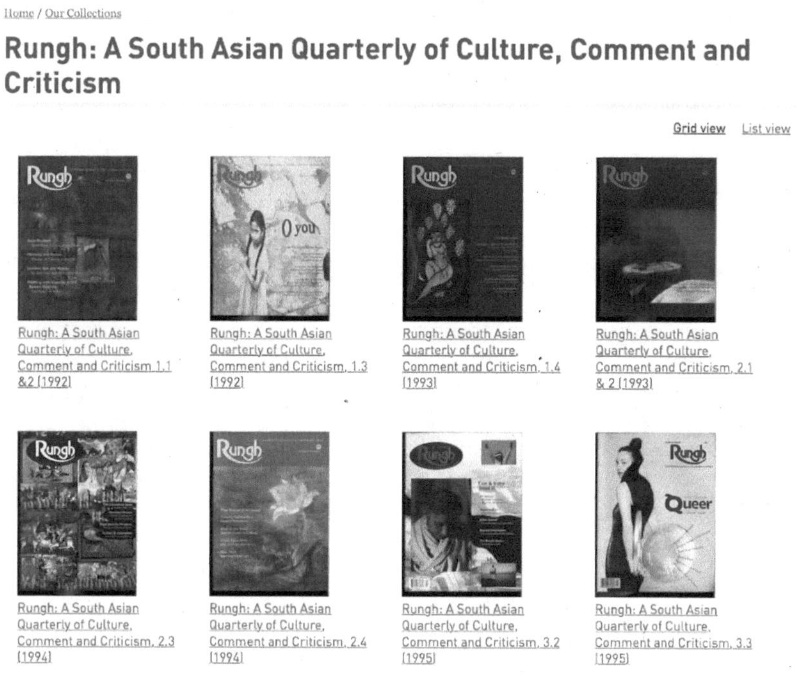

Home / Our Collections

Runqh: A South Asian Quarterly of Culture, Comment and Criticism

Grid view List view

Rungh: A South Asian Quarterly of Culture, Comment and Criticism 1.1 &2 [1992]

Rungh: A South Asian Quarterly of Culture, Comment and Criticism, 1.3 [1992]

Rungh: A South Asian Quarterly of Culture, Comment and Criticism, 1.4 [1993]

Rungh: A South Asian Quarterly of Culture, Comment and Criticism, 2.1 & 2 [1993]

Rungh: A South Asian Quarterly of Culture, Comment and Criticism, 2.3 [1994]

Rungh: A South Asian Quarterly of Culture, Comment and Criticism, 2.4 [1994]

Rungh: A South Asian Quarterly of Culture, Comment and Criticism, 3.2 [1995]

Rungh: A South Asian Quarterly of Culture, Comment and Criticism, 3.3 [1995]

Figure 11.3 | *Rungh*'s archive in collaboration with Simon Fraser University.

increase its international reach by finding sister sites or similar organizations in other countries, using a multi-site approach to increase the chances of academics coming across and studying *Rungh*. In these ways, *Rungh* archives remain vibrant sites of research into Canadian ethnic and alternative media, conserving *Rungh*'s prior communications practices while adopting new technologies to disseminate its original ideas (see figure 11.3).

Mediatization through an Online Format

Since its 2017 relaunch, *Rungh*'s presence is web-based, through its website and newsletter, and offline through participation and organization of community events. On its website, rungh.org, visitors are invited to peruse through the archive, learn about the programs of the Rungh Cultural Society, read the latest issue of the magazine, follow

Figure 11.4 | Archive on *Rungh*'s website.

the news ("samachar" in Gujarati), access the list of artists and contributors, and learn about the history of the organization (see figure 11.4). This online shift has greatly increased *Rungh*'s reach. The web version (2017–present) now counts over 40,000 visits per year and growing, with unique visitors in the 20,000 range. *Rungh*'s free online mailing list is also distributed to approximately 1,000 subscribers (Zool Suleman, personal communication, 2 March 2022).

As an organization committed to furthering the conversation, *Rungh* has embraced a forward-thinking approach in its use of communication technologies. For example, one emerging initiative, pending, of course, funding, is the *Rungh* Redux, a plot-and-scatter site that clearly illustrates *Rungh*'s mandate of seeing the art world through an IBPOC lens. It centres artists of colour as the initial "window" into the Canadian art world and allows for the exploration of IBPOC artists' connections with each other and their past work and invites their reflections on the current moment. According to Suleman, *Rungh*'s historical aspect and its new incarnation "have to talk to each other." He adds: "Histories must be present, but also, what is current? This needs to be on our mind." The constant reflective recontextualization of *Rungh*'s history through different media channels helps *Rungh* to continue its original mandate while adapting to change.

CONCLUSION

Rungh magazine and cultural society, then, constitute a form of alternative media; alternative in the sense of challenging hegemonic interpretations of race, ethnicity, religion, and culture, as well as in its very structure as a non-profit society that is overseen by a voluntary community board. It is also an alternative to mainstream South Asian publications, thus representing a subaltern counterpublic. Finally, it embodies advocacy journalism through its alternative activist stances. However, unlike the DIY style of alternative media that is commonly articulated within the literature on the subject, *Rungh* would best be described as a form of critical alternative media (Sandoval and Fuchs 2010). It is forced to join forces with other institutions, for and not-for-profit, in order to disseminate its works and to create a record of its existence. On the other hand, the content it offers to its readers is critical of the white, neoliberal structures that impede and bury the works of Indigenous, Black, and People of Colour (IBPOC). It seeks to view the art world through the lens of these artists rather than through the predominant viewpoint of white artists.

Whether *Rungh* will continue to survive depends on its ability to draw funding. Situated at margins, it may enjoy some of the benefits of being viewed as avant-garde – on the critical edge – by cultural commentators and academics alike. On the other hand, as one of the few places where Indigenous, Black, and other People of Colour are able to engage with each other and actively contribute to the conversation, *Rungh* fulfills a need. In that sense, its survival and continued evolution are coeval with these needs.

APPENDIX: TIMELINE

1991: *Rungh* was founded in Vancouver, British Columbia by Zool Suleman and Sherazad Jamal and was established as a non-profit with a Canada Council Explorations grant.

Summer 1992: The first issue of *Rungh* magazine was launched at Desh Pardesh in Toronto as a print magazine.

1992–1997: *Rungh* was published as the *South Asian Quarterly of Culture, Comment, and Criticism* under its first editorial team consisting of Jamal and Suleman. It hosted and produced art events like readings, workshops, and creative productions, and fostered a variety of conversations.

1997–1998: *Rungh* had several guest editors, which included Amirali Alibhai, Yasmin Ladha, and Ian Rashid. The last 1998 issue, guest-edited by Sourayan Mookerjea and Ashok Mathur, was pivotal in that it shifted the focus to anti-racism and broadened the approach to include other communities of colour. During that time, *Rungh* also programmed events, engaged in advocacy, and fostered a creative hub of activities.

1999: *Rungh* published volume 4, issues 3 and 4, under a second editorial team: Prem Gill, Jarnail Gill, Sharan Gill, Jagdeesh Mann, and Harry Sadhra.

2000–2004: *Rungh* dormant.

2005–2017: *Rungh* existed as an "in process" webspace.

September 2017: *Rungh* relaunched on Lekwungen territories near Victoria, British Columbia, at the Primary Colours/Couleurs primaires gathering. This was another pivotal moment, reflecting a shift in the direction of *Rungh* to focus on Indigeneity as a starting point, continuing a theme of the 1998 guest-edited issue on critical anti-racism.

NOTES

1 "Race and the Body Politic" was a 1992 artist residency at the Banff Centre that featured twenty POC artists. Through the involvement of Chris Creighton-Kelly, who was also active as a part of *Rungh*, this artist residency indirectly motivated the creation of the Aboriginal Arts Program (Delaney 2020).

2 Sponsored by the Writers' Union of Canada (TWUC), the "Writing Thru Race" conference brought together 180 First Nations writers and writers of colour to discuss issues of "representation, cultural and racial identity, cultural appropriation, and racial and cultural barriers to access in the cultural industries" (Tator, Henry, and Mattis 1998, 86). Although the evening meetings were open to all, daytime meetings were by invitation and exclusively for writers of colour and First Nations writers. This decision provoked six months of debate, which eventually made its way to the House of Commons and into the media.

REFERENCES

Andrews, Marke. 1999. "Revamped *Rungh* Wants to Widen Appeal." *Vancouver Sun*, 12 February 1999.

Appadurai, Arjun. 1990. "Disjuncture and Difference in the Global Cultural Economy." *Public Culture* 2 (2): 1–24.

Artexte. 2020. "About Us." https://artexte.ca/en/about-us/.

Bannerji, Himani. 1986. "Now You See Us/Now You Don't." *Video Guide* 8 (40): 1–4.

Berney, Jane, and David Robie. 2008. "Don't Publish and Be Damned: An Advocacy Media Case Study." *Global Media Journal* 2 (1): 1–21.

Buchignani, Norman, Doreen Marie Indra, and Ram Srivastiva. 1985. *Continuous Journey: A Social History of South Asians in Canada*. Toronto: McClelland and Stewart in association with the Multiculturalism Directorate, Dept. of the Secretary of State and the Canadian Government Pub. Centre, Supply and Services Canada.

Canadian Press. 1988. "CRTC Limits Station's License." *Vancouver Sun*, 6 February 1988.

Carpentier, Nico. 2011. *Media and Participation: A Site of Ideological-Democratic Struggle*. Bristol: Intellect.

Creighton-Kelly, Chris, France Trépanier, and Zool Suleman. 2019. "Centering Indigenous Art Practices." *Rungh* 6 (3).

The Cultch. 2018. "*Rungh*. Means. Colour: An Interview with Our Community Partner." *The Cultch*, 20 November 2018. https://thecultch.com/rungh-means-colour-an-interview-with-our-community-partner/.

Cunningham, Stuart. 2001. "Popular Media as Public 'Sphericules' for Diasporic Communities." *International Journal of Cultural Studies* 4 (2): 131–47.

Delaney, Trynne. 2020. "Episode 2: Chris Creighton-Kelly Interviews Aruna Srivastava." *The Insurgent Architects' House for Creative Writing*, 5 May 2020. https://www.tiahouse.ca/episode-2-chris-creighton-kelly-interviews-aruna-srivastava/.

Downing, John D. 1993. "Spanish-Language Media in the Greater New York Region during the 1980s." In *Ethnic Minority Media: An International Perspective*, edited by Stephen H. Riggins, 256–275. Newbury Park, CA: SAGE.

Downing, John D., Tamara Villarreal Ford, Genève Gil, and Laura Stein. 2001. *Radical Media: Rebellious Communication and Social Movements*. Thousand Oaks, CA: SAGE.

Fraser, Nancy. 1992. "Rethinking the Public Sphere: A Contribution to the Critique of Actually Existing Democracy." In *Habermas and the Public Sphere,* edited by Craig Calhoun, 109–42. Cambridge, MA: MIT Press.

Gagnon, Monika Kin. 2000. *Other Conundrums: Race, Culture, and Canadian Art*. Vancouver BC: Arsenal Pulp Press.

Georgiou, Myria. 2013. "Diaspora in the Digital Era: Minorities and Media Representation." *Journal on Ethnopolitics and Minority Issues in Europe* 12 (4): 80–99.

Griffin, Kevin. 1990. "East Indian Women Find Strong Voice in Mahila Leader." *Vancouver Sun*, 10 December 1990.

Hall, Stuart. 1992. "Cultural Studies and Its Theoretical Legacies." In *Cultural Studies*, edited by Lawrence Grossberg, Cary Nelson, and Paula Treichler, 277–94. New York: Routledge.

Hall, Stuart, Chas Critcher, Tony Jefferson, John Clarke, and Brian Roberts. 1978. *Policing the Crisis Mugging, the State and Law and Order*. New York: Holmes and Meier.

Hesse-Biber, Sharlene, and Patricia Leavy. 2007. *Feminist Research Practice: A Primer*. Thousand Oaks, CA: SAGE.

Karim, Karim H. 2013. "Are Ethnic Media Alternative?" In *Alternative Media in Canada*, edited by David Skinner, Patricia Mazepa, and Kirsten Kozolanka, 165–83. Vancouver: UBC Press.

Kellner, Douglas. 1995. *Media Culture: Cultural Studies, Identity and Politics between the Modern and the Postmodern*. London & New York: Routledge.
Jamal, Sherazad, and Zool Suleman. 1992. "Editorial." *Rungh* 1 (1–2).
Jiwani, Yasmin. 1992a. "Canadian Media and Racism, to Be and Not to Be: South Asians as Victims and Oppressors in the *Vancouver Sun*." *Sanvad* 5 (45): 13–15.
– 1992b. "Culture and Recreation." In *Women's Resource Guide: British Columbia/Yukon*, edited by SFU Public Interest Research Group, 13–15. Burnaby, BC: SFU Public Interest Research Group (PIRG).
Johnston, Hugh J. 1984. *The East Indians in Canada*. Ottawa: Canadian Historical Association.
Lai, Larissa. 2014. *Slanting I, Imagining We: Asian Canadian Literary Production in the 1980s and 1990s*. Waterloo: Wilfrid Laurier University Press.
Raza, Muhammad Munib. 2012. "Social and Human Capital: The Determinants of Economic Integration of South Asian Immigrants in Canada." PhD diss., University of Western Ontario.
Rigoni, Isabelle, and Eugénie Saitta. 2012. *Mediating Cultural Diversity in a Globalised Public Space*. London: Palgrave Macmillan.
Rodríguez, Clemencia. 2001. *Fissures in the Mediascape: An International Study of Citizens' Media*. New York: Hampton Press.
Rosenberg, Ann. 1991. "Racism Charges against Gallery Aired." *Vancouver Sun*, 7 December 1991.
Rungh. 1996. 4 (1 and 2). https://rungh.org/archives/print-magazine/.
Rungh Communications. 2018. "*Rungh* Re-Launch." YouTube. https://www.youtube.com/watch?v=vXnfNqxZXK8&feature=youtu.be.
Said, Edward W. 1978. *Orientalism*. New York: Pantheon Books.
Sandoval, Marisol, and Christian Fuchs. 2010. "Towards a Critical Theory of Alternative Media." *Telematics and Informatics* 27 (2): 141–50.
SAVAC. 2022. "Desh Pardesh – South Asian Visual Arts Centre." https://www.savac.net/about/history.
Sawchuk, Kim. 2013. "Tactical Mediatization and Activist Ageing: Pressures, Push-Backs, and the Story of RECAA." *MedieKultur: Journal of Media and Communication Research* 29 (54): 47–64.
Spivak, Gayatri C. 1988. "Can the Subaltern Speak?" In *Marxism and the Interpretation of Culture*, edited by Cary Nelson, 271–313. Urbana: Univ. of Illinois Press.
Statistics Canada. 1994. "1991 Census Highlights: As Released by *The Daily*." *The Daily Catalogue* 96.

Tator, Carol, Frances Henry, and Winston Mattis. 1998. *Challenging Racism in the Arts: Case Studies of Controversy and Conflict*. Toronto: University of Toronto Press.

Thobani, Sunera. 1992. "Culture Isn't Cause of Violence." *Vancouver Sun*, 3 January 1992.

Tran, Kelly, Jennifer Kaddatz, and Paul Allard. 2005. "South Asians in Canada: Unity through Diversity." *Statistics Canada Catalogue* 11: 20–25.

Verjee, Zainub. 2020. "In Visible Colours: The Making and Unmaking of the Women of Colour and Third World Women International Film and Video Festival and Symposium." Other Places. https://www.otherplaces.mano-ramo.ca/zainub-verjee-in-visible-colours/.

Williams, Raymond. 1977. *Marxism and Literature*. Oxford: Oxford University Press.

CHAPTER TWELVE

Anti-Racist and Feminist Organizing in Canada's Media Industries: A Closer Look at Didihood: The Sisterhood of South Asian Creatives in Canada

Alysha Bains

INTRODUCTION

In 2016, co-founder of Didihood Arti Patel tweeted: "we want to start something for brown [identifying] women in media, who's interested?"[1] which prompted a significant response from South Asian women across the country. Together, Patel, Nikkjit Gill, and Roohi Sahajpal founded and launched Didihood: The Sisterhood of South Asian Creatives in Canada,[2] a collective representing a unique intersectional feminist intervention that reveals the "dialectical tension" between the structure of cultural production in media and South Asian feminine agency (Saha 2018, 47) in the contemporary moment.

The institutional structures of cultural production across the cultural industries have the capability to undermine the disruptive possibilities of creative practice and opportunities implicitly and explicitly for self-definition of racialized communities (Saha 2018, 170). While such structures are embedded within the broader logic of capital and white masculinities, this chapter examines the ways in which Didihood has come to be a curious site that cannot be described as entirely either ethnic or entirely mainstream media.

WHAT IS DIDIHOOD?

Didihood began as a loose idea in 2012, when three South Asian Canadian journalism students started to question not only the lack of diverse representation in the Canadian media, but also the lack of diversity in the industry. After graduating from journalism school and entering the media industry, Patel, Gill, and Sahajpal launched Didihood in Vancouver and Toronto in 2018. The collective was launched both online via Instagram and Twitter and in-person via community in-person events in 2016. Didihood was launched as an effort to create "a space for South Asian women working in the media, art, and creative industries to connect, work together, and inspire the next generation of brown girls to follow their dreams" (Didihood 2020). Didihood locates the complexity of representation in the diaspora and notes that Punjabi representation tends to dominate and "tak[e] up too much space" in the media (personal communication, 2021). The work of Didihood strives to be reflective of the diversity and intersections of the community. Through their active Instagram and Twitter, the collective circulates career and funding opportunities, cultural commentary, and socio-politically conscious content relating to justice and equity. While the collective has an online presence, they also hold events and meet-ups specific to mentorship opportunities, panel discussions, and networking events. Since 2018, they have had a successful mentorship program for South Asian women working across the cultural industries. Didihood, as a multi-modal form of communication that operates both on and in-person via community events, provides a unique mediated critical space for South Asian women to communicate and respond to traditional and institutionalized media landscapes in Canada to challenge common exclusionary practices, such as the overwhelming whiteness of Canadian media, in order to move towards a more equitable and inclusive representation of gender and ethnicity.

This chapter begins by situating the existing literature, outlining community context and the place of South Asian diasporic media in Canada, to set the stage for this chapter. This then lays the groundwork for an intersectional approach and uses analyses of interpersonal, disciplinary, cultural, and structural power. In order to do so, this research draws on a semi-structured interview with Didihood's three founders to explore how second-generation South Asian women are organizing to refashion opportunities in media spaces to build community beyond categories of mainstream or ethnic media. Through this lens, the chapter showcases how power dynamics overlook the experiences of South Asian women employed in Canadian cultural industries.

HISTORICAL COMMUNITY CONTEXT

Situating early South Asian migration patterns helps us understand how historical context continues to "affect" the Canadian diaspora in the contemporary moment (Singh and Singh 2008, 157). Thus, this section offers a snapshot of how the community's location in Canada has been impacted by key historical conditions and colonial forces.[3] While the complexity of the community's migration to Canada goes beyond the scope of this chapter, the purpose here is to have enough historical community context in order to understand (1) how South Asians have come to view Canada as a "homeland," (2) the role diasporic media plays in the South Asian Canadian diaspora, and (3) the relationship diasporic media has had with the children of South Asian immigrants in Canada.

As a result of their direct colonial ties to the British India army, South Asians have had a presence in Canada since the late 1800s. However, explicitly racist and exclusionary public policy ensured that the community did not experience Canada as a hospitable new homeland. At the turn of the twentieth century, the country's national imaginary relied on the construction of a "White Canada" (Kazimi 2011). Whiteness, as an ideological national force, caused South Asians to view Canada as a temporary place of work, rather than a land of settlement (Kazimi 2011). The media representation of South Asians echoed this hostility and suspicion, portraying the brown male body as a source of national threat and pathology. This was especially pertinent in the history of the *Komagata Maru*, which demonstrates how representation of South Asians in Canada as "threatening" or "dangerous" has historical roots in the nation's past.

Immigration shifted in the post–World War II era, where a large influx of South Asians arrived in Canada as a result of Canada's changing economic needs. While South Asians were re-enfranchised and given the right to vote in British Columbia in 1948, race remained a powerful sociopolitical force in Canada. A significant shift in Canadian immigration was introduced in the Canadian Immigration Act of 1952, which introduced a quota system with a focus on the recruitment of general labourers. The points-based assessment focused on "economic" conditions rather than explicit reference to race and nationality (Buchignani, Indra, and Srivastava 1985). The ideological underpinnings of whiteness provide a structure for the consistent refashioning of systemic racism that exists in the contemporary moment. In addressing the changing demographics of Canada because of reformed immigration legislation, Prime Minister Pierre Trudeau responded to the changing cultural and ethnic composition of the nation by establishing the state policy of multiculturalism (Nayar 2004, 10).

A NEW HOMELAND AND SOUTH ASIAN MEDIA IN THE DIASPORA

As the 1970s brought forward a new context of immigration via the introduction of multiculturalism, the South Asian community began to grow nationally. As a result, South Asian–produced media began to take shape with broadcaster Shushma Datt, who became the first key figure of diasporic programming for the South Asian community in Canada (South Asian Stories 2017). Datt made history as the first South Asian female broadcaster when she founded Rim Jhim Radio, the first twenty-four-hour radio station with South Asian content, in 1987 (South Asian Stories 2017). Programming across Datt's radio and television productions was focused on community issues pertaining to the homeland, but also aimed to forge a sense of community and spotlight social issues in the community and nation.

In addition to mainstream media, less conventional forms of diasporic media in the 1980s also aimed to achieve this goal. South Asian playwrights, for example, began "making a concerted effort to engage with the entanglement of issues at home as well in diasporic spaces" (Bhatia 2013, 135). As Stuart Hall (1990) argued, cultural identities have "a continuous 'play' of history, culture and power" (225). As the generation of the post-1965 immigration wave began to grow in Canada (Shariff 2008), Bollywood began responding to the international reach of the diaspora. Films began to acknowledge the "real consequences" of mass migration, which included the generational gaps between immigrant parents and their Canadian-born children (Hirji 2010, 3). While the first generation has a sense of homeland identity or "previous identity" (Rajiva 2005, 26), there are limitations to relying on binary language to describe second-generation identities. As described by Shariff (2008), second-generation South Asian identity construction "call[s] for a sophisticated grasp of cross-cultural dialectics and the sociopolitical dimensions of Otherness that will mark their adult lives" (Durham 2004, 141).

The importance of generational relationships and representation in South Asian media first became visible in the 1990s and early 2000s. The South Asian diasporic film industry brought films such as *Bend It Like Beckham* (2003) and *Mississippi Masala* (1991) to the global South Asian diaspora. Such films were found to be key cultural texts for the participants in Durham's (2004) study on understanding the generational experiences in relation to South Asian identities and diasporic media. Durham's study revealed that these specific hybrid discourses "offered hope" for second-generation South Asian girls in the United States. Hybridity points to a condition of the ongoing construction of identity where Hall (1990) argued there is not only difference but also transformation (235). Durham's findings highlight South Asian diasporic media as a meaningful site of intergenerational dialogue and exchange. Hybrid discourses described by the participants became a site of authenticity and relatability in the construction of their own diasporic subjectivities in relation to gender and sexuality (154). This was also reflected in popular commentaries by both Fariha Róisín (2017) and Rajpreet Heir (2017) when they noted that *Bend It Like Beckham* represented the first time that they, as South Asians growing up in North America, felt they could relate to diasporic media. As Róisín points out, "it means that for a split second we get to see what it means to be us, not an appropriative version of us; us in full definition, spilling with flaws and curiosity, with the quintessential quirks" (n.p.). Such a reflection points to the ways the film captured a snapshot of the multidimensional experiences of second-generation young people. This stands in contrast to the ways mainstream media relies on representations of "culture clash" to simplify understandings of second-generation South Asian experiences by creating a distinct binary between the first generation and dominant white society (Handa 2003, 7). In their respective findings, Durham (2004) and Handa (2003) point to the inadequacies and problematic nature of such explanations for racialized generational relationships and experiences. By constantly relying on a binary experience between generations, emphasis is placed solely on what is deemed "traditional" and "modern" culture

(Handa 2003, 7). The "culture clash" implies conflict in the lives of second-generation women as rooted between two seemingly opposing cultures and works to conceal the workings of institutional powers such as systemic racism (Handa 2003). As Handa highlights, the simplistic notion of "culture clash" fails to recognize the reality of day-to-day experiences that are far more complex. These thin explanations of identity became a stand-in for the absence of a language that can adequately describe the nuances of diasporic South Asian lived experiences of the nation.

As argued by Yu (2018), it is the misrepresentation and underrepresentation of racialized communities in the production and content of media that leads many communities "to create media for and by themselves" (346). This became evident in the early 2000s, when the South Asian community in British Columbia had the largest number of ethnic media outlets in both Punjabi and English (Murray, Yu, and Ahadi 2007, 25). In a recent comparison of diasporic and mainstream media consumption in Ottawa across four ethnocultural and immigrant communities, a high consumption rate of diasporic TV amongst the South Asian community was revealed (Ahmed and Veronis 2020, 306). More specifically, the study indicated that 39 per cent of Canadian-born participants consume diasporic TV, while 63 per cent opted for mainstream TV (Ahmed and Veronis 2020, 306).

Generational relationships in South Asian programming are also at the forefront of the Canadian Broadcasting Corporation's (CBC) *Hockey Night in Punjabi* broadcast (Szto 2020, 42). While mainstream racist outrage on Twitter in response to the broadcast reinforced the "normalization of hockey as a white man's game" (Szto 2020, 215), for the South Asian community, the broadcast provided a bridge of hybridity between generations. Commentators spoke to the positive reception that *Hockey Night in Punjabi* received in multigeneration South Asian family homes, particularly between grandparents and their Canadian-born grandchildren (Szto 2020, 44).

While this chapter draws on examples that have a positive reception and presence in the community, it is careful not to over-romanticize South Asian media, including South Asian–focused programming in the mainstream, as a site of solely positive representation. Rather, this chapter challenges the underlying assumption of race and cultural identity being the sole characteristic of lived experience, thus making South Asian media the answer to all tensions in the community. The dialectical relationships between the South

Asian second-generational experience and the structuration of the broader cultural industries in Canada are problematized. To illuminate this tension, this research seeks to uncover taken-for-granted dynamics which showcase how aspects of gender, cultural identity, and generational experiences take hold in the emergence and work of Didihood.

THEORETICAL FRAMEWORK: INTERSECTIONALITY

Studies concerning South Asian media in Canada have located civic engagement, identity, and well-being as key themes in programming structures and content (Karim 2009). While this work is foundational in taking up questions surrounding the role of ethnic media across racialized communities (Mahtani 2009), it expands on this research and engages with a set of tensions that have since emerged by applying an intersectional analysis of power. Such an approach is instrumental in raising questions of diasporic media and intersectional experience in Canada and goes far beyond simplistic narratives of the "culture clash." More specifically, there is value in spotlighting the experiences of Canadian-born South Asians and their relationship to what has been traditionally thought of as ethnic media, and the role that this has played in their own lives.

While generational differences as a characteristic of lived experience that can help unpack the complexity of contemporary South Asian diasporic media in Canada have been identified, it is crucial to problematize the binary language which tends to appear in generational discourses. Often, the narrative of racialized generational shifts become synonymous with unidirectional and upward social mobility in relation to civic engagement, education, and employment opportunities (Rajiva 2013). Many scholars have addressed the problematic nature of such thin explanations, which reduce experience to an individual's own merit (Handa 2003; Lowe 1991; Rajiva 2013; Shariff 2008; Szto 2020). "Discourses of resilience," which are often associated with such generational shifts, overlook the ideological underpinnings of power in the day-to-day realities of racialized communities (Szto 2020, 130). Robin James (2015) argues that "'good' women and racialized citizens are those who actively commit to 'overcoming their damage' (84) rather than exposing their damage as a problem created by the system itself – 'resilience discourses [naturalize] damage' (83)" (as cited by Szto 2020, 131).

In exploring Didihood, this chapter draws on Sara Ahmed (2017) who writes that "we need to dismantle what has already been assembled; we need to ask what it is we are against, what it is we are for, knowing full well that *we* is not a foundation but what we are working toward" (2). Ahmed describes feminist dwellings as a movement and a process, attuned to the dynamics of institutional powers. Feminism, in this research, is a political orientation that understands how the intersections of power orient bodies in particular ways (Ahmed 2017, 43). To disrupt resilience discourses, the feminist approach of intersectionality is drawn on to critically analyze generations and their intersections of power. More specifically, an intersectional lens helps to identify how a multiplicity of diverse interlocking systems of oppression contribute to the inner workings of gendered cultural production across media spaces. Originating in Black feminist thought, an intersectional frame highlights how social inequality has various inner workings where diverse factors "*mutually influence one another*" (Hill Collins and Bilge 2016, 2).

Intersectionality serves as a heuristic tool that enables us to conduct a critical inquiry into the diverse dimensions of the South Asian experience, which vary significantly based on the intersections of race, gender, ability, sexuality, and class. Failing to use an intersectional approach would result in overlooking the complexity of a South Asian identity, which could potentially reinforce harmful narratives that further marginalize members within and outside the community. The aim of this approach is to illuminate the complexity and many facets of South Asian experience that oftentimes are ignored and therefore "theoretically erased" (Crenshaw 1989, 139). Intersectionality is especially critical in its application to this research, as it highlights the relationships between the micro level of lived experiences, the meso level of Didihood as an organization, and the macro level of the cultural industries (Bilge and Denis 2010, 4).

MULTIPLE MODALITIES AND THE WORK OF DIDIHOOD

Situated as a complex ecology of communication infrastructure, Didihood provides a unique insight into how multiple modalities can co-exist and connect across diverse social agents in the South Asian diaspora. While the collective responds to institutional whiteness in the Canadian media industries, Didihood also actively works to connect and represent the diversity of South Asian cultural production in the diaspora. According to Kim and Ball-Rokeach (2006), "community organizations play storytelling linkage roles in the overall communication infrastructure model of civic engagement" (180). The linkage role of Didihood is a key characteristic that is integral to the collective's functioning. The collective's monthly newsletter can be seen not only as a means of storytelling within their communication infrastructure, but also as a form of feminist archiving and a platform for sharing community resources. For example, in the June 2021 newsletter, Didihood features Vancouver-based artist Jag Nagra, who is the creative director of the Punjabi Market Regeneration Collective. While reflecting on the nostalgia of the market and what it meant to South Asians in the diaspora, Nagra explains: "Over the last few decades, there hasn't been much economic investment in the market. We're trying to change that and revitalize Punjabi Market through an arts and culture-based lens." This chapter argues that the linkage role that Didihood takes on through this newsletter is a feminist intervention in bringing intersectional stories into view for South Asian women. While there is a storytelling element of each newsletter via creator/artist profiles, there are also broader community resources shared. For instance, within the same newsletter, Didihood includes articles that provide support for LGBTQ+ youth, discuss the ways non-Indigenous allies can support Indigenous people and follow their leadership, and explore the complex impact of COVID-19 in India. While unpacking each resource goes beyond the scope of this chapter, it is crucial to highlight how this aspect of Didihood's existence acts as feminist archiving and community resource that questions and interrogates South Asian positionality in the diaspora, including being uninvited guests on this land. In this manner, Didihood's work is complicating the traditional divides between mainstream and ethnic media. Rather, Didihood is situated in between local South Asian media – that are often for first-generation immigrants – and mainstream media, which can be seen as a space of communication, negotiation, and resources for second-generation South Asian Canadians. The collective acts as a feminist and anti-racist organization that addresses and responds to the complex lived experiences of South Asian women in Canada, where mainstream media often fall short. The collective also functions as a capacity-building institution by providing support to South Asian female creatives through a mentorship program.

METHODOLOGY

Feminist Approaches and South Asian Feminine Agency

The emergence of Didihood provides a valuable opportunity to unpack the dialectical tension between the structure of cultural production in media and feminine agency itself (Saha 2018, 18). This chapter aims to examine how particular shifts in institutional sociocultural structures interact with the agency of Didihood founders and their respective experiences in the cultural industries (Saha 2018, 48). To develop this analysis, there is a level of description needed to capture the "entanglements" and ambivalent processes that configure relations of structure and feminine agency within sites of cultural production (Culhane 2017, 3). As described by philosopher Gilbert Ryle, "thicker descriptions" require the researcher to "locate an individual action in terms of its wider meaning and accomplishment" (Ahmed 2012, 8).

In exploring questions of intersectional identities and cultural production, the intersectional approach adds critical nuance to understanding Didihood as a feminist intervention. It is critical to be attuned to the sociocultural conditions and relations that foreground racialized experiences of everyday life which offer a significant level of analysis to examine the dialectical tension of structure and agency. Often, background conditions and relations are rationalized or overlooked where matters of racialized and gendered experience are concerned. This is especially an oversight in the relationship between structure and feminine agency in cultural production. For example, when thinking about institutional whiteness within the cultural industries, a feminist approach can reveal how "whiteness becomes a social and bodily orientation given that some bodies will be more at home in a world that is oriented around whiteness" (Ahmed 2007, 160). This is where there is an opportunity to spotlight characteristics of cultural production that are often naturalized or taken for granted, particularly where diasporic South Asian women are located. Additionally, a feminist lens played a key role in the design of the interview questions, which focused on the dialectical tension between the structure of cultural production in media and feminine agency.

In studies of cultural production (Saha 2018) and ethnic media (Mahtani 2009), it was found that there was not a substantive focus on the relationship between affect and sociopolitical relations in the lives of Canadian South Asian women cultural producers. Therefore, in drawing on interview data and fieldnotes, it was better situated to highlight experienced-based stories to raise critical questions about intersectional diasporic identity and media in the Canadian context. There is an elasticity of experience, which often embodies ambivalent features that are bound to industrial process. For instance, there can become a moment where creative practices that are meant to resist dominant mainstream understandings of "brownness" reproduce problematic tropes. This contradiction is one worth highlighting, particularly in the ways it speaks to the dialectical tension between structure and agency in the lives of South Asian women creatives. It is necessary to also acknowledge that the perspective and research design of this research is informed by the author's experience of being a second-generation South Asian woman in Canada (Mahtani 2009; Hirji 2010; Shariff 2008) where personal positionality and experiences impact not only the relationship of trust between researcher and participants, but also the formation of analysis (Marshall and Rossman 2016, 46).

Semi-Structured Interview and an Intersectional Analysis

This research relies on a semi-structured interview conducted with Didihood founders in January 2021 and field notes that were generated during this time. Interview data were analyzed based on an inductive approach, where the use of theoretical memos enabled an analysis of how the data connects to both the theoretical approach and existing literature in the field (Marshall and Rossman 2016, 221). In drawing on interview data and field notes through theoretical memos, it was aimed to develop "thicker descriptions" of the dialectical tension between structure of cultural production and agency of the Didihood founders (Ahmed 2012, 11). The presentation of findings in this research are structured by an intersectional analysis of power. An intersectional analysis recognizes the multidimensional nature of power to stretch across domains of the interpersonal, disciplinary, cultural, and structural. In the interpersonal domain of power, there is a window into how "axes of social division work together and influence one another to shape each individual biography" (Hill Collins and Bilge 2016, 8). The disciplinary and cultural domains allow a window into how the sociocultural, sociohistorical, and sociopolitical conditions and forces shape opportunity and success. Through the frames of disciplinary and cultural power, there is an unravelling of how myths of opportunity are socially constructed by a neoliberal policy apparatus. With an intense focus on hyper individualism and one's own ability to overcome social inequality, a "neoliberal logic" allows for individuals to "only have themselves to blame" (Hill Collins and Bilge 2016, 17).

MAIN FINDINGS

Desi Nostalgia and the Canadian Experience: An Interpersonal Domain of Power

The experience of second-generation nostalgia and the ways individuals grapple with their own "shifting identities and reified ideals" becomes an important site of exploration (Maira 1998, 368). Didihood founders spoke of the relationship between their shifting identities and nostalgia for ethnic media and narrated their memories in relation to their current adult selves as part of the collective. The nostalgia described by all three women was rooted in their own childhood experiences where South Asian media was a household staple for their parents. Throughout this interview, it became apparent that South Asian media acted as a curious site of reflection and would act as sites of important memory in relation to their career and personal trajectories. Co-founder Arti reflects, "I don't know if any of you remember that *Toronto Star* used to have a magazine back in the day called *Desi Life*?" She described *Desi Life*, a magazine that would come with her father's *Toronto Star* subscription: "I would read it, and I remember it was supposed to be like this 'modern edgier version' of like, you know, 'brown life.'" This publication stood out to her because it was the first time she had seen a publication solely dedicated to exploring the meaning of being South Asian in Canada. Both Roohi and Nikkjit reflected on the importance of South Asian media and the role it played in the lives of their parents in the past and present day. Both noted the important role ethnic media has played amidst the global COVID-19 pandemic as ethnic media are a crucial source of news for many diasporic communities residing in Canada.

When describing their nostalgia of South Asian media, both recalled weekend television programming and the large Punjabi presence, which they believed was a site that needs to become widened to cater to the diversity of the diaspora. Arti located the absence of Gujarati-specific media while growing up, but explained her parents still consumed the Hindi and Punjabi content as a result of understanding these languages. While Roohi suggested her memories are inextricably linked to the ways her parents experienced South Asian media, all three women pointed to the presence of South Asians in the Canadian mainstream media landscape while growing up in the 1990s and early 2000s:

> ARTI: I was always in such awe about old school City TV reporters, like Francis D'Souza and Farah and all these brown faces. They may not be Gujarati, but to me at that time I was like, "wow, there's brown people on TV?"
> ROOHI: It's interesting that we remember all these names. I don't know if that's because they were the only brown people, so it's in our memory that oh – "PJ Aashna from YTV, I remember watching you when I was a kid." Or if it's because we pay more attention anyways to the media, because we work in the media ... yea, in a way they were trailblazers.

While much literature in the field has taken up second-generation diasporic subjectivities in relation to readings of cultural texts (Durham 2004; Shariff 2008; Handa 2003), less work has focused on the relationship between diasporic representation in Canadian mainstream media and second-generation South Asian subjectivities. Second-generation South Asian identities in Canada have not been the subject of much scholarship (Rajiva 2006; Shariff 2008). Those who have taken up scholarship on second-generation South Asian identities in the West have highlighted how such intersections of identity and experience contribute to a larger impact on the social fabric of the nation. As described by both Shariff (2008) and Rajiva (2006), second-generation South Asians in Canada experience exclusion in different forms than their immigrant parents, which becomes an important register to take up further questions of racialized identities in the nation.

Both Arti and Roohi consciously reflected on the impact of seeing South Asians on the screen, not only as a site of nostalgia, but a deeper question of their own professional trajectories into the Canadian cultural industries. The nostalgic recollection of South Asian representation in the Canadian mainstream media landscape pointed to an important pathway of exploration for the collective. Through an intersectional lens, such a reflection highlights the interpersonal domain of power in the lives of Didihood founders. The interpersonal domain of power provides a window into how each individual's race, gender, and citizenship impacted the ways in which they engaged with not only ethnic media, but also the mainstream Canadian media landscape.

Structural and Disciplinary Domains: Consequences for the Invisibility of Intersections

While Arti and Roohi discussed the importance of visibility and their own recollection of South Asian figures on the Canadian screen, Nikkjit identified a problematic gap in formal education structures, as her experiences in journalism school did not prepare her for the realities of being a racialized journalist in a newsroom. The others followed up:

> ROOHI: We had an ethics course, but that was very broad ... there was nothing specific to how people's individual experiences may affect their ability to report on ...
> ARTI: ... there was never this idea that part of your identity will really reflect and shape your career.

The discussion around the lack of intersectional offerings in journalism programs, at the time Didihood founders were in school, demonstrates "how [second-generation South Asian] adult women narrate their past experiences of [race] in terms of their present selves" (Rajiva 2006, 167). Such reflections highlight how structural and disciplinary domains of power materialize in everyday life. While this is specific to the Didihood founders, the invisibility of such discourse pertaining to the complexity of identity and racialized experience works to conceal the ways in which power operates at the structural level of university education. More specifically, the experiences that the three had in journalism school over a decade ago speak to the ways in which structural forces can subtly "discipline" intersectional subjectivities. By adopting a colourblind approach and thus disengaging with the realities of lived experience, educational institutions reinforce institutional whiteness wherein certain bodies become "marked" resulting in "less obvious and more nuanced exclusion"

(Puwar 2004, 10). As I have argued elsewhere (Bains and Szto 2020), colourblind ideology has consequences in everyday life for racialized people. Often colourblind discourses erase race (Jiwani 1999) from sociocultural and sociopolitical contexts, including historical locations. In this sense, instances of racism go unacknowledged, resulting in problematic understandings of race as "individualized issues." These understandings therefore mask the workings of structural power that, in reality, prevent racialized bodies from challenging or confronting race relations and its intersections in the nation.

It is in the above-mentioned context where Didihood's organization confronts the consequences of structural and disciplinary domains of power. While the organizers indirectly respond to the gaps in formal education and media structures, this chapter argues that the collective's own "tactics of resistance" involve multimodal forms and "varied tools," which contribute to "facilitating conscientization" (Freire 1970 as cited by Jiwani 2011, 334). As a site of resistance, Roohi reflected on the Vancouver 2019 event Himmat: Celebrating the Women Around Us. Described as her most memorable event put on by the collective, Roohi explained how the event itself was organized to spotlight South Asian women and their stories that are often overlooked and hidden in various forms of representation. Roohi contextualized the event by explaining, "Himmat is usually thought of as a masculine word, so we named our event Himmat as a counter to that narrative by highlighting the strength and resilience of the women featured at our event" (Johal 2019). The more complex and nuanced narratives of South Asian women were at the forefront of the event, which was a photo exhibition paired with textual narratives. The event revealed how Didihood's organizing is multifaceted and not limited to a single form. Creative expression through feminist organizing can be a means to not only refashion opportunities for community building, but also used as a tactic to unravel aspects of structural and disciplinary domains of power that work to constrain possibilities of self-definition.

The Cultural Domain of Power: The Problem Is Not Solved by Making More of Us "Visible"

> Not being the ideal occupants of privileged positions, "space invaders" endure a burden of doubt, a burden of representation, infantilisation and super-surveillance. Existing under the optic lens of suspicion and

> surveillance, racialized bodies in politics, the arts, universities and bureaucracies are all too easily seen to be lacking the desired competencies. (Puwar 2004, 11)

This chapter draws upon Puwar's description of "space invaders" to highlight the complexity of experience for racialized people existing in spaces that have been historically marked by masculinity and whiteness. As a default, whiteness and masculinity became a structuring force, which is "naturalized" across institutional spaces. In speaking to the generations of South Asian women who worked in the Canadian media and cultural industries, Didihood identified the limited space and lack of resources available to previous generations of South Asian women before them. The cultural domain of power highlights that the playing field is not level, but rather it is disguised by myths of "equal opportunity" (Hill Collins and Bilge 2016, 11).

Although the myths of equal opportunity are present across various institutional spaces, it is important to examine how this power manifests into harmful barriers and limitations for South Asian women and racialized individuals to navigate through. Puwar explains, the "[o]ntological denial of embodiment is implicit in institutional narratives of professionalism" (12). Institutional narratives of professionalism which Puwar identifies point to an invisible criterion that must be adopted by racialized bodies. The embodiment of race and gender is a critical site to recognize when thinking about the agency of the cultural producer herself in relation to structural forces of institutional power.

In thinking about the relationship between race and gender, discourses surrounding the "Canadian dream"[4] for children of immigrants is significant in the facilitation of a false promise, one of "material rewards, status, or job security" (Rajiva 2013, 18). Multicultural discourses, specifically, aid in the construction of the Canadian dream, where one's success is dependent solely on their own efforts and discipline. This understanding of "success" reduces the complexity of racialized experience to one of personal choice. "Choice" is enacted through a set of disciplined actions that are congruent within the confines of multiculturalism, where one does not question or destabilize the national imaginary. In the reflections of those who came before them, Didihood points not only to the limited representations of South Asians, but also to the limited opportunities for South Asians to collaborate and connect in media production:

> ARTI: Now we are in a newer space, where [when] I am the only brown person in the room, I can now bring in all my didis, you know that's my goal. But you know that didn't exist before ...
> NIKKJIT: The definition of representation has changed more since those before us ... at that point the goal [of] representation was to get one brown news reporter on that broadcast show.

Nikkjit's reflection offers an important avenue to unpack and problematize the question of representation. First, this reflection highlights that the problem of representation is not simply "solved" by having more BIPOC cultural producers in the industry (Saha 2018). Second, it locates how the changing cultural politics of "race" acts as a condition in the ways representation becomes defined in the cultural industries. As a structural condition amongst regulatory contexts, technology, and commercial imperatives, the changing cultural politics of race and multiculturalism are key in the production process of "ethnic minority" cultural production (Saha 2018, 37). This is imperative to situate in the contemporary moment, where the COVID-19 pandemic has sparked deeper public discussions of anti-Asian racism, colonial violence existing in the present, inequity, and anti-Black racism following the global Black Lives Matter protests after the police murder of George Floyd in May of 2020. This context stands in contrast with the colourblind era of the 1990s where multicultural rhetoric and discourses worked to produce discourses of tolerance and conceal the inner workings of systemic power and racism (Bains and Szto 2020). This chapter argues that discourses of (multicultural) tolerance create conditions of quietude, which limit the space and potential for having discussions of race and other intersecting facets of identity. As a result, quiet spaces of hesitation and distance end up governing the ways in which race as both lived experience and social structure can be engaged with.

Each of the three women acknowledged the limited space for BIPOC journalists and broadcasters in the newsrooms and the multiple barriers that impede the direct confrontation of institutional whiteness. Arti reflected on the personal responsibility institutions place on BIPOC journalists: "When you're the one who says something, you're the one who has to fix everything." She goes on to explain how meaningful change does not happen by solely placing the responsibility on racialized people in this context, as it must address the structural powers in place (personal communication

2021). However, in the current context and visibility of discussions pertaining to race relations in the current moment, the interviewees are observing a shift where institutions are responding with anti-racism initiatives and policies. Arti explained that while these efforts are becoming more pronounced on the surface, the real social change happens "behind the scenes" across the cultural industries. In locating the dynamics of the production process (Saha 2018), Nikkjit points to the power structures which fundamentally shape representation:

> NIKKJIT: It's not a new thing that South Asian women are creative ... it's that people feel more comfortable going down these career paths now. And we just wanted to encourage that. If you want to see more representation you have to put more bodies in the industry to take up that space.

Didihood's organizing is responding to the complexity of not only representation, but also the cultural domain of power in mainstream media, which determines who is allowed to participate in shaping the narratives consumed by the public. Indeed, the collective's successful mentorship program is a prominent part of their response to this context; here, Didihood pairs two South Asian women working in the same area of the cultural industries to take part in a three-month program, where there is a "focu[s] on interviewing skills, networking and reworking resumes" (Didihood). The technical features and operations of the program reveal the ways in which the collective intentionally carves out a space for professional collaboration and connection. However, a contextual theme which emerged in the interview was how the mentorship program as a strategy is used to challenge the superficial aspects of visibility in the cultural industries. Arti suggested how important the mentorship element is to Didihood in disrupting institutional whiteness across the industry, where for generations before, there were limited spaces for South Asian collaboration and connection. Nikkjit also added,

> There has been a great response from the younger girls who want mentors, but I really found that the really strong response came from people about our age [millennials] ... "I desperately want to give back because it was so hard for me, I want to do whatever I can to make it easier..."

Didihood's emergence reveals that a space for mentorship in the media world was lacking for South Asian women. As described by Ahmed (2017): "to become feminist can often mean looking for company, looking for other girls, women who share in that becoming" (66). Looking for feminist company became a key force in the way that Didihood as a space has not only emerged, but also how it continues to grow and connect to broader communication infrastructure.

CONCLUSION

This chapter has argued that Didihood: The Sisterhood of South Asian Creatives in Canada is a multi-modal communication form of feminist ethnic media organizing in the South Asian diaspora. The collective's presence through feminist archiving (the monthly newsletter), community events (Himmat: Celebrating the Women Around Us), and the mentorship program offers insights into the complicated terrain of what has traditionally been understood as the boundaries around mainstream and ethnic media. As described by Kim and Ball-Rokeach (2006), "community organizations play storytelling linkage roles in the overall communication infrastructure model of civic engagement" (180). This chapter demonstrates how the linkage role of Didihood is a key characteristic that is integral to the collective's functioning in the way the collective circulates career and funding opportunities, cultural commentary, and socio-politically conscious content relating to justice and equity. Didihood's founders challenge the confines of what South Asian feminine agency can look like across media spaces. Didihood acts as a feminist and anti-racist collective that is addressing and responding to the complexities of lived experience as South Asian women in Canada, which media landscapes fail to adequately do. The intersectional analysis unearths the ways in which power operates across interpersonal, disciplinary, cultural, and structural domains.

Future directions of this research could interrogate how community-based organizations are operating across distinct spatial and temporal conditions as a part of ethnic communication infrastructure. Another prominent area of research lies in further locating how cultures of solidarity across broader racialized communities are forged through these types of infrastructures. While this research has only scratched the surface, it raises critical questions surrounding what Nikkjit names as "the beauty and depth" of what it means to be a South Asian woman in Canada.

NOTES

1 "Brown" came up in the ways the founders described themselves. More specifically, "brownness is about an exercise of self-definition and self-determination in white supremacist societies" (Bains and Szto 2020, 3).
2 "South Asian" is a racialized and externally imposed identity, which overlooks the complexity, diversity, and historical locations of the group named (Ghosh 2012, 35).
3 As argued by Bains and Szto (2020), it is critical to interrogate and disrupt how colonial legacies are implicated in the positionality of South Asians in Canada.
4 This is a notion that requires further unpacking in relation to colonial legacies and the connection they have to the current moment.

REFERENCES

Ahmed, Rukhsana, and Luisa Veronis. 2020. "Creating In-Between Spaces through Diasporic and Mainstream Media Consumption: A Comparison of Four Ethnocultural and Immigrant Communities in Ottawa, Canada." *International Communication Gazette* 82 (3): 289–315.
Ahmed, Sara. 2007. "A Phenomenology of Whiteness." *Feminist Theory* 8 (2): 149–68.
– 2012. *On Being Included Racism and Diversity in Institutional Life.* Durham: Duke University Press.
– 2017. *Living a Feminist Life.* Durham: Duke University Press.
Bains, Alysha, and Courtney Szto. 2020. "Brown Skin, White Ice: South Asian Specific Ice Hockey Programming in Canada." *South Asian Popular Culture* 18 (3): 181–99.
Bhatia, Nandi. 2012. "Diasporic Activism and the Mediations of 'Home': South Asian Voices in Canadian Drama." *Studies in Social Justice* 7 (1): 125–41.
Bilge, Sirma, and Ann Denis. 2010. "Introduction: Women, Intersectionality and Diasporas." *Journal of Intercultural Studies* 31 (1): 1–8.
Buchignani, Norman, Doreen M. Indra, and R. Srivastava. 1985. *Continuous Journey: A Social History of South Asians in Canada.* Toronto: McClelland and Stewart in association with the Multiculturalism Directorate, Dept. of the Secretary of State and the Canadian Government Pub. Centre, Supply and Services Canada.

Crenshaw, Kimberlé. 1989. "Demarginalizing the Intersection of Race and Sex: A Black Feminist Critique of Antidiscrimination Doctrine, Feminist Theory and Antiracist Politics." *University of Chicago Legal Forum* (8): 139–67.

Culhane, Dara. 2017. "Imagining: An Introduction." In *A Different Kind of Ethnography: Imaginative Practices and Creative Methodologies*, edited by Dara Culhane and Danielle Elliot, 1–22. Toronto: University of Toronto Press.

Didihood. n.d. "Welcome." https://didihood.com/.

Durham, Gigi M. 2004. "Constructing the 'New Ethnicities': Media, Sexuality, and Diaspora Identity in the Lives of South Asian Immigrant Girls." *Critical Studies in Media Communication* 21 (2): 140–61.

Ghosh, Sutama. 2013. "'Am I a South Asian, Really?': Constructing 'South Asians' in Canada and Being South Asian in Toronto." *South Asian Diaspora* 5 (1): 35–55.

Hall, Stuart. 1990. "Cultural Identity and Diaspora." In *Colonial Discourse and Post-Colonial Theory: A Reader*, edited by Patrick Williams and Laura Chrisman, 222–37. London: Harvester Wheatsheaf.

Handa, Amita. 2003. *Of Silk Saris and Mini-Skirts: South-Asian Girls Walk the Tight-Rope of Culture*. Toronto: Women's Press.

Heir, Rajpreet. 2017. "'Bend It Like Beckham' and the Art of Balancing Cultures." *The Atlantic*, 12 April, 2017. https://www.theatlantic.com/entertainment/archive/2017/04/bend-it-like-beckham-and-the-art-of-balancing-cultures/522477/.

Hill Collins, Patricia, and Sirma Bilge. 2016. *Intersectionality: Key Concepts*. Cambridge, UK: Polity Press.

Hirji, Faiza. 2010. *Dreaming in Canadian: South Asian Youth, Bollywood, and Belonging*. Vancouver: UBC Press.

Jiwani, Yasmin. 1999. "Erasing Race: The Story of Reena Virk." *Canadian Woman Studies* 19 (3): 178–84.

– 2011. "Pedagogies of Hope: Counter Narratives and Anti-Disciplinary Tactics." *The Review of Education/Pedagogy/Cultural Studies* 33 (4): 333–53.

Johal, Rumneek. 2019. "Exhibit celebrates strength of women in Vancouver's South Asian Diaspora." *Daily Hive*, 10 May 2019. https://dailyhive.com/vancouver/exhibit-celebrates-strength-of-women-in-vancouvers-south-asian-diaspora.

Karim, Karim H. 2009. "Other Research Reports on Issues of Race, Ethnicity, and Communication." *Canadian Journal of Communication* 34 (4): 749–56.

Kazimi, Ali. 2011. *Undesirables: White Canada and the Komagata Maru: An Illustrated History*. Vancouver, BC: Douglas & McIntyre.

Kim, Yong-Chan and Sandra J. Ball-Rokeach. 2006. "Civic Engagement From a Communication Infrastructure Perspective." *Communication Theory* 16 (2): 173–97.

Lowe, Lisa. 1991. "Heterogeneity, Hybridity, Multiplicity: Marking Asian American Differences." *Diaspora: A Journal of Transnational Studies* 1 (1): 24–44.

Mahtani, Minelle. 2009. "Critiquing the Critiques about Media and Minority Research in Canada." *Canadian Journal of Communication* 34 (4): 715–20.

Maira, Sunaina. 1998. "Desis Reprazent : Bhangra Remix and Hip Hop in New York City." *Postcolonial Studies* 1 (3): 357–70.

Marshall, Catherine, and Gretchen B. Rossman. 2016. *Designing Qualitative Research*. London: SAGE.

Murray, Catherine, Sherry Yu, and Daniel Ahadi. 2007. "Cultural Diversity and Ethnic Media in BC: A Report to the Canadian Heritage Western Regional Office." Centre for Policy Studies on Culture and Communities. Vancouver, BC: Simon Fraser University.

Nayar, Kamala Elizabeth. 2004. *The Sikh Diaspora in Vancouver: Three Generations amid Tradition, Modernity, and Multiculturalism*. Toronto: University of Toronto Press.

Puwar, Nirmal. 2004. *Space Invaders: Race, Gender and Bodies out of Place*. Oxford: Berg.

Rajiva, Mythili. 2005. "Bridging the Generation Gap: Exploring the Differences between Immigrant Parents and Their Canadian-Born Children." *Canadian Issues* (Spring): 25–8.

– 2006. "Brown Girls, White Worlds: Adolescence and the Making of Racialized Selves." *The Canadian Review of Sociology and Anthropology* 43 (2): 165–83.

– 2013. ""Better Lives": The Transgenerational Positioning of Social Mobility in the South Asian Canadian Diaspora." *Women's Studies International Forum* 36: 16–26.

Róisín, Fariha. 2017. "Kids Like Us." *Hazlitt*, 11 April 2017. https://hazlitt.net/feature/kids-us.

Saha, Anamik. 2018. *Race and the Cultural Industries*. Cambridge, UK: Polity Press.

Shariff, Farha. 2008. "Straddling the Cultural Divide: Second-Generation South Asian Identity and The Namesake." *Changing English* 15 (4): 457–66.

Singh, Milan, and Anita Singh. 2008. "Diaspora, Political Action, and Identity: A Case Study of Canada's Indian Diaspora." *Diaspora* 17 (2): 149–71.

South Asian Stories. 2017. "Shushma Datt: Broadcasting Pioneer." https://southasianstories.com/.

Szto, Courtney. 2020. *Changing on the Fly: Hockey through the Voices of South Asian Canadians*. New Brunswick: Rutgers University Press.

Yu, Sherry S. 2018. *Diasporic Media beyond the Diaspora: Korean Media in Vancouver and Los Angeles*. Vancouver: UBC Press.

CHAPTER THIRTEEN

Constructing Crime in Canadian Ethnic Minority Media: A Qualitative Study of South Asian and Black Newspapers

Aziz Douai and Barbara Perry

INTRODUCTION

Research on media, race, and crime shows the exaggeration of crime in mainstream media outlets and their frequent tendency to racialize crime and criminalize race (e.g., Jiwani 2006). Public perceptions and attitudes regarding crime patterns and appropriate policies, unfortunately, are informed by these media constructions. This calls for an examination of how ethnic media have served as a counterpoint or an echo of mainstream media in their treatment of crime. In other terms, researchers have rarely, if at all, addressed a central question: how do ethnic media targeting racialized ethnic communities cover crime? Our research on ethnic media has sought to address such lacunae and has investigated ethnic media coverage of crime. We have already reported the results of a quantitative content analysis of selected ethnic media from the Greater Toronto Area (GTA) that serve racialized and ethnic communities, specifically, South Asians and African Canadians (Douai and Perry 2018). What struck us about ethnic media coverage of crime was the paucity of attention to crime news, compared to our chosen mainstream media outlet. We scrutinized crime coverage during a six-month period and found that *Share News* (*Share*) targeting the African Canadian community in the GTA featured fewer crime news stories compared to the *Weekly Voice* (the *Voice*) targeting South Asian communities in the GTA and the *Toronto Star*, a mainstream newspaper outlet. As expected, the number of crime stories in mainstream media such as the *Toronto Star* dwarfs both outlets.

In this chapter, we conduct a qualitative analysis of these aforementioned crime stories to delve into their reporting patterns and the construction of crime in these venues. These two minority media outlets, *Share* and the *Voice*, will be used as a case study. We provide a thematic examination of crime coverage. Among other themes, we explore crime coverage patterns in ethnic media and what they tell us about treatment of race and justice issues in the media produced "by and for" ethnic communities (Matsaganis, Katz, and Ball-Rokeach 2010). The next section of the chapter reviews literature and discusses the context of the current study, followed by a qualitative analysis of crime coverage from a select ethnic media sample and concluding remarks. The importance of the findings derives from the fact that ethnic media play a key role in shaping perceptions and awareness of the world around racial and ethnic communities, as well as their place in it. Ethnic media may provide an alternative venue to mainstream media coverage as the latter have failed to represent crime and justice in accurate, representative, or balanced ways (Wortley 2008). Outlets, such as the newspapers under review here, provide spaces that reflect and shape the interests and experiences of the communities they serve. In this respect, this chapter contributes to existing research on ethnic media in Canada, specifically enriching our understanding of their integrative role as information hubs that inform members of broader society about the communities they serve, in line with the objective of this volume.

LITERATURE REVIEW

By ethnic media, this chapter refers to traditional mass and internet-enabled media primarily intended for ethno-cultural and immigrant communities to access a range of information that could be used to facilitate settlement, "integration," and build their communities and/or maintain ties with their homeland (Matsaganis, Katz, and Ball-Rokeach 2010; Ahmed and Veronis 2020). "As a third pillar of communication in Canada," Ziniak (2017) argued, these ethnic media voices facilitate accessible content, and, importantly, "serve as a barometer of positive portrayal, acceptance, self-expression and identity" (24). Similarly, other commentators have underscored the role of these ethnic media voices in empowering ethnic and racialized minority communities as they solidify ties to the "imagined communities" they belong to (Anderson 1991). For instance, ethnographic research in the GTA shows that ethnic newspapers "play a key role in shaping newcomers' sense of place" in particular (Lindgren 2011, 1). At the same time, they facilitate the preservation of identity and connections to the homeland as well as awareness and adaptation to their new country of residence. Such conclusions are well founded since, as Karim (2002, 2) reminds us, ethnic media "function to meet the specific information and entertainment needs of their minority audiences."

Racialized minorities, and people of colour in general, are constructed in mainstream media as threatening in economic, political, and social terms (Perry and Sutton 2006). Racialized minorities who cross the "boundaries" by engaging in interracial relationships are considered transgressors. In a different study, Henry and Tator (2003) showed consistent patterns in criminalization of Blacks in Canadian national newspapers that include media narratives consistent with discourses of the denial of racism in Canada and among police. Discourses of racialization supportive of the status quo, reverse racism and police victimization, and discourses of otherness are commonly found in coverage of Black communities, according to the same study. For instance, Blacks were depicted as being undesirable, problem people, symbols of danger, and a threat to the social order who function outside the boundaries of Canadian "imagined community" (Anderson 1991; Henry and Tator 2003). Through the racialization of crime in the media, racialized minorities collectively lose their status as peaceable and "good" citizens.

Since there are chapters in this volume that offer the history of South Asian media, this chapter will briefly touch upon the history of Black press in Canada. As Ojo (2019, 8) puts it, "Black media have always been important sites of discursive activities and public engagement in the wider sociocultural contexts of political struggles and community building." For example, the early Black press, such as the *Voice of the Fugitive* and the *Provincial Freeman*, two pioneering Black newspapers in Canada established in 1851 and 1853, respectively, highlighted the experiences of Black migrants who moved through the Underground Railroad and settled in Canada (e.g., de B'béri 2015; Reid-Maroney 2017). Their coverage documented the racialized experiences of Black communities and the challenges faced by formerly enslaved Blacks as they settled in a new place. The writing of Mary Ann Shadd, the editor of the *Provincial Freeman*, would later provide the intellectual foundation for the formation of Black identity in Canada (de B'béri 2015; Yee 1997). Demonstrating what Ojo (2006) describes as a "hybridized form of civic and cultural journalism," contemporary Black press provided a communal space for a multiplicity of Black public spheres to debate Black issues and needs ranging from education, discrimination, policing and corruption, religion, and Black political leadership. The growth of Black emigration and diasporic communities in Canada created a new market for the Black press as contemporary Black newspapers gravitated toward urban centers where sizable Black communities reside. For instance, the *Caribbean Camera* and the *Montreal Community Contact* serve the largest metropolitan areas in Canada, Toronto and Montreal, respectively, and offer a mix of local community news with a range of useful information to serve the needs of Black residents. The community and social justice ethos of the Black press continues to inform the Toronto-based *Share* newspaper, founded in 1978, which is one of the largest ethnic newspapers in Canada, and their coverage of crime displays such sensibilities.

RATIONALE AND PROCEDURES OF THE STUDY

We investigated English-language ethnic minority media in Canada and conducted both quantitative and qualitative analyses in the *Voice* and *Share*, two ethnic minority newspapers within the GTA, one of the most ethnically diverse locations in North America. The *Voice* brands itself as "the largest English newspaper providing news catering to the South Asians in the Greater Toronto Area and beyond" and has been in circulation since 2002. *Share* positions itself as "a weekly community newspaper which has served the Black and Caribbean community in the Greater Toronto Area (GTA) of Ontario, Canada since April 9, 1978."

The initial study examined crime-related articles published in the *Voice* (241) and *Share* (n = 20) between November 2012 and April 2013. A follow-up study gathered crime-related stories published in the *Voice* (200) and *Share* (n = 17) between January and July 2019 (table 13.1). The quantitative analysis published in 2018 focused on the extent of crime coverage, such as the frequency of crime news

Table 13.1 | Number of crime articles published in the *Weekly Voice* and *Share News*

Newspaper	Website	Communities/ primary readership	Ownership	No. of crime articles November 2012–April 2013	No. of crime articles January–July 2019
Weekly Voice	http://www.weeklyvoice.com	South Asians	The Voice Media Group	241	200
Share News	http://share-news.com	Black/ Caribbean Canadians	Share Online Inc.	20	17
Total				261	217

and the scope of coverage (Douai and Perry 2018). Lesser attention to crime news in ethnic minority media outlets, compared to mainstream media, seemed striking. The qualitative analysis reported in the present study examined a total of 478 articles dealing with crime published in the two newspapers under study.

The main research question in the current chapter is: How do these minority media outlets cover crime? Specifically, does ethnic media coverage of crime reveal any differences in their treatment of different types of crime such as "serious" crime (e.g., familial homicides, trafficking, terrorism, sexual assault)? How do the *Voice* and *Share* treat crime "at home" (taking place in Canada/in their communities) versus crime happening "abroad"? Lastly, how does crime media coverage in the selected outlets tackle race and social justice issues? An in-depth qualitative analysis of related crime stories explores these reporting patterns and the construction of crime in these venues.

SERIOUS CRIME

Share rarely touches on serious crime stories, with only seven such pieces in 2012 (terrorism and violence against women), and four in 2019 (other serious crime and terrorism). As discussed later, their core focus, even in the context of crime, is on social justice concerns. In contrast, the *Voice* does devote considerable time to serious crime, with particular emphasis on four specific categories: familial homicides; trafficking (drugs, jewels, people, even body parts); terrorism; and sexual assault. In fact, three categories of crime – terrorism, trafficking, and sexual assault – accounted for 90 per cent of all crime stories in the *Voice* in 2019. Terrorism alone was the focus of over half of the stories (n = 112). It is interesting to note, before going on to assess each of these in turn, that the stories often seem to be included because they connect to the larger theme of corruption (discussed below). That is, many of the incidents that are included are described as being a result of or at least enabled by widespread corruption.

Familial Homicides

In 2012–13, the *Voice* featured no fewer than nine articles revolving around familial homicides. The distribution of these was intriguing. When they consider homicides within South Asian communities, mainstream Western news media typically focus on the controversial issue of "honour killings" (Gill 2006). Only two of the articles in the *Voice* in 2012 referred to honour killings. One documents eleven reported cases of honour killings in India in 2013 ("333 Honour Crime Complaints Registered In India This Year"). Another refers to an Afghan girl killed because she rejected marriage proposals ("Afghan Girl Beheaded After Rejecting Marriage Proposal"). Other reported incidents included a mother killing her son for failing to memorize Qur'anic verses, and an alleged homicide of a couple's daughter and a member of their health staff for reasons unknown. What really stood out, however, were reports of contract killings within families. One involved a man who allegedly hired hit men to kill his wife. Two articles were devoted to the murder of a billionaire politician, allegedly contracted by his son. This case resonates with another article, which reported on the deaths of two brothers, described as "liquor barons." In each of these incidents, interfamilial disputes around money and property feature prominently.

It is interesting to note that in 2019, however, there were very few references to familial homicides. The only two exceptions were very brief descriptive pieces about two homicides in Ontario ("Ontario's Police Watchdog Investigating Fatal Incident in Brampton"; "Friends, Co-Workers Mourn 4 Members of Same Family Found Dead in Markham, Ont."). Neither of these stories speculated about motive, nor were they followed up in later stories.

Sexual Assault

It happens that we drew our sample of articles in 2012 shortly after a twenty-three-year-old woman was brutally gang-raped and killed by a group of young men in India. This case seemed to bring the widespread prevalence of violence against women into the limelight, not just in South Asia but across the West as well. That it resonated here is evident in the fact that a protest calling for protection for women was held outside the India consulate in Toronto (Global News 2013). It is not surprising, then, that a significant amount of space was devoted to this tragic event. Like terrorism, the apparently unchecked violence against women affects those living at home and abroad. This particular attack clearly sent shock waves through South Asian communities globally.

While the stories in the *Voice* connected to the Delhi sexual assault case were typically descriptive, there were occasional editorial pieces included. These do not, for the most part, appear to be written by or for the *Voice*. Rather, they are culled from other media sources. The selection is deliberate. A *Times of India* editorial seeks to unpack the patriarchal assumptions that inform such violence: "If what happens to women on the roads of Delhi and Mumbai – other cities, too – is to stop, the change will have to come first at home, from the family. Boys, as they grow up, will have to be taught that their sisters are not there to get the leftovers – the one piece of chocolate that couldn't be eaten, the tricycle with a broken wheel that couldn't be driven, the school with expensive fees that couldn't be afforded."

Alongside articles that described the brutal attack or followed the subsequent arrests and trials of the perpetrators were a number of articles that shone light on calls for policy and legislative reform around violence against women. The *Voice* shares with its Canadian readers assurances from politicians that women would be protected in the future, e.g., "Sweeping Changes Coming to Make Delhi Safe," and that perpetrators would be harshly punished. Oddly, there were more than a dozen articles that, cumulatively, seemed to suggest the *Voice*'s support for the most extreme of punishments: death. Among the relevant headlines were "Salman Calls for Death Sentence to Rapists"; "'Death for Rapists,' An Anguished India Cries Out"; "Delhi Rape Suspects Face Death Sentence"; "People Want Death for Rapists: Survey."

Referencing the Delhi rape, a *Share* article, "The Hazards of Being Born Female," uses that incident as a springboard for a broader critique of the universal risks of violence that face women. The piece reminds readers that North Americans should not be complacent that such things only happen "over there"; Canadian women are also at risk of myriad forms of gender-based violence. Additional articles focus more specifically on initiatives intended to break the silence on violence against women in Caribbean nations. In short, it seems as if the need to create awareness of and subsequent action against violence against women is at the heart of *Share*'s coverage of this class of crime. In comparison, the 2019 coverage of sexual assault was much more diverse than that in 2012–13. Indeed, *Share* published no related articles, which seems odd given their focus on social justice issues. The *Voice* continued to give prominence to the topic with thirty-four related pieces. The influence of the #MeToo movement was very much in evidence, with a number of articles directly referring to it.

Perhaps connecting to the 2012–2013 emphasis on the breadth of sexual assault across South Asia, there were a couple of articles in 2019 that pointed to this as a "push factor" in emigration. One article cited the Canadian Refugee Claims Analysis Report, which argued that, alongside concerns such as environmental degradation, poverty, and widespread corruption, physical and sexual violence against women and girls has shaped refugee claims in Canada. The report also noted "the strong and active Indian diaspora community in Canada, favorable socio-economic opportunities, family reunification, freedom for LGBTQ2 individuals and strong respect for women's rights" ("More Indians Seeking to Migrate to Canada as Refugees Due to 'Push Factors,' Says Canadian Report"). Oddly, given the earlier sympathetic treatment of victims and survivors of sexual assault, the *Voice* featured a particularly cynical op-ed that questioned the legitimacy of the movement, "#MeToo Strikes Where Virtue Means Lack of Opportunity." The claim that "if the intention of the victim is to really see the culprit punished, #MeToo will have to be immediate, not after years" is especially problematic. It fails to recognize the reality that many women are fearful of reporting sexual violence, especially at the hands of men who have some control over their lives and livelihoods (Mendes and Ringrose 2019). The problem is likely exacerbated in countries like India, for example, where reporting is estimated to be at less than 10 per cent (McDougal, Krumholz, Bhan, Bharadwaj, and Raj 2018).

Indeed, the #MeToo movement has underscored the ways in which sexual assault expresses power, and often violates relations of trust. This, too, was a focus in the *Voice*'s coverage of sexual violence in 2019. Aside from the Hollywood/Bollywood exploitation of female actors that was the early focus of the #MeToo movement ("Aditya Pancholi Booked in 10-Year-Old Rape Case"), in the *Voice*, attention is drawn to the abuse of power in workplaces ("Uber Sued for $10 Million in Sexual Assault Case in US"), government agencies ("Ottawa Police Officer Has Been Suspended from Duty for Alleged Sexual Assault of an 18-Year-Old Woman"), places of worship ("Three Children Sexually Assaulted by Toronto Man at Two Churches, Police Allege"), and schools ("Ottawa School Lunch Supervisor Has Been Charged with Sexual Assault and Sexual Interference"). The latter example also points to the *Voice*'s interest in reporting on sexual violence as it is experienced by youth ("Dating Apps Questioned Over Age Verification after Child Abuse Cases"). Interestingly, the bulk of the articles devoted to sexual violence and exploitation in 2019 were focused not on incidents in the subcontinent but in North America, and especially in Ontario, Canada, where the greatest concentration of South Asians resides. This attention to sexual violence in Canada contrasts with the emphasis on such attacks in South Asian nations, and especially India in 2012–13. It seems as if there is an attempt to deflect attention away from the widespread threats to women in home countries.

Trafficking

The processes of globalization that have contributed to the South Asian diaspora in recent decades also have implications for the internationalization of crime. Indeed, the *Voice* pays particular attention to one such phenomenon: international trafficking. Ironically, although India (along with Bangladesh and Nepal) has been recognized as one of the most active countries with respect to trafficking women and girls in the sex trade (Joffres, Mills, Joffres, Khanna, Walia, and Grund 2008), this is not at all evident in the newspaper. There is one brief piece about a grandfather selling his daughter's newborn to a nurse, who then sold the baby to another hospital employee. The infant was sold again – on Facebook. However, this was likely included for much the same reason as the oddities noted above, as the case was described in the report as "a most bizarre and pathetic case" ("Newborn Baby Sold for Rs. 800,000 In Delhi"). Ironically, the article acknowledges that the case represents "the tip of a very big iceberg of child-trafficking; estimates indicate that tens of thousands of children are trafficked each year out of India alone." Yet in spite of this, no further attention is drawn to the phenomenon.

In 2012, there was an almost singular focus on drug trafficking. One article discusses on kidney trafficking, while another focuses on diamonds. The remaining dozen articles survey the movement of drugs across international borders. Perhaps in an effort to link the homeland with newcomers' current locus, there is a heavy emphasis on the alleged drug pipeline between Canada and India. One article title is quite explicit about the Canadian connection: "Police Raid $130 Million Drug Ring with Strong Canada Links."

In a dramatic shift, not only were there far more articles on trafficking in 2019 (thirty-five versus fourteen in 2012), but the emphasis shifted to human trafficking (n = 21), including organ trafficking (the remaining piece features wild animal trafficking). Of equal interest is the fact that eleven of the stories on human trafficking have a Canadian focus, many dealing with Toronto area incidents including articles about the arrests of Toronto area traffickers ("23-Year-Old Man Facing More Charges in Toronto Human Trafficking Case"; "Brampton, Ont. Man Sentenced to Four Years in Prison for Human Trafficking").

Two additional areas of emphasis arose in 2019. The first is a cluster of articles that point to the particular issue of grooming and trafficking youth for the sex trade and/or child bride markets ("In a Marriage Market, Pakistani Christian Girls Are Being Lured to China"; "United Nations: Fixing Climate Change is the Key for Bangladesh's Kids' Lives and Future"). Interestingly, these were matched by a number of articles highlighting efforts to counter child trafficking ("YouTube Changes Policies to Keep Sexual Predators Away from Children"). Indeed, this was part of the other, broader trend that gave prominence to strategies for countering trafficking of all kinds. In addition to those noted above were related articles such as "American Telugu Association Celebrates International Women's Day" and "Killing, Violence toward Indigenous Women, Girls 'Not a Relic of Our Past': PM." This is actually a theme that emerges across most categories of serious crime.

Terrorism

The Global Terrorism Index for 2014 indicates that Pakistan is one of the five nations that accounted for 80 per cent of all terrorism-related deaths. That nation ranks third among 124 nations on the index; India ranks sixth, Bangladesh twenty-third, Nepal twenty-fourth, and Sri Lanka thirty-sixth (Institute for Economics and Peace 2015). Thus, the five nations that constitute the homelands of the target audience are among the top one-quarter of countries impacted by terrorism. This sheds light on why the *Voice* has featured extensive coverage on terrorism news, with over fifty articles. In fact, the *Voice* cites the index findings in one article ("India, Pakistan Among World's Terror Hotspots"). The threat has resulted in thousands of deaths across the region; Pakistan alone suffered over 2,300 terrorism-related fatalities in 2013, and India suffered 404 (Institute for Economics and Peace 2015). The threats are diverse, including from groups associated with fundamentalist Islam, ethnic separatism, and communism. Nonetheless, emphasis was placed on Taliban and ISIS activities which occurred during the period of the study in 2012. However, the bulk of the paper's attention in the first period of study was directed toward following the trials of the accused associated with the Mumbai attacks of 2008, in which the Lashkare-Taiba (LeT) group killed more than 170 people. Given the emotional impact that these attacks had on Indians living abroad, it is no surprise that the paper acts as a conduit for how subsequent events are unfolding. The acts did not only terrorize those living in India, but also Indians living abroad. It left them fearful for the well-being of their family at home (Finseraas and Listhaug 2013).

In light of the time frame for the initial leg of our project, it is perhaps not surprising that both the *Voice* and *Share* also make reference to the Boston Marathon bombing in April 2013. However, their treatment of the bombings is distinct. The *Voice* provides brief, largely descriptive accounts of the attacks. Interestingly, the paper sought to draw connections to South Asia, musing in one headline as to whether there might be a "Pakistani Terror Group Behind Boston Blasts." In contrast, and in line with its general orientation, *Share* offers not just descriptive accounts, but attempts at making sense of the motives for the attacks. In articles entitled "Lessons from Boston" and "The 'Root Causes' Questions Have Been Asked," the paper seeks to put the terrorist attacks in context, both in terms of motives and political reactions. The second article, in particular, criticizes successive Conservative administrations for failing to understand and address the root causes of not only terrorism but also crime more generally. This represents an analytic approach that seeks to engage readers in critical reflection, rather than simply reporting events as they occur.

Given the attention paid to the Boston bombing, it is curious that neither paper gave similar prominence to coverage of the New Zealand Christchurch killings at two of the city's mosques in March of 2019. The *Voice* mentioned it four times, *Share* only once. These limited references were very distinct, however, with *Share*'s single article linking the Christchurch murders with other similar attacks on religious and racialized minorities. *Share* highlights the very real threat of White Nationalism that the authors argue has been ignored by political leaders. It is ironic, then, that in addition to focusing on descriptive accounts of the killings in Christchurch ("The Death Toll in New Zealand Terrorist Mosque Attack Has Risen to 50 Deaths"), the *Voice* also references public condemnations of them ("Statement on New Zealand Terror Attack and Community Safety in Scarborough"). It is important to note, however, that it is generally only in the immediate aftermath of such attacks that Western governments acknowledge the presence and threat associated with White Supremacist terrorism (Perry and Sutton 2019).

Details of a terrorist attack in Sri Lanka in 2019 was also shared with readers of the *Voice* in a number of articles immediately after the attack. Allegedly connected to the Islamic State, the series of bomb attacks in Colombo claimed over 350 lives. While most of the related pieces are descriptive, one op-ed leverages the Easter Sunday attack to warn of the broader threat of Islamist-inspired terrorism to the region, claiming that it was part of the scheme to "establish Islamic state in Pakistan, India, Bangladesh and Myanmar" ("Radicals Trying to Destabilise the Region by Targeting South Asia").

The attention to these two highly impactful attacks is natural. It is an attempt to keep readers up to date on the threats emerging within their homelands. As with the last piece cited above, op-eds are also used to contextualize the attacks for their audiences, some of whom have only recently left the sites of the violence, and some of whom have a much more distant connection. In drawing connections between events in two distinct nations, motivated by distinct ideologies and aims, the aforementioned op-ed and others like it seek to bridge the differences within the South Asian community, reminding them that they are all part of a transnational community at risk.

CRIME "AT HOME" VERSUS CRIME "ABROAD"

Interestingly, aside from references to the Boston bombing, in 2013, *Share* did not feature any other articles referring to crime occurring outside of Canada or the Caribbean. In 2019, *Share* featured just slightly more, with one piece addressing the Christchurch murders, and two others addressing American examples of systemic racism ("Talking on the Phone in a Hotel Lobby While Black"; "Names of Groveland Four Accused Finally Cleared"). *Share* touched on global crime and justice issues, largely as they unfold "at home," that is, in the Caribbean, but only in seven articles ("Report on Gender-Based Violence in Haiti Welcomed"; "Minister Pledges to Stop Violence Against Women"). Although few in number, these references to the homeland nonetheless connect a portion of Canada's Black population to events and patterns in what is, for many, their country of origin. And, as might be expected from the outlet's emphasis on social justice issues, the focus there was generally on concerns around violence targeting vulnerable communities. In short, *Share*'s focus, across time, is largely on justice issues as they impact the Afro-Caribbean community in Canada.

The Canadian content, as described in more detail below, is very much concerned with questions of systemic racism and exclusion as they affect people of colour generally, and especially youth within those communities. Consequently, there is a heavy emphasis on issues like carding of Black people, and other forms of police mistreatment of racialized communities ("New Police Act More Empowering to Cops"; "Justice Tulloch's Carding Report 'Step in the Right Direction'"). Interestingly, countering the focus on Black disempowerment were a number of articles praising role models who dedicated their lives to challenging systemic racism ("Viola Desmond's Courage a Source of Inspiration"; "Documentary Celebrates the Jane & Finch Community").

In contrast, the *Voice* shows an obvious trend toward inclusion of stories "from home." As noted earlier, in 2019, considerable attention was paid to the terrorism attack in Kashmir in March. Additionally, in both years, numerous articles revolved around political and/or financial corruption in the subcontinent. Globally, many of the nations of South Asia are perceived to be significantly impacted by corruption on an array of levels. Transparency International, for example, publishes an array of related indicators, many of which place India, Pakistan, and Bangladesh, especially, among the most vulnerable. None of these nations scored above 40 (out of 100, where 100 is least corrupt) in Transparency International's (2014) Corruption Perceptions Index. Pakistan, Nepal, and Bangladesh all scored in the 20s, India and Sri Lanka in the high 30s. By comparison, Canada's score was 81 out of 100. Consequently, the *Voice* appears to have opted to select items that reflect that reality.

During both periods of study, the *Voice* also featured a sizable number of articles about crime abroad, that is, neither in Canada nor in South Asia. Rather, these stories reflect events across the globe. However, the selections are not random. On the one hand, they are included if a South Asian national is involved in some way, as either a victim or perpetrator of an extraordinary crime. An incident in which a New York City woman pushed an Indian man in front of a moving train garnered attention from the *Voice* in three stories. This case clearly stands out as an Islamophobic hate crime in that the perpetrator was explicit in linking her crime with the 9/11 attacks on the US. Another likely hate crime was reported in the article "Florida Sikh Shot at While Driving." References to the experiences of South Asians abroad are, in some small way, connecting diasporic communities by sharing the misfortunes that are befalling compatriots.

The other cluster of international items revolve around incidents that are noteworthy in their own right or because they have garnered international attention. These typically reflect odd or extreme patterns, or apparently "hypermenacing" situations, as in the following examples caught in headlines: "British Parents Punished for Children Bunking School"; "Over 40 Dangerous Criminals Absconding in Britain"; "Honduran Murder Rate Is 10 Times Global Average";

"Syrian Guilty of War Crimes over Torture Videos Says Germany." As with practices so common in mainstream media, selection of these extraordinary stories is intended to titillate and entertain in a rather dark way.

RACE AND SOCIAL JUSTICE

Given that both the *Voice* and *Share* explicitly define their audiences as communities that are racialized in Canada, one would expect some consideration of race within their respective pages. And indeed, both do refer to race and/or ethnicity, specifically to the identity groups that constitute their audiences. However, their treatment of race is very distinct. In the *Voice*, race is implied by naming individuals involved as victims, offenders, or other actors in the crime dramas that are represented. Very rarely do articles feature what might be thought of as Anglo names, or, important in the Canadian context, Francophone names. Yet race is not problematized, or even explicitly remarked upon. There is silence on the role that race, ethnicity, or even national origin might play in victimization or criminalization. Even those few articles that speak directly to human rights issues avoid issues of race, focusing instead on violations perpetrated against women and children. There is one article, "Sri Lankan Military Charged with Raping Tamils," which discusses widespread sexual violence targeted at Tamil Tigers in custody. However, while the discussion is clearly gendered, it is not raced. Similarly, the references to terrorism, as numerous as they are, refrain from discussing the roles that race, ethnicity or religion might play in either the commission of such crimes or public responses to them. An article describing what was evidently a hate crime in which an African American male allegedly intentionally ran down a South Asian family with his car falls into the common mainstream trap of attributing the violence to mental health issues, rather than systemic racism ("Hate Crime: Indian-Descent Family Mistaken for Muslims Targeted in Car Attack"). In short, the *Voice* is decidedly noncommittal in exploring the nexus of race and crime. The outlet makes no effort to either recreate or deconstruct the mainstream tendency to racialize crime and criminalize race.

In contrast, *Share* explicitly tackles race head on, engaging in commentary and critiques of racism as experienced by Afro-Caribbeans in Canada. It is a much more self-consciously political media outlet, concerned with questions of social justice and inclusion. In one way or another, virtually all of the crime/justice articles in *Share* provide commentary on social justice. This is readily apparent in the many discussions of violence among Black youth. As noted above, the emphasis here is on the ways in which historical and contemporary patterns of racism and racial bias shape experiences of victimization and criminalization. An article chronicling a bus trip to Washington, DC, for a commemoration of Martin Luther King's assassination conjures the memories of not just King, but also Emmett Till, another young victim of white racism ("Charley Roach and Jackie 'Moms' Mabley"); another traces the extent of RCMP surveillance and infiltration of "Black radicals" in the 1970s ("Some Origins of Toronto's Black History Month"), and yet another speaks to investigative findings of police carding of Black youth, especially "Justice Tulloch's 'Street Checks' Review Was Focused."

A significant underpinning of the marginalization of Black communities, according to *Share*, is the representation of Black communities in the media. The article "What's Behind Phenomenon Labeled 'Black on Black Violence?'" asserts that the term has become a "brand" for Black communities. It is "now used to define us, whether or not we as individuals engage in criminality. None of us escapes this global branding insomuch that individuals who might never have met a Black person is nonetheless tainted with this stereotyping." This sentiment is echoed forcefully in news reports which pigeonhole Black life. *Share*, then, offers a counter-narrative. Several articles directly engage in a conversation about the likely roots of violence among Black communities. The common core of these is captured in the piece entitled "Youth Violence Report Should Be Mandatory Reading." In particular, it refers to the "well-documented information that details how chronic economic inequality, neighbourhoods of concentrated poverty and scarcity, absence of opportunity to move out of social deprivation, and anti-Black attitudes lead to the relatively high level of violence in crisis areas." It is not lawlessness or anarchy that accounts for elevated levels of crime in affected communities, but loss of opportunity and thus hope.

Finally, in line with its broader understanding of crime, *Share* promotes *social* justice rather than *criminal* justice responses to crime and violence within the Black community. Indeed, in 2012, *Share* called upon Ontario premier Kathleen Wynne to address Black youth violence through social policy ("New Premier Urged to Make Black

Youth Violence a Priority"). Another article promotes increased funding for outreach work and engagement with youth in "crisis areas," as well as "real social, economic, and psychological interventions such as those recommended in the Alvin Curling and Roy McMurtry "Roots of Youth Violence" report" ("The Real Enemy"). And another urges more effective use and oversight of such bodies as the Ontario Human Rights Commission, and Ontario's Special Investigations Unit ("Using Our Imperfect Institutions").

CONCLUSION

Our analysis suggests that ethnic media outlets vary dramatically in how they represent crime news. The two papers connect their readership to their respective audiences in very distinct ways. The *Voice* highlights factual news coverage as events unfold in South Asia, especially India and Pakistan, along with considerable attention to Canadian content of a localized Ontario sort. It is thus helping to bridge the distance – geographic and social – between the two homelands of its readers. *Share*, on the other hand, places more emphasis on Canadian social justice issues as they affect its audience. It speaks more to accounting for the ways that the justice system disproportionately and negatively impacts people of colour, and especially Black people. It is thus safe to say that the tone of the outlets' crime coverage is also disparate, with the *Voice* concentrating on serious crime and terrorism, sexual assault, and human trafficking in particular. In short, the *Voice* replicates the mainstream media emphasis on extreme acts of violence, often sensationalizing them. *Share*'s focus, in contrast, was on social justice issues rather than on specific categories of crime. Indeed, the greatest departure between the outlets is associated with the papers' respective treatment of the nexus of race and crime.

We noted at the outset that mainstream media tend to overemphasize serious crime, and to both "racialize crime" and "criminalize race." Interestingly, while the *Voice* does appear to pay considerable attention to serious crime, neither *Share* nor the *Voice* explicitly engages in racialized representations of crime. But that is not to say that they then attend to crime stories in the same way. On the one hand, the *Voice* is reserved in its consideration of where crime intersects with race. Indeed, the paper evades the question entirely in that it fails to problematize the intersection of race and crime. Given its heavy concentration on Canadian and especially Ontario news, the failure to address current issues like police carding and hypersurveillance of Muslim communities, for example, is surprising. *Share*, on the other hand, addresses the parallel concerns directly and critically. One of that outlet's core foci, in terms of crime, is, in fact, deconstructing the mainstream representations of Black communities as being inextricably linked to crime.

The two media outlets we examined also, then, play distinct roles in engaging their audiences, particularly with reference to issues related to crime and justice. The *Voice* seems to share the mainstream media preoccupation with serious crime, and especially that in the subcontinent. In this way, they connect their Canadian audience to incidents "at home." *Share*, in contrast, situates crime and justice within the broader matrix of strategies that serve to marginalize and exclude Black Canadians in Canada. The paper critiques, rather than recreates, the racialization of crime and the criminalization of race. It provides its audience with a distinct lens through which to view Black Canadians' experiences with the justice system in Canada.

No doubt, there are other ethnic media outlets that correspond to the trends explored here, but it is even more likely that there is significant diversity across outlets. We encourage others to consider additional media serving distinct communities so that we can better understand the multiple ways in which crime stories are told to their audiences, with an eye to encouraging more critical, reflective treatment of crime news that challenges mainstream representations.

REFERENCES

Ahmed, Rukhsana, and Luisa Veronis. 2020. "Creating In-Between Spaces through Diasporic and Mainstream Media Consumption: A Comparison of Four Ethnocultural and Immigrant Communities in Ottawa, Canada." *International Communication Gazette* 82 (3): 289–315.

Anderson, Benedict. 1991. *Imagined Communities: Reflections on the Origin and Spread of Nationalism*, rev. ed. London: Verso.

de B'béri, Boulou Ebanda. 2015. "La 'Black Press' canadienne du 19ème siècle: Racines et trajectoires des pratiques communicationnelles et d'un activisme intellectuel exceptionnels gommés dans nos études en communication." *Global Media Journal* 8 (2): 15–23.

Douai, Aziz, and Barbara Perry. 2018. "A Different Media Lens? How Ethnic Minority Media Cover Crime." *Canadian Journal of Criminology and Criminal Justice* 60 (1): 96–121.

Finseraas, Henning, and Ola Listhaug. 2013. "It Can Happen Here: The Impact of the Mumbai Terror Attacks on Public Opinion in Western Europe." *Public Choice* 156 (1/2): 213–28.

Global News. 2013. "Toronto Protesters Rally at Indian Consulate over Country's Treatment of Women." Global News, 3 January 2013. https://globalnews.ca/news/324859/toronto-protesters-rally-at-indian-consulate-over-countrys-treatment-of-women/.

Henry, Frances, and Carol Tator. 2003. "Racial Profiling in Toronto: Discourses of Domination, Mediation and Opposition." Presentation at the Canadian Race Relations Foundation. http://www.crr.ca/en/component/flexicontent/items/item/21978-racial-profiling-in-toronto-discourses-of-domination-mediation-and-opposition.

Institute for Economics and Peace. 2015. "Global Terrorism Index 2014." *SIRIUS-Zeitschrift für Strategische Analysen* 1(1): 91–2.

Jiwani, Yasmin. 2006. *Discourses of Denial: Mediations of Race, Gender, and Violence.* Vancouver: UBC Press.

Joffres, Christine, Edward Mills, Michael Joffres, Tinku Khanna, Harleen Walia, and Darrin Grund. 2008. "Sexual Slavery without Borders: Trafficking for Commercial Sexual Exploitation in India." *International Journal for Equity in Health* 7 (1): 1–11.

Karim, Karim H. 2002. *Ethnic Media and Integration: An Empirical Study of South Asian Media in Canada.* CERIS: The Ontario Metropolis Project.

Lindgren, April. 2011. "Front Page Challenge: A Case Study Examining What the Ethnic Media Promises and What It Delivers." *CERIS Working Paper Series* (82): 1–15.

Matsaganis, Matthew D., Vikki S. Katz, and Sandra J. Ball-Rokeach. 2010. *Understanding Ethnic Media: Producers, Consumers, and Societies.* Thousand Oaks, CA: SAGE.

McDougal, Lotus, Samuel Krumholz, Nandita Bhan, Prashant Bharadwaj, and Anita Raj. 2018. "Releasing the Tide: How Has a Shock to the Acceptability of Gender-Based Sexual Violence Affected Rape Reporting to Police in India?" *Journal of Interpersonal Violence* 36 (11–12): 5921–43.

Mendes, Kaitlynn, and Jessica Ringrose. 2019. "Digital Feminist Activism: #MeToo and the Everyday Experiences of Challenging Rape Culture." In *#MeToo and the Politics of Social Change*, edited by

Bianca Fileborn and Rachel Loney-Howes, 37–51. Cham, Switzerland: Palgrave Macmillan.
Murray, Catherine A., Sherry S. Yu, and Daniel Ahadi. 2007. "Cultural Diversity and Ethnic Media in BC. A Report to the Canadian Heritage Western Regional Office." Centre for Policy Studies on Culture and Communities. Vancouver, BC: Simon Fraser University.
Ojo, Tokunbo. 2006. "Ethnic Print Media in the Multicultural Nation of Canada: A Case Study of the Black Newspaper in Montreal." *Journalism* 7 (3): 343–61.
– 2019. "The Early Black Press in Canada." In *Media across the African Diaspora: Content, Audiences, and Global Influence*, edited by Omotayo O. Banjo, 7–17. New York: Taylor & Francis.
Perry, Barbara, and Michael Sutton. 2006. "Seeing Red over Black and White: Popular and Media Representations of Interracial Relationships as Precursors to Racial Violence." *Canadian Journal of Criminology and Criminal Justice* 48 (6): 887–904.
Reid-Maroney, Nina. 2017. "Possibilities for African Canadian Intellectual History: The Case of 19th-Century Upper Canada/Canada West." *History Compass* 15 (12): e12432.
Share News. 2009. https://www.sharenews.com/.
Transparency International. (2014). "Corruption Perceptions Index." https://www.transparency.org/en/cpi/2014.
Weekly Voice. 2022. https://weeklyvoice.com/.
Wortley, Scot. 2008. "Misrepresentation or Reality? The Depiction of Race and Crime in the Toronto Print Media." In *Marginality and Condemnation: An Introduction to Criminology*, edited by Carolyn Brooks and Bernard Schissel, 2nd ed., 104–34. Halifax & Winnipeg: Fernwood Publishing.
Yee, Shirley J. 1997. "Finding a Place: Mary Ann Shadd Cary and the Dilemmas of Black Migration to Canada, 1850–1870." *Frontiers: A Journal of Women Studies* 18 (3): 1–16.
Ziniak, Madeline. 2017. "Ethnic Media in Canada: The Power of Reflection; A Link to Nation Building and Identity." *Canadian Issues*: 22–5.

CHAPTER FOURTEEN

The Ideology of Hindutva in the Canadian Hindu Diaspora's Media: A Critical Examination of the Integrative and Non-Integrative Discourses

Anisha Datta and Indranil Chakraborty

INTRODUCTION

In May 2020, the Canadian multicultural landscape developed a new fault line when a closed Facebook group, "Mississauga Call to Prayer on Loudspeaker Unconstitutional," urged its 8,000-odd members to donate $45 each to create a fund to challenge the temporary Noise Bylaw amendment brought in by the Mississauga Council. The amendment allowed the mosques to broadcast Azaan (sunset prayers) for five minutes during the Ramadan period to compensate for the closed religious services due to COVID-19. The *Toronto Star* reported that this "gesture of compassion" was challenged on the grounds of "preferential treatment" and the founders of the Facebook group stated, "We're not against any religion, we're just against the noise, who live in a city with neighbourhoods around Canada's busiest airport" (Paradkar 2020). The social media comments by the group's members, the majority of whom are from India, ranged from "anti-Muslim hate to equal opportunity racism far-right talking points against the Prime Minister" (Paradkar 2020).

On a YouTube video telecast by TAG TV, the president of the Hindu Forum Canada, Rao Yendamuri, while arguing against the prayer broadcasting said, "Hindu Forum believes in the country's secular foundation that guarantees separation of religion and politics ... as a faith we should not impose any particular faith on other communities."[1] Though this statement invoked the secular principles to disagree with the Mississauga Council's decision, the comment section of the video, mostly contributed by a section of the Hindu diaspora, was filled with hate speech. Some of the comments read: "Loudspeakers should be banned from all the mosques all across the world"; "[T]his marks the start of fall of Great Canada. All of us Asian non-Muslim heritage people know what is about to come, but are helpless."

If we contextualize these contradictory voices, we find that these two lines of thought are not as opposed to each other as it might appear. The Hindu Forum Canada (The Forum) stands for "Oneness of all" (i.e., there is divine in every being and this oneness unifies all beings) (Hindu Forum Canada n.d.). The Forum praises Canada for its secularism. But the Forum's standpoint on secularism is not universal. In 2019, the organization had supported the Indian government's discriminatory move to grant Indian citizenship to all persecuted non-Muslim minorities from Pakistan, Bangladesh, and Afghanistan.[2] The fact that some Islamic sects such as the Ahmadiyya also suffer persecution in Pakistan was not recognized. This implies that the Citizenship Amendment Act (CAA) introduced by the Indian government is Islamophobic in nature.

The idea that India is the holy land for all Hindus based on their ancestry is one of the foundational principles of V.D. Savarkar's ideology of Hindutva, which is a "vigorous assertion of Hindu identity as a tenet of ideological belief" (Lal 2009, 1). This ideology is the inspiration behind the growth of political Hinduism and the Hindu right-wing movement in India. The late nineteenth- and early twentieth-century question "Who is a Hindu?" in India's multifaith and multiethnic society led the Maharashtrian thinker Savarkar (1883–1966) to define the concept of Hindutva (Hinduness) through the three essential features of "a common nation [*rashtra*], a common race [*jati*] and a common civilization [*sanskriti*]" (Savarkar 2009, 116). Savarkar's book, *Essentials of Hindutva*, was first published in 1923 and later republished in 1928 as *Hindutva: Who Is a Hindu*. For the Hindu right wing, the cultural essence of Bharat is "Hinduness" which is the basis of "a very exclusivist form of Hindu nationalism, holding India … as above all a Hindu nation" (Vanaik 2017, 354–5).

The massive growth of political Hinduism in the late twentieth century is a product of several closely related factors. There was the growing communalization of the Indian polity in the post–Babri

Masjid demolition (1992)[3] period, when the Hindu right wing challenged the idea of India as a secular nation. The importance of social change for communalism started increasing in the 1970s, when an Indian Home Ministry study concluded that the persistence of serious social and economic inequalities in rural India had engendered tensions between different classes, which may lead to a situation where the discontented elements are compelled to organize themselves, and the extreme tensions building up within the complex molecule that is the Indian village may end in an explosion. Potentially explosive areas provided the Sangh Parivar[4] targets of opportunity for mobilizing communal antagonism (Ludden 2006).

Since the late 1980s, the globalization of the Indian economy further increased the socio-economic vulnerability of the Indian poor. In this climate of deepening uncertainty, "the BJP and the Sangh Parivar were the one collective force that had the organizational means, ideological clarity and inclination to pursue the politics of sustained [Hindu] mass mobilizations" (Vanaik 2017, 67). This mobilization had led to the destruction of the Babri Masjid and the rise of the Bharatiya Janata Party (BJP) as the party of the future. Soon, India had its first BJP prime minister in Atal Bihari Vajpayee, who held the state power for a full term from 1999 to 2004. Later in 2014, the Hindu right-wing-supported BJP, led by Narendra Modi, ascended to power, and he was re-elected in 2019 with a three-fourths majority. Riding on the wave of Hindu nationalism and India's economic success story in the post-1990s era, the Sangh Parivar (the Sangh Family) actively nurtured various Hindu organizations in countries where the Hindu diaspora had settled. Here, our focus is to look at the important source of the media texts produced by the Hindu organizations in Canada.

The analysis of these media texts could be a valuable contribution to the study of the presence of the ideology of Hindutva in the religious and cultural discourses produced by the Hindu organizations. Here, a text stands for a unit of meaning for interpretation and understanding. In media studies, a text could be a book, film, TV program, website, newspaper article, blog, podcast, or Tweet. Texts are studied "because they are bearers of communication and movers of meaning" (Gray 2017, 196). We attempt to deconstruct the encoded messages (Hall 1973, 1980) of these Hindu cultural texts in order to examine the extent of the presence of Hindutva ideology in them. Second, we also want to examine how far these texts support the Canadian state's secular policy of multiculturalism. Our contribution here examines an understudied form of religious ethnic media in Canada. It is important to note that we have penned this chapter with the academic spirit of exploration and inquiry, and we have no intention of causing offence to any ethnic or religious group.

THEORETICAL FRAMEWORK

In the last two decades, in conjunction with the spread of Hindutva-based Hindu nationalism in India, there has been a surge in academic research to understand the impact of the Hindutva ideology on the Hindu diaspora living in the USA and UK. In contrast, studies on the impact of Hindutva on Canada's Hindu diaspora are comparatively sparse. Based on the socio-economic and cultural analysis of the evolution of Hindu migration and settlement, the scholars cutting across the disciplinary divide (Jaffrelot and Therwath 2007; Kurien 2016; Lele 2003; Rajagopal 2000; Therwath 2012; Vertovec 2000; Warrier 2016) agree that the discourse of political Hinduism has been successful in mobilizing a section of the Hindus in their host countries. However, some of these studies (Vertovec 2000; Warrier 2016) also argue that the markers of Hindutva identity are based on "a common nation [*rashtra*], a common race [*jati*] and a common civilization [*sanskriti*]" (Savarkar 2009, 116), replacing the heterogeneous voices and practices of Hinduism which did not go uncontested. Warrier (2016) researched the challenges posed by the UK-based Hindu organizations in the 1980s and 1990s to the secular fabric of British multiculturalism, and discussed the tension existing between Hinduism as a spiritual journey of diverse practices and orientations, and Hindutva as a project of Hindu nationalism.

These studies investigated the impact of the rising tide of Hindu nationalism on the Hindu diaspora and have exposed the different aspects of the Hindu communal discourse only by observing the diaspora's everyday life, rather than the media intervention undertaken by them in their host countries, where their existence is steeped in the complex interplay of multiculturalism and racism. Research on the Canadian-Hindu diaspora, an ethnic minority, has been scarce, and to fill this gap, we undertake a critical reading of representative media texts produced by five prominent Hindu organizations.

METHODOLOGY

In this study, we have selected Hindu organizations based in Toronto and the Greater Toronto Area (GTA). The organizations were selected from these regions because these have the highest concentration[5] of the Hindu diaspora living in Canada. According to Garamchai.com, there are sixty-nine Hindu temples in these regions.[6] Next, we have classified these organizations into two broad categories: (a) religious-political, where religious discourse has a tendency towards becoming a political instrumental power by trying to influence the legislative and executive decision making at city, provincial, and federal levels (The Hindu Federation and the Hindu Forum Canada both fall under this category); and (b) religious-cultural, where the basic aim is to project religion as a cultural activity. In the latter category falls the BAPS Swaminarayan Temple of Toronto (BAPS), the Bharat Sevashram Sangha Canada (BSS), and the Vedanta Society of Toronto (VS). The dividing line between these two categories is not always distinct since religion, culture, and politics of the diaspora are often entangled. However, what separates these two categories is how religious identity is mobilized, through either politics or culture. Second, our selection of these organizations is based on the following two criteria: (a) the diversity of the Hindu diaspora is reflected in these organizations, i.e., the diaspora's diversity in terms of language, ethnicity, and regions of India, and (b) the organizations have an active media presence through regularly updated websites and frequently published pamphlets and literature. In addition, over the last two years, our interactions with more than 500 members (e.g., friends, relatives, professionals, temple visitors) of the Hindu diaspora have helped us make this selection. These were informal conversations between practising equals, all equally informed and thus equally expert. These persons should not be considered as human subjects, as normally implied in Ethics in Research protocols, the purpose of which is to protect vulnerable populations.

The media texts we are concerned with are religious writings, cultural blogs, videos, festival literature, newsletters, and annual souvenir magazines produced between 2014 and 2020 by the five organizations. The selected period, 2014 to 2020, is significant because our aim is to explore to what extent the ascendency of the Hindutva ideology, as a political force in India during the same period, has influenced the ethnic Hindu diaspora's discourses as represented in the media texts produced by Hindu organizations in Canada. Here, we understand that "ethnic media are media produced for a particular ethnic community ... however not all ethnic media are produced by the ethnic community they serve" (Matsaganis, Katz, and Ball-Rokeach 2010). In this chapter, we examine the ethnic media texts produced by the Hindu organizations in Canada, which represent their religious identity in the Canadian public sphere. Unlike other ethnic media present in Canada like the popular OMNI TV[7] channel, ethnic Hindu media texts are not secular in character. The texts are for, by, and of the Hindus living in Canada.

We have selected the media texts which contain the ideology and mission of each of the aforementioned organizations that are concerned with the integrative and non-integrative aspects of Hindu identity in Canada's secular multicultural context and Hindu identity as a political force. We have accessed the media texts in two ways. First, we visited the places of activity such as the temples and the cultural centers of the organizations to collect the hard copies of the organizations' books, documents, pamphlets, and newsletters. We collected and examined sixteen hard copies of such documents and, finally, we analyzed three of those materials which were relevant to our research. Second, we scanned the Internet to access thirty different online materials posted by the organizations on their web portals, websites, blogs, and other social media platforms (e.g., YouTube). Out of these online materials, we analyzed ten such sources based on the focus of our research. It is important to mention here that our choice of the media text format we used depended on their availability. As the BSS did not have a robust internet presence during the time of data collection, we had to depend on souvenirs and literature produced by that organization. In contrast, BAPS has a considerable media presence across all formats. Therefore, we used websites, blogs, and literature to understand each organization's discourse. The contents of these media texts range from treatises on Yoga and Ayurveda, to expositions of India's glorious culture.

In this work, we view media texts and the discourse embedded in them as an important data source for socio-cultural analysis. In this regard, we draw on the ethnomethodological tradition as found in the works of Garfinkel (1967) and Smith (1993). Thus, we have closely examined the use of language in these discourses to delineate to what effect they are used. In particular, we have looked out for the semantically loaded words (e.g., pure culture; mother of all cultures;

weakened community), the emotionally charged metaphors (e.g., the lamb and the lion), and the politically motivated ideals (e.g., India as the holy land for the Hindus; Hindu persecution in history; India implies Hindu). We have also identified the Hindutva ideological codes (i.e., a common nation, a common race, and a common civilization) that structure these discourses to make them rhetorical. Thus, we view textually mediated discourse as a communicative device through which ideologies are disseminated. We attempt to show how these ideological codes advocate for Hindutva-driven political interests among the Hindu diaspora and how these interests could influence the diaspora's civic life in Canada.

RELIGIOUS-POLITICAL ORGANIZATIONS

The Hindu Federation: Furthering Hindu Canadian Interests

The Hindu spiritual symbol of the AUM[8] embossed on a saffron-coloured rising sun welcomes the visitor on the official web portal of the Hindu Federation (the Federation hereafter). The website informs readers that Dr B. Doobay founded the organization in 1999 and it has seventeen Toronto-based Hindu organizations as its members. The Federation is a platform for the Hindu organizations and individuals that will "ensure the propagation and representation of the Hindu Religion and Culture within Canada" (Hindu Federation n.d.). The organization's aims are to unite all Hindus, to recruit influential Hindus to serve Hindu interests, and to display the greatness of the Hindu religion in all fields of life. The Federation thinks that unity among the Hindus living in Canada would help the Hindus to have a functional body "that will be the focal point of representation to all Federal, Provincial and Municipal levels of government and Media and all other entities in matters relating to Hindus in Canada" (Hindu Federation n.d.).

To the Federation, the unity of Hindus is essential to solve problems pertaining to the Hindu community. Going by the content of the news section and the gallery of pictures posted on the portal, the interests and needs are mostly about the Hindu religion. However, the posts also evince a sense of social concern that economic growth is not taking place among all sections of the Hindu community. The fusion of Hindus coming from different geographies, with their diverse cultural practices into one single Hindu religious identity, could open up spaces of discordance in everyday life unless there are material or spiritual interests to unify various Hindu groups who are divided on the lines of class, caste, sects, linguistic, and geographical backgrounds. Scholars point out that the problem lies in the way Hinduism has evolved, having no single canon that would guide the life of all devotees: "Hinduism was projected largely in terms of its philosophical ideas, iconology and rituals" (Thapar 1989, 211). It is evident that the Federation is aware that the realization of unity would not be an easy task as it mentions that one of its goals is "[to] promote harmony within the Hindu Community through focus [*sic*] efforts to build and maintain relations" (Hindu Federation n.d.). Warrier (2016) observes that "one way which ecumenical umbrella organizations often seek to forge a sense of unity across this [Hindu] diversity at the grassroots level is by arguing that Hindus are vulnerable when disunited and they need to unite if they are to hold their own against threatening forces" (135). In the Canadian context, we find that the Federation, instead of emphasizing the vulnerability of the Hindu community to the forces opposing Hindu interests, urges the community to remain united on a single platform, so that the community would be able to realize "greater achievements socially, culturally and religiously" (Hindu Federation n.d.).

Like its counterparts in the UK and USA, the Hindu Federation in Canada faces strong challenges to bring together the diverse Hindu diaspora. In the UK and USA, the Hindu organizations have devised multiple strategies to minimize this Hindu heterogeneity in order to promote Hindu unity. These strategies range from dog whistling that Hindus are in danger, to serving the community members through professional, educational, and economic support programs.

A close reading of the Federation's website suggests that its project of forging unity is based on a three-pronged approach: (a) delivering community services to the Hindus, (b) visualizing a rich tradition of Hindu culture to bring all Hindus under one umbrella, and (c) representing the Hindus while dealing with the federal, provincial, and municipal levels of government and other agencies. Like the united front alliances in politics, which aim for power through the construction of a gilded future, the Federation also offers the Hindu diaspora a secure and respectful future by telling them to remain united.

The Hindu Forum Canada: Fighting Hinduphobia[9]

According to the website of the Hindu Forum Canada, the Forum is a corporate body formed under Canada's Not-for-profit Corporations Act with the purpose "to combat Hinduphobia." The emblem used by the Forum is a unique symbol – the Hindu AUM is embossed on a dual-coloured (red and saffron) Canadian maple leaf. The picture gallery accompanying the section "Formation of Hindu Forum Canada" displays several pictures depicting its supporters sitting in front of large banners with messages such as "Hindu bashing and Hinduphobia not acceptable" and "We must defend Hindu heritage and Hindu civilization" (Hindu Forum n.d.). Written in first person, the page cites several examples of Hinduphobia in India, the mother country of the writer, accusing Muslims, Christians, and Communists for the persecution and spreading of Hindu hatred. The Hindu life is not valued to the same extent as the other two religions, Christianity and Islam. The author says "Hinduphobia becomes ever so clear when the world media unproportionally [*sic*] reports the instant uproar of a crime against a Christian or a Muslim, but little in the case when it comes to Hindus" (Hindu Forum n.d.). Yet, the webpage does not mention any discriminatory policy that Hindus are facing in Canada to prove its point. Under the "Belief" section of the website, there are several subsections which elaborate on the basic principles that the Forum stands for. As the "Religious Freedom" section states, "we advocate a policy of intolerance towards hatred, violence, and discrimination against all communities and religions. Anti-Hindu hatred or Hinduphobia is the irrational fear of, hostility towards, discrimination against, or hatred directed at Hindus and Hinduism. These have a tragically long history which continues to this day across the globe" (Hindu Forum n.d.). Upon analyzing the paragraph's structure, we can observe that it starts with a secular statement declaring that the Forum endorses policies that do not tolerate any form of disrespect towards any religion. This statement itself could have been sufficient for any organization that supports religious freedom, but the Forum goes on to make a special mention of what anti-Hindu hatred or Hinduphobia signifies in terms of the community's long history of persecution.

Without debating how far this claim of the history of Hindu persecution is an exaggeration, let us examine what else the Forum communicates here: "We request your help in tracking down incidents of identity-based and bias-motivated intimidation, harassment, and violence in [*sic*] our communities. Raise your voices against such prejudice if you or someone you know has experienced or witnessed any incident of intolerance" (Hindu Forum n.d.). This discourse has several significant words and phrases, which are deployed to communicate a politically charged rhetoric.

The rationale against intolerance is arranged and structured in the following way: (a) any religious intolerance should not be tolerated; (b) Hinduphobia is rampant across history; (c) Hindus should come forward if they find any incidence of intolerance toward them. A symptomatic reading of this discourse suggests that the unspoken part is that Hindus can only identify any disrespect and intolerance shown toward their religion. The question evaded by the forum is: what will the Canadian state do in this matter? Will the state follow the Hindu community's opinion, or will it act as a secular institution? The evasion might suggest that the Forum is less inclined to invite the state to intervene, which might lead to a situation where a scholarly critical study of Hinduism is construed as an insult towards the religion.[10]

The Forum also uses a different definition of secularism when talking about secularism in India. This meaning of secularism implies that the interest of the Hindus is first among equals. One of the Hindu Forum participants on a TAG TV telecast reminded the viewers, "Hinduism is overdue [*sic*] over there [India]. As happens in every country, [the] majority has to be respected, for example, as we are in Canada, we have to respect Christianity … it is their country. They have allowed us to stay here, provided us [with] such a good environment, if we start troubling them then they will definitely get against us" (Hindu Forum Canada 2020). This argument is premised on a non-secular assumption about the power and numerical strength of religious groups. We know that Hindus are a minority in Canada, but are a majority in India. This majority-minority political-religious framework is borrowed from the Sangh Parivar. For the Sangh Parivar and the BJP, "democracy has been redefined as Hindu majoritarianism, and secularism as a false and anti-Hindu, minority-favouring construct" (Vanaik 2017, 79).

This Hindutva-inspired definition of secularism and democracy used by the Forum is not specific to Canada. For some Hindu groups in the USA, Australia, UK, and other developed countries, this continues to be the strategy for keeping their community work active among the Hindu diaspora. For organizations such as the Hindu Forum Canada, this strategy of making use of modern secular values to further their cause serves a dual purpose. On one hand, this attempts at erasing the Eurocentric/colonial stigma that Hinduism is intolerant and backward. On the other hand, this strategy conveys a message to the Forum's supporters that they do not need to abandon their ideology of Hindutva to be modern and secular.[11]

RELIGIOUS-CULTURAL ORGANIZATIONS

The BAPS Swaminarayan Mandir of Toronto: An Imagined Hindu Community

The BAPS Swaminarayan group is the most visible face of Hindu public life in the diaspora whose roots go back to Gujrat, India (Hatcher 2020). It is perhaps the most appropriate example of a religious body steeped in "transnationalism" (Kim 2016), representing the "Hindu Nationalist" forces in the "West." Its message of Hinduism expressed through vegetarianism, the authority of the Vedas, and the purity and superiority of Hindu culture has successfully attracted a section of the prosperous Hindu diaspora from the Gujarati Hindu community (Hatcher 2020). The BAPS temple in Toronto (BAPS) is a massive architectural splendour spread over eighteen acres of land. The temple complex consists of the first traditional hand-carved Hindu temple in Canada. It is evident that the temple is a huge financial investment that is backed by its wealthy patrons and followers.[12]

India's Glorious Culture (2015) is a BAPS publication to spread the words of Indian (meaning Hindu) cultural glory. It is a brief booklet in English spanning sixty-five pages, with colourful pictures. It has twenty-eight sections and the topics range from the five moral vows for BAPS followers to the scientific contributions made by the ancient Hindu sages. For our purposes, we will specifically focus on the content of the booklet that converges with the fundamental elements of the ideology of Hindutva. First, Indian culture is equated with Hindu culture without any acknowledgment that India has been shaped by a multitude of religions and sects. The numerous sects within Hinduism can range from practising animal sacrifice to insisting that pure vegetarianism implies good karma. The section "Introduction to Hindu Culture" states, "our eternal Hindu culture means an incredible, timeless tradition of pure thoughts, feelings, social behavior and values which elevate and benefit all. This culture implies unparalleled nobility that was born ... in the vast subcontinent called India. It is also known as Sanatan Dharma, Arya Culture, Hindu Dharma or Indian Culture ... Indian culture is the mother of all cultures. It is also very rare to be born in this culture – Durlabham Bharate Janma" (BAPS 2015, 7). The text also equates Hindu or Indian culture with Aryan culture, which is based on the nineteenth-century European race theory about the preeminence of Hindu upper castes, and this theory also attempted to racialize the caste system.

BAPS believes that there are three unique aspects of "our [Hindu] culture: it is the oldest culture, it is a pure and divine culture (Sanatana Dharma) and it has made contributions in science" (BAPS 2015, 7). Its antiquity is established by the Vedic origin of Hindu culture, which BAPS claims has been proved by archeological excavations. The booklet thus attempts to legitimize its claims by invoking what it takes to be the authority of science and its supposedly irrefutable evidence. At the same time, to embellish the supremacy of Hindu culture, the text makes several unfounded claims that ancient Indian sages had invented technology such as plastic surgery (BAPS 2015, 33).

But in what way is Hindu culture "pure"? The booklet resorts to mystification – since Hindus believe that pure character and spirituality are the pillars of progress. "Indian culture inspires values such as non-violence, truth, self-control and sacrifice right from birth. It nurtures good feelings for everyone – the whole world is one family ... may everyone be united" (BAPS 2015, 11). A symptomatic reading of the section "Indian Culture Is Pure Because" can identify that BAPS is completely ignoring the existence of caste and gender-based inequities and atrocities within Hindu culture. Historically, the sect has tended to support rather than contest the ideology of caste and gender-based hierarchies (Hardiman 1988; Hatcher 2020). Although women are officially accorded respect and protection, they are discouraged from being independent (Williams 1984, quoted in Hardiman 1988, 1911). Women's dependency is further ensured by the denial of rights over family property, inheritance being firmly in the male line (Hardiman 1988, 1911). However, our research did not inquire how far these practices are followed by the BAPS followers in Canada.

Could the above religious-cultural beliefs of a particular kind of Hindu way of life coexist with Canadian multicultural, democratic, and secular values? We can infer that the BAPS' position on gender, caste, vegetarianism, and the 'purity' and supremacy of Hindu culture could potentially generate non-integrative impulses.

The Bharat Sevashram Sangha Canada: A Show of Hindu Strength

The next set of media texts we will look at are produced by the Bharat Sevashram Sangha Canada (BSS). The souvenir magazine *Bharat Sevashram Sangha Inauguration Ceremony 2019* (hereafter *BSS 2019*) states that since Indians (meaning Hindus) living abroad feel isolated from the mainstream of Indian life, there is a need that the lofty ideals of Indian culture and its traditional heritage be preached among them by organizations such as the BSS. The text *BSS 2019* (Bharat Sevashram Sangha) was published in 2019 to celebrate the inauguration of the new Cultural Centre of the BSS Canada Branch at Etobicoke, Ontario.

The Sangha was established in 1923 in undivided Bengal, India, where the 1920s and 1930s witnessed the consolidation of sectarian and communal politics in this region. The ideological impetus behind the emergence of the Sangha came from a strong denial of the materialist Western culture and the regeneration of India with the Vedic ideals of restraint and renunciation. The Sangha has a history of supporting communal politics in late colonial Bengal (Dasgupta 2012). In Canada, the Sangha was established in 1974 when Swami Brahmanandaji established the Canadian chapter in Toronto.

The text *BSS 2019* is written in English, with two chapters dedicated to (a) some brief articles about the history, aims, and mission of the BSS, and (b) the history of the BSS Canadian chapter, respectively. The article "Aims and Objects" highlights Hindu pride by saying that the geography of India has given birth to wise sages and lofty spiritual ideas, and that the country is unparalleled in this regard. Furthermore, Hindus have descended from these wise men. The Hindutva-laced discourse that can be distilled from this section is that India is the Holy land for Hindus, and that Hindus have a superior and special ancestry.

The other article in the *BSS 2019* is focused on why the founder, Pranavananda, had cultivated the order of monk disciples, who would actively participate in nation building along with their sequestered spiritual life. The monk disciples are envisioned to play an active role in the strengthening of the Hindu community and the land so that they are not enslaved as in earlier times by "merciless foreign opportunists" (Moguls and British). A close reading of the discourse reveals the presence of the late colonial "dying Hindu and weakened Hindu" anxiety.

As an exhortation to "weakened Hindus" *BSS 2019* presents the parable of the lamb and lion ("[The] Story of the Lamb and Lion") to illustrate why Hindus need to empower themselves by forging solidarity among themselves. The Sangha's founder understood that the downfall of Hindus is due to their lack of unity as opposed to Christians who are strong because they are united. Hindus lack the united force of a monotheistic faith since they are divided into numerous squabbling sects and factions. Also, Hindus have been perceived as weak by Muslims due to the former's peaceful nature: "Just as a lamb cannot live alongside a lion seeing that the lion could easily devour the poor lamb similarly a weakling or peaceful Hindu cannot coexist with a ruffian member of the other faith. The only way-out for the Hindus was to make themselves lions all [*sic*]." The parable discourse therefore espouses a militant[13] version of the Hindutva, which does not have much respect for the principle of non-violence. For the same reason, the text goes on to say that Gandhi's non-violent movement could not reconstruct Hindu pride and dignity, which was hurt by centuries of oppression by the Moguls and the British.

In the context of the Hindu diaspora, the BSS's anxiety is about the loss of Hindu identity when encountered by alien religious and cultural forces such as the West. According to the BSS, it is crucial to make Indians (referring to Hindus) living abroad aware of and proud of the spiritual roots of their illustrious heritage because they often feel isolated from the mainstream of Indian life. The BSS is concerned not only about the diaspora's loss of "Indian identity" but more importantly, about the demise of "the Hindu way of life" among them. The communal discourse that we have examined above could collide with a core principle of the ethos of Canadian multiculturalism, which is that diverse communities residing in the country should respect each other's belief systems.

The Vedanta Society of Toronto: The Universal Spiritualism of Humanity

The Vedanta Society of Toronto (VS) was established in 1968. It is the overseas Canadian branch of the Ramakrishna (Math and Mission) Order (RKM), which is headquartered in India. The RKM was founded by Swami Vivekananda in 1897. He was a direct disciple of the nineteenth-century Bengali mystic Ramakrishna Paramhansa, whose core philosophy was "*Jato mat tato path*" or "as many faiths so many paths." The main motto of the RKM is "for one's own salvation and for the welfare of the world," formulated by Swami Vivekananda (Belur Math n.d.a).

The RKM describes itself as a "worldwide, non-political, non-sectarian spiritual organization which has been engaged in various forms of humanitarian, social service activities ... without any distinction of caste, religion or race, because they see the living God in them ... Inspired by the idea of the harmony of all faiths, its centres encourage adherents of different faiths to meet in a spirit of friendship and mutual appreciation, and to learn from one another without having to give up one's own faith (Belur Math n.d.b). Thus, the ideology of the VS, which is under the spiritual guidance of the RKM, puts an emphasis on the cultivation of inter-faith dialogue to come to the realization that there are numerous paths to reach God. Given this approach toward universal spiritualism, there is no effort on the part of the VS to assert that the Hindu religion is superior to others due to its "purity" and Vedic antiquity, or that Indian nationhood should be built on the principles of the Hindu religion.

For the Vedanta Society of Toronto's *Newsletter May 2020* (hereafter the *Newsletter*), we find a similar open-minded spiritual quest animating its content. In addition, there is a thrust towards equal respect for all faiths. This open-minded spirit was conspicuously absent in the discourses produced by the BAPS and the BSS. The six-page *Newsletter* is in English. Other than the May calendar of online lectures and scripture classes and the call for donations and volunteering, the newsletter contains several short reflective essays on spiritual topics such as "Many Faiths, One Truth" (by the Dalai Lama), "Buddha's Message to the World," "What Yoga Is," and "The Spirit and Influence of Vedanta."

A passage from the essay by the Dalai Lama states: "A main point in my discussion ... was how central compassion was to the message of both Christianity and Buddhism ... And I've learned how the Talmud and the Bible repeat the theme of compassion ... From this perspective, mutual understanding among these traditions is not merely the business of religious believers – it matters for the welfare of humanity as a whole" (Vedanta Society of Toronto 2020).

Next, let us focus on a quotation in the *Newsletter* from the writings of Swami Vivekananda: "The Vedanta claims that there has not been one religious inspiration, one manifestation of the divine man, however great, but it has been the expression of that infinite oneness in human nature; and all that we call ethics and morality and doing good to others is also but the manifestation of this oneness" (Vedanta Society of Toronto 2020).

The inclusion of the Dalai Lama's essay as well as Vivekananda's understanding of Vedanta evince that the VS provides space to other faiths and it does not preach the superiority of one faith over others. Thus, the spiritual ideas of the VS facilitate the quest for universal spiritualism. This ideology differs from the ideology of Hindutva, and it has a strong potential to have a frictionless co-existence with modern ideas of secularism, multiculturalism, and democracy. Therefore, this ideology can be viewed as more integrative in nature.

CONCLUSION

The Canadian policy of multiculturalism acknowledges "the freedom of all members of Canadian society to preserve, enhance and share their cultural heritage" (Jukier and Woehrling 2010, 155). Further, Canadian multiculturalism is aimed at accommodating "a wide variety of beliefs, diversity of tastes and pursuits, customs and codes of conduct" (158) in a diverse racial and ethnic set-up. This can work as long as believers and non-believers respect each other's belief systems. Vedanta Society's message of spirituality, which is based on the philosophy "*Jato mat tato path*" or "as many faiths so many paths," creates a fertile ground for the cultivation of an integrative force, which can bolster the secular and multicultural principles by respecting and recognizing the non-Hindu ethnic and religious practices. In sharp contrast, messages from the other three organizations (i.e., the BAPS, the BSS, and the Hindu Forum Canada) are layered with the non-integrative ideology of Hindutva, which focuses on the superiority of the Hindu ancestry (*jati* or race), the purity of Hindu culture and religion, India as the holy land for all Hindus, Hindu persecution, and Hindu nationhood. Far less strident are messages from the fourth organization, the Hindu Federation, which are relatively open-minded and less overtly pro-Hindutva. Even so, the burden of the Hindu Federation's message is one of Hindu superiority, though without overt denigration of non-Hindus. However, the ideology of Hindutva is unevenly present in the discourses of these organizations. Among the two religious organizations, the BAPS is more subtle in its delivery of the message of Hindutva when compared with the messages from the BSS. The message from the BAPS is about a meaningful spiritual life based on the idea of a superior and pure Hindu culture and religion. The BSS, on the other hand, is much more overt in its expression of Hindu nationalism and the ideology of Hindutva. For the Hindu Federation, the mission is to consolidate all the members of the Hindu diaspora, hailing from different geographies and ethnicities, on a united Hindu platform. Their message is relatively open-minded, and they draw much less on the ideology of Hindutva when compared to the messages from the Hindu Forum Canada. The Hindu Forum's messages overtly express the ideology of Hindutva, political Hinduism, and Hindu nationalism, and its discourse is distinctly non-integrative in nature.

Why does the unevenness between these organizations exist? We can safely speculate that the membership of these organizations is quite diverse based on heterogeneous social markers of class, caste, sect, language, region, and geography. In addition, the diverse Hindu diaspora's relationship with the Indian state and with the ideology of Hindutva is varied in nature. To come up with a definite answer to the question of unevenness, we need to examine in detail the social composition of the members of these organizations, which is not within the scope of this study, but it can be an area of future research.

In our study, we have also found that when an organization such as the Hindu Forum Canada expresses non-integrative messages, that discourse is precariously positioned on a self-contradictory argument that attempts at balancing secularism with the ideology of Hindutva. For an ethnic minority, it does not usually augur well to act as a rebel, especially when its religious beliefs and practices veer away from Canada's "common culture" (Williams 1989) of democracy, secularism, and multiculturalism. Thus, when the representatives of the Hindu Forum Canada discuss Hinduphobia, and the preferential treatment of some religious groups by the state, they do not forget to add the softening preamble in the "About Us" section of the webpage, that on the whole, they "advocate for policies that enhance the wellbeing of minority groups in Canada, secure their human rights around the world, and promote peace, prosperity, and pluralism in their favor" (Hindu Forum n.d.). How long this precarious balancing act will continue is a matter of speculation. The recent incident of Azaan suggests that in the future, the search for purity and superiority emanating from the Hindutva-influenced discourses of Hindu organizations in Canada might pose challenges for the secular fabric of Canadian multiculturalism.

ACKNOWLEDGEMENTS

We would like to thank Tirthankar Bose, formerly of the Department of English, Simon Fraser University, for his comments and suggestions. We would also like to thank the anonymous reviewers for their comments on the manuscript.

NOTES

1 Hindu Forum Canada, "Hindu Forum Canada Questions Azaan (Adhan) through Mosques' Loudspeakers," YouTube video, https://www.youtube.com/watch?v=N8IYUfkBZnA.
2 Hindu Forum Canada. n.d. "Demonstration in Canada on January 26, 2020 at Consulate General of India," https://hinduforumcanada.org/demonstration-at-consulate-general-of-india/#.
3 In 1992, the Babri Masjid or Mosque (built by Emperor Babur in 1528) was illegally razed to the ground by thousands of supporters of right-wing Hindu groups such as the VHP and the BJP. These groups had pledged to build a Hindu temple at the site of the mosque, since they believe that it was the birthplace of the Hindu deity Ram. The ensuing communal riots led to the deaths of 2,000 people across India.
4 A network of nationalist Hindu organizations led by the Rashtriya Swayamsevak Sangh (RSS – National Volunteers Corps). The RSS and the Sangh Parivar espouse the ideology of Hindutva.
5 According to the 2011 National Household Survey, the total Hindu population in Canada was 497,960. Out of this, in Ontario, the size of the Hindu population was 366,720, with 325,425 Hindus living in the Toronto area (Statistics Canada, "2011 National Household Survey," Statistics Canada Catalogue no. 99-010-X2011032).
6 Garamchai.com, http://www.garamchai.com/canada/GTATemples.htm.

7 OMNI Television is a Canadian television channel owned by Rogers Communications. It currently consists of six Canadian multicultural television stations which offer programs in Cantonese, Italian, Mandarin, Punjabi, and South Asian languages.
8 The symbol of AUM stands for the Param Brahma (the supreme creator).
9 Hindu Forum Canada is not a member of the Hindu Federation in Canada.
10 These kinds of arguments were used against two notable Indologists, Sheldon Pollock and Wendy Doniger, calling them out as intolerant and hateful to the Hindu religion. See Chandra (2016).
11 The supporters of the Forum had demonstrated in favour of the discriminatory CAA of the Indian government.
12 "It is a $40 million vision, hand-carved by Indian artisans out of 24,000 hunks of Italian marble and Turkish limestone … [t]he local Hindu community offered up about 400 devoted volunteers, and it footed the bill for much of the temple, which was erected in 18 months without government funding." https://archive.is/20130704013905/http://www.nationalpost.com/news/story.html.
13 In contemporary India, the Bajrang Dal, a Sangh family organization, often resorts to open physical violence such as lynching of Muslims to show off their Hindu communal strength.

REFERENCES

BAPS Swaminarayan Sanstha. 2015. *India's Glorious Culture*. Ahmedabad: Swaminarayan Aksharpith.

Belur Math. n.d.a. "About Us." *Belur Math*. https://belurmath.org/about-us/.

– n.d.b. "Ideology." *Belur Math*. https://belurmath.org/ideology/.

Bharat Sevashram Sangha. 2019. Bharat Sevashram Sangha Inauguration Ceremony 2019. Toronto, Canada.

Chandra, Naveen. 2016. "Wendy Doniger Is Wrong Again." *Swarajya* magazine, 5 May 2016. https://swarajyamag.com/culture/wendy-doniger-is-wrong-again.

Dasgupta, Kaushiki. 2012. "Hinduizing the Hindus and Politicizing the Consciousness; A Focus on the Bharat Sevashram Sangha in Late Colonial Bengal." *Proceedings of the Indian History Congress* 73: 697–706.

Garfinkel, Harold. 1967. *Studies in Ethnomethodology*. Hoboken, NJ: Prentice-Hall.

Gray, Jonathan. 2017. "Text." In *Keywords for Media Studies*, edited by Laurie Ouellette and Jonathan Gray, 196. New York: NYU Press.
Hall, Stuart. 1973. "Encoding and Decoding in the Television Discourse." Presentation at University of Birmingham, Birmingham.
– 1980. "Encoding, Decoding." In *Culture, Media, Language: Working Papers in Cultural Studies, 1972–1979*, edited by Stuart Hall, Dorothy Hobson, Andrew Lowe, and Paul Willis, 117–28. London: Unwin Hyman.
Hardiman, David. 1988. "Class Base of Swaminarayan Sect." *Economic and Political Weekly* 23 (37): 1907–12.
Hatcher, Brian A. 2020. *Hinduism Before Reform*. Cambridge: Harvard University Press.
Hindu Federation. n.d. "About Us." Hindu Federation. http://www.hindufederation.ca/about-us.
Hindu Forum Canada. n.d. https://hinduforumcanada.org/.
– 2020. "How to Combat Hindu-Phobia in the Western World? HFC Directors Reflect @TAGTV," 6 March 2020. https://hinduforumcanada.org/march-2020-videos/.
Jaffrelot, Christophe, and Ingrid Therwath. 2007. "The Sangh Parivar and the Hindu Diaspora in the West: What Kind of Long-Distance Nationalism?" *International Political Sociology* 1: 278–95.
Jukier, Rosalie, and Jose Woehrling. 2010. "Religion and the Secular State in Canada." In *Religion and the Secular State: National Reports,* edited by Javier Martinez-Torron and W. Cole Durham, 183–212. Provo, UT: International Center for Law and Religious Studies.
Kim, Hanna H. 2016. "Transnational Movements." In *Hinduism in the Modern World*, edited by Brian A. Hatcher, 48–64. New York: Routledge.
Kurien, Prema. 2016. "Hinduism in the United States." In *Hinduism in the Modern World*, edited by Brian A. Hatcher, 143–57. New York: Routledge.
Lal, Vinay, ed. 2009. "Religion in Politics and the Politics of Hinduism." In *Political Hinduism,* 1–32. New Delhi: Oxford University Press.
Lele, Jayant. 2003. "Indian Diaspora's Long-Distance Nationalism: The Rise and Proliferation of 'Hindutva' in Canada." In *Fractured Identity: The Indian Diaspora in Canada*, edited by Sushma J. Varma and Radhika Seshan, 66–119. New Delhi: Rawat Publications.
Ludden, David. 2006. "Preface to the Second Edition." In *Making India Hindu: Religion, Community, and the Politics of Democracy in India.* New Delhi: Oxford University Press.

Matsaganis, Matthew D., Vikki Katz, and Sandra Ball-Rokeach. 2010. *Understanding Ethnic Media: Producers, Consumers, and Societies.* Thousand Oaks, CA: SAGE.

Paradkar, Shree. 2020. "A Small Gesture of Compassion for Muslims during the Pandemic Unleashes Ugly Torrent of Intolerance in Mississauga." *Toronto Star*, 6 May 2020. https://www.thestar.com/opinion/star-columnists/2020/05/06/a-small-gesture-of-compassion-for-muslims-during-the-pandemic-unleashes-ugly-torrent-of-intolerance-in-mississauga.html.

Rajagopal, Arvind. 2000. "Hindu Nationalism in the US: Changing Configurations of Political Practice." *Ethnic and Racial Studies* 23 (3): 476–96.

Savarkar, V.D. 2009 [1923]. *Hindutva*. New Delhi: Hindi Sahitya Sadan.

Smith, Dorothy. 1993. *Texts, Facts and Femininity*. New York: Routledge.

Thapar, Romila. 1989. "Imagined Religious Communities? Ancient History and the Modern Search for a Hindu Identity." *Modern Asian Studies* 23 (2): 209–31.

Therwath, Ingrid. 2012. "Cyber-Hindutva: Hindu Nationalism, the Diaspora and the Web." *e-Diasporas Atlas*, April 2012. http://www.e-diasporas.fr/working-papers/Therwath-Hindutva EN.pdf.

Vanaik, Achin. 2017. *The Rise of Hindu Authoritarianism*. London: Verso.

Vedanta Society of Toronto. 2020. *Newsletter May 2020*. http://newsite.vedantatoronto.ca/documents/Newletters/NM20.pdf.

Vertovec, Steven. 2000. *The Hindu Diaspora*. London: Routledge.

Warrier, Maya. 2016. "Hinduism in Britain." In *Hinduism in the Modern World*, edited by Brian A. Hatcher, 128–42. New York: Routledge.

Williams, Raymond B. 1984. *A New Face of Hinduism: The Swaminarayan Religion*. London: Cambridge University Press.

– 1989. "Culture Is Ordinary." In *Resources of Hope: Culture, Democracy and Socialism*, edited by Rabon Gable, 3–14. London: Verso.

CHAPTER FIFTEEN

Innovative Models in Ethnic Media 2.0: A Practitioner's Reflections

Naser Miftari

INTRODUCTION

What are some of the dimensions in which ethnic media becomes contextualized in Canada, how, and by whom? From a practitioner's perspective, this chapter explores the role and functioning of three distinct entities – New Canadian Media, a diversity initiative dedicated to immigrant and ethnic reporting; Multilingual International Research and Ethnic Media Services, a for-profit media monitoring and analysis service; and *Multicultural Meanderings*, a public policy blog. The main question that is explored here is whether these three initiatives, alone or in peer cooperation, reflect capacity to bridge the gap or fill the void (real or perceived) between ethnic and mainstream media.

This chapter explores how these initiatives negotiate their place in the broader Canadian media and public opinion landscape while operating at the intersection of ethnic and mainstream media, and examines their functioning in the context of what Ball-Rokeach, Kim, and Matei refer to as a "(Multicultural) Communication Infrastructure" consisting of a web of community organizations and media outlets that function as "connective tissues" which facilitate communication between immigrant communities and the broader society (2001, 398). As argued, without the existence of a well-functioning communication infrastructure, it becomes more difficult for immigrant communities to form and function, both as a socially and physically concrete entity, and as units within the larger dominant culture (Matei and Ball-Rokeach 2001; Ahadi and Murray 2009).

These three initiatives stand out because they reflect an "emerging model" alongside traditional ethnic media outlets, or "ethnic media 2.0," which represents the evolving nature of ethnic media in the digital sphere. They are located at the intersection between the mainstream and ethnic and play important roles as (a) promoters of ethnic media perspectives by sifting and sorting through a plethora of ethnic media voices; (b) liaisons or connectors between ethnic and mainstream media landscape; and (c) contextual articulators, through reflection and analysis of ethnic media reporting on issues related to immigrants and immigration, and offering the broader Canadian public opinion the possibility to become informed on the prevailing views among various ethnic communities on matters that are of relevance to the rest of Canada.

These initiatives also emphasize an educational role in their mission statements, a role that is reflected in the activities they undertake in their individual or joint projects. Despite facing challenges and constraints (financial or otherwise), the three initiatives play a vital role in bridging the gap between the mainstream media's inability to provide comprehensive coverage of various ethnic communities' issues, challenges, and concerns, and the ethnic media's unwillingness or inability to reach beyond its immediate audience. All three initiatives identify themselves as having an important role in shaping the public's perception of a united national community, shared citizenship, and common values. They do so by promoting multiculturalism and Canadian diversity and citizenship. Their operational context and contribution, which will be outlined below, reflect on these efforts and objectives. Additionally, a commonality of the three is their facing toward broader society, unlike the (primarily) in-group oriented traditional ethnic media (Fleras 2011) that have a rich history in Canada (National Ethnic Press and Media Council of Canada 2021).

NEW CANADIAN MEDIA

Mission

New Canadian Media (NCM) is a member-based non-profit that exists to showcase immigrant journalism and amplify the work of journalists from various immigrant/ethnic backgrounds (Medford n.d.). It was launched in 2011 and incorporated as a non-profit in

2014 to represent the immigrant perspective in Canadian discourse through news, views, and comments from an immigrant perspective (Mark Do 2014). According to NCM's publisher's perspective, mainstream media outlets tend to capture major trends effectively, but they fall short in depicting the subtler undercurrents. Further, and perhaps most importantly, the immigrant point of view is not accurately or comprehensively represented in mainstream media (Abraham 2018). According to Abraham (2014), the focus of NCM is not to "break" stories, but rather to offer the "pulse of immigrant Canada" through original news articles, opinion pieces, and headlines aggregated from English-language ethnic media. Hence, New Canadian Media has been characterized as a mongrel among media, neither mainstream nor entirely ethnic, making it a hybrid model (Abraham 2018).

NCM operates under the leadership of the board of directors. Its key officers are George Abraham, founder-publisher and executive director; Brent Jolly, editorial advisor, who is also the director of communications, research, and community management with the National NewsMedia Council of Canada (NNC); and Fabian Dawson, a multiple-award-winning journalist and an internationally acclaimed author, filmmaker, and media expert who serves as its business development advisor (NCM 2022).

In terms of demographics, most NCM subscribers are in Ontario and British Columbia, and are more likely to live in larger cities rather than small urban or rural areas (Medford n.d.) Subscribers outside of Canada are from many parts of the world, including South Asia (Pakistan, India, Sri Lanka, etc.), the Middle East/ Western Asia (Lebanon, Turkey, Iraq, Egypt, etc.), Africa (South Africa, Nigeria, Somalia, etc.), Southeast Asia (China, Vietnam, Korea, etc.), Eastern Europe (Poland, Russia, Bulgaria, ex-Yugoslavia, etc.), Latin America (Brazil, Chile, Mexico), and the Caribbean (Jamaica, Trinidad, Haiti, etc.) (Medford n.d.).

The inception of NCM, according to its publisher, was unconventional because "there was no template to follow [and] NCM charted its [own] course" (Abraham 2018). The principal journalism vehicles for NCM are its news portal and the newsletter. Originally supported with funding from the Department of Canadian Heritage and the federal government's Inter-Action: Multiculturalism Funding Program, in 2017, NCM moved to launch the Collective, a group of journalists and paid members across Canada to take part in the organization's training and mentorship program. It sustained itself on the backs of volunteer directors and pro bono time from members of its editorial board (Abraham 2018).

Organizational Structure and Operation

When it was established, NCM had several initial partnerships and supporters, including iPolitics.ca and the *Walrus* magazine, which both provided mentoring. These outlets believed that NCM is an essential voice in Canada and supported its mission (Mark Do 2014). In 2020, NCM earned the status of Qualified Canadian Journalism Organization, recognizing it as a producer of original news content that adheres to established journalistic processes and principles (Government of Canada n.d.). Initially, the editorial team consisted of dedicated individuals who strongly believed in NCM's mission, including immigrant journalists, publishers from the ethnic press, academics, as well as corporate and editorial experts with exceptional skills and experience (Mark Do 2014). Currently, NCM has a diverse virtual newsroom that relies on a consultative editorial board and board of directors alongside scores of freelance writers and immigrant contributors from many parts of the world. The content that NCM produces falls largely into two broad categories: news and commentary on Canadian current affairs from an immigrant perspective, and stories on topics that are of particular relevance to immigrants (Abraham 2018). It features original content, and recently it has also started publishing articles in French.

To date, NCM has successfully executed a series of needs-based training workshops for newcomer journalists. It has created Canada's first ethnic media style guide, published weekly newsletters, and produced hundreds of stories through the Local Journalism Initiative (LJI) portal. Notably, its LJI contributions are also being picked up by mainstream media outlets across Canada. It has also successfully initiated a journalist mentorship program, and in partnership with the *Walrus*, organized a range of public discussion series relating to the role of ethnic media, immigrant journalists, and media in general in Canadian society. In 2020, in cooperation with the Canadian Association of Journalists (CAJ), NCM initiated a joint membership in CAJ for members of the Collective of NCM, offering an opportunity for many ethnic journalists to feel more included professionally in the

Table 15.1 | Increase in the number of articles published by New Canadian Media between 2018 and 2021, and trends in training and website traffic

	Data from 23 June 2018	Data from 19 June 2021
Original stories published on the NCM platform	855	1,875 + editorial in French (9)
Web traffic	10,840 unique monthly visitors in Nov. 2015 (22,448 page views)	67,962 unique visitors in 2020 (171,402 page views)
E-newsletter distribution list (no. of subscribers)	1,433	1,531
Twitter followers	3,811	4,845
Facebook followers	1,630	2,146
Reporters/commentators published	220	298
Journalists enlisted for NCM's professional development program	102	298

Canadian community of journalists. Aside from the board and editorial team, NCM relies on the support of 200 members of the Collective who speak more than fifty different languages other than English or French and have deep connections within their communities. Most of the Collective members are also active contributors to the content of NCM (New Canadian Media 2022).

The efforts of NCM have been, to date, largely sustained through project-based public funding (roughly $275,000 through 2018 and about $200,000 in 2020–21), enabling NCM to demonstrate the calibre and depth of its journalism and showcase the work of a growing roster of new reporters in every province. Comparing the data from 2018 and the more recent updates in 2021 tells a story of the growing influence of NCM with distribution of its Collective Newsletter as shown in table 15.1.

In November 2021, NCM celebrated a milestone of publishing 2,000 articles, including 352 articles in 2021 alone, and over 1,000 articles in the last three years. These figures demonstrate the growing potential and impact of NCM. In 2020, NCM collaborated on a project with Multilingual International Research and Ethnic Media Services to analyze the coverage of COVID-19's impact on newcomers, refugees, international students, and temporary foreign workers by the ethnic media. The project also sought to compare the level of similarities and differences in the coverage by mainstream media on the same issues (Hayder 2021).

MULTILINGUAL INTERNATIONAL RESEARCH AND ETHNIC MEDIA SERVICES (MIREMS)

Mission

Multilingual International Research and Ethnic Media Services (MIREMS) is the only for-profit monitoring service recognized by the Government of Canada. It is dedicated to monitoring, researching, and analyzing ethnic and multilingual media sources in Canada and globally. MIREMS was established initially as Ethnomedia Monitor Services in 1988 and is currently managed by Andrés Machalski, a linguist by profession and a University of Toronto graduate in linguistics and fine arts. He is an Argentinian immigrant with Anglo-Polish heritage (MIREMS "Blog" 2018). In addition to being an acronym for Multilingual International Research and Ethnic Media Services, MIREMS derives from the Spanish "miremos" which means "let us look" (MIREMS "Team" 2018).

MIREMS strives to increase awareness of the central role that ethnic media plays in giving a voice to newcomers in Canadian society, and to respond to the needs of corporations as well as governments and NGOs to encourage them to include perspectives from diverse communities in their communication strategies.

Organizational Structure and Operation

MIREMS has a team of consultants representing forty languages who monitor, analyze, summarize, and translate stories from more than 1,000 ethnic media outlets daily to provide analysis of current news, opinions, and insights from a whole range of ethnic groups. In performing this task, the MIREMS team provides summarized coverage of ethnic media content in over thirty language groups/communities (MIREMS "Media List" 2018).

Founded in 1988, under the name Ethnomedia Monitor Services, and after a brief transition as Andrew Machalski and Associates, MIREMS rebranded in 2009 as a service with thirty-two years of operation. MIREMS has assisted corporations, government agencies, and non-profit organizations with a variety of media monitoring and translation services, providing them with a unique look at diverse ethnic communities in Canada. Its clients include all three levels of government, from municipalities such as the City of Brampton, provincial governments of Alberta and Ontario, and Immigration, Refugees and Citizenship Canada (IRCC) and the Privy Council Office (PCO). Also among their clients are companies such as Canada Post and General Motors, and organizations like the Canadian Blood Services (MIREMS "Our Work" 2018).

In its methodology statement, MIREMS notes that while utilizing all the advantages of computerized media monitoring (search by keywords, automated topic compilation, reports, and analysis), it is an ethnic media monitoring company with consultants who read the papers, listen to the radio and TV programs and broadcasts, and manually select and summarize stories based on clients' topics of interest. Monitoring and communicating with ethnic media is one sure way to find out the reach of ethnic media (MIREMS "Our Approach" 2018).

The guide to Ethnic Media Essentials published by MIREMS notes that its inventory of sources runs to over 1,000 sources, including specialized publications such as sports and entertainment magazines, directories, and real estate guides. They are spread across more than thirty languages from over forty-five cultural groups, the top five being Chinese, Punjabi, South Asian English, Russian, and Spanish (MIREMS "Ethnic Media Essentials" 2016).

MIREMS also runs a public service blog using its exclusive ethnic media feed to highlight the opinions and analyses reflected in the blog with plans for further educational moves to support outreach to ethnic media. In recent years, through its blog, MIREMS has highlighted many issues that its monitoring and analysis team has followed, including the Syrian refugee crisis; refugees, immigrants and asylum-seekers in the context of Canada-US cross-border issues; US and Canadian politicians in ethnic media; COVID-19 and reporting in ethnic media; Black Lives Matter protests; US and Canada foreign policy; and reactions in the former Eastern Bloc countries when Canada's House of Commons passed the Magnitsky Law (MIREMS "Blog" 2022).

MULTICULTURAL MEANDERINGS

Mission

Multicultural Meanderings (*MM*) refers to meandering, an act of wandering in a leisurely or aimless manner, as the name of their blog denotes. Despite the connotation of the name, the content they produce is highly relevant to public policy. The driving force behind the blog is Andrew Griffith, former director-general for the Citizenship and Multiculturalism Branch, Department of Citizenship and Immigration, where he led policy and program development to strengthen citizenship, inclusion, participation, and inter-cultural understanding. He is also the author of *Multiculturalism in Canada: Evidence and Anecdote* and a fellow of the Environics Institute and the Global Affairs Institute of Canada (*Multicultural Meanderings* 2011).

At *MM*, Griffith brings his policy and data analysis expertise to focus on the whole nexus of immigration, settlement, citizenship, and multiculturalism to assess what works and what does not work in the Canadian context. The approach of *MM* has been to explore the available data, whether it be census data, equity employment data, other diversity data, or public polling, and contextualize them to offer a more comprehensive analysis behind the data. In this sense, *MM* has been a relevant voice on these topics over the years, with over 100 analyses and opinions on these issues. Griffith, for one, has been cited in more than 100 articles and opinion pieces in the last four years alone, demonstrating the impact and relevance of *MM*'s contributions to these conversations (*Multicultural Meanderings* 2011).

The Content and Perspectives

Since 2011 when the blog was introduced, *MM* has published dozens of analyses on the topics of immigration, settlement, citizenship, and multiculturalism (*Multicultural Meanderings* 2011). The blog is published solely by Griffith, without any outside support. The blog features Griffith's analyses, including those published on the *Policy Options* website, alongside summaries of his work. Griffith's contributions are not limited to the blog, as he has also been featured in various national media outlets, such as the *Hill Times*, *iPolitics*, *Ottawa Citizen*, the *Globe and Mail*, and *Toronto Star*. Additionally, he has contributed to think tanks across Canada, including the Canadian Immigration Historical Society, MacDonald Laurier Institute, Pearson Centre, and Migration Policy Institute. Beyond that, the blog aggregates the issues and topics from Canada and around the world from five core areas of focus including multiculturalism, immigration, citizenship, government, and refugees, while keeping the emphasis on Western democracies that have sizable immigrant populations. Also relevant are the subheadings under the multiculturalism section, which focus on religion, radicalization, racism, and anti-Semitism. Griffith's main interest, however, is in issues around citizenship.

In 2018, in cooperation with MIREMS, Griffith launched diversityvotes.ca to reflect on ethnic media coverage of election issues and to assist voters in learning what federal issues are resonating in ethnic media and what potential effects they will have on voting (Wright 2019). The website is now terminated. However, the original idea behind diversityvotes.ca was to connect comprehensive statistics about Canada's minority communities with ethnic media stories. The mission statement pointed out that diversityvotes.ca is a national project that aims to bring together national expertise in diversity demographics and diversity discourse together to connect, empower, and educate (diversityvotes.ca 2019b). The goal was to combine the impact of statistics and stories into a new, useful, and powerful tool for citizens, journalists, researchers, academics, government agencies, and non-governmental organizations.

As a partner in the diversityvotes.ca project, MIREMS provided the financial resources and in-kind donations of translated materials from Canada's ethnic media to help diversityvotes.ca provide better insight into the issues and concerns of different ethno-cultural communities across Canada. The support from MIREMS included 1,200 articles in two dozen different languages, collected and summarized in English, and processed for the analysis of the federal by-elections in 2019. Additionally, MIREMS produced dozens of blogs and reports, as well as the building of the first stage of the diversityvotes.ca website, which was launched at the Metropolis Conference in Halifax. The market value of these contributions was estimated at up to $15,000 (Machalski 2019).

In 2019, the Canadian Ethnic Media Association (CEMA) announced its partnership in the launch and ongoing support of diversityvotes.ca, which also partnered with other relevant organizations in Canada (Cision 2019). Another important partner of diversityvotes.ca has been the Canadian Race Relations Foundation (CRRF), which announced its sponsorship and support of the website in the same year (CRRF 2019). The Clayton H. Riddell Graduate Program in Political Management at Carleton University is yet another important partner that has pledged its support for diversityvotes.ca. Stephen Azzi, the director of the Riddell Program, has called the online hub essential for anyone working in the political field to understand Canada's ethnic media (diversityvotes.ca 2019a). At this point, NCM played a role in publishing the analyses produced before and after the elections, adding another layer of cooperation between the three initiatives.

The approach of diversityvotes.ca was to engage a team of media consultants who produced numerous stories related to the elections and election campaign. They posted weekly round-ups on the website highlighting key themes, from foreign relations to climate change. The media consultants were provided by MIREMS. The website also featured samples of headlines from ethnic media and maps, indicating where these outlets were operating across Canada. The website further used charts and statistics to show how immigrant populations were represented in each electoral riding to underline their potential stake in the vote (Bolger 2019).

In 2019, the team at diversityvotes.ca sought to identify what political topics were most important to different communities. The conclusion drawn, based on the analysis of ethnic media coverage of elections, was that ethnic media were relevant in the riding by riding electoral contest, as well as in the whole national conversation. The analysis showed that in the 2019 election, the People's Party of Canada, with its focus on limiting immigration, received more than twice as much coverage in the ethnic media than the New Democratic Party and Green Party combined (Griffith 2019).

In an opinion piece written for the *Vancouver Sun*, Douglas Todd credited diversityvotes.ca for providing a great service to Canada by establishing the online hub, noting that the founders of the site, Griffith and Machalski, are trying to make ethnic journalism more transparent to the public, bringing it out of its language silos (Todd 2019). Although the metrics for measuring the impact of the blog are not the same as for NCM, the blog has close to 3,000 followers, making it a valuable point of reference on the debates around multiculturalism, immigration, citizenship, government, and refugees, as well as on issues concerning ethnic voting in Canada.

PRACTITIONER'S REFLECTIONS

New Canadian Media

NCM is a multimedia portal that represents the voice of immigrant Canadians from across Canada. By featuring immigrant and ethnic issues not reflected in national media, it gives immigrant issues a national attention. Based on its mission, NCM was born primarily from the need for professional development of ethnic journalists, as an NGO, with a mandate to inform and educate. Since its establishment in 2011, it has managed to gain traction among ethnic journalists throughout Canada who serve as its contributors. NCM performs well in reflecting issues faced by immigrants and newcomers to Canada by offering a distinctive coverage of the challenges they face in accessing services, health and wellbeing, support, recognition of credentials, housing, education, and more. It also reflects often on crisis points from around the world or about stifling of media rights in growing authoritarian regimes such as Syria, Nicaragua, China, and Turkey. Such a perspective makes NCM stand out from typical ethnic media that primarily focus on communicating information and updates from homelands, offering a flavour of countries of origin, or engaging in limited ways in pushing forward the efforts of local settlement agencies by posting community event calendars and PACs. Here, NCM affirms its mandate to deliver "the beat of immigrant Canada" from a more comprehensive perspective. Its cooperation with MIREMS on the COVID-19 reporting project and other issues of importance, or with MM on the impact of immigrant votes in various elections in Canada, reflects the potential of the initiatives to continue to work together on similar projects in the future for higher impact.

One of the shortcomings that influence the work and commitment of NCM is that it is a non-profit but remains still heavily government subsidized due to the lack of opportunities offered for cooperation and partnership by mainstream media institutions and other journalism institutions across Canada.

In order to realize its full potential, NCM must secure a steady flow of income. The success of NCM relies, to some degree, on audience growth as well as the expansion of its programs to reach a wider audience. However, in order to meet such objectives, it must continue to inspire trust in its collective of around two hundred members to ensure their ongoing contribution. The decision to introduce a joint membership with the Canadian Association of Journalists (CAJ) is a promising move forward, as it gives NCM members greater recognition in the Canadian media landscape. Its mentorship programs and efforts to bridge the gap between mainstream and ethnic media journalists through a series of debates are also steps in the right direction. Its participation in the Local Journalism Initiative (LJI) gives ethnic journalists opportunities for greater exposure and cross-referencing in the Canadian media. Through its original content and participation in the LJI, it can present this unique perspective and increase the likelihood that its pool of successful writers become mainstream or get invited to work with Canadian mainstream media in the future. Simultaneously, NCM aspires to raise the standards of ethnic journalism, enabling professionals to become more prepared and engaged in the Canadian media market.

The recent growth of NCM is indicative of its potential to become an important hub, uniting media professionals with international credentials who otherwise might have limited opportunities to get employed in the mainstream media. Its ongoing mentorship and potential training programs in the future could make NCM a hub for professionals from other parts of the world who move to Canada and want to pursue careers in journalism. Most recently, NCM has formalized the kick-off of a micro-credentialing program with Seneca College to help the participants develop equity and inclusion-informed skills to incorporate into their reporting process.

Beyond these accomplishments, NCM needs to be more assertive in creating additional partnerships to be seen, heard, valued, and connected. Its ability to grow, then, could be realized in the future by being able to formalize a long-term training centre for newcomer journalists to help consolidate the ranks of some of the existing ethnic media across Canada, and also prepare immigrant journalists for work in the mainstream media.

To create a sustainable operation, NCM will still need to be supported through government-funded programs as well as pursue non-profit fundraising routes such as private donors, sponsorships, memberships, and events, and push more assertively in its coverage of topics of interest to immigrants, broadening their scope of coverage and consistency. Moreover, NCM needs to better communicate and connect with mainstream media and ethnic media managers to effectively channel pitches and continue to bring stories about ethnic communities to their daily agenda. There will be a requirement for initiatives like NCM to advocate to policy makers at the national, provincial, and municipal levels for a better understanding of immigrant and ethnic issues. NCM initiatives are a valuable conduit to promote pluralism in news coverage, helping to shape the public discourse around the need to fight and address bias and ethnic and racist stereotypes, and striving for greater inclusion and diversity in the public opinion.

MIREMS

MIREMS maintains a non-partisan attitude and is client-focused. It has been around for a long time. It was initially a newspaper clippings business that operated prior to the Internet, providing its clients with clippings via courier. Over time, MIREMS expanded its services from newspapers to include radio, television, and eventually online content, enabling it to continue operating in the digital era. MIREMS's media content analysis has directly and indirectly fostered a greater sense of accountability among ethnic media in Canada. For example, it has enabled ethnic media to regain a sense of legitimacy by promoting accountability to the broader Canadian public. In their monitoring and analyzing ethnic media content, particularly for the needs of their government clients, MIREMS has established certain benchmarks. Their content analysis of ethnic news, for one, has allowed decision-makers in the government's advertising sector to gain a better understanding of the ethnic media landscape, including the amount of original content produced, the benchmarks for editorial content versus advertising space, the coverage of difference issues, and the challenges and problematic areas. MIREMS has highlighted some of these contributions and examples of their analyses in their blog. One such analysis was on advertising in the ethnic media from former Eastern Bloc countries of immigration consultants, promoting fast-track immigration to Canada for exotic dancers. Through this analysis, MIREMS assisted one of its main clients, Citizenship and Immigration

Canada, in addressing loopholes in the immigration sector related to such anomalies. Additionally, MIREMS has examined how much Canadian content versus international content is typically carried by ethnic media newspapers.

Although over the last decade the service has successfully executed contracts with different government agencies, MIREMS remains a lean operation with a turnover of less than one million dollars annually over the last decade. One challenge that MIREMS faces is the inconsistent interest from its principal clients, government institutions, in having ethnic media perspectives analyzed in their departments. The drive of successive Canadian governments to hear more of what is said in ethnic media seems to have been uneven and shifting in scope, even though certain institutions such as IRCC and PCO maintain a continued interest in MIREMS services. While MIREMS's blog brings attention to important issues related to ethnic media, it could potentially benefit by offering paid subscriptions allowing media scholars and other interested individuals access to the content it monitors. Additionally, establishing institutional arrangements with colleges and universities to provide paid access to its content and therefore help expand opportunities for research and analysis related to ethnic media could be further beneficial to MIREMS.

Multicultural Meanderings

While the *MM* blog is not on the same organizational resources level as MIREMS or NCM, the blog remains a relevant and credible source of information in academic and policy debate circles on matters of immigration, multiculturalism, diversity, and citizenship. Operated solely by Griffith, the blog nurtures an important segment of the audience in Canada and serves as an essential resource for those interested in those issues. Dozens of analytical contributions over the last decade by Griffith, published on the *Policy Options* website and reflected on the *MM* blog, bring attention to important discussions relating to immigration, citizenship, multiculturalism, and diversity perspectives. While its manager is not interested in expanding the *MM*, the focus on citizenship, in particular, can be elevated to new levels by inviting more elaborate research. Although it was a relevant project, diversityvotes.ca received minimal support from institutions and grant providers and was terminated after 2019. Nonetheless, the groundwork provided by Griffith can serve as a good basis for its reintroduction, and the project could remain as a focal point for relevant matters to voting and ethnic ridings in the future. Furthermore, the blog could also benefit by inviting contributors and seeking out further engagement from media and public policy students and scholars who are interested in the field, and could possibly increase its scope of coverage pending new partnerships and future projects. Potential partners and donors could also assist this project by supplementing it with additional staff and resources to be able to deliver more coherent and comprehensive studies in the future regarding electoral issues, perspectives, and options in ethnic minority communities, even though its publisher is more interested in maintaining it as a lean operation. *MM*, on the other hand, can pursue important topics regarding immigration, citizenship, multiculturalism, and diversity, and encourage further the research on those topics. Increased publicity for initiatives such as *MM* could help to raise awareness of its importance and increase its reach.

NCM has a prominent social media presence, with approximately 5,000 followers on Twitter, 2,254 followers on Facebook, and 528 on LinkedIn as of July 2021. NCM also has a YouTube channel although it remains underutilized. The social media presence of *MM* is likewise sizable: the public policy blog had 2,853 followers, as of July 2021. MIREMS, on the other hand, seems to have a lesser focus on social media; its operation for more than thirty years nonetheless shows that the service is highly valuable and useful to its clients, and is expected to continue playing an important role in the monitoring and analysis of ethnic media content in the future.

CONCLUSION

The main question explored in this chapter was whether the three entities analyzed here – New Canadian Media, a diversity initiative dedicated to immigrant and ethnic reporting; Multilingual International Research and Ethnic Media Services, a for-profit media monitoring and analysis service; and *Multicultural Meanderings*, a public policy blog – can, alone or in partnership with one another, reflect the unique capacity to bridge the gap between ethnic and mainstream media, and, if yes, how, and to what extent? Based on the analysis, each of the three initiatives has demonstrated success in filling the gap, to the extent that this is possible, within the current ethnic media landscape, and each serves as an important conduit filling in the void left behind by the inherent inability of mainstream media to provide inclusive coverage of diverse community issues as well as the inability of traditional ethnic media to tread outside their immediate cohorts. All three outlets serve as good examples to illustrate the potential of ethnic media 2.0.

While the challenges they face are not the same, these initiatives provide valuable input to a Canadian audience, reflective of a multitude of ethnic media voices across Canada. They also offer valuable reflections on the changing demographic trends in Canada and affirm ethnic media in the broader societal debate. At the same time NCM, MIREMS, and *MM* are caught between the need to grow, expand, and remain lean, sustainable, and consistent in their operations within the precarious landscape of the media sector. Nonetheless, they remain important conduits in the communication infrastructure in Canada, and offer valuable contributions in the socio-political context of Canada while being at the intersection of ethnic and mainstream media, aiming to reach out toward the broader audience.

REFERENCES

Abraham, George. 2014. "Keeping the Faith – Nieman Storyboard." *Nieman Storyboard*, 13 February 2014. https://niemanstoryboard.org/articles/keeping-the-faith/.

– 2018. "A Mongrel among Media." *New Canadian Media*, 24 June 2018. https://newcanadianmedia.ca/a-mongrel-among-media/.

Ahadi, Daniel, and Catherine A. Murray. 2009. "Urban Mediascapes and Multicultural Flows: Assessing Vancouver's Communication Infrastructure." *Canadian Journal of Communication* 34 (4): 587–612.

Ball-Rokeach, Sandra J., Yong-Chan Kim, and Sorin Matei. 2001. "Storytelling Neighborhood." *Communication Research* 4: 392–428.

Bolger, Katrya. 2019. "Online Tool Views Election Coverage through the Eyes of Ethnic Media." *Review of Journalism*, 4 December 2019. https://rrj.ca/online-tool-views-election-coverage-through-the-eyes-of-ethnic-media/.

Canadian Race Relations Foundation (CRRF). 2019. "Canadian Race Relations Foundation Announces Sponsorship of New Project: diversityvotes.ca." 25 April 2019. https://www.crrf-fcrr.ca/en/news-a-events/articles/item/26996-canadian-race-relations-foundation-announces-sponsorship-of-new-project-diversityvotes-ca.

Cision. 2019. "CEMA Partners Launch of Diversity Electoral Website." 20 June 2019. https://www.newswire.ca/news-releases/cema-partners-launch-of-diversity-electoral-website-856450755.html.
diversityvotes.ca. 2019a. "The Clayton H. Riddell Graduate Program in Political Management Announces Its Support for diversityvotes.ca." *Diversity Votes*, 18 June 2019. https://diversityvotes.ca/the-clayton h-riddell-graduate-program-in-political-management-announces-its-support-for-diversityvotes-ca/.
– 2019b. "The Mission." https://diversityvotes.ca/team-mission/.
Fleras, Augie. 2011. *The Media Gaze. The Representations of Diversity in Canada*. Vancouver: UBC Press.
Government of Canada. n.d. "Qualified Canadian Journalism Organization." Ottawa, ON: Canada Revenue Agency. https://www.canada.ca/en/revenue-agency/services/tax/businesses/topics/corporations/business-tax-credits/canadian-journalism-labour-tax-credit/qualified-canadian-journalism-organization.html.
Griffith, Andrew. 2019. "How Does Ethnic Media Campaign Coverage Differ?" *Policy Options*, 2 October 2019. https://policyoptions.irpp.org/magazines/october-2019/how-does-ethnic-media-campaign-coverage-differ/.
Hayder, Reedah. 2021. "What COVID-19 Teaches Us about the Divide between Mainstream and Multilingual Media." *JSource*, 18 March 2021. https://j-source.ca/what-covid-19-teaches-us-about-the-divide-between-mainstream-and-multilingual-media/.
Machalski, Andrés. 2019. "Support Inclusive Diversity in Canadian Politics." *Diversity Votes*, 27 May 2019. https://diversityvotes.ca/support-inclusive-diversity-in-canadian-politics/.
Mark Do, Eric. 2014. "New Canadian Media Looks to Give Immigrants a Voice." *JSource*, 25 February 2014. https://j-source.ca/new-canadian-media-looks-to-give-immigrants-a-voice/.
Matei, Sorin, and Sandra J. Ball-Rokeach. 2001. "Real and Virtual Social Ties: Connections in the Everyday Lives of Seven Ethnic Neighborhoods." *American Behavioral Scientist* 45 (3): 550–64.
Multilingual International Research and Ethnic Media Services (MIREMS). 2016. "Ethnic Media Essentials." http://www.mirems.com/uploads/8/1/4/2/8142628/mirems_ethnic_media_essentials_2016.pdf.
– 2018. "Blog." http://www.mirems.com/mirems-blog.
– 2018. "Media List." http://www.mirems.com/mirems-media-list.html.
– 2018. "Our Approach." http://www.mirems.com/mirems-approach.html.

– 2018. "Our Work." http://www.mirems.com/mirems-work.html.
– 2018. "Team." http://www.mirems.com/mirems-team.html.
Multicultural Meanderings (MM). 2011. "About." 2 May 2011. https://multiculturalmeanderings.com/about/.
National Ethnic Press and Media Council of Canada. 2022. "Working to Make Canada a True Community of Communities." http://nepmcc.ca/basic/ethnicpress1.htm.
New Canadian Media (NCM). 2022. https://newcanadianmedia.ca/.
Todd, Douglas. 2019. "Douglas Todd: The Political Use and Misuse of Canada's Ethnic Media." *Vancouver Sun*, 7 July 2019. https://vancouversun.com/opinion/columnists/douglas-todd-the-political-use-and-misuse-of-canadas-ethnic-media.
Wright, Teresa. 2019. "New Tool Launched to Shine Light on Ethnic Media Coverage of Election Issues." *Toronto Star*, 18 June 2019. https://www.thestar.com/politics/federal/2019/06/18/new-tool-launched-to-shine-light-on-ethnic-media-coverage-of-election-issues.html.

Contributors

DANIEL AHADI, PhD, is senior lecturer in the School of Communication and an affiliated faculty member at the Digital Democracies Institute at Simon Fraser University. His research focuses on the development of self and identity within the context of media, migration, globalization, and formation of transnational diasporas.

AHMED AL-RAWI, PhD, is associate professor of news, social media, and public communication at the School of Communication at Simon Fraser University. He is the director of the Disinformation Project that empirically examines fake news discourses in Canada on social media and news media. His research expertise is related to social media, news, and global communication with emphasis on Canada and the Middle East.

ALYSHA BAINS is a PhD candidate at Simon Fraser University's School of Communication. Through spotlighting the creative work of South Asians across the nation, Alysha's research is driven to locate how industry processes and practices are contradictory spaces that have both limitations and opportunities for South Asian storytelling and resistance. She is passionate about creating social change by bridging systems of care, critical thought, and storytelling through her writing and teaching.

MARIE BERNARD-BRIND'AMOUR is a PhD student researching alternative media and social movements at Concordia University. Her work currently focuses on historical artist-driven resistance in Quebec. She has a background in public relations and communications management, and has co-authored articles for journals such as the *International Journal of Communication*.

SYEDA NAYAB BUKHARI earned her PhD in gender, sexuality, and women's studies at Simon Fraser University and completed her postdoctoral fellowship at McGill University. Her areas of interest include race, class, and gender; immigration and integration studies; mainstream and ethnic media; and community-based programming for disadvantaged groups. Interested in qualitative research, she has engaged with several ethnic/minority communities in Canada, analyzing and documenting their lived experiences and challenges. Currently, she is serving as part-time faculty at Concordia University and as a research associate with the Simone de Beauvoir Institute. She is also acting as the director of the South Asian Film Festival of Montreal.

INDRANIL CHAKRABORTY is a Horizon Postdoctoral Fellow at Concordia University and his current research examines how deindustrialization and reindustrialization in the retail sector in North America are changing the labouring population's everyday life experiences. He holds a PhD in information and media studies from Western University. In 2021, he published his first monograph, *Invisible Labour: Support-Service Workers in India's Information Technology Industry*. His research interests include media, technology, labour, and South Asia.

ANISHA DATTA is associate professor of sociology at King's University College at Western University. She also works as an expert for UNESCO's Inclusive Policy Lab and holds a PhD in sociology from the University of British Columbia. Her research interests include postcolonial studies, diaspora and transnational studies, neoliberalism, social and cultural theories, historical sociology, and South Asia.

AZIZ DOUAI, PhD in mass communications, Pennsylvania State University, is professor of journalism and dean of the Faculty of Graduate Studies and Research at the University of Regina. He currently researches disruptive media technologies and the politics of global media, and he is the author of *Arab Media and the Politics of*

Terrorism: Unbecoming News (2020, Peter Lang) and co-editor of *Mediated Identities and New Journalism in the Arab World: Mapping the Arab Spring* (2016, Palgrave Macmillan) and *New Media Influence on Social and Political Change in Africa* (2013, IGI Global).

AUGIE FLERAS received his doctorate in Maori studies and anthropology at Victoria University, Wellington, New Zealand. His teaching career has spanned nearly five decades, primarily at the University of Waterloo in addition to the University of Canterbury in Christchurch, New Zealand, McMaster University, and Wilfrid Laurier University. Fleras is the author of some thirty-five books, including eight editions of *Unequal Relations: A Critical Introduction to the Politics of Race, Ethnic, and Indigenous Dynamics in Canada*, with a proposed ninth edition to be published in 2024. Fleras has been a recipient of the Lifetime Achievement Award from the Canadian Ethnic Studies Association.

MARK HAYWARD is associate professor in the Department of Communication Studies at York University. He is the author of *Identity and Industry: Making Media Multicultural in Canada* (2019, MQUP) and the co-editor (with Joshua Hanan) of *Communication and Economy: History Value Agency* (2014, Peter Lang). He has published essays on media history, the philosophy of technology, and minority media.

YASMIN JIWANI is professor in the Department of Communication Studies at Concordia University, Montreal. She is the author of *Discourses of Denial: Mediations of Race, Gender and Violence*, as well as lead editor of *Girlhood, Redefining the Limits*, and co-editor of *Faces of Violence in the Lives of Girls*. Her work has appeared in a wide variety of journals and anthologies. Her research interests include mediations of race, gender, and violence in the press, as well as representations of women of colour in popular media. She was the Concordia University Research Chair in Intersectionality, Violence, and Resistance (2017–2022).

NASER MIFTARI is an independent researcher based in Ottawa. He has a PhD in political science from the University of Nebraska-Lincoln and a master's in journalism from Temple University in Philadelphia. He has worked for many years in the media sector in

Southeast Europe with a range of publications as a writer and editor and has taught at different journalism schools in the region, including the Southeast Europe University in Northern Macedonia; the Kosovo Institute of Journalism in Pristina; the University of Pristina Department of Journalism; Bilgi University-Istanbul; the University of Nebraska-Lincoln; and the Ole Miss School of Journalism in Mississippi.

PAUL S. MOORE is professor of communication and culture at Toronto Metropolitan University. His media histories of cinema exhibition and newspaper distribution in North America have focused on the relation between audiences and publicity, appearing in *Canadian Journal of Communication*, *The Moving Image*, *Film History*, and the book *The Sunday Paper: A Media History* (2022, Illinois), co-authored with Sandra Gabriele. His recent work maps early transnational and diasporic circuits of cinema.

KARIM H. KARIM, Chancellor's Professor at Carleton University, is editor of *The Media of Diaspora*, an international reference work, and co-editor of *Diaspora and Media in Europe*. He received the inaugural Robinson Prize for the monograph *Islamic Peril: Media and Global Violence*. Dr Karim has also published extensively on Ismailis and organized the Second International Ismaili Studies Conference. His writings have been critically acclaimed and translated into several languages. Dr Karim has held visiting positions at Harvard University, Simon Fraser University, and Aga Khan universities, and has delivered distinguished lectures around the world. He has served as director of Carleton's School of Journalism and Communication, the Carleton Centre for the Study of Islam, and the Institute of Ismaili Studies in London, England.

ELIM NG, PhD, is a researcher based in Edmonton, Alberta. Her doctoral research investigated how Chinese-language media practitioners in Canada navigate overlapping governance from Canada and the PRC. Her current work includes community-engaged research, local politics and community development, transnational migration, and Chinese politics. In her spare time, she explores art and music that reflect the diverse places where she and her partner have lived and travelled.

BARBARA PERRY is professor in the Faculty of Social Science and Humanities at Ontario Tech University, and the director of the Centre on Hate, Bias and Extremism. She also holds a UNESCO Chair in Hate Studies, a field in which she has written. She is currently working in the areas of anti-Muslim violence, antisemitic hate crime, the community impacts of hate crime, and right-wing extremism in Canada. She is regularly called upon by policy makers, practitioners, and local, national, and international media as an expert on hate crime and right-wing extremism.

ANGELO PRINCIPE, PhD, is a retired professor. He is the author of several books, including *The Darkest Side of the Fascist Years: The Italian-Canadian Press, 1920–1942* and *Enemies Within: Italian and Other Internees in Canada and Abroad*, with Franca Iacovetta and Roberto Perin.

DANIELA SANZONE is a researcher, journalist, and novelist. She is a PhD candidate in communication and culture at York University, researching Canadian ethnic broadcasting policy and journalism. She has worked as an "ethnic" journalist in Toronto for the newspaper *Corriere Canadese* and for the Italian News at OMNI Television.

JESSICA L. WHITEHEAD is assistant professor at Cape Breton University. Her research on screen cultures in North America has appeared in the *Canadian Journal of Film Studies*, *Transformative Works and Cultures*, *Italian Canadiana*, and chapters in *Rural Cinema-Going from a Global Perspective* and *Mapping Movie Magazines*. Her current book projects are exploring Italian-Canadian cinema cultures for McGill-Queen's University Press and celebrating the impact of Federico Fellini for the University of Toronto Press.

SHERRY S. YU, PhD, is associate professor in the Department of Arts, Culture and Media, and the Faculty of Information at the University of Toronto. Her research explores multiculturalism, media, and social integration. She is the author of *Diasporic Media beyond the Diaspora: Korean Media in Vancouver and Los Angeles* (2018, UBC Press) and the co-editor of *Ethnic Media in the Digital Age* (2019, Routledge). Her research also has been published in scholarly journals such as *Journalism: Theory, Practice & Criticism*, *Journal-*

ism Studies, Television & New Media, Canadian Journal of Communication, Journal of Ethnic and Migration Studies, and *Canadian Ethnic Studies.*

SZYMON ZYLINSKI, PhD, is assistant professor in the Institute of Journalism and Social Communication, University of Warmia and Mazury in Olsztyn, Poland. He researches diasporic media, media in Bhutan, and mediatization. He has taught at Maltepe University, Royal Thimphu College, and was a visiting scholar at Toronto Metropolitan University, University of Turku, and Simon Fraser University.

Index

Page numbers in italics indicate references to tables and figures.